Affluence and Influence

Affluence and Influence

ECONOMIC INEQUALITY AND POLITICAL
POWER IN AMERICA

Martin Gilens

RUSSELL SAGE FOUNDATION

NEW YORK

PRINCETON UNIVERSITY PRESS

PRINCETON AND OXFORD

Library of Congress Cataloging-in-Publication Data
Gilens, Martin.
    Affluence and influence : economic inequality and political power in America /
Martin Gilens.
        p. cm.
    Includes bibliographical references and index.
    ISBN 978-0-691-15397-1 (hardcover : alk. paper) 1. Political planning—United
States. 2. Decision making—United States. 3. Equality—United States. 4. Representative
government and representation—United States. 5. Pressure groups—United States.
I. Title.
    JK468.P64G55 2012
    320.60973—dc23   2012002445

British Library Cataloging-in-Publication Data is available

This book has been composed in Sabon

Printed on acid-free paper. ∞

Printed in the United States of America

3 5 7 9 10 8 6 4

Chapter 1 was previously published as "Two-thirds full? Citizen Competence and
Democratic Governance." Copyright 2011. From *New Directions in Public Opinion*
by Martin Gilens, edited by Adam J. Berinsky. Reproduced by permission of Taylor
and Frances Group, LLC, a division of Informa plc.

Chapter 4 was previously published in Gilens, Martin. "Policy and Consequences
of Representational Inequality." In *Who Gets Represented?* © 2011 Russell Sage
Foundation, 112 East 64th Street, New York, NY 10065. Reprinted with Permission.

To Janet, and to Naomi and Josh
Who brighten my life every day

Contents

List of Tables ix

List of Figures xi

Acknowledgments xiii

Introduction 1

CHAPTER 1
Citizen Competence and Democratic Decision Making 12

CHAPTER 2
Data and Methods 50

CHAPTER 3
The Preference/Policy Link 70

CHAPTER 4
Policy Domains and Democratic Responsiveness 97

CHAPTER 5
Interest Groups and Democratic Responsiveness 124

CHAPTER 6
Parties, Elections, and Democratic Responsiveness 162

CHAPTER 7
Democratic Responsiveness across Time 193

CHAPTER 8
Money and American Politics 234

Appendix 253

Notes 279

References 305

Index 323

253
12

241

List of Tables

2.1 Observed and Imputed Percent Favoring Policy Change 62
2.2 Alternative Question Wordings for Reliability Estimates 64
2.3 Consistency vs. Correlation as Measures of Policy Responsiveness 68
3.1 Policy Responsiveness by Income Percentile 76
3.2 Policy Responsiveness by Size of Preference Gap across Income Percentiles 79
3.3 Policy Responsiveness When Middle-Income Preferences Align with Those of the Affluent or the Poor 84
3.4 Alternative Estimates of Policy Responsiveness by Income Percentile 87
4.1 Policy Responsiveness by Policy Domain 98
4.2 Characteristics of Proposed Policy Changes by Policy Domain 99
4.3 Decline in Policy Responsiveness as Preferences across Income Groups Diverge 102
4.4 Foreign Policy and National Security Preferences 106
4.5 Religious/Moral Values Issue Preferences 110
4.6 Economic Issue Preferences 114
4.7 Social Welfare Issue Preferences 118
5.1 Distribution of Interest Group Alignments 131
5.2 Interest Group Alignment and Public Preferences as Predictors of Policy Outcomes 137
5.3 Interest Group Engagement and Public Preferences as Predictors of Policy Outcomes 139
5.4 Interest Group Alignment, Public Preferences, and Their Interaction as Predictors of Policy Outcomes 141
5.5 Correlations between Public Preferences and the Net Interest Group Alignment Index 144
5.6 Interest Group Alignment and Public Preferences as Predictors of Policy Outcomes by Policy Domain 148
5.7 Correlations between Public Preferences and Interest Group Positions 156
6.1 Restructuring the Dataset to Create Two Annual Observations from Each Policy Question 169
6.2 Policy Responsiveness and the Federal Election Cycle 171
6.3 Policy Responsiveness and the Length of the Presidential Partisan Regime 176
6.4 Party Control Score 179

6.5   Policy Responsiveness and Partisan Control   181
6.6   Policy Responsiveness and Partisan Control by Policy
        Domain   184
6.7   Multivariate Analyses of Policy Responsiveness   191
7.1   Policy Responsiveness by President by Income Percentile   200
7.2   Policy Responsiveness by President When Preferences across
        Income Levels Diverge   202
7.3   Characteristics of Proposed Policy Changes by President   204
7.4   Policy Responsiveness under G. W. Bush and Johnson by
        Income Percentile (in Comparison with Reagan, G.H.W. Bush,
        and Clinton)   219
7.5   Policy Responsiveness under G. W. Bush in 2001–02 vs. 2005–06
        by Income Percentile   228
A3.1   Policy Responsiveness by Size of Preference Gap across Income
        Percentiles   254
A3.2   Policy Responsiveness by Income Percentile When Preferences
        across Income Levels Diverge   255
A3.3   Alternative Estimates of Policy Responsiveness by Income
        Percentile   256
A3.4   Policy Responsiveness When Preferences across Income or
        Education Levels Diverge   259
A4.1   Policy Responsiveness by Policy Domain by Income
        Percentile   260
A4.2   Policy Preference, Preference Divergence, and Their Interaction
        as Predictors of Policy Outcome by Policy Domain by Income
        Percentile   261
A4.3   Social Welfare Policy Preferences, Preference Divergence, and
        Their Interaction by Income by Interest Group Alignment   262
A5.1   Expanded Power 25 List of Interest Groups in
        Washington, DC   263
A6.1   Policy Responsiveness and Length of Presidential Partisan
        Regime   264
A6.2   Policy Responsiveness and Partisan Control   266
A6.3   Policy Responsiveness and Partisan Control by Policy Domain   267
A6.4   Policy Responsiveness by Direction of Redistributive Policies by
        Partisan Control   269
A6.5   Multivariate Analyses of Policy Responsiveness   270
A7.1   Linear and Quadratic Time Trends in Policy Responsiveness by
        Income Percentile   273
A7.2   Gridlock and Policy Responsiveness by Income Percentile   274
A7.3   Size of Majority Party Seat Advantage and Policy Responsiveness
        by Income Percentile   276
A7.4   Policy Responsiveness under Johnson and G. W. Bush   277

List of Figures

3.1   Stylized Models of Policy Responsiveness   71

3.2   Observed Association between Policy Preferences and Policy Outcomes   73

3.3   Observed and Predicted Associations between Policy Preferences and Policy Outcomes   75

3.4   Policy Responsiveness for the 10th, 50th, and 90th Income Percentiles   77

3.5   Policy Responsiveness When Preferences across Income Levels Diverge   80

3.6   Policy Responsiveness When Preferences Diverge between the 90th and Other Income Percentiles   82

3.7   Percent "Don't Know" and Strength of Opinion by Income Percentile   89

3.8   Homogeneity of Preferences by Income Percentile   92

3.9   Policy Responsiveness When Preferences across Income or Education Levels Diverge   94

4.1   Policy Responsiveness by Policy Domain by Income Percentile   101

4.2   Policy Responsiveness Overall and When Preferences across Income Levels Diverge   103

5.1   Percent of Proposed Policy Changes Adopted by Interest Group Alignment   133

5.2   Predicted Probability of Policy Change by Interest Group Alignments, Preferences of the 90th Income Percentile, and Their Interaction   142

6.1   Policy Responsiveness by Year in the Federal Election Cycle When Preferences across Income Levels Diverge   172

6.2   Policy Responsiveness by Length of Partisan Regime When Preferences across Income Levels Diverge   177

6.3   Policy Responsiveness under Maximum Republican or Democratic Party Control When Preferences across Income Levels Diverge   182

7.1   Time Trends in Policy Responsiveness   199

7.2   Policy Responsiveness by President   200

7.3   Time Trends in Policy Responsiveness When Preferences across Income Levels Diverge   201

7.4   Policy Responsiveness by President When Preferences across Income Levels Diverge   203

7.5   Total U.S. Congressional Campaign Expenditures (in millions of 2010 dollars)   207

7.6   Income Inequality in the United States   208
7.7   Change over Time in Percentage of Proposed Policy Changes
       Adopted   210
7.8   Relationship of Partisan Regime Change and Gridlock as
       Influences on Policy Responsiveness   211
7.9   Gridlock and Policy Responsiveness   212
7.10   Gridlock and Policy Responsiveness When Preferences across
       Income Levels Diverge   213
7.11   Size of the Majority Party Seat Advantage, 1964–2006   215
7.12   Majority Party Seat Advantage in the Senate and Policy
       Responsiveness   216
7.13   Majority Party Seat Advantage in the Senate and Policy
       Responsiveness When Preferences across Income Levels
       Diverge   217
7.14   Policy Responsiveness under Johnson and G. W. Bush (in
       Comparison with Reagan, G.H.W. Bush, and Clinton)   220
7.15   Association of Presidential Job Approval with Respondents'
       Party Identification and Income during July/August of First Year
       in Office   225
8.1   Forms of Political Involvement by Income   240

Acknowledgments

DEMOCRACY SEEMS LIKE A SIMPLE IDEA: that government policy should reflect the preferences of the governed. But thousands of years of theorizing and decades, if not centuries, of empirical study have revealed the enormous complexities that this seemingly simple idea contains.

This book also started out as a seemingly simple idea: that the association between government policy and public preferences could tell us something important about the responsiveness of our government to the public and the extent to which political influence is reserved for the affluent. But as the following pages reveal, the complexities contained in this idea also turned out to be substantial.

Although I have spent neither decades nor centuries pursuing this research, I have spent many years doing so and have accumulated many debts along the way, debts that I am happy to acknowledge here. The inspiration for this project grew from the work of Alan Monroe, who was the first to assess democratic representation by relating public preferences to government policy outcomes across large numbers of issues. Although Alan did not examine inequalities in responsiveness to different subgroups of the public, he encouraged my plans to do so, and that was all it took to set me off down the path that led, many years later, to the book you are now reading.

I began thinking about this project while I was at Yale in the 1990s, and it blossomed into a serious research effort when I moved to UCLA in 2000. I was fortunate to have wonderful colleagues in both departments who inspired by example and created supportive and stimulating environments for pursuing this work. I am especially grateful to my Yale colleagues Alan Gerber, Donald Green, Eric Patashnik, and Rogers Smith and my UCLA colleagues David Sears, Lynn Vavreck, and John Zaller for their friendship, encouragement, and advice.

In 2003 I left UCLA for Princeton. Princeton has a large and diverse group of scholars with interests in politics and inequality, and my research has benefited greatly from comments and suggestions from my colleagues Chris Achen, Doug Arnold, Larry Bartels, Chuck Cameron, Brandice Canes-Wrone, Fred Greenstein, Kosuke Imai, Steve Macedo, Nolan McCarty, Devah Pager, Betsy Paluck, Markus Prior, Tali Mendelberg, Kathy Newman, and Jonas Pontusson. Also at Princeton I was fortunate to take advantage of the many benefits provided by the Center for the Study of Democratic Politics, and I am grateful to CSDP director Larry Bartels and to CSDP staff Michele Epstein and Helene Wood for creating such a wonderfully warm and intellectually enriching environment.

Feedback from far-flung scholars and interested laypeople has greatly enhanced the quality of this research (and perhaps slowed its completion as I pursued many of the excellent suggestions I received along the way). I am grateful to seminar discussants and participants at Cornell, Columbia, Harvard, Michigan, MIT, Rutgers, Temple, and Yale universities and to the Russell Sage Foundation (which sponsored the 2008 Conference on Homogeneity and Heterogeneity in Public Opinion at Cornell University) and the Tobin Project in Cambridge, Massachusetts (which sponsored the 2010 Conference on Democracy and Markets). Through these presentations, and in other conversations, I have received helpful comments and useful data from Dennis Barr, Sarah Binder, Will Bullock, Ted Carmines, Nick Carnes, Kevin Collins, Peter Enns, Michele Epstein, Janet Felton, Alan Gerber, Josh Gilens, Naomi Gilens, Jim Glaser, Marissa Golden, Jacob Hacker, Will Howell, Larry Jacobs, Beth Leech, Michael Malbin, George Marcus, Lynda Powell, Wendy Rahn, Elizabeth Rigby, Tom Romer, Theda Skocpol, Sidney Verba, Chris Wlezien, Jerry Wright, and John Zaller.

I have been especially fortunate to have had the extensive help and support of Kay Schlozman, Ben Page, and Larry Bartels, and all of whom read the entire manuscript and offered scores of helpful suggestions. Kay is an expert in the study of interest groups and served as a valuable guide on a topic that I had little familiarity with when I began this research. Ben has long been both an ardent supporter and a valued critic of this work, and I am deeply grateful for the time and thought he has so generously given. Larry is an extraordinarily talented political scientist and an extraordinarily generous colleague. His own research on inequality and democracy has inspired me, and his unfailing helpfulness in talking through one or another issue in my own work—whether of statistical methodology, substantive argument, or clarity of presentation—has been hugely helpful.

A project of this magnitude requires a virtual army of research assistants. It would have been impossible to collect the thousands of survey questions from dozens of different organizations over four decades, and to code the policy outcomes and interest-group alignments associated with each, without the able assistance of Marty Cohen, Jason Conwell, Andrea Vanacore, and Mark West at UCLA, and Oleg Bespalov, Daniel Cassino, Kevin Collins, Shana Gadarian, Raymond Hicks, and Lee Shaker at Princeton.

Armies cost money (even virtual armies), and I am grateful for the financial support I received for this project from the Institute for Social Science Research and the Academic Senate at UCLA, the Bobst Center and the Committee for Research in the Humanities and Social Sciences at Princeton University, and the Russell Sage Foundation. The Russell Sage Foundation and the Institute for Advanced Study generously provided sabbatical funding for this research, and I am grateful to Eric Wanner, president of the foundation, and Eric Maskin, the Albert O. Hirschman Professor at the Institute for Advanced Study, for their support. I am also indebted to the Russell Sage Foundation for a wonderful July spent at its offices (and in its Upper East Side condominiums in New York) with an extremely engaging group of inequality scholars in 2010.

Chuck Myers, my editor, and Princeton University Press have been a pleasure to work with.

My parents, Gwen and Al Gilens, have been a constant source of love and support. Their enthusiastic embrace of people and ideas, their devotion to community, and their commitment to making the world a better place are an inspiration.

Over the decade or so that it took for this research to mature, my children Josh and Naomi somehow grew from lovable preteens to independent, engaging, vivacious (and just as lovable) young adults. It has been an enormous delight to have them in my life. My wife Janet has changed less over the past decade, but the delight of having her in my life has only grown. Her love, humor, wisdom, and encouragement make life's challenges manageable and life's joys so much sweeter.

Affluence and Influence

DECADES AGO Supreme Court Justice Louis Brandeis wrote, "We can have democracy in this country, or we can have great wealth concentrated in the hands of a few, but we cannot have both." We now live in what has been christened a "new gilded age." Wealth in the United States is indeed concentrated in the hands of a few—more so than at any time since the 1920s. In this book I examine the relationship between individual Americans' financial resources and their political power, seeking to understand the extent to which contemporary America confirms Justice Brandeis's grim assertion.

Citizens in every society are unequal in many ways. But democracy is commonly understood to entail a substantial degree of *political* equality, even in the face of social and economic inequalities. In Robert Dahl's formulation, a central characteristic of democracy is "the continuing responsiveness of the government to the preferences of its citizens, considered as political equals." This ideal of political equality is perhaps impossible to fully achieve in the face of economic inequality—in every democracy citizens with greater resources are better able to shape government policy to their liking. But the *degree* of political inequality in a society, and the conditions that exacerbate or ameliorate it, tell us much about the quality of the society's democracy.

My goal in this book is to document and explain patterns of representation in the United States over the past few decades by examining the relationship between the policy preferences expressed by the American public and the policies adopted by decision makers in Washington. To do so I have assembled a dataset of survey questions reflecting the policy preferences of Americans at different income levels. These data reflect the answers given by hundreds of thousands of respondents to questions about all sorts of government policies—from raising the minimum wage, to restricting abortions, to sending U.S. troops to Bosnia. In the chapters that follow, I analyze these data by comparing the support for specific changes in national policy expressed by lower- or higher-income Americans with the course of actual policy as determined by the president and Congress. What I find is hard to reconcile with the notion of political equality in Dahl's formulation of democracy. The American government does respond to the public's preferences, but that responsiveness is strongly tilted toward the most affluent citizens. Indeed, under most circumstances, the preferences of the vast majority of Americans appear to have essentially no impact on which policies the government does or doesn't adopt.

As I show below, representational inequality is widespread across time, political circumstances, and domains of government policy. Yet there are exceptions to this pattern, and conditions that are more conducive to the representation of the middle class and low-income people. In identifying these conditions, I aim not only to document the variation in representational inequality in the United States, but to identify more and less promising strategies for expanding the responsiveness of government policy makers to more equally encompass all Americans.

What This Book Is and Is Not

This book is not about plutocrats or corporate titans. America's tycoons certainly have inordinate influence over our government. For many Americans the great recession that began in 2007 confirmed the extraordinary power and unchecked greed of the country's top financial institutions and the millionaires and billionaires who run them. Moreover the apparent failure to hold responsible the people and institutions accountable for the economic crisis, and the difficulty in strengthening government regulation of financial institutions, suggest that the government in Washington is far too beholden to these powerful interests.

The political influence of Wall Street moguls and the financial industry more generally surely helps to explain why the government's response to the financial crisis took the form it did. I will address the power of interest groups in chapter 5 and the influence of wealthy individuals in chapter 8. But most of my attention to the affluent will be devoted not to millionaires and billionaires but to the larger group of Americans at the 90th income percentile. In 2010, 90 percent of American households earned less than $135,000 a year—a substantial sum, but hardly enough to qualify as "rich" by most people's standards. The reason I concentrate on this income level rather than the smaller number of even more prosperous Americans at the 99th or 99.9th income percentile is simply that I lack sufficient data on the preferences of the truly rich. The number of rich Americans is small to begin with, and they are even scarcer among respondents to typical national surveys. Despite the obvious importance of this privileged class, we simply do not have much hard evidence about their policy preferences and how those preferences differ from those of less advantaged Americans.

The existing evidence (which I discuss in chapter 8) suggests that, in general, the policy preferences of the rich are somewhat more extreme than those at the 90th income percentile (whom I call "the affluent") but follow the same patterns in their divergence from the preference of the middle class and the poor. Nevertheless there may be some issues, like corporate regulation or the tax treatment of investment income, that differentially affect the rich, and on which the preferences of rich Americans differ significantly from those of the affluent. Different subsets of individuals and interest groups are of course likely to exert influence on different policies at different times. (Indeed, much of the analysis in the chapters that follow involves an effort to identify these sorts of patterns in the responsiveness of policy makers to subgroups of the public.) It may be that a small group of rich Americans dominate policy making on a subset of issues about which they care most intensely. Assessing that influence, however, will require different kinds of data and perhaps a very different strategy for identifying influence over government policy from the one I adopt here.

This book is also not about good versus bad government policy. My interest here is in how the public's preferences shape policy outcomes, not in whether those preferences are wise or misguided. In chapters 1 and 7 I discuss the formation of public preferences, the role of elite manipulation, and the extent to which public preferences can serve as a useful foundation for democratic policy making. My conclusions in this regard are fairly positive, certainly more so than those of the many observers who see the American public as typically misinformed or hoodwinked by powerful interests. Nevertheless I hold no illusion that citizens' policy preferences are in fact the best policies, or even the policies best suited to advance the interests and values of those citizens. If public policy better reflected the preferences of the majority, our country would be more democratic. But that doesn't always mean it would be better. Citizens are often shortsighted and unsophisticated in forming their judgments about public policy, just as they are often shortsighted and unsophisticated in making decisions in their own private lives, and numerous elites are more or less constantly trying to influence the public, with varying degrees of success. Yet however imperfect the public may be as a guardian of its own interests, it is a more certain guardian of those interests than any feasible alternative.

Finally, the approach I use to assess government responsiveness to public preferences does not account for all aspects of democratic representation or assess all dimensions of representational inequality. I don't examine inequalities by race or sex or age or geographic location. Nor do I consider inequalities in the administration of policies once they are adopted, or unequal opportunities to articulate one's preferences or attempt to shape the public debate. My focus is confined to the expressed preferences of Americans at different income levels and the differential association of these preferences with policy outcomes. To measure Americans' policy preferences, I assembled a dataset of survey questions asking whether respondents favored or opposed specific policy changes. Most of the analyses in this book assess how the level of support or opposition to a policy among poor, middle-class, or affluent Americans affects the probability of that policy being adopted. I call this association between policy preferences and policy outcomes the "preference/policy link" and use interchangeably the terms "responsiveness," "policy responsiveness," and "representation" to refer to this association between what citizens want and what government does. A strong positive preference/policy link for a particular income group indicates a high degree of responsiveness to the preferences of that group. To the extent that policy responsiveness is both strong and equal across income levels, it approaches the idealized condition I call "democratic responsiveness." In my analyses I estimate the strength of the preference/policy link in order to determine how much and under what conditions policy outcomes reflect the desires of more and less economically advantaged Americans.

Responsiveness, then, can be democratic (to the extent that it reflects the preferences of all citizens) or antidemocratic (to the extent that it reflects the preferences of only a privileged subgroup of citizens). But this specific kind of responsiveness—the strength of the preference/policy link—is not the only important feature of the connection between citizens' desires and government activity. For example, if government policy makers are gridlocked and little policy change is adopted during some period, then many important issues may go unaddressed. Yet if the policies that are adopted during this period are highly popular, then the preference/policy link will be strong and responsiveness in the sense that I am using it will be high.

PLAN OF THE BOOK

I begin by addressing the role of public opinion in a democracy. Many observers view the policy preferences expressed by survey respondents as largely reflecting ill-informed "nonattitudes." Given citizens' demonstrably low levels of knowledge and engagement in public affairs, I ask whether the public's policy preferences are worthy of shaping government policy. Chapter 1 takes up this question by considering the claims of public ignorance raised by scholars of public opinion. I argue that despite the failure of the public to live up to many observers' standards of citizen knowledge and engagement, the policy preferences that Americans express in public opinion surveys do in fact deserve respect as criteria from which to judge the degree of democratic responsiveness in the United States. That doesn't mean that policymakers should always follow majority opinion. But it does suggest that substantial deviations of public policy from public preferences are prima facie indications of a failure of democratic governance, and that inequality in the responsiveness of policy makers to the preferences expressed by more and less advantaged citizens is a prima facie indication of a violation of the norm of democratic equality.

Chapter 2 describes my approach to analyzing democratic representation. I first consider the difficulty of identifying a set of actual and potential policy changes that is neither too broad (e.g., encompassing minor and obscure issues about which few Americans could be expected to have meaningful opinions) nor too narrow (e.g., neglecting important issues that political actors have failed to include on the government's agenda). Next I describe the survey data and policy outcome coding that form the basis of my analyses. Finally, chapter 2 addresses the advantages and disadvantages of alternative approaches to assessing government responsiveness to the public. In particular I point to the benefits of using actual policy rather than congressional votes as the outcome of interest. For one thing, examining only congressional roll-call votes (a common approach in analyses of representation) fails to account for the importance of agenda-setting power in determining which among the many potential issues government takes up and which it ignores. In addition, many of the key decisions concerning even those issues that do result in congressional roll-call votes are made behind closed doors earlier in the legislative process. Finally, I argue that understanding representational inequality requires the analysis of discrete policy choices rather than broad measures of liberal or conservative leanings. Affluent Americans tend to be more conservative on economic policies but more liberal on issues like abortion, gay rights, and foreign aid. Consequently preference differences across income groups are canceled out when these countervailing issues are combined into broad ideological indices.

In chapter 3 I assess the link between public preferences and government policy in broad terms. I find a fairly strong association between policy outcomes and the preferences of the affluent, and weaker associations for the preferences of the middle class and the poor. I also find that most of the observed association between preferences and policies for these latter groups is accounted for by shared preferences with the affluent. When less-well-off Americans hold preferences that diverge from those of the affluent, policy responsiveness to the well-off remains strong but responsiveness to lower-income groups all but disappears.

My examination of policy responsiveness also shows that the impact of preferences on policy outcomes is most apparent at high levels of support for or opposition to a proposed policy change. For example, a difference of 20 percentage points in support for a policy has little effect if opinion is evenly divided (e.g., the difference between 40 percent and 60 percent favorability) but a much greater effect if opinion leans in one direction or the other (e.g., between 20 and 40 percent or between 60 and 80 percent favorability). This pattern implies that the most politically significant aspect of public preference is less likely to lie in the simple distinction between majority support and opposition than in the *degree* of support or opposition among the relevant group.

Chapter 3 also addresses alternative explanations for the representational inequality I find. First, I show that the reliability of my policy-preference measures does not differ significantly across income groups. Nor is differential responsiveness caused by differences in the breadth of opinionation across income groups (i.e., the proportion of respondents at different income levels that have opinions on the issues contained in my dataset). Differences in the strength of opinion (i.e., the extent to which respondents' preferences are held "strongly" versus "somewhat") also fail to explain patterns of representational inequality. Finally, I address the possibility that the link between preferences and policy outcomes reflects not the influence of the public (or of the affluent segment of the public) over government policy, but rather the influence of policy makers and other elites on the public's preferences. Drawing on a variety of evidence from my own data and from previous scholarship, I argue that while both these processes contribute somewhat to the observed association of preferences and policy outcomes, the influence of the public over government policy likely accounts for the bulk of the association I observe in my analyses.

While chapter 3 shows dramatic representational inequalities between lower- and higher-income Americans, chapter 4 looks at the variation in this inequality across substantive issue domains. For the most part I find the overall pattern of unequal responsiveness reproduced across each of the four issue domains I examine. A detailed look at preferences and policy outcomes in each domain shows how government policy would differ if it more equally reflected the preferences of all Americans. For example, in the economic domain we would expect a more progressive tax system, stricter corporate regulation, and a higher minimum wage; foreign policy would reflect a more protectionist trade regime and less foreign aid; policies on "religious" or "moral" issues such as abortion and gay rights would be more conservative. On many of these policies, the differences across income groups are matters of degree rather than differences in which side of an issue the majority favors. But as chapter 3 shows, degree of support (or opposition) can be as politically consequential as whether a majority favors or opposes the policy, if not more so.

My analyses in chapter 4 do show a partial exception to the general pattern of representational inequality in the case of social welfare. On issues such as Social Security, Medicare, school vouchers, and public-works spending, policies are more responsive to the preferences of poor and middle-class people than is true for the other issue domains I examine. The reason, I argue, is that poor and middle-income Americans have interest-group allies on these issues that they lack elsewhere. The American Association of Retired People (AARP), teachers' unions, the health care industry, and other lobbying interests share the preferences of less-well-off Americans on these issues and serve to pull policy outcomes in the direction that both the less advantaged and the interest groups prefer.

The identification of interest groups as important in explaining variation in representational inequality in chapter 4 leads to a broader examination of the role of interest groups in chapter 5. For these analyses I develop a measure of interest-group alignment on each of the proposed policy changes in my dataset. Using this measure I show that while interest group alignments are strongly related to policy outcomes, they do not explain the representational inequalities documented in the previous chapters. Nor is it the case that the preferences of the public (or of affluent members of the public) are more or less influential when interest groups are more strongly engaged on an issue. Instead I argue that interest groups form an essentially parallel channel of influence over government policy. When interest groups and affluent Americans agree, policy makers are very likely to follow suit. When these two influences work at cross-purposes, they typically prevent policy from changing—whether it is interest groups or affluent members of the public that favor the status quo. I conclude that interest groups help to explain the patterns of policy outcomes in my data and to account for anomalous cases such as outcomes that are more consistent with the preferences of the poor or the middle class than of the affluent. But interest groups as a whole cannot be held accountable for the economic biases in policy responsiveness.

In chapters 6 and 7 I examine changes over time in political conditions and the impact of those changes on policy responsiveness. Chapter 6 begins by describing additions to my dataset and modifications to its structure to better assess how representation has differed across time and political context. I then examine the role of the electoral cycle, showing that responsiveness to all income groups is highest in presidential election years, but that this "representational boost" is greatest for the least-well-off Americans. Consequently representational inequality is lowest during presidential election years (although even in these periods, the preference/policy link remains strongest for the affluent and weakest for the poor). I also show in chapter 6 that responsiveness to the preferences of well-off Americans increases in the first years after control of the presidency shifts from one party to the other. This pattern is much weaker for the middle class and wholly absent for the poor. Thus the flurry of policy making that typically characterizes a new partisan regime in Washington tends to advance the preferences of the affluent but not those of the less well-off.

Finally, chapter 6 explores the impact of political parties on representation by contrasting periods in which Republicans had greater control of Congress and the presidency with periods in which the Democrats dominated the federal government. The Democratic Party has long been recognized as the party of the working class, and less-well-off Americans continue to identify as Democrats to a greater extent than do the affluent. But, unexpectedly, representational inequality is greater and responsiveness to all income levels (including the poor) lower under Democratic control. Analyses of the specific issues that account for these partisan patterns of representation show that they are largely a consequence of the core policy commitments of the two parties, including the broad unpopularity of tax increases (and popularity of tax cuts), approval of the Reagan defense buildup, support for the Afghan and Iraq wars (at least in their early stages), opposition to loosening restrictions on immigration, and support for George W. Bush's "faith-based initiative." In addition the Democratic Party's long-standing alliance with organized labor has eroded as the party has adopted a more free-market orientation toward regulation and trade policy over the past decades (exemplified by the ratification of the North American Free Trade Agreement under unified Democratic control). A different partisan pattern does emerge in the social welfare domain, however, where responsiveness to the poor is greater under Democratic Party control and responsiveness to the affluent is greater under Republican control (the policy responsiveness for the middle class is about equal under Democrats and Republicans).

It is important to note that the stronger policy responsiveness for poor Americans under Republican than Democratic control does not mean that policies that benefit the poor in material terms are more likely to be adopted when the Republicans hold power. I show in chapter 6 that policies with clearly downwardly redistributive consequences, such as increases in the minimum wage, are considerably more likely to be adopted under Democratic rule, while policies with upwardly redistributive consequences, such as reductions in the estate tax, are more common when Republicans are in control. But these redistributive policies, while very important, are a small fraction of the policies in my dataset, and preferences on these policies do not differ as consistently or as strongly across income levels as one might suppose.

Chapter 7 addresses broader trends in policy responsiveness over the past decades. My expectation was that representational inequality had grown in the United States along with the growth in economic inequality. I did find evidence of this pattern in the steadily rising responsiveness to the well-off—but not to other income levels—over the four decades covered by my data. But the story is more complicated than this, and short-term fluctuations in political conditions are powerful influences that overlay long-term trends and shape responsiveness to all income levels. Specifically, chapter 7 shows that an evenly divided Congress enhances responsiveness to poor, middle-class, and affluent Americans alike, as parties and politicians (temporarily) neglect their own policy commitments in an effort to bolster their support among the public. I also show that the policy gridlock that grows out of partisan polarization serves, counterintuitively, to enhance responsiveness as well. Gridlock reduces the *amount* of policy change and consequently diminishes the extent to which the federal government addresses the public's concerns. But gridlock, I show, impedes unpopular policies more than popular policies. As a result policy outcomes during periods of high gridlock are more consistent with public preferences, as only those policies with the broadest public support are able to generate sufficient political pressure to overcome the "gridlock filter."

Political conditions like partisan regime change, majority party strength in Congress, and gridlock help to account for some unexpected patterns of policy responsiveness over time. For example, I anticipated a high degree of responsiveness to the poor and the middle class during the Lyndon Johnson years but found low levels of responsiveness to all income levels instead. I argue in chapter 7 that the strong Democratic control during this period insulated the Johnson administration from public pressures and allowed the Democratic Party to pursue its own policy agenda—an agenda that included both broadly popular policies like Medicare and federal aid to education, and broadly unpopular policies like (many aspects of) the war on poverty and immigration reform. In stark contrast the early years of George W. Bush's first administration were characterized by an evenly divided Congress and a highly polarized political climate following the disputed 2000 presidential election. Policy outcomes in this period were highly responsive to the preferences of all income levels—a significant and unexpected departure from the lack of responsiveness to poor and middle-class Americans characteristic of Bush's predecessors. But as I show in chapter 7, this unique set of circumstances was short-lived, and responsiveness to public preferences plummeted during the period of strong Republican control that characterized the middle years of Bush's presidency. Political conditions, then, not a predisposition of the Bush administration to respond to the preferences of the less advantaged, account for this unexpected finding.

The patterns of responsiveness that emerge from my analyses in chapters 6 and 7 support a view of political parties as "policy maximizers" captured by activists and interest groups with strong commitments to enacting their preferred policies. My findings seem to support the notion that parties in the United States have evolved from broad-based, vote-maximizing organizations attentive to the preferences of large and diverse publics to coalitions of intense, narrow "policy demanders." Yet the fact that parties and politicians must be forced by political circumstances to respond to the preferences of the public means that they *can* be forced by those circumstances. Thus there is reason to hope that reforms that enhance political competition can intensify the beneficial impacts of electoral proximity and equal partisan division of Congress and thereby strengthen the responsiveness of policy makers to poor and affluent Americans alike.

In my concluding chapter I further explore the role of money in American politics and seek to identify the most promising strategies to enhance representational equality. I focus on citizens' engagement with the political system, showing that affluent Americans are more likely to vote, to volunteer in political campaigns, and to donate money to political causes. But donating money is the only component of political participation that mirrors the patterns of representational inequality revealed in earlier chapters. This finding, which parallels those of other studies of political influence, suggests that the disproportionate responsiveness to the preferences of the affluent cannot be attributed to their higher turnout rates or their greater involvement with political campaigns. Money—the "mother's milk" of politics—is the root of representational inequality, and as political campaigns have become more expensive over the decades, the responsiveness to those who supply the necessary resources has grown.

I close by exploring efforts to tame the flow of money in politics and suggest possible avenues by which democratic responsiveness might be increased and representational inequalities lessened. Achieving even modest gains in this regard will be difficult. Campaign finance reform has been likened to squeezing a balloon; if you push in one place the balloon simply pops out in another. Moreover, the increasing concentration of income and wealth in an ever smaller slice of well-off Americans raises the specter of an ever increasing concentration of political power as those with the means to influence the government shape policy in ways that further reinforce their advantaged position.

But American democracy did not spring fully grown from the Revolution of 1776. Voting rights were limited at first to white, male property holders, and it took long decades—indeed centuries—of struggle to include poor people, women, and African Americans among the electorate. My analyses suggest that the power to shape policy outcomes has not been following this hopeful trajectory. In recent decades the responsiveness of policy makers to the preferences of the affluent has steadily grown, but responsiveness to less-well-off Americans has not. Our country faces huge challenges in the years ahead in responding to economic uncertainty, increasing ethnic diversity, shortcomings in our educational system, and the emergence of new global military and economic powers. How we respond to these challenges will depend significantly on whose preferences guide government policy making, and those policies in turn will significantly shape the life circumstances of more- and less-advantaged Americans.

CHAPTER 1

Citizen Competence and Democratic
Decision Making

THIS BOOK IS ABOUT the relationship between what the American public wants government to do and what government does. I analyze the relationship between public preferences and government policy in order to determine the conditions under which government responds to the will of the governed, and to identify who it is among the governed that government responds to. In the chapters that follow I document enormous inequalities in the responsiveness of policy makers to the preferences of more- and less-well-off Americans, inequalities that have both practical implications for the lives of the rich and the poor and normative implications for our understanding of the society in which we live.

The radical idea at the core of democracy—that the power to shape public policies should be widely and more or less equally shared among citizens—presupposes that citizens are widely (and more or less equally) competent to exercise that power. It is helpful, therefore, before setting off to assess public preferences and their relationship to government decision making, to identify the role assigned to such preferences according to different understandings of democracy, and to assess the role the public reasonably can be expected to play in the process of democratic governance, given what we known about the nature of public opinion and the modest levels of political knowledge and engagement of the American citizenry.

Critics of democracy since Plato have questioned the ability of citizens to guide their political rulers. If citizens' preferences on policy issues are fickle or misinformed, or if they are too easily manipulated by powerful interests, then equality of influence over government decision making would produce undesirable, if not disastrous, results. However appealing equality of representation may be from a normative perspective, the limitations of the public may present a practical impediment to meaningful democracy. If the public is incapable of forming sensible preferences on matters of public policy, then the representational inequalities that I document in the following chapters take on a very different normative hue. In this case inequality in responsiveness to the public may reflect not the shortcomings of government decision makers in responding to the public, but the failures of the public to form meaningful policy preferences to begin with.

In this chapter I address the problem of citizen competence. Drawing on the extensive empirical research on public opinion, I argue that democracy's critics are in many ways right in their understandings of citizens' limited political knowledge and abilities. But they are wrong in the implications of those understandings. Citizens, I argue, need not be informed about and attentive to every issue on the agenda as long as they are reasonably knowledgeable about the subset of issues they care about most. In addition, citizens need not become experts in the technical complexities of public policy as long as they can identify experts who share their general values and outlooks and can guide them in forming their political preferences. Finally, the shortcomings in individual citizens' political knowledge are substantially mitigated when individuals' preferences are aggregated; collective opinion is more consistent, more predictable, and more cogent than the individual opinions that make it up. In short, the public's preferences, imperfect as they are, constitute a reasonable basis for democratic decision making.

If the public, as I argue, is reasonably competent in forming policy preferences, then the failure of government policy to reflect those preferences, or stark inequalities in the responsiveness of policy makers to the preferences of more- and less-advantaged Americans, imply a failure of democratic governance. While we would not expect, and perhaps not desire, a perfect correspondence between majority opinion and government policy on every issue, large and persistent inequalities in responsiveness to public preferences impugn our understanding of America as a democratic society.

In the following pages I look first at the role assigned to the public according to different understandings of democracy and then assess how well the public can be expected to fulfill this role, given what we known about the nature of public opinion and the modest levels of political knowledge and engagement of the American citizenry. After concluding that the public is indeed capable of fulfilling its assigned function in democratic governance, I address some of the practical challenges involved in measuring public attitudes and assessing the responsiveness of government to citizens' preferences.

WHAT IS A DEMOCRACY?

Democracy is not one idea or even one set of ideas about the way a political community might be governed, but a disparate array of related conceptions. Rousseauean notions of the General Will and the direct participation of citizens in lawmaking contrast with republican conceptions of checks and balances in a government of elected representatives, while both are distinct from substantive conceptions of democracy involving human rights, freedoms of expression, due process of law, and universal suffrage.

Common to all conceptions of democracy is the idea that the power to shape political decisions should be shared widely. But just how citizens are expected to exercise this power varies widely across different democratic theories and different democratic polities. One school of democratic theory highlights the role of citizen engagement in democratic decision making. Such participatory conceptions of democracy call for the direct involvement of the citizenry in the process of deliberation and collective decision making, bringing to mind New England town meetings or ancient Athens. Theorists of deliberative democracy have identified an array of institutional forms that might facilitate deliberation in larger polities as well, like neighborhood councils or stakeholder meetings that bring together representatives of the various interests involved in a particular issue or policy decision. Central to theories of deliberative democracy is the notion that citizens' preferences and their understanding of their own interests are not exogenous to the political process but can and should be shaped by it. Through deliberation, by this account, citizens come to better understand both the issue at hand and their fellow citizens' perspectives on that issue, and through this understanding refine and revise their preferences and beliefs.

In contrast to deliberative theories, aggregative theories of democracy take citizens' preferences and interests as given and focus on the mechanisms by which those preferences are incorporated (or aggregated) into political decisions. The more demanding versions of aggregative democracy require citizens to be well informed about the issues of the day and the alternative policies proposed by candidates and parties. In one widely quoted formulation of this conception of democracy, Bernard Berelson, Paul Lazarsfeld, and William McPhee write, "The democratic citizen is expected to be well informed about political affairs. He is supposed to know what the issues are, what their history is, what the relevant facts are, what alternatives are proposed ... [and] what the likely consequences are."[1] As Berelson, Lazarsfeld, and McPhee note, actual citizens rarely meet this lofty ideal.

Minimalist conceptions of democracy view citizens of modern polities as too uninterested and uninformed about politics and social policy to fulfill their assigned role in either the deliberative or aggregative theories of democracy sketched above. The most influential formulation of the minimalist conception of democracy is Joseph Schumpeter's. Schumpeter believed that most citizens, including the most educated and successful in society, simply do not apply much effort to formulating political opinions.

As one person among a huge multitude, the average citizen lacks any clear sense of responsibility for political matters and thus lacks the motivation to acquire information or to use the information he or she has in a disciplined, rational manner. "The typical citizen," Schumpeter writes, "drops down to a lower level of mental performance as soon as he enters the political field. He argues and analyzes in a way which he would readily recognize as infantile within the sphere of his real interests."[2]

Believing that few citizens hold preferences worthy of shaping government policy, Schumpeter put forward a model of democracy in which the role of the public is limited to choosing between competing candidates for political office. Democracy, for Schumpeter, is strictly a mechanism of governance based on the competitive selection of political leaders. "The principle of democracy then merely means that the reins of government should be handed to those who command more support than do any of the competing individuals or teams."[3] But once those leaders are selected, the preferences of the citizenry should have no bearing on government decision making. "The voters," he writes, "must understand that, once they have elected an individual, political action is his business and not theirs."[4]

Citizens' Role in Democratic Governance

To explore the role of citizens in democratic governance, I start by looking at the expectations or requirements of the public as embodied in the minimalist conception of democracy. The central task for the public, according to Schumpeter and other theorists of "minimal democracy," is to choose among alternative political parties or candidates.[5] But what might the basis of this choice be? If voters are unable to form sensible policy preferences, as minimalist theories of democracy suggest, how can they decide which candidate they prefer?

The least demanding basis for choosing among competing candidates is a simple evaluation of the incumbent officeholder's performance, as elaborated in theories of retrospective voting. According to the retrospective voting model, citizens need not form preferences on a multitude of political issues but simply assess the performance of the incumbent politician or administration. The voter returns the incumbent to office if he or she has performed above some threshold, and if not the voter casts a ballot for the challenger. Central to this view of the public's democratic role is the ease with which it can be carried out. As Morris Fiorina writes, "In order to ascertain whether the incumbents have performed poorly or well, citizens need only calculate the changes in their own welfare."[6]

Many voters do seem to behave in accord with the retrospective model, as reflected in the strong association between economic conditions and election outcomes.[7] But other voters have strong ties to political parties and are unlikely to be swayed by economic conditions. Moreover retrospective voting in this simple form applies directly only to "consensus issues" on which all voters prefer the same outcome, like a good economy or low crime rates.[8] Yet many prominent issues that government addresses are matters of contentious disagreement: the level and progressivity of taxes, gun control, abortion, foreign military engagements, environmental and energy policy, and so on. As Fiorina points out, judging retrospective performance on these issues requires a preference or criterion by which success or failure can be measured. Far from being undemanding, retrospective voting on nonconsensual issue requires *both* a policy preference and the knowledge of whether the incumbent candidate has helped advance the desired outcome.

Consensus issues like economic well-being may appear to avoid the necessity for citizens to form preferences on complex policy issues. But even as seemingly simple a judgment as economic well-being can be quite complex. For example, individual voters must assess the degree to which their own economic fortunes reflect those of the country. If they've lost a job and the national unemployment rate has increased, voting against the incumbent seems straightforward. But what if they've lost their job while the national unemployment rate has declined? In that case citizens must make some assessment of the tie between their personal situation and broader national conditions. Studies show that voters do attempt to make these sorts of distinctions.[9]

Furthermore, accurate retrospective evaluations require citizens to distinguish between those aspects of current conditions for which incumbent politicians might plausibly be held responsible and those that are clearly outside their control. For example, voters are more likely to reelect their governors when state economic conditions are good and cast them out of office when times are bad. But when state economic conditions appear to reflect national conditions (which are presumably beyond any governor's control), voters adjust accordingly and attribute less blame or credit for state conditions to their incumbent governor.[10] While such patterns suggest a degree of rational accounting among members of the public, apportioning blame for current conditions, economic or otherwise, is a difficult task (even for economists), and voters seem to do a mediocre job of it at best.[11]

Minimalist democracy could persist, of course, even if voters do a poor job of forming retrospective evaluations, ignoring concerns about the extent to which incumbent politicians are responsible for changes in social conditions or using such simple but misleading criteria as only the most recent trends in economic performance.[12] But uninformed or misguided retrospection is no more viable a basis for democracy than uninformed policy preferences. In short, even the least demanding conceptions of democracy require citizens to form preferences and to make difficult assessments of the responsibility of political leaders. But are citizens capable of fulfilling even this least demanding understanding of their role in democratic governance? Skeptics of democracy since Plato have held that ordinary citizens are ill-equipped to guide government decision making, and a half-century of survey data on political knowledge lends credence to this skepticism. My view is that few Americans fulfill the stringent expectations of the more demanding conceptions of democracy, but that public opinion is nevertheless a worthy, if imperfect, guide for government policy.

Does the American Public Hold Meaningful Policy Preferences?

Scholars of American public opinion can be roughly divided into two schools of thought: One concludes that Americans' low level of political knowledge and apparent lack of clear and consistent policy preferences show that the public is indeed incapable of providing meaningful guidance to government decision makers on policy matters. The other school of thought acknowledges the gap between traditional expectations and the public's performance but believes that compensatory mechanisms allow citizens to form meaningful preferences, at least in the aggregate, even in the face of low information levels and considerable inconsistency in preferences as revealed by survey responses.

In his seminal paper "The Nature of Belief Systems in Mass Publics," Philip Converse paints a bleak picture of the American public as largely lacking coherent political preferences. Converse observed that survey respondents are apt to express different preferences when presented with the identical question on different occasions, that preferences on one policy issue are at best weakly associated with preferences on seemingly related issues, and that most Americans poorly understand broad organizing principles like liberalism or conservatism. Confronted with this evidence, Converse concludes that the preferences respondents report on surveys consist largely of "non-attitudes" and that "large portions of [the] electorate do not have meaningful beliefs, even on issues that have formed the basis for intense political controversy among elites for substantial periods of time."[13]

Many subsequent assessments of Americans' political preferences have been only slightly more hopeful. After examining hundreds of survey measures of political information, for example, Michael Delli Carpini and Scott Keeter conclude that "more than a small fraction of the public is reasonably well informed about politics—informed enough to meet high standards of good citizenship. Many of the basic institutions and procedures of government are known to half or more of the public, as are the relative positions of the parties on many major issues of the day."[14] But the flip side of this coin is that a large proportion of the public does not rise to this level. "Large numbers of American citizens are woefully underinformed," Delli Carpini and Keeter write, and "overall levels of knowledge are modest at best."[15]

These two analyses address the two most troubling aspects of public opinion, casting doubt on the feasibility of meaningful democratic government: the public's lack of knowledge about political affairs and the seeming randomness of policy preferences expressed in surveys as reflected in their lack of stability over time, and the weakness of associations between related issues or across similar formulations of the same policy issue.

Scholars who take a more sanguine view of the quality of citizens' policy preferences point to three aspects of mass political attitudes to explain how a public with minimal political information can nevertheless form meaningful issue preferences. First, citizens with modest levels of information might turn to more knowledgeable others for cues about the desirability of alternative policies or politicians. Second, individual citizens are not equally interested in the full range of political issues at play at any given time but tend to specialize in a subset of issues about which they are more knowledgeable and have more stable and well-thought-out preferences. The division of citizens into these issue publics means that the ability of any individual citizen to participate meaningfully in shaping government policy should be judged relative to the set of issues that that individual cares about; all citizens need not hold equally well-developed preferences on all issues for the public to fulfill its role in democratic governance. Finally, the fickle element of individual citizens' policy preferences will, to some degree at least, tend to cancel out when preferences are aggregated across the public as a whole (or across distinctive subgroups of the public). Aggregate opinion, by this reckoning, will typically be more stable, with a higher signal to noise ratio than the individual opinions that make it up.

CUE TAKING AS A BASIS FOR POLITICAL PREFERENCES

Given the stringent standards for the democratic citizen laid out by Berelson, Lazarsfeld, and McPhee, it is not surprising that these authors view the American public as falling short. Political opinions, they write, are more frequently "matters of sentiment and disposition rather than 'reasoned preferences' ... characterized more by faith than by conviction and by wishful expectation rather than careful prediction of consequences."[16] Yet Berelson and his coauthors believe that despite the public's general lack of politically relevant information and poor quality of reasoning about policy matters, the ignorant many are able to leverage the expertise of the well-informed few who are politically knowledgeable and engaged. If most citizens are indifferent to and uninformed about public affairs, it is nevertheless true that some are absorbed in the world of politics and policy. Moreover social networks, they maintain, allow for a division of labor in which more informed opinion leaders provide policy insights and endorsements to their less-informed friends and acquaintances. "The political genius of the citizenry," they conclude, "may reside less in how well they can judge public policy than in how well they can judge the people who advise them how to judge public policy."[17]

Taking cues from more knowledgeable elites or acquaintances is a sensible strategy for citizens who lack the ability or inclination to gather the information needed to formulate a preference on a given policy issue. Anthony Downs, writing shortly after Berelson, Lazarsfeld, and McPhee, notes that the average citizen "cannot be expert in all the fields of policy that are relevant to his decision. Therefore, he will seek assistance from men who are experts in those fields, have the same political goals he does, and have good judgment."[18]

A substantial literature has developed over the past decades that identifies the wide range of cue-givers that citizens can rely on in forming political judgments.[19] The simplest cue-taking models posit that citizens adopt the policy positions expressed by like-minded elites and ignore those of the non-like-minded (judged on the basis of partisan or ideological compatibility, or the more specific affinities associated, for example, with a citizen's religious, union, or professional organization). Cue-givers of this sort can be either social leaders whose views are transmitted through the media or individual acquaintances who are perceived as comparatively well informed on the issue at hand.

A somewhat more complex understanding of cue taking as a basis for political preference formation allows citizens to adapt cues to their own purposes by adopting the positions of like-minded cue-givers and adopting the opposite positions of those espoused by the non-like-minded. Arthur Lupia illustrates this process nicely in an experiment in which respondents were told either that Jesse Jackson or that Patrick Buchanan favors or opposes no-fault automobile insurance.[20] Democratic respondents tended to shift their own preference on no-fault insurance in the direction of the position attributed to Jackson and away from the position attributed to Buchanan, while the opposite was true for Republican respondents. Interestingly, Democrats were more influenced by Buchanan's purported position on the issue than by Jackson's, while Republicans reacted more strongly to Jackson's position than to Buchanan's. That is, the dissuasive impact of the non-like-minded cue-giver was stronger than the persuasive impact of the cue-giver with perceived compatibility of ideological leanings.

The strategy of turning to those with greater knowledge when faced with a challenging decision is hardly limited to political novices. Even citizens who follow politics closely will inevitably lack sufficient information (or technical expertise) to form opinions from scratch on many issues. In a modern nation there are simply too many detailed and technical issues for even the most motivated members of the public to keep abreast of. Indeed, even elected representatives who have abundant informational resources and who follow politics for a living turn to experts in specific issue areas for advice and take cues from other representatives in their own party who specialize in particular issue domains.[21]

Issue Publics

Cue taking is one mechanism by which citizens may be able to form meaningful preferences on issues despite a lack of knowledge and expertise, and the relationship between cue-taker and cue-giver highlights the large differences in political knowledge held by different members of the public. But large differences in knowledge can also exist from one policy issue to another for the same person.

Among the many enduring contributions of Converse's seminal paper is the concept of issue publics—the obvious but often overlooked fact that different people care about different political issues. To participate in democratic governance, citizens must be able to form meaningful preferences on the policy issues that government addresses. But that does not mean that every citizen must have a preference on every issue. Given the broad range of backgrounds, interests, and situations that citizens in a large and diverse society face, it would be surprising if there were not substantial variations in the specific political issues that different citizens care about and attend to.

Converse based his negative assessment of the mass public's political preferences in part on the substantially stronger intercorrelations of preferences on related issues among the political elites he surveyed. (Converse's sample of political elites consisted of candidates for the U.S. Congress, arguably an unrealistically sophisticated comparison group.) Nevertheless, when Converse restricted his analysis of the public's policy positions in a given issue domain like foreign aid or racial policy to those respondents whom he judged to be members of a given issue public,[22] he found that the intercorrelations among ordinary Americans resembled those among his political elites: "removal from analysis of individuals who, through indifference or ignorance, lie outside the issue publics in question serves to close much of the gap in constraint levels between mass and elite publics."[23]

Subsequent analyses confirm Converse's insight regarding issue publics.[24] Jon Krosnick, for example, sorted survey respondents into issue publics on the basis of the level of importance they attached to a dozen different political issues. Krosnick reports that the greater the importance a respondent attached to a given policy issue, the more likely he or she was to mention that issue as a reason for liking or disliking the presidential candidates, the less likely he or she was to change an issue preference in response to persuasive communications, and the more stable his or her reported issue preference was over time.

Research on issue publics suggests that assessments of the quality of public preferences that look only at the average level of knowledge, preference stability, or other measures across the public as a whole may strongly understate the degree to which a typical citizen holds meaningful policy preferences. True, the typical citizen may attend to only a few of the many issues facing the country at any time. But if citizens have sensible and reasonably informed preferences on the subset of issues that they care most about, and if they use those issues disproportionately as a basis for choosing among parties and candidates, then the public can fulfill its assigned role in democratic governance, even if most citizens lack meaningful opinions on most issues.

THE "MAGIC OF AGGREGATION" AND THE QUALITY OF PUBLIC PREFERENCES

Cue taking suggests that even citizens with minimal information may be able to form meaningful preferences by relying on others who share their general outlook or political orientation, and the division of the citizenry into issue publics suggests that meaningful participation in democratic governance does not require all citizens to hold meaningful preferences on all issues. A third factor relevant to the assessment of the public's role in democracy is that the aggregate preferences of the public as a whole have different characteristics from the individual preferences that make them up.

The eighteenth-century French philosopher and mathematician Condorcet explained in his famous "jury theorem" that if each individual in a group has even a modest tendency to be correct, the group as an aggregate can have a very high probability of reaching the correct decision (and the larger the group, the higher the probability that the collective judgment will be correct). This insight has been applied to the political attitudes expressed in surveys to suggest that the errors in respondents' reports of their own preferences will, at least under some circumstances, tend to cancel out, resulting in a measure of aggregate opinion that is more stable and more reliable than the individual opinions that make it up.[25]

But how can respondents be "wrong" about their own preferences? Two different kinds of errors in survey-based measures of policy preferences can be distinguished. First, even if respondents had perfectly fixed and certain views on a particular policy option, the reports of those views as captured in surveys would contain some degree of error. The ambiguities of question wording, the difficulty in matching a specific sentiment to the available response options, and mistakes in reading or hearing the survey question or recording the respondent's answer will all introduce some degree of measurement error.

Second, most respondents are not likely to have perfectly fixed and certain views on most political issues. Current understandings of political attitudes suggest that citizens typically hold a variety of considerations relevant to a given policy issue and use those considerations to construct a position on a policy question when asked by a survey interviewer.[26] For example, if asked whether he or she favors cutting government spending on foreign aid, a survey respondent might consider his or her views about taxes and government spending, about humanitarian needs in developing countries, about waste and corruption in those countries, about competing domestic needs, and so on. This process of canvassing considerations and constructing positions is an imperfect one, however. Given the time and motivational constraints typical of a survey interview, only a subset of all possible considerations bearing on a particular question are likely to be brought to mind. Moreover this subset of considerations may be biased toward those that are at the top of the head as a result of earlier questions in the survey, stories that have been in the news, recent experiences the respondent may have had, specific aspects of the question wording, or any number of other reasons.

From this perspective most citizens cannot be said to "have attitudes" corresponding to a particular survey question on a political issue, in the sense that those attitudes existed in a crystallized form before the question was asked. But individual citizens can be said to have "response tendencies" or "long-term preferences" that represents their (hypothetical) average opinion if it were to be ascertained repeatedly over time.[27] This Platonic "true attitude" is nothing more than the imperfectly revealed average of these hypothetical repeated preference constructions (in the same way that a "true circle" is a hypothetical shape that any actual circle in the real world can only approximate).

It is impractical, of course, to measure citizens' long-term preferences by repeatedly surveying the same individuals. But aggregating survey responses across many individuals will produce much the same result (without the problem of dealing with new information or changed circumstances that might alter the set of relevant considerations). To the extent that the biases in formulating a preference from a given set of considerations are randomly distributed across individuals they will balance out, just as the errors in individuals' judgments in a jury context cancel each other out. If randomly distributed idiosyncratic factors lead individual citizens to report preferences that differ from their true or long-term preferences, those errors will lead some citizens to underreport support for a policy while leading others to overreport support. With a large enough sample of citizens, these errors will cancel out, resulting in aggregate preferences that closely match the average of the individuals' long-term preferences. Of course, not all factors that lead citizens to wrongly report their issue preferences will be random and therefore offsetting, a concern I'll return to below.

The most thorough examination of aggregate opinion toward public policy is Benjamin Page and Robert Shapiro's influential book *The Rational Public*. Page and Shapiro do not view aggregation as a cure for all the shortcomings of public opinion. But they argue that collective preferences display a degree of stability and cogency that far exceed the typical individual-level preferences that make them up.

> While we grant the rational ignorance of most individuals, and the possibility that their policy preferences are shallow and unstable, we maintain that public opinion as a *collective* phenomenon is nonetheless stable (though not immovable), meaningful, and indeed rational ... it is able to make distinctions; it is organized in coherent patterns; it is reasonable, based on the best available information; and it is adaptive to new information or changed circumstances.[28]

Moreover, they maintain, "surveys accurately measure this stable, meaningful, and reasonable collective public opinion."[29] The collective rationality of public opinion stems, Page and Shapiro argue, from the aggregation of individual opinions that cancel out both random measurement errors in surveys and temporary fluctuations in individuals' opinions. The aggregate preferences that result from this process tend to be quite stable but also exhibit sensible responsiveness to changing conditions. For example, public support for unemployment assistance increases as unemployment rates rise, public support for defense spending increases when the threat of war goes up, public support for tax cuts declines when tax rates are lowered, and so on.

Page and Shapiro also show that trends in public opinion among sub-groups of Americans tend strongly to move in parallel. That is, even when preferences diverge across income, racial, or age categories, social conditions that shift preferences in a given direction for one subset of the public do so for the other subsets as well; the rich and poor, blacks and whites, the old and the young tend to shift in the same direction and by similar amounts in response to changes in political and social conditions.[30]

FALSE CONSCIOUSNESS AND ELITE MANIPULATION

Two principal objections have been raised about the "miracle of aggregation." The first, which Page and Shapiro discuss at some length, is that errors in individuals' policy preferences will not always be randomly distributed. One source of nonrandom error in preference formation is misinformation that leads most or all members of the public to shift their policy preferences in the same direction. For example, John Kennedy and others claimed during the late 1950s that the United States was facing a "missile gap" with the Soviet Union. In retrospect it is clear not only that was there no missile gap (the United States maintained a considerable advantage in nuclear missiles), but that good evidence was available at the time demonstrating the absence of such a gap. This sort of misinformation will inevitably pervert the preferences that the public would otherwise hold on related policy issues (in this case, defense spending and foreign policy).

Military and foreign policy have long been identified as domains in which elite actors (especially the president and administration) have an informational advantage over other elites and the public at large, and many of the most glaring examples of elite manipulation of public opinion concern foreign policy. In addition to Kennedy's purported missile gap, apparently successful attempts to shape public opinion through misinformation include the 1964 Gulf of Tonkin incident, which Johnson used to pressure Congress into expanding U.S. military involvement in Vietnam, and efforts by the George W. Bush administration to tie Saddam Hussein to the September 11 terrorist attacks.[31] While these cases are troubling, and many more could be cited, a clear assessment of the significance of the problem of elite manipulation must consider counterexamples as well. Despite years of effort, for example, the Reagan administration was never able to convince the public to support its policy of military intervention in Central America.[32] A similar failure to shape public views was displayed in the G. W. Bush administration's resistance to creating a cabinet department of homeland security. Bush insisted for months that domestic antiterror efforts should be located within the executive office of the president, but the public was unmoved, and in an abrupt turnaround Bush came out in June 2002 in favor of establishing the Department of Homeland Security.[33]

By its very nature, foreign policy is a domain in which the executive branch has an informational advantage over both the public and other elites. The practical control of this information, and the perceived legitimacy of restricting access to information with national security implications, will perhaps always present a challenge to government accountability in foreign policy.

While foreign policy may always be a problematic domain for democratic decision making, concerns about the manipulation of the public by elites have frequently focused on economic and redistributive issues. The concept of "false consciousness" has come to refer to the acceptance by those who are disadvantaged of beliefs that justify social inequalities or policies that promote those inequalities, especially when the segments of society that are advantaged by existing arrangements encourage those beliefs and policies.[34]

Without discounting this understanding, I believe there are three considerations that should make us wary of attributing the preferences of the disadvantaged (or any other social group) to false consciousness. First, efforts to convince others to support or oppose a given policy are central to political life, and these efforts nearly always involve some degree of biased information, dubious argument, and so on. While the degree of bias, misinformation, and misleading argument need not be equal among all parties to political debate, such tactics are employed by the Left as well as the Right, by Democrats, Republicans, Tea Party activists, and liberal and conservative bloggers, and even by friends and acquaintances who are more likely to make a case for favoring or opposing a given policy than to attempt to lay out a set of arguments highlighting both the pros and cons. For example, after studying the course of Bill Clinton's efforts to pass health care reform in the mid-1990s, Lawrence Jacobs and Robert Shapiro concluded that "Clinton and Republican leaders were engaged in a kind of double deception: they crafted misleading claims and they used the cover of promoting rational and critical discussions about the 'national interest' ... to obscure the play of special interests behind the scenes."[35] From this point of view, efforts to convince low-income Americans to support tax cuts that primarily benefit the rich are no different in kind from the arguments that all parties to policy debates frequently make.

Second, as observers we have a strong tendency to attribute support for positions we disagree with to false information or manipulation but attribute support for positions we agree with to sensible reasoning based on relevant facts. Many on the left, for example, attribute low-income

Americans' opposition to the inheritance tax to false consciousness since it so clearly contradicts their material interests. But these same observers view the support for the inheritance tax by George Soros or Bill Gates as resting on sensible, clear-sighted evaluations of fairness, broader benefits to society, and so on. The point is not that these interpretations are necessarily wrong (they are surely correct for some subset of low-income Americans), but that they are too easy to embrace when they hold congenial political implications.

Finally, as the previous observation suggests, outside observers must acknowledge the difficulty of identifying the true interests of another individual or social group. If we conceive of interests narrowly, as reflecting only individuals' material well-being (or that of their families), then people often hold preferences that conflict with their interests. Affluent liberals, for example, may value the perceived benefits of progressive taxation for society more generally or may hold conceptions of fairness and virtue that demand greater contributions to social welfare from those most able to pay. There is no reason to think that less-affluent or less-educated Americans do not also consider nonmaterial factors and arrive sometimes at policy preferences that contradict their narrow economic interests but fit with their broader values or conceptions of justice or fairness.

Support for the G. W. Bush administration's efforts to eliminate the estate tax, for example, might appear to be a clear case of false consciousness on the part of the public since the benefits of eliminating the tax were restricted entirely to a very small number of extremely well-off Americans. But despite the clear and divergent interests for rich Americans and everyone else, preferences regarding the estate tax are complicated by the apparently strong and widely shared noneconomic concern that the estate tax is unfair. Scholars who disagree about the political forces that led to the estate tax reforms of 2001 nevertheless agree that public opposition to the estate tax was rooted primarily in perceptions of fairness (or unfairness, to be more exact) and not in calculations of economic self-interest.[36]

My argument is not that false consciousness and elite manipulation are absent from American politics or that they should not concern us. On the contrary, elites' attempts to mislead the public are often deeply troubling. The Bush administration's efforts to link Saddam Hussein with 9/11 and the selective use of intelligence about Iraqi weapons of mass destruction in the lead-up to the Iraq War undoubtedly boosted public support for a policy with enormous consequences for America and the world.[37] My claim, instead, is that clear-cut cases of successful elite manipulation are rare, and that we should be cautious in attributing others' preferences to manipulation, especially when we disagree with those preferences.

The possibility of elite manipulation does complicate the assessment of government responsiveness to public preferences. But concerns about such manipulation typically focus on the vulnerability of the least engaged, least educated, and least-well-off members of the public. To the extent that these citizens are most susceptible to elite manipulation, we would expect to find stronger associations between the preferences they express and the policies government adopts. In fact, as the chapters that follow will show, quite the opposite is true. The link between preferences and policy outcomes is strongest for the most affluent Americans and weakest for the poor. If elites are manipulating the preferences of these arguably most vulnerable citizens, they are doing a poor job of it indeed.

Elite manipulation is one potential impediment to an informed citizenry, but shared misinformation need not result from purposeful attempts to mislead the public. Sizable misperceptions of changes in the crime rate, spending levels on foreign aid, the racial composition of the poor, or the typical length of time beneficiaries receive welfare have all been widespread among the American public at various times.[38] This kind of misinformation may result from media practices that tend to stereotype social groups (as in the overly racialized depictions of poverty) or that cater to audiences' appetite for bad news (as in the extensive coverage of crime stories in TV news, even when crime rates are in decline).

The extent of collectively held misinformation among the public is difficult to assess, in part because the truth about many politically relevant facts may not become known until later, if ever. After canvassing some of the sources and content of misinformation held by Americans, Page and Shapiro conclude that "we cannot hope to offer a precise or definitive account of the extent (or, for that matter, the nature) of information biases in the United States. But if we are on track concerning important instances of opinion manipulation and general patterns of biased and misleading information, these pose troubling implications for the workings of democracy."[39]

Just how troubled we should be about biased or misleading information is difficult to judge. To the extent that misinformation is universal (or nearly universal) among elites and the public at large, it is hard to see how any form of government could make optimal decisions. If the best information available at the time a decision is made turns out in retrospect to be wrong, it hardly makes sense to blame the public for relying on that information. The consequences of misinformation that are unique to democracy, on the other hand, are those in which large numbers of citizens fall prey to *avoidable* misperceptions or biases. For example, if misinformation that the best-informed citizens knew to be untrue influenced the preferences of the majority of citizens, then a democratic government that reflected the public's collective preference might do a poor job of serving the public's true interests. Misinformation always has the potential to bias preferences under any form of government, but the special challenge to democracy arises from situations in which the collective preferences of the public would be different if the public had the same level of relevant information that the most politically knowledgeable and engaged members of society hold.

In the following section I discuss the degree to which this sort of misinformation appears to bias public preferences and undermine democratic governance. But there is a second principled objection to the optimistic account of aggregate opinion that we must consider as well. As Scott Althaus explains, the notion that errors in the individual preferences reported on surveys will cancel out when those individual reports are aggregated rests on the assumption that preferences are measured in such a manner that errors in one direction and errors in the other direction are equally likely.[40] But this is not always the case. For example, consider a question with only two response options (in addition to "Don't know"), such as those gauging support or opposition to some proposed policy change. Among citizens who really favor the proposed change, some proportion will mistakenly be recorded as opposing it because they misunderstood the question, they were misinformed about the policy, or the interviewer simply entered the wrong code. But if these sources of error are randomly distributed across the survey respondents, then (approximately) the same proportion of citizens who really oppose the policy will be recorded as favoring it.

It might appear that this balancing out of opposite errors will leave the aggregate preference on this policy as measured by this hypothetical survey question unchanged. But that is only the case if equal numbers of citizens support and oppose the policy. If true supporters outnumber opponents by, say, three to one, then the number of survey respondents erroneously counted as opponents will be three times as great as the number erroneously counted as supporters. In this example if 20 percent of all respondents are misclassified, then 15 percent of the respondents will be erroneously shifted from supporters to opponents (20 percent of 75) while 5 percent will be erroneously shifted from opponents to supporters (20 percent of 25). As a result, it will appear that 65 percent rather than 75 percent of respondents favor the proposed policy, and 35 percent rather than 25 percent oppose it.[41]

More generally, random errors will shift the apparent distribution of preferences on questions with only two valid responses toward 50 percent. (If the true distribution of preferences on such an item is 50 percent, then random errors will in fact be equal and offsetting.) The same logic applies to survey questions with more than two valid response categories to the extent that the preferences of respondents who belong in the highest category can only be moved downward while those in the lowest category can only be moved upward. If the true distribution of long-term preferences is asymmetrical, then random errors will not cancel out but will tend to move the recorded mean toward the center of the scale.

This sort of nonoffsetting error on policy issues with asymmetric distributions of preferences will dampen the apparent extremity of preferences for the public as a whole. This in itself is not likely to present much of a problem for the analyses of public preferences and government policy in the following chapters. The distribution of preferences across issues would appear to be somewhat more centrist and less extremist than is really the case, but the relationship between those preferences and the probability of a proposed policy change being adopted would look much the same.

A greater concern would arise if the tendency to provide wrong answers to the policy preferences measures varied systematically across groups. A group might appear to hold more centrist views simply because more of its members' preferences were recorded with error. If so, the apparent relationship between this group's preferences and actual policy outcomes would appear stronger than it otherwise would.[42] Most analyses of measurement error in political attitude questions focus on differences in question format rather than differences among types of respondents. There is some evidence, however, that somewhat higher levels of measurement error exist for less-educated respondents.[43] Since education and income are related, we might expect higher levels of measurement error among lower-income respondents as well. If so, the apparent relationship between preferences and policy outcomes for low-income respondents would be biased upward somewhat relative to the relationship for higher-income respondents. As chapter 3 reveals, the relationship between preferences and policy outcomes is considerably weaker for low-income than for high-income respondents. If anything, then, the greater responsiveness of policy to the preferences of the well-off may be somewhat understated by the lower reliability of preferences measures among low-income respondents.

In sum, the magic of aggregation cannot be assumed to cancel out all the random error inherent in measures of political preferences (nor, of course, can it help alleviate nonrandom errors based on shared ignorance or misinformation). But to the extent that the moderating bias toward more centrist aggregate views that results when aggregating asymmetric preferences influences the results presented in the following chapters, this bias works to dampen the differences observed across income groups.

How Well Do Cue Taking and Aggregation Work?

To what extent do cue taking, preference aggregation, and issue publics ameliorate concerns about low levels of political information and the low quality of public preferences on political issues? No actual public in a large society is likely to meet the classical expectations of the well-informed citizen as laid out by Berelson, Lazarsfeld, and McPhee. But does the existing public display enough wisdom in its political preferences to recommend a system of governance that strongly reflects the preferences of the public? We know that cue taking *can* be an effective strategy for forming policy preferences on complex issues. In one study, for example, respondents who were poorly informed about the details of five competing insurance-reform initiatives on a California ballot but knew where the insurance industry stood on each initiative were able to closely emulate the voting behavior of their better-informed peers.[44] But just because cues *can* serve as effective shortcuts does not mean the necessary cues are always available or that citizens will make use of them when they are.

One way to assess the quality of public preferences that emerge from the processes described above is to compare the actual preferences expressed in surveys with some hypothetical standard of well-informed preferences that citizens would hold if they had the ability, time, and inclination to gather the relevant information on any given set of policy issues.

The most straightforward way to assess how far actual preferences diverge from hypothetical well-informed preferences is to inform a representative group of citizens about some set of policy issues and see how their preferences shift as a result. James Fishkin and Robert Luskin have done just this in a series of "deliberative polls."[45] For example, the 1996 National Issues Convention brought 466 participants, selected at random from the U.S. population, to Austin, Texas, for four days, during which they read briefing materials on various economic, foreign policy, and family issues, discussed those issues in small groups, and participated in question-and-answer sessions with experts. When initially contacted, and once again at the end of their stay in Austin, participants answered identical questions concerning their policy preferences in these three issue areas. To provide a comparison group, members of the initial sample who elected not to come to Austin completed the same surveys.

The participants in the National Issues Convention did shift their preferences somewhat on many of the forty-eight political attitude questions they were asked. But the average change in aggregate preferences was not large and barely exceeded the aggregate change of preferences expressed by the control group that was not provided with the information or opportunity to deliberate. On a 100-point scale, the average net (i.e., aggregate) difference in pre/post preferences across these forty-eight issue questions was about 5 points for the deliberation group and about 3 points for the control group.[46] The four days of focused study and deliberation, it appears, resulted in an aggregate change in policy preferences that was 2 percentage points greater than would otherwise be expected by simply resurveying the same respondents with no intervening activity.

The results of the National Issues Convention study suggest that on the topics addressed, participants' preexisting aggregate preferences closely resembled the well-informed preferences they expressed after four days of education and deliberation. But these conclusions hinge on the specific information provided to the deliberating respondents. If the information provided was not new to the participants, was not different enough from what they already knew, or was not relevant enough to the policy judgments they were asked to make, then the possibility remains that different information might have shifted aggregate preferences to a greater degree. Nevertheless, since the organizers' goal was to provide just the sort of educational experience that critics of the quality of public opinion view as lacking, these results do lend some credibility to the notion that cue taking and aggregation result in collective judgments that differ little from what a well-informed and engaged citizenry would express.

A different way to compare actual to hypothetical well-informed preferences is to use statistical tools to simulate a well-informed citizenry. This approach takes advantage of the fact that, as Philip Converse observed, the mean level of political knowledge among the electorate is very low, but the variation in knowledge is very high.[47] By modeling the vote choices or policy preferences of the best-informed segment of the electorate, one can impute preferences for citizens who share a given set of characteristics but have lower levels of political information.

Larry Bartels, for example, compared the presidential votes of the best-informed respondents with those of less-informed respondents of the same age, education, income, race, sex, occupational status, region, religion, union membership, urban residence, homeowner status, and labor force participation.[48] Bartels found an average individual deviation of about 10 percentage points between actual and well-informed votes for the six presidential elections between 1972 and 1992. Many of these deviations were offsetting, however—some poorly informed citizens reported casting a Republican vote when they would have been predicted to vote Democratic if well informed, but other poorly informed citizens "mistakenly" voted Democratic when they would have been predicted to vote Republican. The more relevant *aggregate* deviation between actual and well-informed presidential votes was only 3 percentage points.[49]

In an even more directly relevant study that used a similar methodology, Scott Althaus compared respondents' expressed preferences on 235 political opinion questions with imputed preferences calculated by assigning to each respondent the predicted preference of someone with the maximum level of political knowledge but otherwise identical in terms of education, income, age, partisan identification, race, sex, marital status, religion, region, labor force participation, occupational category, union membership, and homeownership.[50] Althaus found that in the aggregate, imputed "fully informed preferences" differed from expressed preferences by an average of about 6.5 percentage points—not a trivial amount, but hardly enough to dismiss existing preferences as an unsuitable guide to government decision making.[51]

Two lessons can be drawn from the research on enlightened preferences. First, while heuristics or informational shortcuts might, in theory, be extremely effective at allowing citizens to reach the same preferences they would if they were more fully informed, in practice a gap remains between actual and hypothetical well-informed preferences, whether those preferences are statistically imputed or arrived at after exposure to new information and deliberation. Second, the size of the aggregate gap is rather modest. The two most directly relevant analyses that focus on policy preferences find gaps of 2 and 6.5 percentage points, with a gap of 3 percentage points in presidential voting. Differences of this size might be enough to swing a close election or to shift aggregate preferences from slightly favorable toward some policy option to slightly opposed. But the policy proposals I examine in the following pages range widely from strong opposition to strong support (about two-thirds of the proposed policy changes in my dataset were favored by under 40 or over 60 percent of the respondents). Thus the relatively small differences in favorability that might be expected from a better-informed, more enlightened citizenry would be unlikely to lead to substantially different conclusions.

QUESTION-WORDING AND FRAMING EFFECTS

Even casual consumers of survey data are aware that subtle differences in how a question is worded can sometimes produce large differences in responses. But just how ubiquitous and how consequential are such question-wording effects? Some of the most frequently cited examples of question-wording effects do raise doubts about the ability of survey measures to accurately capture the public's policy preferences. For example, Tom Smith reports that 64 percent of Americans thought the government was spending too little on "assistance to the poor," but only 22 percent thought too little was being spent on "welfare."[52] Howard Schuman and Stanley Presser found that in the 1970s two in five Americans felt that the United States should "not allow" public speeches against democracy, but only half that number felt that the United States should "forbid" public speeches against democracy.[53] Finally, George Quattrone and Amos Tversky found that 64 percent of their respondents preferred a program that would *reduce unemployment* from 10 percent to 5 percent (at the cost of somewhat higher inflation), but only 46 percent made the same choice when the program was described as *increasing employment* from 90 percent to 95 percent.[54]

Each of these examples reveals substantial effects from apparently minor changes in the words used to describe a policy choice, and each has been replicated numerous times, so we cannot dismiss them as statistical flukes. Yet their implications for how we understand citizens' policy preferences (or their lack of preferences) and our ability to gauge those preferences is far from clear. For example, the greater appeal of "assisting the poor" over "welfare" has often been interpreted as indicating the sensitivity of the public to particular positively or negatively loaded terms. If the preferences expressed toward the same policy can be shifted so dramatically by calling it one thing rather than another, can we even say the public has a real and discernible preference toward that policy? Yet this example can be viewed another way entirely. There are many different government programs that assist the poor by providing medical care, housing subsidies, legal aid, child care, job training, and so on. For some respondents all these programs might be included under the rubric "welfare," but for many Americans welfare is understood as cash assistance to the able-bodied, working-age, unemployed poor. The public tends to be strongly supportive of these other antipoverty programs,[55] so the lesser appeal of "welfare" in comparison to "assisting the poor" can be understood not as a superficial response to an emotionally laden term, but as a sophisticated differentiation between kinds of government antipoverty programs.

The broader lesson from this alternative perspective on the welfare question-wording experiment is that much of what passes for question-wording effects are actually differences in responses resulting from differences in the policy that respondents are asked to respond to. The same survey that showed more support for "assisting the poor" than for "welfare" also found greater support for "halting the rising crime rate" than for "law enforcement" and for "dealing with drug addiction" than for "drug rehabilitation" (General Social Survey). But these alternative question wordings are not simply different formulations of the identical policies; they are references to different aspects of their respective issues.

In the example above that contrasts "forbid" and "not allow," the alternative wordings do appear to have identical meanings. The substantial differences in responses to these two formulations are a bit of a mystery, especially since the alternate question wordings sometimes produce dramatically different responses (as in the case of "speeches against democracy" described above), sometimes modest differences (e.g., in a parallel experiment focused on "speeches in favor of communism"), and sometimes no differences at all (e.g., in questions about "showing x-rated movies" or "cigarette advertisements on television").[56] Sometimes respondents seem to react differently to "forbid" and "not allow," but at other times these alternative wordings seem to make no difference.

Quattrone and Tversky's study revealed different evaluations if a policy choice was presented in terms of its effect on the percent of the workforce that would be *employed* or on the percent of the workforce that would be *unemployed*. These sorts of mathematically equivalent alternative descriptions have been labeled "equivalency frames."[57] This example is explained by recognizing that people tend to evaluate differences in magnitude (like the employment or unemployment rates) at least partly in terms of ratios. The difference between 10 percent and 5 percent unemployment appears large because the former is twice as big as the latter. In contrast, the difference between 90 percent employment and 95 percent employment appears small because the ratio is close to one.[58]

These sorts of framing effects have led many scholars to doubt whether the public can plausibly be said to have preferences on the underlying policies. But other scholars point out that such framing effects in survey experiments take place under highly artificial conditions. In the real world alternative ways of characterizing a policy choice are typically encountered not in isolation (as in survey experiments) but simultaneously as part of the political debate. The availability of competing frames and the give-and-take of political debate have been shown to undermine framing effects, reducing or eliminating differences in responses.[59]

Question-wording and framing effects potentially challenge the notion that the public holds meaningful preferences and that we can use survey interviews to discern what those preferences are. Yet the real-world impact of these problems may be small, as two recent examples suggest. In the first example, opponents of the inheritance tax were said to have boosted their cause by relabeling it the "death tax."[60] But the best evidence suggests that the label made little difference. In a survey experiment using two alternative wordings administered to randomly selected halves of the sample, 69 percent of respondents favored doing away with the "estate tax" while 73 percent favored doing away with the "death tax."[61]

In a parallel example, observers have claimed that the label "climate change" generates greater concern among the public than does "global warming."[62] But the only randomized survey experiment to pit these two formulations against each other found little difference: 57 percent of Americans believed that "global warming" would become a "very serious" or "extremely serious" problem if nothing was done, compared with 60 percent who felt that way about "climate change" and 58 percent about "global climate change."[63]

In sum, we cannot entirely dismiss concerns about question-wording and framing effects. The evidence is strong that how a policy is described can have an impact on the level of support or opposition expressed toward that policy. However, the conclusion that these effects mean that the public has no real attitudes toward these policies, or that we cannot know (at least approximately) what those attitudes are, seems unjustified. James Druckman, a leading expert who has conducted numerous studies of framing effects, concludes that "framing effects appear to be neither robust nor particularly pervasive. Elite competition and heterogeneous discussion limit and often eliminate framing effects."[64]

FEIGNED ATTITUDES AND FEIGNED NONATTITUDES

Two additional problems are sometimes viewed as affecting survey measures of political attitudes. First, respondents who lack opinions may be reluctant to say "Don't know" either out of embarrassment or in an effort to be helpful to the interviewer. In such cases claims to support or oppose some policy represent "nonattitudes" that distort the observed measure of public preferences. In other cases respondents who in fact do have relevant opinions nevertheless may answer "Don't know" perhaps because they think their true preference is embarrassing or out of step with perceived social norms. In either situation respondents who engage in these behaviors may be distinctive in ways that result in a misleading assessment of what the true distribution of preferences in the population looks like.

Scholars have examined both kinds of "misreported" attitudes. Respondents' tendency to feign preferences on issues on which they lack opinions has been assessed by asking respondents about wholly fictitious issues. For example, 24 percent of respondents in one survey expressed a preference on whether the "1975 Public Affairs Act" should be repealed, and 39 percent offered an opinion on the "Agricultural Trade Act of 1984," despite the fact that neither of these supposed pieces of legislation existed.[65] This suggests that some of the opinion preferences that survey interviewers collect about policies (or potential policy changes) that really do exist are in fact nonattitudes reported by respondents who are reluctant to say "Don't know." Yet the 76 percent and 61 percent of respondents who did say "Don't know" in response to these two questions about fictitious legislation is far higher than the percentage of respondents saying "Don't know" to any of the real issues represented in my dataset.

Since most respondents do seem able to resist the pressure to express a preference on an issue they have never heard of, most of the preferences that are expressed in response to the questions I examine in this study are likely real preferences, even if the respondents offering those preferences are only vaguely familiar with some of the issues they were asked about. Taking the worst-case scenario above as a guide, if only 61 percent of those who really don't have an opinion on an issue say "Don't know" and the rest offer a substantive preference anyway, the observed proportion of "Don't knows" will be an underestimate of the true proportion by 1/0.61. Thus if we observed that 5 percent of respondents said "Don't know" (about the average for my data), we could infer that the real percentage of respondents who lack an opinion is about 8.2 percent (5/0.61).

The hidden nonattitudes in the example above consist of the 3.2 percent of respondents who gave a substantive answer despite having no real opinion. Of course if the question concerned a more obscure policy on which a larger percentage of the respondents in fact had no opinion, the size of the hidden nonattitudes group would be proportionately larger. Since few of the policy questions in my dataset produce observed "Don't know" rates of greater than 10 percent, the extent of such hidden nonattitudes is simply too small to seriously distort the real information contained in the substantive survey responses that form the basis of my analyses.[66]

The second threat to the validity of survey data mentioned above is the opposite of hidden nonattitudes. In this second scenario respondents who hold opinions give "Don't know" responses. Adam Berinsky offers the most extensive analysis of this phenomenon.[67] Berinsky hypothesizes that survey questions on political attitudes are most likely to elicit "Don't know" responses from people who do have opinions if the issue being discussed is complex or if the respondent's views run counter to perceived social norms. In the former case, for example, a question about tax policy might require considerable effort from respondents to connect the proposed policy to their own interests and preferences on taxes. Rather than engage in this effortful processing, respondents may simply say "Don't know." In the latter case a respondent who opposes laws protecting homosexuals from discrimination may prefer to avoid the risk of embarrassment or social sanction by saying "Don't know" instead.

Berinsky tests this theory with a series of questions about race, social welfare policy, and the Vietnam War. Of concern here is the extent to which observed measures of policy preferences are distorted by respondents with real attitudes who say "Don't know." Using a sophisticated statistical model to impute preferences to respondents who said "Don't know," Berinsky finds virtually no such distortion for questions that lack complexity and have no clear socially normative answer (consistent with his hypotheses). In contrast he does find distortions on questions with one or the other of these qualities. But like the impact of hidden nonattitudes, the size of the distortions uncovered in Berinsky's analysis is quite small. The largest distortions occur on racial policy questions asked during the 1990s for which he estimates that opposition to school integration would appear 3 to 5 percent higher if the hidden attitudes of respondents saying "Don't know" were statistically taken into account. The distortions on the other questions hypothesized to produce hidden attitudes are even smaller: observed preferences on social welfare policy in the 1990s and on the Vietnam War in the 1960s never differ from the estimated true preferences by more than 2 percentage points.

Survey questions are imperfect measures of public preferences in many ways. The question for scholars and others interested in what the public thinks is whether the distortions inherent in survey data are small enough that such data can be relied on to gauge public sentiments. With regard to both potential threats to validity examined above, it appears that these distortions are minor. Neither hidden attitudes nor hidden nonattitudes appear to be substantial enough to significantly affect the value of survey-based preference measures for analyzing Americans' preferences on matters of public policy.

PREFERENCE INTENSITY AND DEMOCRATIC RESPONSIVENESS

Many democratic theorists consider political equality to be the hallmark of democratic government. Robert Dahl, for example, writes that "a key characteristic of democracy is the continued responsiveness of the government to the preferences of its citizens, considered as political equals."[68] But exactly what political equality means, and how it might be achieved, are difficult questions that generations of scholars and theorists have debated. One prominent issue in democratic theory concerns the variation in preference intensity across individuals on a given issue and across issues for a given individual. As noted above, citizens differ in the extent to which they care about different issues. The existence of multiple issue publics raises the question of whether policy makers *should* respond equally to the preferences of all citizens on every issue, or whether policy in a given domain should be shaped more by the subset of citizens who are most passionately concerned about that set of issues. In discussing the limitations of majoritarian rule, Dahl notes: "By making 'most preferred' equivalent to 'preferred by the most' we deliberately bypassed a crucial problem: What if the minority prefers its alternative much more passionately than the majority prefers a contrary alternative? Does the majority principle still make sense?"[69]

At first blush it may appear that a system of policy responsiveness tilted toward citizens who, on any given issue, are the best informed and hold the most intense preferences might, in the long run, produce the most optimal outcomes for all. If I care deeply about foreign policy and am indifferent to education, and you care strongly about education and not foreign policy, a government that responds to my preferences on foreign policy and yours on education would make us both happier than one that took each of our views equally into consideration in both issue domains.

The problem, of course, is that citizens with the greatest information and most intense preferences on a given issue may have interests that are quite distinct from, and often in conflict with, the less strongly held preferences of the majority. Such special-interest politics are particularly likely to arise when the benefits of a policy are concentrated in a small number of citizens and the costs are diffused to a larger group.[70] Each individual in the larger group lacks an incentive to become engaged in the issue, yet the total cost to the group as a whole can be substantial. Dairy price supports, for example, impose a small cost on each consumer of dairy products and provide a substantial benefit to dairy producers. Not surprisingly, it is the dairy producers who are most knowledgeable about and hold the most intense preferences about this transfer of resources from consumers to producers.

I will not try even to lay out the complexities of such considerations here, much less attempt to resolve them.[71] My analyses in the following chapters will for the most part ignore differences across respondents in the intensity of preferences and simply weight each individual who expressed an opinion equally with every other. This is partly because my data do not for the most part allow me to distinguish between more and less intensely held preferences and partly because the normative implications of differential responsiveness to more and less strongly held views are so complex.

There is one aspect of preference intensity that does play a central role in my analyses, however. Although I lack measures of individuals' preference intensities, I do, in a sense, have measures of *groups'* preference intensities. Although a group of people as such cannot strictly be said to have a preference (or any other psychological state), we often attribute to a group those characteristics that are widely shared by the individuals who make it up. Much of my analysis of representation in the chapters that follow rests on measures of how widespread a particular preference is among a specific group. If 60 percent of poor people express support for a particular tax cut, for example, and 80 percent of the affluent support that same tax cut, I might say the affluent supported the tax cut more strongly than did the poor. As I discuss in chapter 2, taking into account the extent of support for a given policy rather than focusing simply on the congruence of policy outcomes with majority preference reveals more about the strength of the connection between citizens' desires and government decision making.

MANIFEST AND LATENT PREFERENCES

To the extent that electoral incentives compel politicians to respond to the preferences of the public, it is not the public's existing preferences that are likely to be most influential, but rather the preferences that the public might be expected to hold at the time of the next election.[72] From a strategic point of view, therefore, we might expect democratic responsiveness— to the degree that it occurs—to reflect the public's "latent opinions"[73] or "potential preferences"[74] rather than its manifest opinions. From a normative point of view, we might even *want* government to respond not to the preferences the public expresses at any given time, but rather to the preferences the public would express if the issue were raised in the context of an election, with opposing candidates raising arguments for and against the policy, other elites weighing in with information and recommendations, and citizens giving more attention to the issue. Democratic responsiveness, from this perspective, would consist not in policies that mirror the public's expressed preferences, but in policies that would receive the greatest support at some future point when the wisdom of those policies could be subjected to a public debate.

The question, then, is whether comparing government policy to manifest (i.e., expressed) opinion, as I do in the following chapters, provides a superficial or misleading account of policy responsiveness. If policies diverge from expressed opinion because policy makers are responding to the opinions they anticipate the public will hold at some future date, we might deem government *more* rather than *less* democratic.

Without denying that there are occasions when a lack of fit between manifest opinion and government policy might reflect a deeper form of responsiveness to *latent* opinion, I believe that opinions expressed at the time policies are adopted constitute a reasonable basis for assessing policy responsiveness. First, one of the reasons manifest and latent preferences might differ is that opinions change in response to new information or changing circumstances. Deteriorating conditions in Iraq and Afghanistan led to sharp drops in the initially high public support for these wars. But it would be silly to base our assessment of whether government policy reflected the preferences of the public on the latent or potential opposition that materialized only years later. In cases like this, policy makers and the public alike must form preferences based on the information available at the time a policy decision is made, and it is this manifest opinion that counts as the basis for assessing democratic accountability.

Dramatic new information or changing conditions may lead the public to change its preferences, but when conditions remain stable, preferences almost always remain stable as well. In their study of fifty years of survey data discussed above, Page and Shapiro conclude that "collective policy preferences of Americans have been quite stable, ... when opinion change does occur, it is usually modest in magnitude, ... [and] most abrupt opinion changes represent understandable responses to sudden events."[75]

Still, potential preferences might differ from manifest preferences even in the absence of changing conditions or sudden events if the public were exposed to new policy-relevant information or arguments of the sort that opposing candidates might raise during an election. While preferences do undoubtedly change in this way on occasion, the "deliberation experiments" described above suggest that exposing citizens to this sort of information and these sorts of arguments has a very minor impact on their policy preferences.[76]

Some will find my comparison of *expressed* opinion and government policy in the pages that follow too impoverished to reflect a normatively desirable model of democratic responsiveness. I too recognize the appeal of a more sophisticated account of democracy in which the latent or enlightened preferences of the public form the basis for evaluating democratic governance. But the empirical evidence suggests that such potential or hypothetical preferences are strongly correlated with expressed opinions, and when they differ it is most often because the relevant social conditions have changed. In addition, manifest opinion has the very desirable quality of being measurable in a direct and concrete way while latent opinion, as V. O. Key put it, is a "singularly slippery" problem that "so long as it remains latent ... cannot well be inspected."[77]

DEMOCRACY: THE WORST FORM OF GOVERNMENT ...

The account of public preferences sketched above is consistent with Winston Churchill's oft-quoted remark that "Democracy is the worst form of government except for all those other forms that have been tried from time to time."[78] Individual citizens' policy preferences are often unstable and ill-informed, but the specialization of multiple issue publics and the ability of citizens to use cues in place of raw policy-relevant information go a long way toward redeeming the public as a source of policy guidance. Moreover, some of the shortcomings attributed to public preferences are inherent in the complex nature of policy formation. Additional cues or information might shift the preferences the public holds on a given policy,[79] but experts too shift their preferences on public policies as their understanding evolves or as new information comes to light.

There is surely much room for improvement in the quality of the American public's preferences on policy matters. But those preferences, imperfect though they may be, are worthy of guiding government policy makers—at least on the many issues that gain some prominence on the public agenda. Given the lack of a compelling alternative to letting the public determine its own preferences as best it can based on its values and interests, the pressing question is how responsive the government is to the public's preferences, and in particular whether that responsiveness privileges the preferences of more advantaged subgroups of the public over those of the less well-off.

ASSESSING POLICY RESPONSIVENESS

My approach to assessing policy responsiveness involves three elements that collectively distinguish it from previous research. First, my outcome measure consists of actual policy rather than representatives' votes in Congress, presidents' proposals, or other intermediate steps in the policy-making process. We may learn much from studying these intermediate outcomes, but the bottom line of democratic governance is the public's ability to shape actual policy. If representatives' votes reflect their constituents' wishes, but other elements of the legislative process prevent those wishes from being realized in policy outcomes, the resulting responsiveness is of little benefit to the public.

Second, my analyses are based on a large number of specific proposed policy changes rather than an aggregate measure reflecting broad preferences for more versus less government activity or liberal versus conservative policy. Such broad measures can sometimes help analysts discern general patterns, but they also obscure differences that emerge when specific policies are examined. Affluent Americans, for example, tend to hold more conservative views on economic issues but more liberal views on moral or religious issues than those who are less well-off. Broad measures of liberal versus conservative leanings conceal this distinction and hinder the ability to identify inequalities in responsiveness to different income groups.

Finally, my approach is based not on dichotomous judgments of whether policy conforms with majority preference, but on the strength of the association between policy outcomes and the *degree* of support expressed by the public (or a subgroup thereof). That is, I estimate the probability of a proposed policy change being adopted as a function of the proportion of the relevant group favoring that change. By using the degree of support for a proposed policy change as a predictor, I don't need to impose a predetermined level of support (like 50 percent) as my criterion but can allow the data to reveal the relationship between public preferences and policy outcomes. As I show in chapter 3, the difference between modest opposition to a policy and modest support (e.g., between 40 percent in favor and 60 percent in favor) has little political consequence. But the difference between modest opposition and strong opposition, or modest support and strong support (e.g., between 20 percent and 40 percent in favor or between 60 percent and 80 percent in favor), has far more impact.

Each of these elements of my analytic approach has been used in one form or another in previous studies on policy responsiveness. But the combination of these elements, and the way they are incorporated into my estimates of the policy responsiveness, allow me draw conclusions about representational inequality that extend beyond previous research.

Alternative Gauges of Policy Responsiveness

Quantitative analyses of the link between public preferences and government decision making have taken three main forms.[80] The most prevalent approach, often labeled "dyadic representation," examines the relationship between constituency opinion and the behavior of representatives or candidates across political units like U.S. states or congressional districts.[81] This work typically finds strong correlations between constituents' preferences and legislators' voting behavior.

A second approach examines changes over time in public preferences and the corresponding changes (or lack of changes) in public policies. For example, if support for spending on space exploration declines over some period of time, does actual spending on the space program also decline? Using this technique, Page and Shapiro found fairly high levels of congruence between the direction of change in opinion and the direction of change in government policy, especially for salient issues or cases with large changes in public preferences.[82] Robert Erikson, Michael MacKuen, and James Stimson also related changes in public preferences to subsequent government policy.[83] Rather than focusing on individual policy issues, however, Erikson, MacKuen, and Stimson used a broad measure of "public mood" concerning the size and scope of government and a similarly broad measure of actual government policy. Taking into account the reciprocal relationship between public preferences and government policy, they report an extremely strong influence of public mood on policy outputs, concluding that there exists "nearly a one-to-one translation of preferences into policy."[84]

Finally, using a third approach, Alan Monroe compared public preferences for policy change expressed at a given time with subsequent changes
(or lack of changes) in government policy.[85] For example, if the public
expresses a preference for cutting spending on space exploration at a
given time, does actual spending on the space program decline in the following years? Monroe found only modest consistency between public
preferences and subsequent policy change during the 1960s and 1970s
and even less consistency during 1980s and 1990s. Mirroring Page and
Shapiro's results, however, Monroe found a better match between public
preferences and government policy for issues that the public deemed more
important.[86]

Previous research, then, suggests a fairly high level of correspondence
between constituency preferences and legislators' behavior, a more modest match between Americans' specific policy preferences and specific government policies (with stronger correspondence on more salient issues),
and a strong aggregate relationship between broadly defined public mood
and broad measures of government activity.

In contrast to the substantial body of research examining the preference/
policy relationship for the public taken as a whole, only a small number
of studies use quantitative data to assess the variation in this relationship
across social groups. John Griffin and Brian Newman conduct dyadic
analyses of congressional voting and constituent opinion, looking separately at the preferences of black, white, and Latino constituents.[87] Taking into account the different size of each racial group within a congressional district, they find that the fit between legislators' voting patterns and
constituents' views is strongest for whites and weakest for blacks.

Taking a different approach, Lawrence Jacobs and Benjamin Page assess the impact on U.S. foreign policy of various elite groups as well as the
public as a whole.[88] Using parallel survey measures of policy preferences
administered to the general public and a variety of foreign policy leaders
over almost thirty years, they find that business leaders and experts have
the greatest ability to sway foreign policy, but that the public as a whole
has little or no influence.

Finally, in the study that most closely relates to my concerns with economically based representational biases at the national level, Bartels relates
U.S. senators' roll-call votes to the preferences of their high-, middle-, and
low-income constituents. Examining civil rights, the minimum wage, government spending, abortion, and broad measures of liberal/conservative
ideology, Bartels finds senators to be consistently and substantially more
responsive to the opinions of high-income constituents (this bias being
somewhat greater for Republican than for Democratic senators).[89]

As the description of past research indicates, previous analyses of government responsiveness have used a variety of techniques to assess the fit

between what the public wants and what the government does. In the United States, dyadic analysis, which links individual senators' or representatives' voting behavior with the preferences of their constituents, has been by far the most common approach. One advantage of this approach is that data are plentiful. A single congressional vote can provide the researcher with 435 distinct observations (House districts) or 100 Senate votes from the 50 states. Dyadic analysis also allows researchers to take into account other factors that affect representatives' voting behavior, such as political party, personal background, and district characteristics.

But the dyadic approach to assessing policy responsiveness has some serious limitations as well. Most obviously, analyses of congressional roll-call votes limit studies of policy responsiveness to those potential policy changes that actually make it to a floor vote in Congress. But political power, and hence responsiveness, may rest as much in the ability to determine what policies will be considered as what decisions about those policies will be made.[90] Consequently congressional scholars sometimes view agenda control, including the power to determine which potential policy changes receive floor votes, as the key to partisan influence in Congress.[91] In chapter 2 I discuss in more detail the distinction between the "public agenda" of issues that receive attention from citizens, the media, interest groups, and so on and the "government agenda" of issues that are taken up by Congress and the president. Limiting one's analyses to congressional roll-call votes severely restricts the range of issues and misses entirely that portion of policy responsiveness that consists of the process by which some issues and not others are brought to a vote in Congress. To the extent that the potential policies that receive roll-call votes in Congress differ systematically from those that do not, studies of roll-call votes will fail to reflect the degree of responsiveness across the wider range of potential issues that the federal government might plausibly have addressed.

The importance of "what didn't happen" in understanding policy responsiveness is central to the notion of "policy drift" that Jacob Hacker and Paul Pierson develop in their exploration of rising economic inequality in the United States.[92] Hacker and Pierson point out that the impact of existing policies can shift as circumstances change. In such cases not acting results in changes in the impact of government policies just as much as explicit changes in policy do. For example, if inflation erodes the value of the minimum wage and policy makers do not act to adjust the minimum wage, then the impact of this policy changes over time. Another example of the importance of considering governmental nonactions as well as actions comes from Sarah Binder's analysis of legislative gridlock.[93] Where previous studies looked only at policies that were adopted by Congress and concluded that divided government was not a hindrance to enacting significant legislation, Binder considers potential policy changes that were prominent in public debate but not adopted by Congress and comes to the opposite conclusion.[94]

Not only are dyadic analyses of roll-call votes limited to the subset of possible policy changes for which floor votes in Congress are recorded, but legislators' behavior with regard to roll-call votes may systematically differ from their behavior with regard to less visible aspects of their jobs. Members of Congress have electoral incentives to behave in ways that reflect the preferences of their constituents. But the strength of those incentives varies according to the degree of visibility and clarity of the behavior in question.[95] Final-passage votes on substantive legislation are typically the most visible and easily interpretable actions that legislators take (at least with regard to policy issues; I leave aside district-specific pork barrel activities, which may also be highly visible and easily interpretable). Thus constituent influence over legislators' behavior is likely to be strongest on final-passage votes on hot-button issues and weakest on activities like committee votes, floor votes on procedural matters and legislative amendments, and the substantial behind-the-scenes work that is needed to move potential policies onto the congressional agenda and secure passage.

If constituents' preferences were the *only* factor influencing legislators' behavior, we might be safe in assuming that whatever degree of responsiveness we observe with regard to roll-call voting would be reflective of the broader range of activities that members of Congress undertake. But legislators must balance constituent desires against a range of other factors including party leaders, interest groups, campaign donors, and their own personal political orientations.[96] Roll-call votes, and especially final-passage votes on high-profile legislation, are most likely to be noticed by voters (and most easily brought to voters' attention by electoral opponents, interest groups, and legislators themselves). Therefore it is these votes on which members of Congress have the greatest incentives to conform to their constituents' desires. This is particularly true because the other interested parties attempting to shape legislators' behavior have a greater ability to monitor the less-visible aspects of congressional activity than does the public. Party leaders, interest groups, and legislators themselves are all able to consider a wider range of activity, thereby increasing the incentives for members of Congress to be more responsive to constituents on roll-call votes and more responsive to other influences (including their own personal policy preferences) on other activities that shape policy outcomes.

Donations to members of Congress from political action committees (PACs), for example, do not appear to influence legislators' roll-call votes, but they are strongly related to behind-the-scenes activities such as offering amendments during subcommittee markup and negotiating with other legislators.[97] We might therefore expect legislators to respond to their constituents' preferences most strongly on highly visible roll-call votes and least strongly on these sorts of behind-the-scenes activities that are difficult or impossible for constituents to monitor.

Dyadic analyses based on roll-call votes, then, are likely to overestimate the extent to which legislators behave in ways that further the preferences of their constituents. The extent of this overestimate will depend on the extent to which constituent preferences diverge from the other forces that shape legislators' behavior. For some representatives on some issues, there may be no conflict between the policies their constituents prefer and the policies the representatives would otherwise be inclined to pursue. But in other cases legislators will be pressed to pursue their constituents' preferences in their most visible actions and to pursue competing preferences in activities that are unlikely ever to come to their constituents' attention.

The evidence concerning the differential impact of constituents on different legislative activities is scant but appears to be consistent with the expectations outlined above. Michael Crespin, for example, shows that members of Congress whose districts have been redrawn adjust some, but not all, of their roll-call voting to better match the preferences of their new districts.[98] Change is most evident, Crespin finds, on highly visible final-passage votes and not at all on procedural votes that are hard for observers to interpret but important to the party for controlling the congressional agenda. Along the same lines Vincent Hutchings, Harwood McClerking, and Guy-Uriel Charles show that the proportion of African Americans in a congressional district is most strongly related to representatives' final-passage votes on prominent racial policies and least related to the less visible but equally consequential votes on racial policy amendments.[99]

In this book I ignore the behavior of individual legislators and other specific political actors and focus on the end product of the policy-making process: the actual policies that are adopted—or not adopted—by the federal government. This approach requires a far larger number of policy issues to serve as the input into the analysis than does the dyadic approach. But it avoids the problem of relying on a partial and potentially misleading aspect of policy making and concentrates instead on the policies themselves, which, after all, is presumably the reason we find legislative voting (and other aspects of the political process) of interest to begin with.

By focusing on policy adoption, I incorporate into my analyses the influence of the public (or subsets of the public) over both agenda formation and policy decisions. That is, for a policy to be adopted, it must be accepted onto the government agenda and then acted on. Whether influence is exerted primarily at the agenda-setting stage or primarily at the policy-decision stage, it will be reflected in the associations of public preferences with policy outcomes. Finally, by focusing on individual policies rather than broad measures of ideological orientation, I allow the association of income and policy preference to vary across the different issues.[100] As noted previously, affluent Americans, for example, tend to be more conservative on economic issues but more liberal on "moral" issues like gay rights or abortion. Combining too broad an array of issues into one measure will tend to obscure these differences and make representational inequalities impossible to detect.

There is no single right way to assess something as complex as government responsiveness to public preferences; alternative approaches offer different sets of trade-offs and limitations. By using the end product of the policy process as my outcome measure, discrete proposed policy changes as my unit of analysis, and the strength of the preference/policy link as my measure of responsiveness, I have sought to maximize the benefits and minimize the limitations inherent in any analysis of this complicated relationship. My hope and expectation is that other scholars will further pursue the study of representational inequality using a variety of methods and data, providing additional insights, extensions, and corrections of the results reported here.

DEMOCRACY AND REPRESENTATION

The quality of democratic governance in any society must be judged on a range of considerations. Are elections free and fair? Do citizens have access to the information necessary to evaluate their political leaders and competing candidates? Do government agencies perform their duties in a competent and unbiased manner?

In this book I concern myself with only one aspect of democratic governance—the extent to which government policy reflects the preferences of the governed. My aim is to document and explain the patterns of "representation" or "policy responsiveness" (terms that I will use interchangeably) reflected in the link between public preferences and government policy. My focus is description rather than prescription. In documenting the ways in which policy fails to reflect (or reflect equally) the preferences of the public, I do not mean to imply that a perfect (or perfectly equal) responsiveness to the public is best.

There are good reasons to want government policy to deviate at times from the preferences of the majority: minority rights are important too, and majorities are sometimes shortsighted or misguided in ways that policy makers must try to recognize and resist. But the association of public preferences and government policy—and the variation in that association across subgroups of the public— does provide a descriptive baseline from which to understand the nature and judge the quality of democratic representation.

Perfect equality in the responsiveness of policy makers to the wishes of the public is neither attainable nor, perhaps, even desirable. Particular segments of the public may hold preferences on particular issues that are harmful to the community, violate important democratic values, or are misinformed and detrimental to the interests of those citizens themselves. On the other hand, gross levels of inequality—of the sort I document in the pages that follow—do seem incompatible with notions of political equality that Americans embrace. Furthermore, the increasing concentration of economic resources at the very top of the income distribution that we have witnessed over the past few decades intensifies concerns with political inequality. America's richest citizens have enjoyed astonishing increases in income and wealth since the 1970s while the incomes of poor and middle-class people have barely risen—and would have fallen if not for the substantial increase in the hours they work per year.[101] Other nations have adopted policies to ameliorate the increases in economic inequality brought, at least in part, by changes in the global economy. America has not. Tax cuts for the wealthy, financial deregulation, attacks on unions, and cutbacks in funding for public education serve to exacerbate economic inequalities. In the face of these changes, and the continuing economic challenges facing less-well-off Americans, the representational inequalities described in the pages that follow are all the more significant.

The findings reported in this book can at best provide a broad sense of the extent to which the American political system works to incorporate citizens' preferences into government policy. By illuminating the conditions that lead to stronger and weaker, and more and less egalitarian, patterns of responsiveness, I hope to provide an empirical foundation on which normative evaluations (and further empirical analyses) can be built. In chapter 8 I discuss the policy implications of my findings, focusing on mechanisms that seem more or less promising in redressing inequality in government responsiveness. Some readers may not view existing inequality as something that needs addressing, but I suspect that many will feel otherwise. For those who share my concern that responsiveness to public preferences is tilted too far in the direction of the most advantaged Americans, a challenging task of political reform lies ahead.

• • •

In the next chapter I discuss the sorts of potential policy changes that are suitable for inclusion in a study of government responsiveness to public preferences and describe the nature of my preference measures and policy outcome coding. With that groundwork laid, chapter 3 begins my analysis of policy responsiveness and takes up the important issue of causal influence: Do associations between public preferences and government policy reflect the influence of the public over policy makers, the ability of policy makers to sway public opinion, or the operation of some other, unobserved factor?

CHAPTER 2

Data and Methods

To WHAT EXTENT does government policy reflect the preferences of the governed? To answer this seemingly straightforward question we must address a host of practical and conceptual issues. First, should all government policies be included in our assessments, even the most technical and obscure? If not, by what criteria can we distinguish an appropriate set of policies to include? Second, since control over the government's agenda is one important form of influence over policy outcomes, how can we account for the failure of some policy options to even make it onto the agenda in Washington? Third, what sort of time frame is appropriate for assessing the responsiveness of policy makers to the preferences of the public? The wheels of government sometimes turn slowly, but at what point does "policy delayed" become "policy denied"? Finally, what are the practical considerations in collecting and coding measures of public preferences and policy outcomes and in choosing among alternative ways of measuring the strength of association between those measures?

In this chapter I lay the groundwork for my analyses of policy responsiveness by identifying my data sources and analytic procedures. Along the way I address conceptual issues such as those raised above that any effort to understand the role of the public in shaping government policy making must confront.

DEFINING A SUITABLE SET OF POLICY PREFERENCES

Any assessment of the impact of public preferences on public policy must grapple with the difficulty of identifying a suitable collection of policy preferences to assess. Federal government activity extends to a huge array of policy areas. In addition, any comprehensive assessment of public attitudes needs to consider not only preferences toward the policies government adopted, but toward policies that could have been, but were not, adopted as well. For example, in the realm of education policy, one would want to know what the public thinks about both the No Child Left Behind program, which was adopted, and federally funded school vouchers, which have been frequently discussed but never adopted.[1] One challenge, then, is to develop a set of criteria by which to assess the suitability of the virtually infinite number of possible policy changes that the public might favor or oppose.

John Kingdon's discussion of agendas, alternatives, and policies provides a helpful start. Kingdon distinguishes between the "systemic agenda" of issues being discussed by the media, interest groups, political parties, and the general public and the "formal government agenda" of issues taken up by Congress or the president.[2] Practical constraints preclude government from addressing all the issues on the broader public agenda at once, even if policy makers were inclined to do so. As Herbert Simon put it, "the environment makes parallel demands on the system, but the system can respond only serially."[3] Since government cannot address all the policies on the public agenda, influence over government policy can take the form of shaping what issues government addresses as well as what policies government adopts on the issues that are addressed.

In addition to considering the process by which issues become part of the government agenda, Kingdon notes that policy depends as well on the set of alternatives that government policy makers seriously consider. Just as an issue on the public's agenda may fail to make it onto the government's agenda, so too a particular response or alternative approach to an issue may be popular with the public but not seriously considered by the government. Thus any assessment of the role of the public in shaping policy must consider the degree of support for or opposition to policies the government adopted, to policies the government considered but failed to adopt, and to policies that were in some sense on the public agenda but that the government never considered at all. In short, we want to include in our analyses policies the government plausibly could have adopted, even if they never made it onto the formal agenda.

One difficulty in defining such a set of policies is that an almost infinite array of policies could, in principle, be adopted. Thus criteria are needed to exclude policies that are clearly impractical or that fall far outside the realm of plausible public support. For example, if tires, for technical reasons, could not be made from recycled rubber, then the failure to pass a law requiring tire companies to use recycled rubber would not be very informative, even if such a policy was popular with the public.

In addition to excluding policies judged as clearly impractical, analyses of government responsiveness should also exclude policies that fall outside the realm of plausible public support. For such policies the correspondence between public preferences and government policies is trivial and uninformative (assuming, of course, that they are not adopted). For example, the fact that the public opposes and the government hasn't adopted a policy outlawing bicycles should not be taken as an example of democratic responsiveness to the preference of the public. In this example it's hard to imagine the public holding any other position, so the policy is unsuitable for assessing government responsiveness. In contrast the public's strong opposition to switching to the metric system for federal highways is less obvious (and, indeed, one could imagine this opposition softening over the years). In this case the correspondence between public preferences and government policy does seem to reflect a substantively meaningful observation.

The challenge, then, is to identify a reasonable set of possible policies or policy changes that the government might adopt. One approach that has been taken to address this challenge is to consider all bills introduced in Congress, whether passed into law or not.[4] This approach has the advantage of providing a clearly defined universe of possible policies to include. But as Kingdon points out, nonresponsiveness to the public (or other constituencies) may take the form of excluding particular issues or policy alternatives from consideration altogether. If the process of government agenda setting is biased against less-well-off Americans, any analysis that is limited to bills introduced in Congress will miss this aspect of democratic inequality.

An alternative approach that catches some prominent policy issues that Congress doesn't address but misses many less prominent issues that it does take up is to use media sources to identify issues on the public agenda.[5] The weakness with using the media as a reference point is that many enduring issues of public interest receive very irregular coverage in the media. Moreover, much of this coverage is driven by political actors themselves. Abortion, for example, is an ongoing issue salient to many Americans. But it rarely receives media coverage unless a dramatic incident creates a news event, or it becomes the subject of a court decision, or politicians raise the issue during an election.

Finally, not every kind of policy issue the federal government addresses is appropriate for inclusion in analyses of the role of public preferences in shaping policy outcomes. Some policies are simply too technical or too obscure to reasonably be held to the delegate model of representation. While citizens might have attitudes or orientations that would inform their views on such issues, it is unreasonable to expect citizens to hold actual preferences on questions like which high-definition television standard should be adopted or whether anabolic steroids should be changed from a schedule III prescription drug to the more restrictive schedule II category.

If sufficiently clear cues are available, citizens can form meaningful opinions even on very complex and technical issues (see chapter 1). For example, the impact of free-trade agreements on the U.S. economy are quite complex with different effects on different industries, different effects on employers and consumers, and different impacts on different segments of the labor force. Some citizens will have cue-givers they trust on questions like this—perhaps their union or an advocacy group such as the Chamber of Commerce. But when issues are both technical and obscure, citizens are much less likely to encounter cues on which to base their preferences. Citizens can attend to cues and information about only a limited subset of the issues on the agenda at any given time, and the more obscure the issue, the less likely it is that any given citizen has any basis whatsoever for forming a preference.

When an issue gains prominence on the public agenda, citizens are likely to encounter some discussion of the issue and become aware to a greater or lesser degree of the positions of potential cue-givers on the issue. But we cannot expect citizens to form opinions on the thousands of issues that government decides every year that never arise on the public agenda. Representatives must serve as trustees on issues like these, making decisions that they deem to be in their constituents' (or the country's) best interest rather than reflecting their constituents' existing preferences.

In sum, a set of policies suitable for assessing democratic responsiveness to public preferences should be broader than those taken up by Congress or prominent in the media but at the same time restricted to the subset of issues that at least a reasonable proportion of the public might be expected to hold preferences on. To approximate this vaguely defined set of policies, I've relied on the judgments of multiple polling organizations over the period my study covers. Using online data bases of survey questions from news media and national polling firms, I collected as many questions as possible that asked whether respondents favored or opposed some specific change in federal government policy.[6] Since my ultimate objective in collecting these data is to analyze the relationship between public preferences and actual policy outcomes, I included only policy questions that were specific enough to be able to determine whether the proposed policy change was adopted. My primary dataset (described below and analyzed in chapters 2–5) covers the years 1981–2002. As detailed in chapter 6, I later augmented these data with additional survey questions from 1964–68 and 2005–06.

My set of survey questions covers a broad array of public policies and ranges from quite specific questions about particular policy proposals to broader questions reflecting general orientations with regard to some policy area. For example, a broad question about national health care included in the dataset reads: "Do you favor or oppose national health insurance, which would be financed by tax money, paying for most forms of health care?" A more specific (and less popular) version reads: "Do you favor or oppose a national health plan, financed by the taxpayers, in which all Americans would get their insurance from a single government plan?" Finally, specific aspects of health care reform were addressed in questions like "Please tell me if you favor or oppose charging all Americans the same for health care, regardless of factors like their age and where they live."

Many of the questions in my dataset refer to specific proposals on the government agenda, including specific bills before Congress, but many other questions reflect policies that might garner some public support but that Congress or the president is quite unlikely to consider seriously. For example, during the mid-1990s a majority of Americans expressed support for "a five-year ban on all legal and illegal immigration into the United States." Bills to cut back on legal immigration were introduced in Congress during this period, but none called for an outright ban on legal immigration (for any length of time).

The public policy questions that polling organizations asked during the years I examined tilt toward the more prominent policy debates of the day but extend to a wide range of relatively obscure issues as well. For example, I have twenty-nine questions in my 1981–2002 dataset relating to health care reform, seventeen questions about missile defense (asked mostly during the Reagan and G. W. Bush administrations), twenty-six questions about military action against Iraq, and eighteen questions about the North American Free Trade Agreement. But I also have questions about allowing motorized vehicles in federal wilderness areas, adopting a federal income tax credit for purchasing high-mileage cars, classifying tobacco as a drug subject to government oversight, and making the birthday of Martin Luther King, Jr., an official federal holiday.

In sum, the questions collected from polling organizations range broadly across policy areas, degrees of specificity, and centrality to the formal government agenda of the time. While I make no claim that these data are the only or even the best set of policy-preference questions with which to assess government responsiveness, I do believe they are a reasonable set of questions that match the criteria outlined above. Before describing my dataset in more detail, I address some specific issues that have been raised concerning the use of survey questions to assess policy responsiveness.

POLICY PREFERENCES AND THE SURVEY AGENDA

For practical reasons many authors have used archived survey data of the kind I employ to study the relationship between public preferences and government policy.[7] But other scholars have raised questions about the suitability of the "survey agenda" as a basis for assessing policy responsiveness.[8]

The most pressing reservation concerns possible biases in the set of policies that survey organizations ask about. Benjamin Page and Paul Burstein have argued that the policies that survey organizations ask about over-represent the most salient and important issues and underrepresent those that are obscure or technical in nature.[9] Since the link between public preferences and government policy tends to be stronger for more salient issues, this leads, these authors argue, to an upwardly biased estimate of the strength of the preference/policy link.

This is an important objection, and it is certainly true that survey organizations tend to focus more on questions of broad interest. Given the wide range of often obscure issues government deals with, we would expect survey organizations to ignore many—indeed the vast majority of—specific policy proposals. On the other hand, survey organizations do sometimes ask surprisingly obscure questions of the general public. For example, the Roper Organization asked Americans whether they favored or opposed "U.S. companies selling telecommunications systems such as high-tech telephone switches, telephone communications satellites, and microwave transmission systems to Mainland China."[10] More important, the proper mix of more- and less-obscure policies that would produce an unbiased estimate of policy responsiveness depends on one's conception of the nature of representation. As discussed above, it would be unreasonable to expect the public to hold preferences over the full range of policies the government does or might pursue. In a modern nation there are simply too many detailed and technical issues for the public to possibly keep track of. Even elected representatives with large staffs and substantial resources appear to have difficulty following the details of many policy issues. Based on his extensive interviews with members of the U.S. House of Representatives, Kingdon concludes that "like most busy people, congressmen have limited time to devote to any one activity and are faced with much more information than they can systematically sift and consider."[11] What we care about most is how much influence the public has over policy on that subset of issues that Americans do or reasonably could hold preferences on.

From this perspective the tendency of survey organizations to neglect obscure and technical policy issues is desirable as long as it doesn't go too far. Of course, defining exactly how far is too far may be difficult; a dataset consisting of only the most prominent policies over a given time period is likely to be a misleadingly narrow basis on which to judge responsiveness. But a dataset reflecting *all* the policies on the formal government agenda (or, equivalently, a representative sample of all the policies) is also unlikely to provide a suitable basis for assessing responsiveness to public preferences.[12]

A second form of bias in the survey agenda may be equally problematic and equally difficult to assess. In choosing questions to pose to the public, survey organizations may tend to overrepresent issues that political elites or they themselves consider important, or policy options that they consider feasible or desirable. If the public as a whole—or subgroups of the public like the economically disadvantaged—place more importance on other issues or gravitate toward other policy options, the groups whose priorities survey organizations ignore may be even less well represented by government policy makers than appears to be the case. For example, creating federal government jobs to alleviate unemployment is quite popular among poor and middle-income Americans (and only modestly less popular among the affluent) but rarely asked about by survey organizations. Since no such programs were adopted during the decades covered by my primary dataset, additional survey questions on this policy would have reduced the apparent responsiveness of policy makers to public preferences (and somewhat more so for the less well-off).

The magnitude of such biases in the survey agenda is difficult to gauge for the public as a whole, but my data do allow me to compare the extent to which the proposed policy changes in my dataset privilege the priorities or policy alternatives of one economic level versus another. To the extent that survey organizations favor the preferred policy options of one subgroup of Americans and ignore the preferred options of another group, the average level of support for the proposed policy changes should be higher among the former than the latter. In fact my data show virtually no difference across income levels in the average support for the proposed policy changes posed to Americans by survey organizations. The average support for the proposed policy changes in my dataset is 54.8 percent for respondents at the 10th income percentile, 56.0 percent for those at the 50th percentile, and 56.3 percent for respondents at the 90th income percentile.[13] Particular policies, of course, often generate differing levels of support among Americans at different income levels. But averaged across the full set of policy questions I've collected, the preferences of all economic levels appear to be equally well represented. At the very least, then, whatever tendency survey organizations may have to neglect certain policy options favored by the public does not seem to differentially advantage or disadvantage one income level or another.

I make no claim that my set of policy-preference questions constitutes a definitive collection of federal policies from the years I examined, only that it constitutes a broadly defined group of policies that plausibly reflect the range of issues that were on the public agenda over this time period and is, on average, equally reflective of the preferences of Americans at all income levels. To the extent that news media and survey organizations tailor their questions to the more prominent policy issues of the day, the set of questions I collected should reflect at least in a loose way the set of concerns that the federal government and the American public were grappling with.

DATASETS

The main dataset used for my analyses of policy preferences consists of 1,923 survey questions asked of national samples of the U.S. population between 1981 and 2002. For my analyses of change in policy responsiveness over time, I supplement these data with additional survey questions asked during 1964–69 and 2005–06 (as described in chapter 6). Each survey question in these datasets asks respondents whether they support or oppose some proposed change in U.S. government policy: raising the minimum wage, sending U.S. troops to Haiti, requiring employers to provide health insurance, allowing gay people to serve in the military, and so on. The survey question is the unit of analysis in the dataset, with variables indicating the proportion of respondents answering "Favor," "Oppose," or "Don't know" within each category of income and education.[14]

The survey questions in my dataset were identified using keyword searches of the iPOLL database maintained by the Roper Center at the University of Connecticut and the Public Opinion Poll Question database maintained by the Odum Institute at the University of North Carolina. I obtained the actual data indicating the distribution of responses to these questions by demographic categories from these two sources when possible, or from the Inter-University Consortium for Political and Social Research, the Institute for Social Science Research at UCLA, the Kaiser Family Foundation, or the Pew Research Center for the People and the Press. Dozens of different survey organizations collected the original survey data, with the largest number of questions coming from Harris, Gallup, CBS, and *Los Angeles Times* surveys.

To be included my dataset, a survey item had to meet four criteria: First, it had to pose a dichotomous choice of supporting or opposing some specific policy change.[15] Second, it had to be specific enough to allow for a reasonably confident judgment of whether the proposed policy change was implemented. For example, a question asking whether or not the respondent favored the government doing more to help small business would be very difficult to code since there are so many programs that could plausibly be thought to help (or hurt) small businesses. Assessing whether the sum of changes in tax policies, Small Business Administration programs, trade policy, and so on were a net help for small business would be virtually impossible. On the other hand, a question asking whether or not the respondent favored a reduction in federal corporate tax rates could be coded with a fair degree of certainty. (Even in the case of this more specific question, however, coding the outcome as consistent or inconsistent with the preference addressed by the survey question can be complicated. For example, statutory rates might be cut but exemptions reduced, resulting in higher effective taxes.)

Third, all survey questions included in my dataset had to concern an issue that is or plausibly could be addressed by the federal government. I excluded questions about state or local policies, such as whether tenure for public schoolteachers should be abolished. Finally, the questions had to be categorical rather than conditional. For example, a question asking whether the United States should take military action against Iraq even if the United Nations Security Council were to vote against such action would be excluded.

To find questions that meet these criteria, I first combed through hundreds of questions from the relevant time period in the iPOLL database. This exploratory exercise revealed that the vast majority of appropriate questions contained the words "favor" and "oppose" or "support" and "oppose" in the question text. Consequently I used the word "oppose" as a keyword to identify questions that were candidates for inclusion in the dataset. I examined all the questions from the iPOLL and Public Opinion Poll Question databases containing this word in the relevant time period and retained those that met the criteria outlined above.

If identical questions were asked in the same calendar year, I used only the most recent instance of the question. This was done to avoid allowing a prominent topic (say, the Clinton health care reform efforts) from dominating the dataset. On the other hand, alternative questions about the same topic were allowed for two reasons. First, I wanted the dataset to reflect to some degree the amount of attention different issues were getting. To include only one question about the Clinton health plan would put it on a par in shaping my findings with a single question on an obscure topic, such as whether alcohol advertising should be banned from radio and television.

In addition, allowing alternative versions of questions about the same policy gives me the best chance of capturing the public's "response tendencies" or "long-term preferences" and the range of considerations on a given issue.[16] As I argued in chapter 1, there are two distinct sources of variation in individuals' responses to alternative questions about the same policy issue. For individuals with weakly held preferences on the issue at hand, alternative question wordings or framings may evoke different sets of considerations. If one question about Social Security privatization, for example, reminds respondents that individuals might lose money if the stock market performs poorly and another question reminds respondents that reforms have been proposed to deal with the future financial problems facing Social Security, Americans without firm preferences on Social Security privatization are likely to express less support in responding to the first than to the second version.[17] For these respondents the closest we can come to identifying a true underlying preference is to average across a range of plausible question wordings. By including multiple question wordings in my dataset, I am in essence doing just that.

The second source of variation in responses to alternative questions about the same policy issue stems from the complexities of social policy and the sensitivity of (some) respondents to alternative formulations of related policy options. For example, a question asking whether respondents favor a proposal to "allow Americans to take all of their Social Security taxes out of the Social Security system and invest them on their own" generated support that was about 9 percentage points lower than that for a question asking whether respondents favor or oppose "people having individual accounts and making their own investments with a portion of their Social Security payments." In a case like this the best estimate of the public's support or opposition to Social Security privatization would reflect both these questions since they are both plausible formulations of proposals that were being debated at the time: one suggesting private accounts as an alternative to traditional Social Security and the other referring to the partial privatization of "a portion" of Social Security payments.

A final aspect of the selection of questions for the dataset is that I included even identical survey questions if they were found in different calendar years. There are some policy issues that are never completely resolved but remain at least potentially on the agenda decade after decade. For example, taxes could always be raised or lowered, irrespective of whatever choices on tax rates had been made in the past. Social conditions, political control, and public preferences can all change over time. Consequently it is important to have multiple measures over time of these kinds of enduring issues.

Even when public preferences remain fixed, the inclusion of multiple measures allows the analysis to reflect the reality of changing responsiveness on that issue. For example, large majorities of the public supported raising the minimum wage throughout the 1981–2002 period. But the minimum wage remained at $3.35 an hour from 1981 through 1990 and then increased four times over the next seven years. Thus the policy history on this issue shows a substantial period during which public preferences supporting an increase were not reflected in government policy, followed by a substantial period during which policy was (at least more) consistent with the public's preferences. The fifteen separate questions in my dataset about the minimum wage allow me to capture the pattern of government responsiveness and nonresponsiveness in a way that would be impossible with either a single measure or a summary of multiple survey questions across these decades. In chapters 6 and 7, where I examine change in policy responsiveness over time, I take advantage of the temporal spread of my preference data to assess the impact of changing political and economic conditions.

CODING POLICY OUTCOMES

Once I identified appropriate survey questions, I used historical information sources to determine whether or not the proposed policy change occurred.[18] If the proposed change took place within four years of the date of the survey question, the change was coded as having been adopted. More specifically, if federal policy makers completed their task within the four-year coding window, the policy was coded as having been adopted even if it did not go into effect within this time frame. For example, if Congress passed and the president signed legislation, then I considered the policy to have changed on the date it was signed into law, even if the implementation was delayed until the next fiscal year or beyond. In his analysis of public preferences and policy change, Alan Monroe looked for policy changes over a long time period and found that 88 percent of the changes that eventually took place occurred within two years of the date of the survey questions he examined.[19] In my data 90 percent of changes that took place within the four-year window occurred in the first two years (with an additional 7 percent occurring in year three and 3 percent in year four).

In coding outcomes for survey questions with specific quantified proposals (e.g., raising the minimum wage to six dollars an hour or increasing fuel efficiency standards to forty miles per gallon), coders considered a change to have occurred if it represented at least 80 percent of the change proposed in the survey question. If the actual policy change represented less than 80 percent of that proposed in the survey question but more than 20 percent, the outcome was given a "partial change" code. Only 3 percent of the outcomes were coded as partial changes; these cases were dropped in all the analyses reported below.

Additional codes were developed indicating the policy area addressed by the question (e.g., tax policy, abortion) and whether the proposed change would require a Supreme Court ruling or a constitutional amendment. After I eliminated proposed policy changes that would require a constitutional amendment or Supreme Court ruling, proposed changes that were partially but not fully adopted, and questions that lacked income breakdowns, 1,779 questions from 1981–2002 remained for the analyses reported below.

IMPUTING PREFERENCES BY INCOME AND EDUCATION

Because the surveys employed were conducted by different organizations at different times, the demographic categories are frequently inconsistent. In particular income and education are divided into different numbers of categories and use different break points in various surveys. To create consistent measures of preferences that can be compared across surveys and across years, I used the following procedure. For ease of exposition, I describe the procedure for imputing preferences by income; I applied the identical procedure to education.

For each survey, respondents in each income category were assigned an income score equal to the percentile midpoint for their income group based on the income distribution from their survey. For example, if on a given survey 10 percent of the respondents fell into the bottom income category and 30 percent into the second category, those in the bottom group would be assigned a score of 0.05 and the second group a score of 0.25 (the midpoint between 0.10 and 0.40, the bottom and top percentiles for the second group).

After rescoring income for each survey, I estimated predicted preferences for specific income percentiles using a quadratic function. That is, for each survey question, I used income and income-squared (measured in percentiles) as predictors of policy preference for that question (resulting in 1,779 separate logistic regressions, each with two predictors). I then used the coefficients from these analyses to impute policy preferences for respondents at the desired percentiles.[20]

This approach has three advantages. First, it allows easy comparisons across survey questions with different raw income categories. Second, in basing the imputations on the continuous functions of policy preference by income for each policy question, this approach smoothes out some of the noise inherent in estimating preferences for population subgroups with limited numbers of respondents. Finally, by converting income categories to percentiles for each survey, this approach generates policy preferences based on relative rather than absolute measures of income level. Relative income levels are more appropriate for my purposes both because inflation changes the value of a given dollar level of income and because they allow me to hold constant over time the proportions of the population whose influence I am comparing. (If I used absolute income levels, the proportion of the population in the top income category, for example, would have grown considerably over time, making comparisons difficult.)

To assess the accuracy of the preference imputation process, I identified a subset of the survey questions that used identical income categories. The largest such subset is from 1981 to 1987 and contains 451 questions,

Table 2.1 Observed and Imputed Percent Favoring Policy Change

Income Category	Average Absolute Difference between Observed and Imputed Percent Favoring	Correlation between Observed and Imputed Percent Favoring
Under $7,500	1.95	.991
$7,500–$15,000	2.63	.987
$15,000–$25,000	1.60	.995
$25,000–$35,000	1.86	.993
$35,000–$50,000	2.45	.988
Over $50,000	2.45	.987
Average across income categories	2.16	.990

Based on the 451 questions with identical income categories asked between 1981 and 1987. Imputed percent favoring based on quadratic estimates for each survey question using income and income-squared as predictors of policy preference. See text for details.

each using the same six income categories. For this subset of questions I compared the observed percentage of respondents in each category favoring each proposed policy change with the imputed percentage based on the quadratic imputation procedure described above. As shown in table 2.1, the average size of the absolute difference in the percent favoring policy change between the observed and imputed preferences is about 2 percentage points, and the correlations between the observed and imputed preferences ranges range from 0.987 to 0.995. For this set of survey questions where the observed and imputed values can be directly compared, the estimated percent favoring each policy change for each income group based on the imputation equations is quite close to the observed percent favoring change in that income group. While only a quarter of the questions in my dataset can be easily compared in this way, the similarity of imputed and observed values for these questions suggests that the imputation procedure can be relied on to produce reliable preference estimates for the dataset as a whole.

RELIABILITY OF PREFERENCE AND OUTCOME MEASURES

As indicated above, policy outcomes were coded according to whether or not the proposed policy change was adopted within the four-year coding window, with a third category used to indicate partial change in the direction indicated in the survey question. Partial change codes (representing about 3 percent of all cases) are excluded from my analyses. Of the remainder, the proposed policy was adopted within the coding window for 30.6 percent of all questions. Intercoder agreement for policy outcome (whether the proposed change occurred within four years of the survey question) was 91 percent, equivalent to an alpha reliability coefficient of 0.81.[21]

The reliability of the policy-preference measures is more difficult to assess because I lack the ability to compare multiple measures of the same characteristic (like the outcome codes produced independently by two separate coders referenced above). For a subset of my survey questions, however, I can approximate multiple measures by using alternative question wordings relating to the same policy collected around the same time. Of the 1,779 questions available for my analyses, 387 had at least one alternative version relating to essentially the same policy change asked within the same calendar year. Most of these questions had a single alternative form, but 75 of them had two alternatives and 80 had three or more alternatives asked within the same year. By treating the pairs of alternatives among these 387 questions as parallel measures, I can estimate the reliability of the preference measures for the imputed preferences at various income levels.

To give some sense of the nature of these paired questions, table 2.2 shows four examples of policies from the early 1980s that were identified as having multiple measures of aggregate preferences for the same policy. Note that the alternative question wordings embody alternative contextualizations of the policies being asked about. For example, one version of the question about selling airborne warning and control systems (AWACS) to Saudi Arabia gives pro and con arguments while the other version does not. To the extent that the arguments contained in the first version reflect prominent considerations that were being raised in public debate about this policy, the first question is more likely to reflect the existing opinions of those attending to this issue and the potential or latent opinions of those who are not attending. On the other hand, to the extent that public preferences on this issue typically rest on other considerations, the bare version of the question that doesn't provide any framework of considerations for respondents may be a better gauge of public preferences. Such uncertainties contribute to the unreliability of my measures of public preferences, even if they do not reflect measurement error per se.

To assess the reliability of survey questions, classical test theory employs parallel measures of the same underlying construct asked of the identical respondents at a single point in time. Since my reliability estimates are based on different samples of respondents at different (but close)

Table 2.2   Alternative Question Wordings for Reliability Estimates

Selling AWACS to Saudi Arabia (1981)

Version 1: Saudi Arabia wants the U.S. to supply it with our highly sophisticated system for detecting hostile military activity, called AWACS. Supporters of the sale say the system will help Saudi Arabia defend itself against outside attack, and that providing them with the AWACS will demonstrate our friendship. Opponents of the sale say the AWACS could be used in a war against Israel, or that the top-secret system could fall into hostile hands. Do you favor or oppose the U.S. sending the AWACS system to Saudi Arabia?

Version 2: Do you favor or oppose the sale of AWACS to Saudi Arabia?

Criminalizing privacy violations (1983)

Version 1: Would you favor or oppose federal laws that would make it a criminal offense if the privacy of an individual were violated by an information-collecting business or organization?

Version 2: Would you favor or oppose federal laws that could put companies out of business which collected information about individuals and then shared that information in a way that violated the privacy of the individual?

Supplying 136 million dollars in military aid to El Salvador (1983)

Version 1: As you may know, President Reagan has charged that the Russians and Cubans are supplying arms to the left-wing guerrillas in El Salvador. Do you favor or oppose the U.S. taking each of the following steps to help the government in El Salvador: sending in 136 million dollars in military aid to the El Salvador government troops for 1983?

Version 2: President Reagan has taken a number of steps in Central America to meet what he says is the mounting supply of arms from Russia and Cuba going to left-wing rebel forces in El Salvador and to the Sandinista government in Nicaragua. Let me ask you if you favor or oppose sending in 136 million dollars in military aid to the El Salvador government troops for 1983?

Providing government money to faith based organizations (2001)

Version 1: Do you think it is a good idea or a bad idea for the federal government to give money to religious organizations so they can provide social services like job training and drug treatment counseling?

Version 2: Do you favor or oppose allowing churches and other houses of worship to apply, along with other organizations, for government funding to provide social services such as job training or drug treatment counseling to people who need them?

Version 3: Do you favor or oppose giving government funding to churches and other houses of worship so they can provide social services such as job training or drug treatment counseling to people who need them?

points in time, my estimates will reflect not only the degree of unreliability inherent in the survey measures, but also the additional unreliability due to sampling error in comparing two different samples and whatever systematic change may have taken place in respondents' preferences during the time between the two surveys.[22] On the other hand, my measures are aggregate preferences for the respondents as a group or imputed preferences for respondents at a particular income level. Because unreliability is assumed to result from random measurement error, aggregated measures are considerably more reliable than the individual-level measures they are based on. (That is, the random errors inherent in individuals' responses tend to cancel out when those responses are aggregated.)

In one of the broadest efforts to assess the reliability of survey-based political attitude measures, Duane Alwin and Jon Krosnick found an average reliability of 0.53 for the 33 policy questions they examined.[23] In comparison the average correlation (equivalent to the classical reliability coefficient) across alternative measures among my 387 paired policy-preference questions is 0.82. (In chapter 3 I show that the reliability of my imputed preferences is quite similar for low-, middle-, and high-income respondents.)

As explained above, only 387 of the questions from my larger dataset can be used to estimate the reliability of my policy-preference measures. While this number of questions is sufficient for my purposes, the broader applicability of the results depends on the extent to which these 387 questions are representative of the broader set of preference questions in my data. Of particular concern is the possibility that survey organizations might ask more questions (and thus be more likely to produce multiple measures in my dataset) about more prominent policies. Since respondents' views on more prominent policies might well be more crystallized, this set of 387 questions might be measured with greater reliability than questions about the less prominent policies for which I have only single measures.

As I show in the appendix, the 387 multiple-measure questions do closely resemble the remaining questions in my dataset in terms of the average level of support for the proposed policy change and the percentage of respondents saying "Don't know" (an indication of the salience of the policy the question addresses). While it is impossible to assess the reliability of the questions that lack multiple measures, I can compare the reliabilities of questions with two, three, or four alternative measures. If responses to multiple-measure questions are more reliable than responses to questions with only single measures, we might also expect reliability to increase as the number of multiple measures increases. In fact this turns out not to be the case: the reliabilities for questions from two-item, three-item, and four-item sets of alternative measures are 0.79, 0.82, and 0.77, respectively.

In sum, the aggregation of individual-level responses in my preference measures appears to generate data that are quite reliable by the standards of survey research. As I discuss in chapter 3, the aggregation process also equalizes the reliability of these measures across levels of income and education—an important advantage given my interest in comparing the strength of policy responsiveness for different demographic groups.

Assessing Responsiveness: Consistency vs. Influence

Measures of public preferences and policy outcomes can be used to assess two conceptually distinct aspects of the preference/policy link. With these data we can examine the extent to which the public as a whole, or various subgroups of the public, get what they want from government. Alternatively we can examine the extent to which the public or subgroups of the public shape what they get from government. It may be true that the more a social group shapes government policy, the more that group is going to get the policy it wants. Nevertheless, a group's preferences can coincide with government policy even in the absence of any actual influence of the former over the latter. In an absolute theocracy, for example, any group of citizens that shares the preferences of the theocratic rulers will get the policies they desire, but it would clearly be a mistake to see in that correspondence the influence of those citizens over policy makers.

As described more fully in chapter 1, previous analyses of the association of public preferences and government policy have taken one of two forms. One set of scholars has related changes in public preferences across time to subsequent changes (or lack of changes) in government policy.[24] This approach has its advantages and disadvantages, as discussed above, but is impossible with my data, which most often contains preference measures for a given policy at only one point in time.

The second approach to assessing the relationship between preferences and policies—the one I take here—is to measure support for specific changes in policy and relate that support (or opposition) to subsequent policy. Previous analyses using this approach have relied primarily on consistency between majority opinion and policy outcome as their measure of policy responsiveness.[25] But raw consistency (defined as the conformance of a policy outcome with majority preference) is a rough measure that does not take into account the *degree* to which policy outcomes are influenced by the public's preferences. For example, a policy change opposed by 51 percent of the public and one opposed by 99 percent of the public would both be inconsistent with public preferences, but the latter clearly represents a greater failure of policy to reflect public preferences.

More important for my purposes, raw consistency reflects whether a majority of the public (or a subgroup of the public) got what it wanted on the policy in question. But it is a poor measure of the extent to which the public (or a subgroup) shaped what it got. Consistency can be particularly misleading in trying to assess the relative influence of different subgroups over government policy making. In my dataset 56 percent of the proposed policy changes received majority support, but only 32 percent of the proposed changes actually took place—a substantial status quo bias that I return to in chapter 3.[26] Consequently if the majority of population group X prefers policy change less often than population group Y, X will *ceteris paribus* have higher consistency scores. But *influence* over policy outcomes is reflected in the degree to which policy change is more or less likely to occur depending on whether or not members of that group support it. A group that favors only 10 percent of proposed policy changes will inevitably have a high consistency score, but if the probability of a change being implemented bears no relationship to the group's preferences, the group cannot be said to have influence over policy outcomes.

The weakness of raw consistency as a measure of policy influence is illustrated with a hypothetical example in table 2.3. The preferences of groups A and B are each consistent with policy outcomes ten out of sixteen times (63%). But for group A, policies are three times as likely to be adopted if they are favored as if they are opposed (3/8 vs. 1/8), while for group B, policies are equally likely to be adopted whether they are favored or opposed (1/4 vs. 3/12). The consistency scores are 0.63 for both groups, but the measure of association (in this case, correlation) reveals the stronger relationship between preference and policy for group A (0.29 vs. 0.00). For group B in this example, consistency results from the lower number of favored policies combined with the status quo bias in policy outcomes, not from the association of preferences and outcomes.

Finally, consistency scores are problematic for assessing influence over government policy because any specific cutoff point for this purpose (such as 50 percent or majority preference) is arbitrary. The 50 percent mark may be a logical criterion for assessing the extent to which a group gets what it wants, but there is no reason to expect influence over policy outcomes to be focused around this level. That is, there is no reason to think the difference in impact on policy outcomes between 45 percent favorability and 55 percent favorability is any greater than the difference between 55 percent and 65 percent. Because public preferences are only one factor affecting policy outcomes, the degree of favorability needed to tip a policy from not being adopted to being adopted may be more or less than 50 percent. Since policies requiring federal legislation to be adopted need to garner the support of the president, congressional committees and

Table 2.3 Consistency vs. Correlation as Measures of Policy Responsiveness

Policy	Group A's Preference	Group B's Preference	Outcome
1	1	1	1
2	1	0	1
3	1	0	1
4	1	0	0
5	1	0	0
6	1	0	0
7	1	0	0
8	1	0	0
9	0	0	1
10	0	1	0
11	0	1	0
12	0	1	0
13	0	0	0
14	0	0	0
15	0	0	0
16	0	0	0
Consistency of preference and outcome	0.63	0.63	
Correlation of preference and outcome	0.29	0.00	
Group A:	Favors eight policies of which three are adopted Opposes eight policies of which one is adopted		
Group B:	Favors four policies of which one is adopted Opposes twelve policies of which three are adopted		

subcommittees in both houses of Congress, a majority of House members, and a supermajority of Senators (to avoid a filibuster),[27] we might very well expect the tipping point for public support to be considerably higher than 50 percent. On the other hand, if powerful forces such as interest groups are aligned in favor of a particular policy change, that change may require only a modest level of public support to be adopted (that is, such a policy may have a high probability of adoption unless the public overwhelmingly opposes it).

In chapter 3 I look more closely at the probability of policy change associated with different levels of public support. For now the important point is that there is no magic number in terms of public support, and the politically relevant threshold may be lower or higher than 50 percent depending on the other forces at work in shaping any particular policy outcome.

In the analyses that follow, I use a measure of association (the logistic regression coefficient) rather than raw consistency scores to assess the strength of the relationship between policy preferences and policy outcomes across groups. Regression coefficients (and the associated probabilities of policy change that I report) overcome the various shortcomings of consistency scores—they incorporate the degree of support (or opposition) to a specific policy proposal, they reflect the extent to which different levels of policy support are associated with different probabilities of policy implementation within each group, and they don't impose an arbitrary tipping point in assessing the strength of policy responsiveness.

With the preliminaries of data description and analytic approach now out of the way, I turn in the next chapters to the substantive examination of policy responsiveness. Chapter 3 presents some key findings on variation in responsiveness across income groups and considers the alternative causal processes that might account for those associations. In chapters 4 through 7 I examine additional aspects of representational inequality, looking at the variation across substantive issue domains (chapter 4), the role of interest groups (chapter 5), and changes in policy responsiveness under different political circumstances and over time (chapters 6 and 7).

CHAPTER 3

The Preference/Policy Link

FEW WILL BE SURPRISED that the link between preferences and policies turns out to be stronger for higher-income Americans than for the poor. But the magnitude of this difference, and the inequality in representation that I find even between the affluent and the slightly less well-off, suggest that the political system is tilted very strongly in favor of those at the top of the income distribution. After presenting my core findings on representational inequality, I show that alternative methodologies for estimating the independent influence of Americans at different income levels produce similar results. The final section of the chapter discusses alternative explanations for the representational inequalities I find. I show that the stronger link between preferences and policies for the affluent does not result from different reliabilities in measuring preferences at different income levels. Neither can representational inequality be explained by differences in the scope of the issues on which Americans at various income levels hold preferences or to the strength of those preferences. I argue instead that the association of policy outcomes and the preferences of affluent Americans primarily reflects the influence of this subgroup of the public over policy outcomes.

STYLIZED MODELS OF POLICY RESPONSIVENESS

Democratic responsiveness implies a positive association between the level of public support for a policy and the likelihood of that policy being adopted. In any actual democracy, of course, this relationship is likely to be imperfect. First, there are many other factors that influence government policy in addition to public preferences; second, electoral structures can generate countermajoritarian outcomes (e.g., the overrepresentation of citizens from small states in the U.S. Senate); and third, governing structures can impose restraints on policy making leading to a bias favoring the status quo (for example, by requiring supermajority support for some kinds of policy change or by the imposition of constitutional constraints).

Four stylized representations of the relationship between public preferences and government policy are shown in figure 3.1. The two diagrams at the top reflect perfectly nonresponsive and perfectly responsive rela-

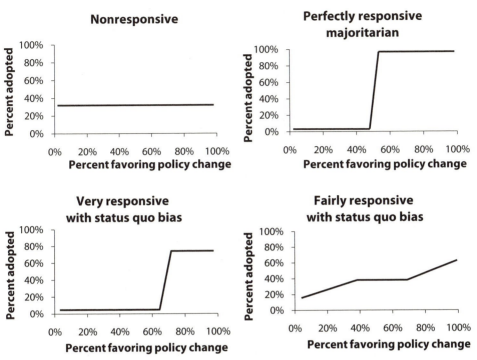

Figure 3.1. Stylized Models of Policy Responsiveness

tionships. In the top left panel the probability that a policy change will be adopted is unrelated to the percent of the population favoring that change. In the top right panel, in contrast, potential policy changes with majority support are always adopted while those lacking majority support are never adopted. These hypothetical examples represent the extreme ends of the continuum of democratic responsiveness and are presented to help clarify the graphical representation of different kinds and degrees of government responsiveness to public preferences.

The bottom left panel of figure 3.1 shows a still-stylized but somewhat more realistic hypothetical example in which government policy is strongly related to public preferences but with a substantial bias toward the status quo. In this diagram policies that lack majority support are never adopted, but policies favored by a majority of citizens are adopted only 70 percent of the time (compared with 100 percent in the "perfectly responsive majoritarian" example in the upper right panel).

Finally, the lower right panel reflects a fairly responsive government with a strong status quo bias. In this hypothetical world, even policies with near unanimous opposition are sometimes adopted (in contrast to the perfectly responsive systems in the previous two diagrams), but the status quo bias is reflected in the asymmetry in response to very unpopular and very popular policies. In this diagram 85 percent of the least popular policies are rejected, but only 60 percent of the most popular policies are adopted. In addition, government responsiveness to public preferences is less dramatic than in the preceding example. In this last case, there is a zone of indifference that ranges from mild opposition (40 percent favorable) to mild support (60 percent favorable). Within this range the probability of a policy being adopted does not change. As support declines further below 40 percent, however, the chances of a policy being adopted diminish. Likewise, as support grows above 60 percent, the chances increase.

These hypothetical examples of policy responsiveness are intended to illustrate the ways plausible, real-world elements of American politics might be reflected in macrolevel analyses of policy responsiveness like those reported below. The zone of indifference around the point at which roughly equal numbers of Americans support and oppose a policy reflects the room to maneuver that politicians have when the public in the aggregate does not lean heavily in one direction or the other. If proponents and opponents of a policy are roughly equal in numbers (and assuming that they are also equal in their intensity of preference regarding the relevant policy), politicians have no strong incentive to act one way or the other, at least in terms of satisfying public opinion. It should be emphasized that an evenly split public can be said to be indifferent to the proposed policy change in an aggregate sense even though many or most individual members of the public are strongly in favor or strongly opposed. For purposes of both the electoral incentives that politicians face and responsiveness of the government to aggregate preferences, an evenly split public is, in the aggregate, indifferent to the adoption of the policy in question.[1]

Both the zone of indifference and status quo bias illustrated in the bottom right panel of figure 3.1 are consistent with the American system of divided government with its multiple veto points and supermajority requirements. In contrast to many parliamentary systems, which concentrate power and facilitate policy making, the American system of checks and balances was expressly designed to protect against the "tyranny of the majority."[2] For majority sentiment (or any sentiment) to be translated into law, legislation must successfully pass through committees and subcommittees of both the House and Senate, receive majority votes on the floor of both houses of Congress, and be signed by the president.[3] As we'll see shortly, the hypothetical status quo bias embodied in the bottom panels of figure 3.1 is also reflected in the actual patterns of association between public preferences and government policy.

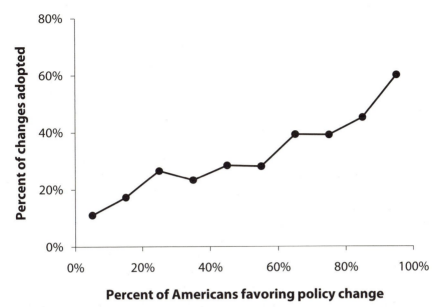

Figure 3.2. Observed Association between Policy Preferences and Policy Outcomes. Cases consist of survey questions about proposed policy changes asked between 1981 and 2002. Changes are coded as adopted if the proposed policy change took place within four years of the survey date (N = 1,779).

EMPIRICAL EVIDENCE OF POLICY RESPONSIVENESS

Turning now from stylized models to real-world data, figure 3.2 shows the relationship between the percentage of survey respondents favoring a proposed policy change and the proportion of proposed changes that were adopted. As expected, the association between public support and probability of adoption is positive, with the percentage of changes adopted increasing from only 11 percent for those policies favored by fewer than one in ten respondents to 60 percent for policies favored by at least nine out of ten Americans. Figure 3.2 clearly displays the status quo bias embodied in the hypothetical examples in the bottom of figure 3.1. Policies that are strongly opposed have little chance of being adopted, but policies with strong public support still face uncertain prospects.[4] Of the 240 proposed policy changes that were favored by at least 80 percent of survey respondents, only 48 percent were adopted (the two rightmost dots in figure 3.2).

Figure 3.2 also appears to show a zone of indifference in which the probability of a policy being adopted changes little between about 25 percent approval and 55 percent approval among the public. This leftward shift in the zone of indifference suggests a bias toward change rather than toward the status quo. That is, the increase in the probability of a policy being adopted as support rises from 50 to 75 percent is much greater than the decrease in probability as support drops from 50 to 25 percent. On the other hand, this change bias must be assessed in relation to the low probability of policies with 50 percent support being adopted in the first place (only 28 percent of policies on which the public was evenly split were adopted). The net result is that any given level of support for policy change is less likely to be reflected in policy outcomes than is an equivalent level of support for keeping the status quo. (For example, when three out of four Americans support a policy change, that change occurs about 39 percent of the time, but when three out of four Americans oppose a policy change, that change is rejected about 78 percent of the time.)

As discussed above, the status quo bias evident in figure 3.2 reflects the design of the American political system. No sensible observer of American government would be surprised that unpopular policies are more likely to be rejected than popular policies are to be adopted. But few scholars have made any effort to quantify the magnitude of the status quo bias in federal policy making, and the results presented in the figure arguably represent the best existing evidence on the strength of this bias.[5] The bias, in short, is enormous. As reported above, the probability of seeing majority preferences reflected in policy outcomes is only half as large when three-quarters of Americans favor a policy change as when three-quarters oppose a change (39% vs. 78%). Of course, some degree of status quo bias in policy making may be beneficial, preventing policy from shifting too frequently or in response to small changes in public preferences. But the low probability of policy changes desired even by quite large majorities of Americans does seem to indicate a very substantial democratic deficit.

The shape of the relationship between preferences and policy outcomes shown in figure 3.2 is somewhat unusual in that the steepest parts of the curve are at the low and high extremes of public support and the flattest part is in the middle values. (This is opposite the common logit or probit functional form in which the marginal change in probability is largest in the middle of the distribution and smallest at the tails.) To capture the nature of the observed relationship between preferences and policy outcomes, I take the log of the odds ratio of the percent favoring a given policy as my predictor in a logistic regression on my dichotomous policy outcome measure (coded 1 if the proposed change was adopted and 0 otherwise). That is, my predictor (x) is a function of the proportion favoring a given policy (p) as given by $x = \ln(p/(1-p))$.

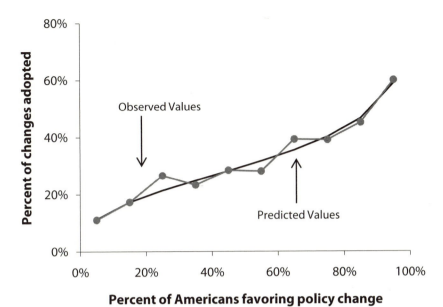

Figure 3.3. Observed and Predicted Associations between Policy Preferences and Policy Outcomes. Cases consist of survey questions about proposed policy changes asked between 1981 and 2002. Changes are coded as adopted if the proposed policy change took place within four years of the survey date. Predicted probabilities based on the logistic regression shown in the first column of table 3.1 (N = 1,779).

Figure 3.3 shows both the observed and predicted probabilities of policy adoption by level of public support using the transformation above. The predicted probabilities, shown by the dark line in the figure, do not follow every bump in the observed values (no single transformed predictor could), but they do nicely capture the general form of the observed relationship and in particular the steeper slope of the preference/policy link at high and low levels of support for proposed policy changes.

The regression results that produced the dark line in the figure are shown in the first column of table 3.1. The logistic coefficient of 0.41 is not easily interpretable, but the magnitude of the preference/policy link can be gauged by comparing the predicted probability of adoption for highly popular versus highly unpopular policies. Row 4 of the table shows the predicted probability of a policy change occurring if 20 percent of respondents favor the proposed change, row 5 shows the predicted probability if 80 percent favor the proposed change, and row 6 shows the ratio of row 5 to row 4—that is, the factor by which the predicted probability

Table 3.1 Policy Responsiveness by Income Percentile

	All Respondents	Income Percentile				
		10th	30th	50th	70th	90th
Logistic coefficient	.41	.31	.34	.37	.42	.49
(Standard error)	(.05)	(.05)	(.05)	(.05)	(.05)	(.05)
Intercept	−.85	−.80	−.82	−.84	−.87	−.90
Predicted probability if 20% favor	.19	.23	.22	.21	.19	.17
Predicted probability if 80% favor	.43	.41	.41	.42	.43	.45
Relative difference in predicted probability (row 5/row 4)	2.2	1.8	1.9	2.0	2.3	2.7
N	1779	1779	1779	1779	1779	1779
Log Likelihood	2198	2223	2213	2203	2188	2169
Likelihood ratio χ^2	$\chi^2(1) = 60$ $p < .001$	$\chi^2(1) = 35$ $p < .001$	$\chi^2(1) = 45$ $p < .001$	$\chi^2(1) = 55$ $p < .001$	$\chi^2(1) = 70$ $p < .001$	$\chi^2(1) = 88$ $p < .001$

Cases consist of survey questions about proposed policy changes asked between 1981 and 2002. Dependent variable is policy outcome coded 1 if the proposed policy change took place within four years of the survey date and 0 if it did not. Predictors are the logits of the percentage of respondents favoring the proposed policy change (column 1) or the imputed percentage of respondents at a given income percentile favoring the proposed policy change.

of policy change increases as opinion shifts from strong opposition to strong support.

The first column, which reflects policy responsiveness for the public as a whole, shows that the predicted probability of a policy being adopted rises from 0.19 among policies with only 20 percent support to 0.43 for policies with 80 percent support. The ratio of these two probabilities is 2.2, meaning that a highly popular policy is about twice as likely to be adopted as a highly unpopular policy.

Turning next to the differences in policy responsiveness for respondents at different income levels, we find, as expected, that higher-income respondents' views are more strongly related to government policy. The logit coefficients relating preference and policy rise from 0.31 for those at the 10th income percentile, to 0.37 for median income respondents, to 0.49 for those at the 90th percentile. These coefficients are translated into

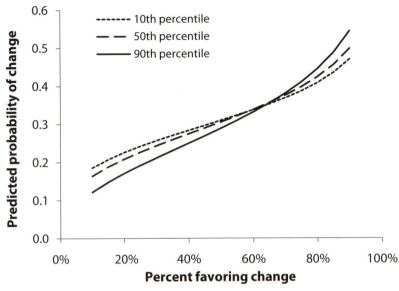

Figure 3.4. Policy Responsiveness for the 10th, 50th, and 90th Income Percentiles. Predicted probabilities are based on the logistic regressions reported in table 3.1.

probabilities in rows 4 and 5 of table 3.1 and displayed graphically in figure 3.4. For respondents at the 10th income percentile, the probability of policy change rises from 0.23 with 20 percent favoring to 0.41 with 80 percent support. Thus a policy that those at the 10th income percentile strongly favor has just under twice the probability of being adopted as one that they strongly oppose.

For those at the top of the income distribution, the probability of policy change rises somewhat more dramatically, from 0.17 to 0.45 (a factor of 2.7). Looking across the columns in table 3.1, we see that the strength of the relationship between preferences and policy outcomes not only increases with each step up the income ladder but does so at an increasing rate: the differences in the logit coefficients and the 80/20 ratio are smaller between the 10th and 50th income percentiles than they are between the 50th and 90th percentiles.

POLICY RESPONSIVENESS WHEN PREFERENCES ACROSS INCOME GROUPS DIVERGE

It is hardly surprising that the preferences of the well-off are more clearly reflected in government policy than those of poor or middle-income citizens. But the results in table 3.1 understate the true differences in the ability of different economic groups to influence policy. On many of the policy issues in the dataset, low- and high-income Americans do not differ substantially in their policy preferences. If the well-to-do are better able to exert influence over government policy, the observed association between policy outcomes and the preferences of poor or middle-income respondents may simply reflect those proposed changes on which Americans of all income levels agree.

To assess the ability of citizens at different economic levels to influence government policy, we need to know not the strength of the overall preference/policy link for each income group, but rather the strength of this association net of the impact of other income groups. That is, after parceling out the preferences that are shared across income groups, how much of an association do we find between policy outcomes and the unique preferences of affluent, middle-income, or poor Americans?

The most common technique for identifying the unique contribution of each predictor on some outcome of interest is multivariate analysis, which holds all other variables constant in estimating the impact of any given factor. For reasons explained below (and in detail in the appendix), my ability to use this approach is limited by the distinctive characteristics of my data.

As an alternative to multivariate analysis, I assess the influence of Americans at various income levels by separating out those proposed policy changes that elicit similar levels of support across the economic spectrum from those on which the preferences of low-, middle-, and high-income respondents diverge. (In the following section I show that this technique produces results comparable to a multivariate model when the multivariate approach is feasible.) Low- and high-income respondents express comparable levels of support (within 5 percentage points) on about one-third of the proposed policy changes in my dataset, and middle- and high-income respondents agree on about half the proposed changes. Examples of agreement across income groups include opposition to new taxes, government support for higher education, strengthening antidrug efforts (but legalizing marijuana for medical use), and providing welfare recipients with job training and child care. In contrast the affluent and the poor often disagree on issues like stem cell research, gay rights, abortion, the progressivity of the tax system, and market-oriented reforms of Social Security and Medicare. Even in the same general issue area, lower- and higher-income Americans are sometimes in agreement and sometimes not. For example, while Americans at all income levels favor job training and child care for welfare recipients, the poor are far less supportive than the affluent when it comes to welfare time limits or efforts to reduce welfare spending overall. In chapter 4 I discuss these patterns of policy support and opposition in detail; I focus here on how the overall strength of the

Table 3.2 Policy Responsiveness by Size of Preference Gap across Income Percentiles

	10th vs. 90th Income Percentiles		50th vs. 90th Income Percentiles	
Size of Preference Gap	10th	90th	50th	90th
Less than 5 points	.54 (.09)***	.54 (.09)***	.48 (.07)***	.50 (.07)***
Between 5 and 10 points	.41 (.11)***	.52 (.11)***	.33 (.10)***	.51 (.12)***
Greater than 10 points	.02 (.09)	.46 (.10)***	−.01 (.14)	.47 (.18)**

Cases consist of survey questions about proposed policy changes asked between 1981 and 2002. Dependent variable is policy outcome coded 1 if the proposed policy change took place within four years of the survey date and 0 if it did not. Predictors are the logits of the imputed percentage of respondents at a given income percentile favoring the proposed policy change. N ranges from 322 to 936. See appendix table A3.1 for full results.
**$p < .01$; ***$p < .001$

preference/policy link differs for policies that generate more or less agreement across economic groups.

For questions that generate comparable levels of support across different income groups, the preference/policy link is necessarily the same irrespective of income. For the next set of analyses, then, I divide the proposed policy changes into three categories based on the size of the preference gap between respondents at the 10th and 90th income percentiles. To the extent that policy responsiveness for low-income respondents is an artifact of those issues on which they agree with the affluent, the strength of this association should decline as the preferences between low- and high-income Americans diverge. At the same time, if government policy reflects the preferences of the affluent to the exclusion of other groups, policy responsiveness for those at the top of the income distribution should not decline as preference divergence across income groups increases.

The first two columns of table 3.2 show exactly this pattern: as the size of the preference gap between low- and high-income respondents increases, the association of preferences and policy outcomes declines dramatically for the poor but only marginally for the affluent (full results in appendix table A3.1). On those proposed policy changes where the preferences of low- and high-income respondents coincide (top row), the logistic coefficients for the preference/policy link are 0.54 for both the 10th and 90th income percentiles ($p < 0.001$ for both). As the bottom row of table 3.2 shows, policy outcomes for questions that generate preferences gaps of over 10 percentage points between low- and high-income respondents continue to show a strong association with the preferences of the affluent ($b = 0.46$, $p < 0.001$) but no association with the preferences of the poor at all ($b = 0.02$, $p = 0.85$). The top panel of figure 3.5 shows

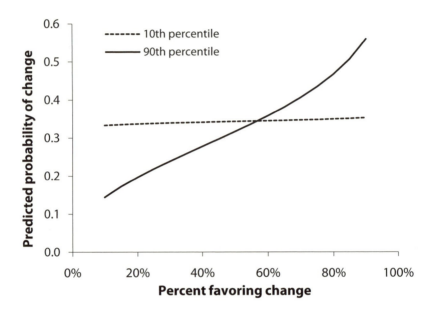

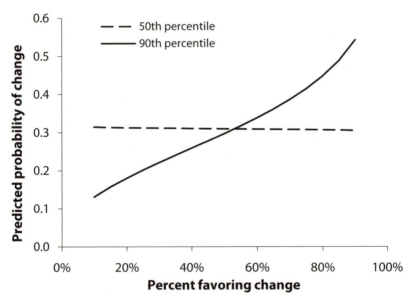

Figure 3.5. Policy Responsiveness When Preferences across Income Levels Diverge. Predicted probabilities are based on the logistic regressions reported in table 3.2.

these two relationships graphically, conveying the fairly steep relationship between preferences and policy outcomes for the well-off and the
virtually flat relationship for the poor for those policies on which their
preferences diverge.

The complete lack of government responsiveness to the preferences of
the poor is disturbing and seems consistent only with the most cynical
views of American politics. These results indicate that when preferences
between the well-off and the poor diverge, government policy bears ab-
solutely no relationship to the degree of support or opposition among the
poor. But these results could be compatible with an egalitarian and majoritarian polity if poor people hold attitudes that consistently differ from
those held not only by the wealthy but by the middle class as well. If the
preferences of the poor were systematically at variance with the majority of Americans, the lack of responsiveness to their preferences might
actually reflect a well-functioning democracy. Middle-income respondents
better reflect the preferences of the median voter on most issues, and the
responsiveness of government policy makers to the preferences of the
middle class might therefore serve as a more appropriate test of biases in
representation.

The right two columns of table 3.2 and the bottom panel of figure 3.5
show that median-income Americans fare no better than the poor when
their policy preferences diverge from those of the well-off. For those proposed policy changes on which middle- and high-income respondents'
preferences diverge by at least 10 percentage points, policy responsiveness for the 90th income percentile remains strong ($b = 0.47, p < 0.01$)
but is indistinguishable from zero for the 50th percentile ($b = -0.01, p =
0.93$).

The lack of responsiveness to the preferences of the 10th and 50th
income percentiles does not mean that those groups never get what they
want from government, or that high-income Americans always see their
preferences enacted in government policy. On the policy questions on
which low- and middle-income respondents share the same preferences as
those with high incomes, they are, of course, just as likely as high-income
Americans to get what they want. But when their views differ from those
of more affluent Americans, government policy appears to be fairly responsive to the well-off and virtually unrelated to the desires of low- and
middle-income citizens.

To provide a more complete picture of the relative influence of different economic groups, figure 3.6 repeats the analyses shown in the bottom row of table 3.2 for the 10th, 30th, 50th, and 70th income percentiles for those proposed policy changes where the preference gap with the
90th percentile is larger than 10 percentage points (the numeric results of
these analyses are in table A3.2).[6] This figure makes clear the dramatically

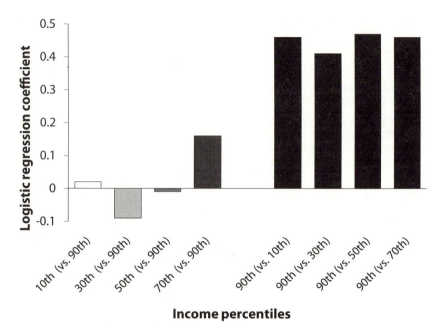

Figure 3.6. Policy Responsiveness When Preferences Diverge between the 90th and Other Income Percentiles. Predicted probabilities are based on the logistic regressions reported in table A3.2.

greater influence of the affluent when their preferences diverge from those of less-well-off Americans. In the four leftmost columns in figure 3.6 the only hint of a link between preferences and policies is for Americans at the 70th income percentile (when the preferences of each of these groups are pitted against those of the 90th percentile). But even for the 70th income percentile, the coefficient is small ($b = 0.16$) and nonsignificant ($p = 0.28$).

In stark contrast, responsiveness to the preferences of the 90th percentile are equally strong whether their preferences diverge from the poor, from the middle class, or even from respondents at the 70th percentile of family income (and the four estimates of policy responsiveness for the 90th percentile all are statistically significant at $p < 0.01$). Of course the number of proposed policy changes that elicit divergent preferences is greatest between groups farthest apart on the income distribution—in this case the 10th and 90th percentiles. Nevertheless, when preferences did diverge from the affluent, Americans at the 70th income percentile appear as powerless to shape government policy as their less-well-off fellow Americans.

In short, figure 3.6 suggests that for Americans below the top of the income distribution, any association between preferences and policy outcomes is likely to reflect the extent to which their preferences coincide with those of the affluent. Although responsiveness to the preferences of the affluent is far from perfect, responsiveness to less-well-off Americans is virtually nonexistent, at least based on the proposed policy changes in my 1981–2002 dataset. (In subsequent chapters I look for exceptions to this lack of influence across different substantive policy domains, years in the federal election cycle, partisan control of the national government, and so on.)

The concentration of political influence among Americans at the top of the income distribution is incompatible with the core democratic principle of political equality. More prosaically, it is also incompatible with the expectation that the policy positions of parties and candidates will tend to converge on the preferences of the median voter.[7] A large literature has developed that elaborates, criticizes, and defends the median voter theorem as a model of democratic politics.[8] Whatever empirical validity median voter models may hold with regard to the professed positions of parties and candidates, the findings presented above clearly show that actual government policy does not respond to the preferences of the median voter.

Although the median voter theorem, in its most straightforward formulation, is clearly inconsistent with the results presented above, one of the variations that build on the median voter model is particularly relevant in evaluating the patterns of responsiveness my data reveal. Noam Lupu and Jonas Pontusson contend that a key determinant of redistributive policy is whether middle-income voters align with the poor (in favoring greater redistribution) or the affluent (in opposing it).[9] Lupu and Pontusson argue that when the income distance between the median income and the poor is small relative to the distance between the median and the affluent, middle-income voters will tend to align with the poor and push policy toward greater redistribution. But when the median income is relatively farther from that of the poor and closer to the affluent, the middle class will tend to align with the affluent and push policy in a less redistributive direction. Using data from eighteen advanced democracies, Lupu and Pontusson show that middle-income voters hold more redistributive preferences, and government policy is in fact more redistributive, when the median income is closer to the income of the 10th percentile and farther from the income of the 90th percentile.

Lupu and Pontusson look only at preferences and policies concerning economic redistribution, but a similar dynamic of cross-class coalitions could be at work on the wider range of policies I examine. To assess the

Table 3.3 Policy Responsiveness When Middle-Income Preferences Align with Those of the Affluent or the Poor

	When the Preferences of the 50th and 90th Percentiles Align			When the Preferences of the 50th and 10th Percentiles Align		
	10th	50th	90th	10th	50th	90th
Logit coefficient	.07	.42	.39	.03	.06	.54
(Standard error)	(.20)	(.16)	(.15)	(.16)	(.18)	(.25)
Intercept	−.69	−.83	−.84	−.82	−.82	−.88
N	235	235	235	192	192	192
Log likelihood	300	293	293	237	237	232
Likelihood ratio χ^2	$\chi^2(1) = .12$ $p = .73$	$\chi^2(1) = 6.9$ $p = .01$	$\chi^2(1) = 7.2$ $p = .01$	$\chi^2(1) = .03$ $p = .87$	$\chi^2(1) = .11$ $p = .74$	$\chi^2(1) = 4.8$ $p = .03$

The first three columns are restricted to policies on which preferences of the 50th and 90th income percentiles are within 5 percentage points and both diverge from the 10th percentile by at least 10 percentage points. The last three columns are restricted to policies on which preferences of the 50th and 10th income percentiles are within 5 percentage points and both diverge from the 90th percentile by at least 10 percentage points. Cases consist of survey questions about proposed policy changes asked between 1981 and 2002. Dependent variable is policy outcome coded 1 if the proposed policy change took place within four years of the survey date and 0 if it did not. Predictors are the logits the imputed percentage of respondents at a given income percentile favoring the proposed policy change.

extent to which preference alignments across income levels influence patterns of responsiveness, I isolated two sets of policies in my data: those on which the preferences of middle-income Americans resemble those of the poor but diverge from those of the affluent, and those on which middle-income Americans' preferences resemble those of the affluent but diverge from those of the poor.[10] The associations of preferences and policy outcomes for these two sets of policies do not fit the pattern that Lupu and Pontusson find (see table 3.3). When preferences of the middle class and the affluent align in my data, responsiveness is strong and (necessarily) equal for these two groups and essentially nonexistent for the poor (columns 1–3). But when middle-class preferences align with those of the poor, responsiveness to the affluent remains strong while responsiveness to the poor and middle class is completely absent (columns 4–6).

We saw above that less-well-off Americans have little influence over policy outcomes when their preferences diverge from those of the affluent. These additional findings show that this is true not only for the poor and the middle class considered separately (as shown in table 3.2), but for those policies on which the poor and middle class are closely aligned in opposition to the affluent. These results are inconsistent with the broad cross-national pattern that Lupu and Pontusson find, but not with their analysis of the United States, which is somewhat of an exception among the eighteen advanced democracies they examine. As Lupu and Pontusson explain, income growth in the United States over the past few decades has been concentrated at the top of the distribution (pushing median incomes relatively closer to those of the poor), but this has not produced the same increase in government redistribution that other countries with similar patterns of income growth over this period have experienced.[11] Perhaps other advanced democracies are generally more responsive to the preferences of middle-income citizens than the United States is, or perhaps this pattern reflects the particular characteristics of the redistributive policies that Lupu and Pontusson examined. At any rate my data suggest that across the spectrum of policy issues I examine, the representational biases that privilege the affluent are not diluted by the shared preferences of the middle class and the poor.

In sum, the responsiveness of policy makers to the preferences of the American public is highly skewed in favor of the most affluent, and this remains true even when we isolate those policies on which the preferences of the poor and the middle class converge. Whether this broad pattern holds less strongly in other democratic societies, as Lupu and Pontusson's examination of redistributive policy suggests, must await future analysis. In the following chapters we'll see that representational inequalities in the United States extend widely, but not universally, across time, policy domains, political conditions.

An Alternative Approach to Estimating Income Groups' Policy Influence

Dividing my set of proposed policy changes into those with greater and lesser agreement across income groups, as I did above, is a straightforward technique to assess the influence of different groups. But this method necessarily entails an arbitrary cutoff for defining the sets of policy changes. The more common approach to estimating the independent effect of multiple predictors on some outcome of interest is to use multivariate analyses that include all the relevant predictors simultaneously (in this case, the policy preferences of low-, middle-, and high-income respondents). Unfortunately, correlated error in my measures of policy preferences at different income levels makes this approach difficult to apply.

All data contain some amount of error, and survey measures of subjective phenomena (such as support or opposition to proposed policy changes) are especially prone to measurement error.[12] The consequences of measurement error depend on the nature of the errors and, in particular, whether the errors in measurement of one variable are correlated with the errors in measurement of other variables included in the same analyses. Random measurement error biases bivariate associations toward zero, but correlated errors can either weaken or strengthen observed bivariate associations.[13] In the multivariate context the consequences of both random and correlated errors can bias estimates in either a positive or a negative direction.

The unique nature of my data—aggregated measures of preferences for subgroups of survey respondents—helps reduce random measurement error by averaging across many individual respondents within each income group. At the same time the aggregated nature of my data generates correlated error since the same survey questions are used to gauge the preferences of respondents at different income levels. To the extent that question wording or other idiosyncratic features of a particular survey question lead respondents at all income levels to express more (or less) support for the proposed policy change, the preferences across income levels will be more strongly correlated than would otherwise be the case.[14] Correlated errors, in other words, artificially inflate the degree to which policy preferences appear to be shared across income levels.

The inflated associations of policy preferences across income levels that result from correlated measurement error in my data would cause biased estimates of the preference/policy link if multiple preference measures were included together in predicting policy outcomes. The most direct remedy for this problem is to deflate the observed covariances among the predictors by the estimated size of their error covariances. The details of this procedure are described in the appendix. As I explain there, these estimates can be applied with confidence only to the dataset as a whole, and not to smaller subsets of my data. This limitation precludes using this covariance deflation technique for the analyses of substantive policy sub-areas and change over time in chapters 4–7. Nevertheless, this approach does allow me to conduct a traditional multivariate analysis for assessing the independent impact of preferences at different income levels for the dataset as a whole and therefore provides a check on the results presented above.

The associations of policy outcomes with the preferences of the 10th, 50th, and 90th income percentiles when all three are simultaneously included as predictors are shown in table 3.4 (with details in table A3.3). For comparison, table 3.4 also shows the analogous measures of policy responsiveness based on analyses that restrict the dataset to questions on which preferences across income levels diverge by more than 10 percentage points (based on the bottom row of table 3.2). These two techniques for estimating the independent influence of Americans with differing incomes produce very similar results. In both cases the association between

Table 3.4 Alternative Estimates of Policy Responsiveness by Income Percentile

Income Percentile	Multivariate OLS Regression Based on a Deflated Covariance Matrix	Marginal Impact Based on Bivariate Logistic Regressions When Preference Gap Is > .10	
		10th vs. 90th Percentiles	50th vs. 90th Percentiles
10th	−.10 (.09)	.02	
50th	.08 (.10)		−.01
90th	.51 (.09)***	.44***	.45***

The coefficients in the first column are from an ordinary least squares (OLS) model for which the covariance matrix was deflated to correct for correlated measurement error among the predictors, as explained in the appendix. The marginal impacts in the last two columns are based on the logistic regressions for policies in which preferences for the indicated income percentiles diverged by more than 10 percentage points (reported in tables 3.2 and A3.1) and are estimated at the mean of the dependent variable. N is 1,779 for the OLS regression, 723 for the 10th vs. 90th income percentile logistic regressions, and 322 for the 50th vs. 90th logistic regressions. See table A3.3 for details.
*** $p < 0.001$

government policy and the preferences of low- and middle-income Americans is weak and not significant, while the association for high-income Americans is strong and highly significant (with all three estimates for the 90th percentile significant at $p < 0.001$).

EXPLAINING THE ASSOCIATION BETWEEN PREFERENCES AND POLICY OUTCOMES

The analyses above show that the policy preferences of affluent Americans are strong predictors of whether potential policy changes are adopted, while the preferences of less-well-off Americans are essentially unrelated to policy outcomes. The most straightforward explanation for this pattern is that it reflects the causal impact of affluent Americans' preferences on policy outcomes. That is, policy makers attend to the preferences of the affluent but largely ignore the preferences of other constituents, at least when their preferences diverge from those of the well-off. Yet there are a number of other factors that may account for at least part of the association of policy outcomes with the preferences of the well-off and for the lack of association with the preferences of the middle class and the poor. In this section I address some of these alternative explanations; others will be taken up in later chapters.

Reliability of Preference Measures

One possible concern is that the differences in the strength of policy responsiveness across income groups described in this chapter may stem, at least in part, from differences in the reliability of the policy-preference measures. I could not locate any studies that compare the reliability of survey measures across income levels, but political-attitude measures from respondents with more education have been shown to be somewhat more reliable than those of less-educated respondents.[15] But as I discussed in chapter 1, what is true for individuals is not necessarily true for groups, and the random measurement error that compromises the reliability of survey measures tends to cancel out when responses are aggregated. If I use the same multiple-measure technique for estimating reliability from my 387 survey questions with alternate versions described in chapter 2, the estimated reliabilities for the 10th, 50th, and 90th income percentiles are virtually identical at 0.77, 0.80, and 0.77, respectively. (The reliabilities for respondents at different education levels are also highly similar at 0.78, 0.81, and 0.77 for the 10th, 50th, and 90th education percentiles, respectively.)[16]

Strength of Preferences

A second explanation for the stronger association of policy outcomes with the preferences of high-income Americans is that the affluent tend to hold opinions on a wider range of policy issues or to feel more strongly about the opinions they do hold. The data used in the analyses above reveal the distribution of preferences among respondents who express an opinion in favor or opposition to each proposed policy change. But what about respondents who say "Don't know" or who express preferences that they care little about?

The top panel in figure 3.7 shows the average percentage of respondents saying "Don't know" in response to the policy questions in my dataset for the 10th through 90th income percentiles. As the figure shows, poor respondents are about twice as likely, on average, to say "Don't know" than those at the median income, but there is no discernible difference between the propensity of middle- and upper-income Americans to respond in this way. Since the apparent influence over policy as shown in figure 3.5 is essentially zero for both low- and middle-income Americans, but fairly strong for the well-off, the pattern of responsiveness does not fit well with the propensity of different income groups to hold (or at least to express) policy preferences.[17]

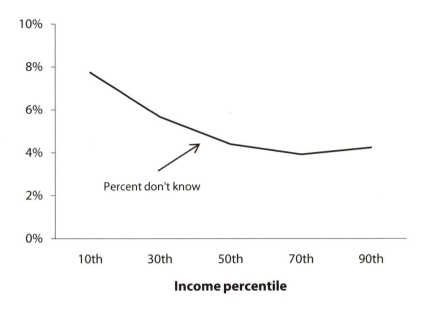

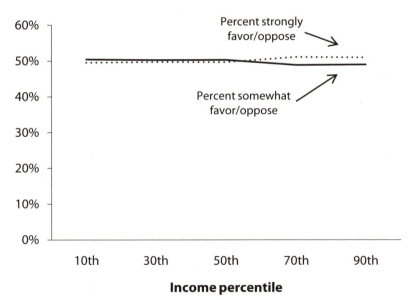

Figure 3.7. Percent "Don't Know" (top) and Strength of Opinion (bottom) by Income Percentile. Percent "Don't know" is based on imputed percent of respondents saying "Don't know" at each income level. Percent strongly and somewhat favor/oppose is based on the 160 survey questions in the dataset that ask respondents to qualify their support or opposition in this way.

Most telephone and in-person survey questions do not explicitly provide a "Don't know" option to respondents, forcing those with no opinion on a topic to volunteer that response on their own. As discussed in chapter 1, some proportion of respondents who in fact have no opinion will nevertheless offer a substantive response, out of a sense either that they ought to have a view on the matter or that saying "Don't know" would somehow be less helpful to the interviewer. The question arises, therefore, whether respondents at different income levels might differ in their tendency to give a substantive response even if they really have no opinion on the question.

The only research I am aware of that sheds light on this question distinguishes respondents by education rather than income. Three studies looked at the propensity of survey respondents to offer substantive opinions on policy questions that referred to fictitious issues like the "1975 Public Affairs Act" or the "Agricultural Trade Act of 1984" discussed in chapter 1. One of these studies finds no difference across educational levels in the percent of respondents reporting "fictitious opinions,"[18] another finds about a 5 percent higher rate of fictitious opinions among those with no college education compared with those with at least some college,[19] and a third finds about a 6 percentage point difference between these two educational groups.[20] More tellingly, substantial majorities of even the least educated groups said "Don't know" in response to these questions about fictitious policies. Averaging across the two studies that found educational differences, about 63 percent of low-education respondents and 71 percent of high-education respondents said "Don't know" despite the lack of an explicit "Don't know" option among the response categories offered. If differences across income groups are roughly similar to differences across educational categories, the different proportions of "Don't know" responses across income levels in my data must be fairly close to the actual differences in opinionation (or lack of opinionation) among these groups. In other words, inflating the percentage of "Don't knows" shown in figure 3.7 by the proportion of respondents who give substantive answers even in the absence of any real opinion would do little to change the pattern of nonopinions across income groups.

The proportion of respondents expressing opinions at different income levels does not appear to play an important (if any) role in explaining differential responsiveness. However, not everyone who expresses a preference feels equally strongly about that preference. If high-income Americans care more about the policy attitudes they express, or hold more extreme views, policy makers might be justified in attending more closely to their preferences than to those of the less well-off.

Conclusive evidence of subjective evaluations like the importance of policy preferences to different groups of Americans is hard to come by.

Yet two kinds of evidence suggest that high-income Americans do not hold stronger views of policy issues or consider such issues to be more important to them. First, surveys occasionally ask respondents to indicate their policy preferences and then to report how important that policy issue is to them. The 2004 American National Election Study, for example, asked a series of questions about gun control, government health insurance, defense spending, aid to black people, and environmental protection. Each policy item was followed by a question asking, "How important is this issue to you personally?" with five options ranging from "extremely important" to "not at all important." The patterns differed slightly across these five issues, with gun control eliciting slightly greater "personal importance" ratings from low-income Americans and health insurance slightly greater importance from those with high incomes. But averaged across the issues, low-, middle-, and high-income respondents expressed nearly identical levels of importance; the percentage indicating these issues were "extremely" or "very" important to them was 58, 61, and 58 percent for low-, middle-, and high-income Americans, respectively.

The second indication that high-income Americans are no more fervent in their policy preferences than those of more modest means comes from the subset of my data that contains measures of both direction and strength of preference. One hundred sixty of my survey questions ask respondents to indicate not only their support or opposition to the proposed policy change, but whether they support or oppose that change "strongly" or only "somewhat." The bottom panel in figure 3.7 shows no difference across income levels in the propensity of respondents to say they "strongly" as opposed to "somewhat" favor or oppose a given policy.

None of these assessments of opinion holding and opinion strength is definitive, but collectively they provide strong evidence that little if any of the representational inequality documented above can be explained by a greater tendency of the affluent to hold opinions on policy questions, to consider the issues personally important, or to feel more strongly about the policy preferences they hold.

Preference Homogeneity

Even if affluent Americans are no more likely than the middle class to hold or express policy opinions, the affluent might be distinctively homogenous in the opinions they do hold. If the well-off are typically in agreement about policy issues but the poor or middle class are more often divided, a stronger apparent preference/policy link for the affluent might result. Since all my preference measures are dichotomous (reflecting simply support for or opposition to a proposed policy change), a higher level

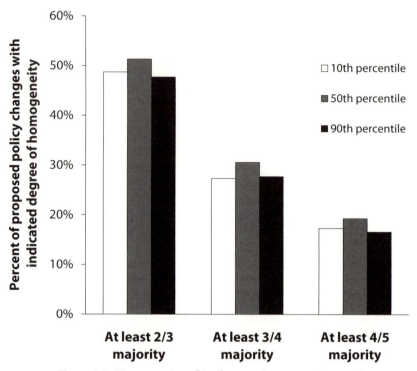

Figure 3.8. Homogeneity of Preferences by Income Percentile

of agreement on a policy is equivalent to a more lopsided distribution of opinion. That is, a 50/50 split on an issue would represent both the lowest level of agreement and the least lopsided distribution, while unanimous support or opposition would represent the highest level of agreement and most lopsided distribution.

Figure 3.8 shows the proportion of proposed policy changes in my dataset that generated varying degrees of agreement for respondents at the 10th, 50th, and 90th income percentiles. The first set of columns shows that at least two-thirds of respondents were in agreement (either in favor of or opposed to the proposed change) for about 50 percent of the questions in my dataset, and this percentage varied little across income levels. Not surprisingly, fewer proposed changes resulted in preference majorities of three-quarters or four-fifths of respondents. But as the second and third sets of columns show, these more homogenous policy proposals occurred with similar frequency across income levels. In short, the affluent are no more (or less) likely to be of one mind on the proposed policy changes in my dataset than are Americans with low or middle incomes.

Public Receptiveness to Elite Persuasion

The stronger link between preferences and policies for high-income Americans appears to be real in the sense that it is not an artifact of differential measurement error. But is it causal? That is, does it arise from the *influence* of affluent Americans over policy outcomes?

The preference/policy link is typically understood to reflect the democratic responsiveness of government policy makers to the will of the people. But this relationship can run in the other direction as well. Both common sense and considerable evidence suggest that citizens form their policy preferences at least in part on the basis of cues from political decision makers and other elites.[21] If higher-income Americans are more attentive to such cues, their preferences may correlate more strongly with government policy than do those of Americans with lower incomes—not because they have more influence, but because they are more easily led to hold the preferences that policy makers favor.

If the stronger preference/policy link for those at the high end of the income distribution reflects greater attentiveness to elite political discourse, we would expect to find an even stronger pattern across levels of education, since education is more closely associated with interest in and attention to politics than is income.[22] In fact the increase in strength of policy responsiveness as education rises is similar to, if slightly weaker than, that which we observe with income. Table 3.1 showed the estimated coefficients for the 10th and 90th income percentiles to be 0.31 and 0.49, respectively; the analogous coefficients for the 10th and 90th education percentiles are 0.37 and 0.50.[23]

A more telling analysis would separate out the effects of income and education on policy preferences before examining their impact on policy outcomes. Chapter 2 described the imputation process I used to estimate policy preferences at specific percentiles of income or education. In a parallel procedure I used both income and education as predictors of policy preferences within each survey in order to estimate a series of imputed preferences for various combinations of low, middle, and high income and education. That is, using income, income squared, education, and education squared, I estimated the joint relationship of income and education with each policy outcome.[24] Then, using the coefficients from these equations, I imputed policy preferences for each of the nine combinations of income and education (the 10th income and education percentiles, the 10th income and 50th education percentiles, and so on).

Figure 3.9 shows the results from nine logistic regression equations using each of these imputed preferences as predictors of policy outcomes (this analysis parallels that used for income alone in figure 3.5 and the bottom row of table 3.2; complete results for these nine logistic analyses

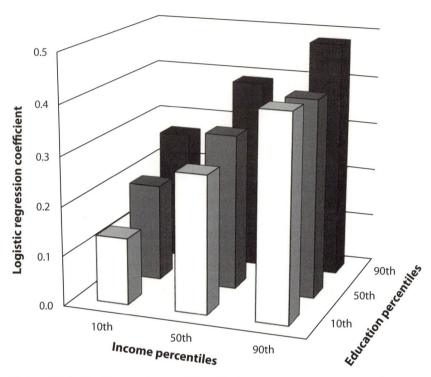

Figure 3.9. Policy Responsiveness When Preferences across Income or Education Levels Diverge. Figure shows logistic regression coefficients from nine separate regressions. Dependent variable is policy outcome coded 1 if the proposed policy change took place within four years of the survey date and 0 if it did not. Predictors are the logits of the imputed percentage of respondents at a given combination of income and education percentiles favoring the proposed policy change. Analysis is restricted to the 1,050 questions on which preferences diverged by at least 10 percentage points between the 10th and 90th income percentiles or the 10th and 90th education percentiles. See table A3.4 for full results.

are provided in table A3.4). Clearly both income and education matter in determining the strength of the preference/policy link. But equally clearly, income is the more important determinant of how strong the link is. At each income level there is a modest increase in the association of preferences and policy outcomes as education increases from the 10th to the 90th percentiles (that is, from the front row to the back row of figure 3.9). But this association increases much more dramatically as income increases within each level of education (from the left side to the right side of the figure). Even among the highly educated, the shift from the 10th to the 90th income percentile is associated with a change from 0.27 to 0.48 in the strength of policy responsiveness (see table A3.4). But among those with high incomes, a shift from the 10th to the 90th education percentiles only increases the estimated coefficient from 0.41 to 0.48. In other words, high income alone seems sufficient to ensure a strong association between preferences and outcomes, while high education alone does not.

The greater attentiveness to politics that characterizes highly educated Americans does not seem to explain the stronger association between preferences and policy outcomes among the affluent than among less-well-off Americans. Consequently the ability of decision makers and other elites to sway public opinion is not a likely explanation for the differential relationships between preferences and policy outcomes across income groups.

In addition to this evidence in my own data, other research bolsters the general notion that public preferences have a causal impact on government policy. First, the strong associations between constituency preferences and representatives' votes found in the dyadic representation literature reviewed in chapter 1 are unlikely to arise from the influence of representatives on their constituents. Only 29 percent of Americans can name their representative in the House of Representatives, much less describe his or her position on any particular issue, and only 25 percent can name both their senators.[25] A far more plausible explanation is that representatives' votes are shaped by their constituents' preferences, operating through incumbents' desire to avoid providing potential challengers with campaign issues and through the election of like-minded officeholders to begin with.[26]

The second kind of evidence that the preference/policy link reflects the influence of the public on government decision makers comes from studies of public policy and the electoral cycle. For example, Brandice Canes-Wrone and Kenneth Shotts show that the association between public preferences and presidential budget proposals is strongest not when the president is most popular (and presumably most able to influence public preferences) but when the president is most in need of public support (i.e., when facing reelection with a moderate level of popularity).[27] Similarly, research on congressional voting shows that legislators' positions tend to be more moderate and more consistent with constituency preferences when an election is near.[28]

The representational inequalities documented in this chapter cannot be explained by any of the alternative possibilities explored above. The reliability of my preference measures is virtually identical across income levels, poor and affluent Americans show no clear differences in strength or breadth of their policy opinions, and preferences are equally heterogeneous among those with higher and lower incomes. Nor does it appear that differential receptiveness of the public to elite persuasion can explain much of the dramatic inequality in policy responsiveness that the analyses in this chapter reveal.

In subsequent chapters I examine other possible explanations for these patterns, including the role of interest groups (which may be more aligned with the preferences of the affluent); the different propensities of lower- and higher-income Americans to vote, contribute, and involve themselves in politics in other ways; and the fact that members of Congress and other influential policy makers all fall well within the top decile of the income distribution themselves.

In the next chapter I look at the substantive content of policy responsiveness (and nonresponsiveness) in order to understand the consequences of the inequalities this chapter revealed. I also begin the search for exceptions to the general conclusion that influence over government policy is restricted to affluent Americans. If there are cases—even if few in number—where poor or middle-class Americans prevail over the preferences of the well-off, there may be lessons to be learned about how representational inequality can be lessened.

CHAPTER 4

Policy Domains and Democratic Responsiveness

THE PREVIOUS CHAPTER documented the stark inequality in policy responsiveness to the preferences of low- versus high-income Americans. In this chapter I look at the substantive content of this inequality. That is, I examine the specific policies that account for the differential responsiveness across income groups in order to understand which policies contribute to the observed inequality and how national policy would differ if responsiveness were more egalitarian. Dividing my dataset of policy questions into foreign policy/national security, social welfare, economic policy, and issues with strong moral or religious components shows that the representational inequality documented in chapter 3 is replicated in varying degrees across these diverse issue domains. Policy responsiveness is always strongest for Americans with the highest incomes, but differences across domains do emerge both in the extent to which government policy reflects the public's preferences in general, and in the degree to which affluent Americans are advantaged. In particular, moral/religious issues show the strongest level of responsiveness to public preferences overall, while representational inequality is lowest for social welfare policies. Toward the end of this chapter, I explore the relatively equal responsiveness in the social welfare domain and begin to examine the role of organized interest groups in shaping policy responsiveness—a topic I then take up in more detail in chapter 5.

The 1,779 policy questions analyzed in chapter 3 contain proposals for changes in dozens of different policy areas, from taxes, to gun control, to abortion policy, to foreign military engagements. Three-quarters of these questions fall into the four major domains of foreign policy/national security, social welfare, economic policy, and issues with strong moral or religious components. Taking each of these domains in turn, I start by applying the same logistic model of policy outcomes used in the previous chapter. Table 4.1 shows the raw logistic regression results as well as the predicted probabilities of a policy being adopted if favored by 20 percent or 80 percent of respondents and the relative differences in predicted probabilities of adoption for popular versus unpopular policies.

The regression coefficients in the top row of the table show roughly similar levels of responsiveness in the domains of foreign policy, social welfare, and economic policy, but greater responsiveness to public preferences

Table 4.1 Policy Responsiveness by Policy Domain

	Foreign Policy/ National Security	Social Welfare	Economic Policy	Religious Issues
Logit coefficient	.59	.51	.66	.93
(Standard error)	(.12)	(.12)	(.13)	(.26)
Intercept	.12	−1.50	−.84	−1.61
Predicted probability if 20% favor	.33	.10	.15	.05
Predicted probability if 80% favor	.72	.31	.52	.42
Relative difference in predicted probability (row 5/row 4)	2.2	3.1	3.5	8.1
N	428	399	389	161
Log likelihood	562	403	482	161
Likelihood ratio	$\chi^2(1) = 28$	$\chi^2(1) = 20$	$\chi^2(1) = 27$	$\chi^2(1) = 15$
χ^2	$p = <.001$	$p < .001$	$p < .001$	$p < .001$

Cases consist of survey questions about proposed policy changes asked between 1981 and 2002. Dependent variable is policy outcome coded 1 if the proposed policy change took place within four years of the survey date and 0 if it did not. Predictors are the logits of the percentage of respondents favoring the proposed policy change.

on moral or religious issues (a similar pattern is reflected in the sixth row, which reports the relative difference in predicted probabilities). A more nuanced picture of policy responsiveness in these four domains can be seen in the fourth and fifth rows, which report the predicted probabilities of adoption when policies are either opposed or supported by 80 percent of Americans. The fourth row shows that both popular and unpopular policies are much more likely to be adopted in the foreign policy/national security domain than in the other three issue domains. The weaker status quo bias on foreign policy issues reflects the ability of the president to act independently of Congress and avoid the multiple veto points that allow minority factions to thwart policy changes they oppose.

Table 4.2   Characteristics of Proposed Policy Changes by Policy Domain

	N	Percent Favored	Percent Adopted	Percent Lopsided	Percent High Salience	Respon-siveness	Percent Divergent
Foreign policy/ national security	428	0.52	0.54	0.33	0.49	.59	.40
Social welfare	399	0.57	0.22	0.37	0.65	.51	.44
Economic policy	389	0.57	0.36	0.35	0.59	.66	.45
Religious issues	161	0.57	0.24	0.30	0.66	.93	.44

The four major policy domains contain 75 percent of all policy questions in the 1981–2002 dataset. Percent lopsided shows the percentage of questions in each policy domain for which at least two-thirds of the respondents either favor or oppose the proposed change; percent high salience shows the percentage of questions in each policy domain with less than 5 percent "Don't know" responses; responsiveness shows the logistic coefficient for policy outcomes regressed on policy preferences from table 4.1; percent divergent shows the percentage of questions for which preferences of the 10th and 90th income percentiles diverge by more than 10 percentage points.

In contrast to the foreign policy domain, the status quo bias is strongest for social welfare issues. As the fifth row of table 4.1 shows, fewer than one-third of proposed social welfare policy changes that garnered 80 percent support from the public were adopted. Many of these popular but not adopted policies concern proposed expansions of programs or increases in regulation (e.g., increasing government support for preschool or college education or mandating various aspects of health insurance), but some involve cutting back on existing programs or benefits (e.g., imposing work requirements on welfare recipients). In the pages below I examine each of these four issue domains in turn, identifying the specific policies that give rise to the patterns of responsiveness shown in table 4.1.

Policy issues vary across numerous dimensions, such as their popularity, the extremity of the preferences citizens hold, or the extent to which preferences differ by income. Because these sorts of characteristics might contribute to the patterns of representational inequality I describe below, I begin by examining some of the key characteristics of the issues in each of the four policy domains. Table 4.2 shows that, in most respects, the issues within the different domains are quite similar. For example, the proposed policy changes were, on average, about equally popular across the four domains, with 52 percent of respondents favoring the proposed changes in foreign policy and 57 percent favoring the proposed changes in each of the other three domains. The percentage of proposed changes with large preference gaps across income groups was also similar in the four domains: the proportion of policy changes generating preference gaps of more than 10 points between the 10th and 90th income percentiles ranged from 40 percent (for foreign policy) to 45 percent for economic policy issues. Finally, the proportion of proposed changes that generated lopsided preferences for the public as a whole varied only modestly across policy domains, ranging from 39 to 51 percent. (Lopsided issues are those for which at least two-thirds of the respondents who expressed a preference were on one side of the issue or the other.)

In contrast to these characteristics, proposed policy changes in these four domains did differ in terms of their salience to respondents and the likelihood that they would be adopted. As indicated by the percentage of respondents saying "Don't know," proposed changes in the foreign policy/ national security domain were the least salient, with economic issues, social welfare, and religious issues somewhat more salient to respondents. The politics of policy making in the foreign policy domain are somewhat distinct in that the president not only has more power to act unilaterally but (partly for that reason) is more frequently able to set the foreign policy agenda as well.[1] This independence may account, at least in part, for the higher proportion of proposed policy changes that are adopted in the foreign policy domain. If the president is more likely to set the agenda in foreign policy and less constrained by Congress in foreign policy decision making, policies that the administration opposes are less likely to make it onto the national agenda, and those that do make it onto the agenda are more likely to have the support of the political actors needed to implement the proposed changes.

In short, the characteristics of proposed policy changes do not differ substantially across the four issue domains in most respects. The modest differences evident in table 4.2 seem to correspond with expectations about the different policy domains. For example, foreign policy is the least salient domain and religious/moral issues the most contentions (with the lowest percentage of lopsided consensus issues on which the public falls predominantly on one side of the issue or the other). But these differences are modest and show no apparent relationship with differences in responsiveness. For example, the more salient social welfare and moral/ religious issue domains have both the lowest (social welfare) and highest (moral/religious) levels of overall responsiveness. The generally similar characteristics of proposed policy changes suggest that there may be more commonalities than differences in the dynamics of agenda formation and policy change across these four substantive domains.

Of central interest, of course, are variations in representational inequalities across these four domains. The strength of the preference/policy link for the 10th, 50th, and 90th income percentiles is shown in figure 4.1 (the

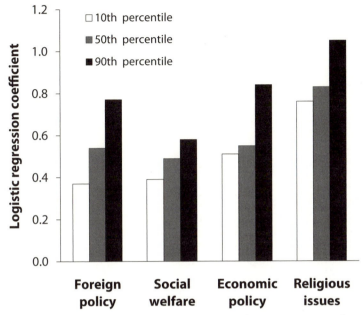

Figure 4.1. Policy Responsiveness by Policy Domain by Income Percentile. Figure shows coefficients from twelve logistic regressions. Dependent variable is policy outcome coded 1 if the proposed policy change took place within four years of the survey date and 0 if it did not. Independent variables are income groups' preferences as measured by the logits of the imputed percentage of respondents favoring the proposed policy change at each income level. Full results appear in table A4.1.

full logistic regression results are in table A4.1). In each policy domain, responsiveness is strongest for high-income Americans and weakest for the poor, but the inequality across income levels is highest for foreign policy and lowest for social welfare. The figure also shows that the starkest difference in responsiveness to the affluent and the middle class occurs on economic policy, a consequence of high-income Americans' stronger opposition to taxes and corporate regulation, as we'll see below.

Chapter 3 showed that patterns of differential responsiveness emerged more clearly once we distinguished between policies on which preferences diverged across income groups and those that did not. Since the number of policy questions in some of the domains is quite limited, I don't divide up the proposed policy changes into categories as in table 3.2. Instead I use the interaction between the preferences at a given income level and the size of the preference gap across income levels to assess how the strength of the preference/policy link varies depending on the size of the preference gap. Negative interactions in these models indicate that the associa-

Table 4.3   Decline in Policy Responsiveness as Preferences across Income
Groups Diverge

	N	Income Percentile		
		10th	50th	90th
Foreign policy/ national security	428	−.62** (.22)	−.42* (.22)	−.06 (.21)
Social welfare	399	−.26* (.14)	−.13 (.14)	−.03 (.16)
Economy and tax policy	389	−.43* (.24)	−.45* (.23)	−.16 (.24)
Religious issues	161	−.79* (.38)	−.46‡ (.33)	−.27 (.34)

Table shows logistic regression coefficients (with standard errors in parentheses)
indicating the interaction of policy preference at each income level, with preference
divergence across income levels. Policy preference measured by the log of the odds ratio
of the imputed percentage supporting the proposed policy change at each income level.
Divergence measured by the log of the mean absolute difference between the 10th and
50th and the 50th and 90th income percentiles. Full regression results in table A4.2.
‡$p < .10$; *$p < .05$; **$p < .01$ (one-tailed tests)

tion of preferences and policy outcomes for the particular income level
being examined declines as the magnitude of the preference gap across
income levels increases.

The interaction coefficients reflecting the change in responsiveness as
preferences across income levels diverge are shown in table 4.3 (with full
results in table A4.2). For those at the 10th income percentile, this decline
is significant for all four policy domains but smallest for social welfare
and largest for religious values issues. For median-income Americans, declines in policy responsiveness are quite small and nonsignificant for social welfare and about equal for the other three domains. For those at the
top of the income distribution, there are no statistically significant declines
in the association of preferences and outcomes as the preference gap
across income groups increases. The lack of significant interactions for
the 90th income percentile echoes the findings in chapter 3: the affluent
do not always get the policies they favor, but differences of opinion with
other income groups do not seem to blunt the influence they do exert.
Similarly echoing the findings in chapter 3, policy responsiveness for the
poor and the middle class declines as preference divergence across income levels grows (with the partial exception of social welfare issues).

The substantive significance of the interaction coefficients in table 4.3
can be gauged by calculating the impact of each income level's policy
preferences at a particular degree of preference divergence. Figure 4.2
repeats the estimates for the overall strength of policy responsiveness at

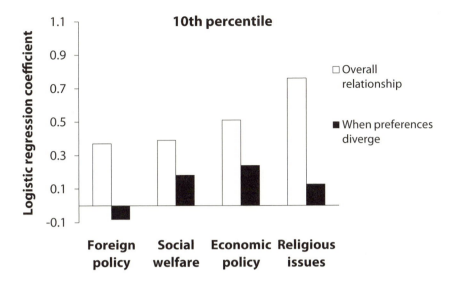

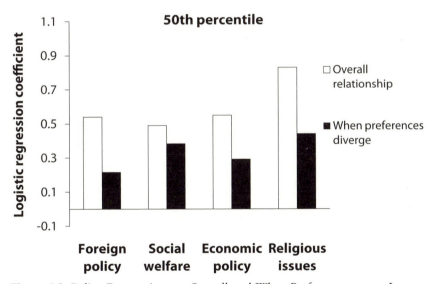

Figure 4.2. Policy Responsiveness Overall and When Preferences across Income Levels Diverge. Figure shows logistic regression coefficients from analyses in tables A4.1 ("overall") and A4.2 ("when preferences diverge") with the latter calculated for preference divergence of 10 percentage points across income levels. Policy preference measured by the log of the odds ratio of the imputed percentage supporting the proposed policy change at each income level. Divergence measured by the log of the mean absolute difference between the 10th and 50th and the 50th and 90th income percentiles. (*Continued on next page*)

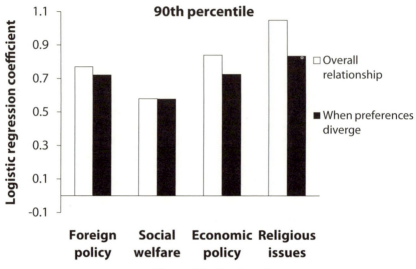

Figure 4.2. Continued

each income level from figure 4.1 and contrasts these estimates with the analogous measures when preferences across income groups diverge by 10 percentage points. The top panel of figure 4.2 shows the substantial weakening of the preference/policy link for the 10th income percentile when preferences across income groups diverge. (All the overall associations of preferences and policy outcomes for the 10th percentile shown in the white columns in figure 4.2 are statistically significant at $p < 0.001$, but none of the conditional associations for the 10th percentile shown in the black columns is statistically significant.) For the 50th income percentile, the decline in responsiveness is also substantial for all domains expect social welfare (of the four conditional associations shown for the 50th percentile in the figure, only the estimate for social welfare is statistically significant). Finally, the last panel shows only modest declines in responsiveness for the 90th income percentile (and all four of the conditional associations for this income level are statistically significant at $p < 0.05$ or lower).

In the following pages I examine the specific policies within each domain that contribute to the broad patterns documented above. This more fine-grained exploration will not only reveal the substantive content of representational inequality but suggest some of the factors that contribute to these unequal outcomes as well as the infrequent but important exceptions in which government policy reflects the preferences of poor and middle-class Americans more than those of the affluent.

FOREIGN POLICY, DEFENSE, AND TERRORISM

In the domain of foreign policy and national security, responsiveness to low- and middle-income Americans declines sharply as their preferences across income levels diverge (table 4.3 and figure 4.2). To better understand the substantive policy issues that underlie these patterns, table 4.4 shows the policy preferences for the 10th, 50th, and 90th income percentiles for those proposed changes that attracted the greatest attention from polling organizations or that resulted in the largest preference divergence across income levels. To make the data in this table and subsequent tables for the other policy domains easier to absorb, I rescored preferences from percentages to a 11-point scale in which –5 represents strong opposition, +5 strong support, and 0 an approximately equal division of support and opposition (the top left cell of these tables contains the legend, which shows the relationship between percentage favorable and the 11-point scale).

The first section of table 4.4 shows support for U.S. involvement in foreign military engagements, including Latin America in the 1980s, the former Yugoslavia in the 1990s, and Afghanistan and Iraq starting in 2001 and 2003. Public support for these foreign interventions varied considerably, with the invasion of Afghanistan in the aftermath of the 9/11 terrorist attacks receiving the strongest support and aid to anticommunist forces in Latin America during the 1980s the strongest opposition. With the exceptions of Afghanistan and (to a lesser degree) Iraq, the public has been ambivalent toward or opposed to the various proposed military interventions that survey organizations have asked about. When queried in advance, majorities expressed opposition to most of the direct foreign military operations the United States did engage in (including Panama in 1989, Haiti in the early 1990s, and the former Yugoslavia in the mid-1990s), as well as possible operations the United States did not engage in (taking military action against Iran, invading Libya, invading Nicaragua).

Consistent with previous research, public support was strongest when risks to American lives appeared small, when the prospects of being drawn into an extended imbroglio were low, when the United States acted as part of an international force rather than unilaterally, and in response to an attack on Americans.[2] In sum, U.S. military policy was sometimes consistent with public preferences (invading Iraq and Afghanistan but not Iran, Libya, or Nicaragua) and sometimes not (invading Panama, sending troops to Haiti and Bosnia, supporting anticommunist forces in Central America). As the last column in table 4.4 shows, preferences on issues of military engagement tended to be quite similar across income groups.

The preferences of high- and low-income Americans also coincided on most aspects of nuclear weapons policy. In the mid-1980s, for example,

Table 4.4 Foreign Policy and National Security Preferences

Between 45% and 55%	0
Over 55% or under 45%	+/–1
Over 60% or under 40%	+/–2
Over 65% or under 35%	+/–3
Over 75% or under 25%	+/–4
Over 85% or under 15%	+/–5

	Income Percentile			Difference
	10th	50th	90th	(90th – 10th)
Foreign military engagements				
Invade Afghanistan	+4	+4	+5	+1
Invade Iraq	+2	+2	+1	–1
Use air power against Serbia	0	0	0	0
Send U.S. ground troops to Serbia	–3	–2	–2	+1
U.S. troops in international peace-keeping force in Bosnia	–1	0	0	+1
Send U.S. troops to Haiti	–1	–2	–2	–1
Give military aid to El Salvador or Sandinistas	–3	–2	–2	+1
Nuclear weapons				
Negotiate a nuclear freeze with Soviet Union	+4	+4	+4	0
Build the MX missile	–3	–1	+1	+4
Build a missile defense system	+3	+4	+4	+1
War on terrorism				
Restrict Americans' freedom of speech	–1	–2	–4	–3
Relax legal protections (e.g., habeas corpus)	+3	+4	+5	+2
Monitor Americans' phone calls, etc.	+1	0	0	–1
Torture known terrorists	0	0	–1	–1
Attack nations that harbor terrorists	+3	+4	+5	+2
Foreign economic policy				
Development aid generally	0	+1	+2	+2
Development aid to former Soviet Union	–2	0	+2	+4
GATT, NAFTA, free trade	–1	0	+1	+2
Mexico loan guarantees	–4	–4	–3	+1

support was strong across the board for a nuclear freeze agreement be-tween the United States and the Soviet Union. Despite the popularity of the nuclear freeze among the public, the policy ran strongly counter to the hard line the Reagan administration adopted against the Soviet Union.[3]

Americans at all income levels also expressed strong support for anti-missile defense. Reagan's 1983 Strategic Defense Initiative vastly increased the resources devoted to developing a defense against nuclear attack. Despite continued doubts about the technical feasibility of such a system, funding remained relatively steady throughout the 1980s and 1990s and increased dramatically under George W. Bush.[4]

Preferences of high- and low-income Americans did diverge on one aspect of nuclear weapons policy. The development of the MX missile in the 1980s was strongly opposed by those with low incomes but weakly favored by the affluent. Intended to enhance the ability of the U.S. nu-clear arsenal to survive a Soviet attack, the MX became mired in contro-versy over its feasibility, its potential impact on the nuclear arms race, and how it was to be based. While alternative basing strategies were pro-posed and rejected, development of the missile itself proceeded. The drawn-out compromise over the MX missile and the funding it received over the years despite the brouhaha about its basing were more consis-tent with the mild support of the well-off than with the strong opposition of poor Americans.

Larger differences of opinion across income groups sometimes emerged concerning the war on terrorism, although it would be hard to character-ize either the poor or the affluent as consistently more hard-line in the policies they supported. For example, well-off respondents were more likely to oppose restrictions on Americans' freedom of speech but more supportive of proposals to relax legal protections such as habeas corpus and more willing to attack nations that harbor terrorists. For most as-pects of antiterrorism policy, however, differences in preferences across income groups were minor.

In general, policies on terrorism have been fairly consistent with public preferences. Policies with strong public support have been adopted (e.g., attacking nations that harbor terrorists, relaxing detainees' legal protec-tions, assassinating terrorists in foreign countries) and policies with strong opposition have not (e.g., restricting speech that might incite terrorism).

The most consistent divergence in preferences across income groups in the realm of foreign policy and national security concerns trade policy and foreign aid. Affluent Americans tend to be at least somewhat supportive of free-trade policies such as NAFTA and the General Agreement on Tariffs and Trade (GATT), and somewhat supportive of nonmilitary aid to developing countries including the former Soviet Union. Low-income Americans tend to be somewhat opposed to all these aspects of foreign policy. U.S. policy on tariffs and trade during the past few decades has clearly been more consistent with the preferences of the affluent and has become more so over time as trade barriers have fallen and bipartisan support for an open trade regime has strengthened.[5] On the other hand, U.S. foreign aid in general and development aid in particular declined somewhat during the 1980s and 1990s (a trend more congenial to lower-income than to higher-income Americans) before increasing sharply beginning in 2002.[6]

In sum, policy making in the foreign affairs and national security domain reflects a mix of popular and unpopular decisions on military engagement and weapons policy over the decades examined, and the generally popular antiterror policies in the wake of the September 11 attacks. In contrast, the drop-off in responsiveness to middle- and low-income Americans as their preferences diverge from the affluent is accounted for largely by trade and foreign aid policies and second by divergent views of the war on terror. Affluent Americans' greater support for free trade, for development aid in general, and for aid to the states of the former Soviet Union in particular, along with their stronger support for curtailing the legal rights of suspects but greater opposition to restricting freedom of speech to combat terrorism, all contributed to inequality across economic groups in responsiveness to preferences in this domain.

Previous research has documented large gaps between the general public's preferences in foreign policy and the preferences of business and government elites.[7] The findings presented above show that preference gaps also exist between less- and more-affluent Americans. If foreign policy had more equally reflected the preferences of all Americans over the past decades, we would have seen a more protectionist trade policy and even lower levels of foreign aid than we did.

RELIGIOUS VALUES ISSUES

A wide range of policy issues—from taxes to health care to terrorism—may involve moral or religiously based considerations, but such considerations typically play a more direct or more dominant role in most people's preferences on issues like abortion, school prayer, and gay rights. As table 4.1 and figure 4.2 show, policy responsiveness for religious values issues is strong in general but falls significantly for the middle-class and even more dramatically for the poor when preferences across income groups diverge. In contrast, responsiveness to high-income Americans in this domain is only modestly lower on issues with divergent preferences, reflecting the weak and nonsignificant interaction for the 90th income percentile in table 4.3.

When preferences across income levels diverge, affluent Americans consistently express more liberal views on these moral/religious issues than those with low or middle incomes. Table 4.5 shows that affluent Americans were significantly more liberal on abortion policy, school prayer, stem cell research, and mandatory AIDS testing (a highly moralized policy debate when these questions about AIDS were asked in the mid-1980s). The affluent were also slightly more liberal on gay rights than were low- and middle-income Americans, though on this set of issues the differences across income groups tended to be smaller.[8]

On other religious values issues, preferences were shared across income groups. Majorities at all income levels opposed gay marriage, supported G. W. Bush's faith-based social services initiative, favored strengthening laws restricting sex and violence on television, and favored intensifying the fight against illegal drug use and teenage smoking. On most of these issues, federal policy was consistent with majority opinion. George W. Bush established his faith-based initiative by executive order shortly after coming into office in January 2001 and expanded its scope in subsequent years.[9] Also consistent with public preferences, federal policy throughout the 1980s and 1990s moved in a direction of greater regulation of sex and violence on television. The Supreme Court struck down the restrictions on TV content that had been adopted into law, but Congress did succeed in mandating a new rating system for television content, requiring TV manufacturers to install V-chips in new televisions enabling parents to block objectionable shows, and increasing fines for broadcasting indecent material.[10]

Americans at all income levels expressed similar, and typically strong, opinions on federal policy toward recreational drugs. The poor and the well-off alike strongly favored both strengthening the fight against drugs and teenage smoking and encouraging mandatory drug testing in the workplace. Similarly strong majorities opposed legalizing marijuana for personal use, but perhaps surprisingly, strong majorities at all income levels favored allowing use of marijuana for medical reasons with a doctor's prescription.

Federal policy during these decades reflected public support for fighting recreational drug use, with spending on antidrug efforts increasing sixfold (in inflation-adjusted dollars) between 1981 and 2004.[11] In addition, workplace drug testing expanded greatly between the mid-1980s and the early 1990s.[12] The clearest exception to the consistency of federal policy and majority preferences on religious values issues concerns medical marijuana. Federal policy never reflected the strong public support for legalizing medical marijuana; to the contrary, both the Clinton and G. W. Bush administrations tried to shut down growers and distributors of medical marijuana in states that had legalized marijuana for medical use.[13]

Table 4.5 Religious/Moral Values Issue Preferences

Between 45% and 55%	0
Over 55% or under 45%	+/–1
Over 60% or under 40%	+/–2
Over 65% or under 35%	+/–3
Over 75% or under 25%	+/–4
Over 85% or under 15%	+/–5

	Income Percentile			Difference
	10th	50th	90th	(90th – 10th)
Abortion and birth control				
Approve RU-486	–1	0	+2	+3
Constitutional ban on abortion	–2	–3	–4	–2
Federal funding for abortions (e.g., for low-income women)	–2	–2	0	+2
Ban "partial-birth abortion" procedure	+2	+2	+1	–1
Require biological father's consent or notification for abortion	+3	+3	0	–3
Require parental consent for birth control assistance for teens	0	0	–2	–2
Gay rights				
Extend legal protection to gay people	+1	+3	+3	+2
Gay marriage	–2	–2	–1	+1
Gay civil unions	–1	0	0	+1
Gays in the military	0	0	+1	+1
Recreational drugs and teen smoking				
Strengthen fight against drugs and teenage smoking	+4	+4	+4	0
Legalize marijuana for medical use with doctor's prescription	+4	+4	+4	0
Legalize marijuana for personal use	–3	–3	–3	0
Encourage mandatory drug testing in workplace	+4	+3	+3	–1
Miscellaneous moral/religious issues				
Constitutional amendment to permit school prayer	+4	+3	+1	–3
Stem cell research:				
Source unspecified	+1	+1	+3	+2
From discarded embryos	0	+1	+3	+3
From newly created embryos	–2	–1	+1	+3
Mandatory AIDS testing of all citizens (mid-1980s)	+3	+2	0	–3
G. W. Bush's faith-based initiative	+3	+3	+2	–1
Strengthen TV rating system or time restrictions; require V-chip	+4	+5	+4	0

While federal policy on consensual issues in the religious values domain generally reflected public preferences, policy on nonconsensual issues fell largely in line with the preferences of the affluent. The issue in this area that received the greatest attention from survey organizations (and the media) in the decades under study was reproductive policy. For example, high-income Americans opposed laws that would have required parental consent for teenagers to receive birth control assistance from federally financed clinics (low-income Americans were split on this). Despite repeated efforts by Republican legislators to require parental notification for federally funded contraception services to minors, federal law continues to guarantee the confidentiality of such services, regardless of age.[14]

Opinions also differed on approving the abortion pill RU-486, which the affluent supported and the poor opposed. President George H. W. Bush delayed FDA approval of RU-486 for a few years, but the Clinton administration eventually approved the drug.[15] Since few survey questions concerning RU-486 were asked until the late 1990s, coded outcomes (reflecting final approval of RU-486 in 2000) were consistent with the more liberal preferences of the well-off on this issue for most of the questions in my dataset.

One aspect of abortion law that has clearly favored the stronger antiabortion sentiments of low-income Americans is—perhaps ironically—the prohibition on federal funding of abortion services for low-income Americans. Although the specific exceptions (e.g., in cases of rape or danger to the life of the woman) have changed over the years, the exclusion of abortion services from Medicaid and other federal government health programs has been in effect continuously since 1976.[16]

The highly moralized debate about AIDS in the mid-1980s also reflected very different attitudes among less- and more-affluent Americans. During the early stages of the AIDS epidemic, some called for compulsory universal AIDS testing of all American citizens.[17] Affluent Americans were split on this policy, but it was strongly favored by the poor and somewhat less strongly favored by the middle class. Public health officials unanimously rejected such large-scale compulsory testing and the policy was never adopted.[18]

Federal policy in the religious values domain did not always reflect the preferences of the affluent. High-income Americans strongly supported efforts during the Clinton years to expand the scope of civil rights laws to include sexual orientation while low-income Americans were only mildly supportive. Despite this favorable public opinion, no new federal legislation of this kind was adopted.

Finally, federal funding for stem cell research was arguably more consistent with the preferences of lower- and middle-income Americans, although the degree of support among all groups varied depending on the source of the stem cells in question. During the 1990s federal funding of stem cell research was limited. Under G. W. Bush funding became available for work with cells that came from embryos that had already been destroyed, but not for cells extracted from additional embryos. On the whole the strict conditions on federal funding for stem cell research were more consistent with the split opinions of low-income Americans than with the generally strong support of the well-off.[19]

Of the four major policy domains examined, moral and religious values policies stand out as being the least affected by logistical or economic factors and the least influenced by the economic interests of organized groups or identifiable classes of citizens. In addition the moral and religious values policies in table 4.5 do not impose significant economic costs on government. Extending legal protections, restricting abortion procedures, or permitting federal research dollars to be used on one or another source of stem cells does not require significant government expenditures the way many social and economic policies do. Consequently politicians are freer to follow the public's preferences in this domain, a pattern reflected in the stronger responsiveness of policy to preferences shown in figure 4.2.

Despite the lack of government costs and constraints for most moral/religious policies, some consensually popular policies in this domain were not adopted during the decades under study. In particular over 80 percent of Americans at all income levels supported a twenty-four-hour waiting period before a woman could have an abortion, and over 90 percent supported a government requirement that doctors inform patients about alternatives to abortions. The inconsistency between federal policy and public preferences on these aspects of abortion law is explained by the polarized nature of abortion politics, especially at the federal level, and the shift in focus of abortion opponents to state reproductive laws.[20] Surveys show that most Americans hold moderate positions on abortion law, supporting some restrictions on the availability of abortion but not strict bans.[21] But the groups that have been most central in shaping abortion politics have typically adopted extreme positions favoring either universal (or near universal) bans on abortion or the complete elimination of any legal restrictions. Thus even restrictions popular with large majorities of the public have been strenuously resisted by abortion rights advocates, who tend to view such restrictions as the thin end of the wedge that will inevitably lead to greater restrictions.

By refocusing their efforts on state abortion laws, antiabortion groups have been able to achieve policy goals that could not be won at the national level. While federal law does not require a waiting period before a woman can obtain an abortion, twenty-four states do have laws requiring a waiting period. The even more popular requirement that doctors inform patients of alternatives to abortions is absent from federal law but has been adopted by thirty-three states, with varying stipulations of the information that must be provided.[22]

In a more equally responsive political system, moral/religious policies at the national level would be more conservative than they currently are. In particular we might expect to find greater restrictions on abortion, such as requirements for the notification or agreement of the biological father and a ban or limitation on the availability of RU-486. Also likely would be a requirement of parental consent for minors to receive birth control, at least when funded through federal government programs. Although abortion rights supporters often view federal lawmaking over the past few decades as gradually eroding abortion rights, federal abortion policy remains in many respects more liberal than the preferences expressed by the American public as a whole.[23]

ECONOMIC POLICY

Unlike foreign policy or religious values issues, economic policies tend to have clear and distinct consequences for Americans at different income levels. Yet as reported above, preferences across income groups do not differ more in the domain of economic policy than they do on religious values issues (table 4.2). This attests both to the important role of non-interest-based considerations in shaping Americans' policy views and to the substantial number of economic issues on which low- and high-income Americans agree.[24] As table 4.6 shows, for example, Americans of all incomes opposed proposals for a federal sales tax, opposed across-the-board increases in income tax, favored across-the-board income tax cuts, and favored unpaid family leave laws. Americans at all income levels also strongly supported corporate accounting reform in the wake of the Enron scandal and differed only modestly on cutting taxes for low- and middle-income taxpayers and increasing taxes on extremely high earners.[25]

Federal government policy on many of these consensual economic issues did reflect the predominant preferences of the public. Lawmakers have never seriously considered a federal sales (or "consumption" or "value-added") tax, and the marginal income tax rate for the average taxpayer fell from about 31 percent in 1981 to about 24 percent in 2002.[26] Also consistent with public preferences, a national family and medical leave law was adopted in 1993, requiring employers to grant up to twelve weeks of unpaid leave per year. The 2002 Sarbanes-Oxley Act strengthened corporate accounting rules in the wake of the Enron, Tyco, and other corporate scandals, again reflecting strong public support. In contrast, changes

Table 4.6   Economic Issue Preferences

Between 45% and 55%	0
Over 55% or under 45%	+/−1
Over 60% or under 40%	+/−2
Over 65% or under 35%	+/−3
Over 75% or under 25%	+/−4
Over 85% or under 15%	+/−5

	Income Percentile			Difference
	10th	50th	90th	(90th − 10th)
Income taxes				
Cut personal income tax (across the board)	+3	+3	+3	0
Cut income tax rates for low- or middle-income earners	+4	+4	+3	−1
Raise income tax rates to reduce the deficit (1980s)	−3	−3	−3	0
Raise taxes on very high income earners	+4	+4	+3	−1
Cut top marginal tax rate	0	+1	+2	+2
Flat tax	−1	0	+1	+2
Other taxes				
Support a federal sales or consumption tax	−2	−2	−2	0
Cut capital gains taxes	0	+1	+3	+3
Cut/eliminate inheritance tax	+1	+2	+3	+2
Raise gas/energy taxes	−2	−1	0	+2
Other economic issues				
Unpaid family leave law	+3	+3	+3	0
Reform corporate accounting rules (post-Enron)	+3	+3	+3	0
Raise minimum wage	+5	+4	+3	−2
Extend/increase unemployment benefits	+2	+1	−1	−3
Increase government regulation of oil/gas industry	+1	+1	−2	−3
Increase miscellaneous corporate regulation	+3	+2	+1	−2

in income tax rates for very high earners did not consistently reflect the consensus for increases expressed by Americans at the 10th through 90th income percentiles. Effective (average) income taxes on the top 1 percent of earners fell during the Reagan years but rose under Clinton, ending slightly higher in 2002 than they were in 1981.[27]

On many other economic policies, preferences across income groups did diverge, reflecting the differing interests at stake for lower- and higher-income Americans. In these cases there was little decline in policy responsiveness to affluent Americans, but substantial decline in responsiveness to both the middle class and the poor (table 4.3 and figure 4.2). Poor people were evenly split on cutting both the top income tax rate and the capital gains tax rate, for example, while the affluent strongly supported both ideas. During the period under study, the top tax rates for both capital gains and ordinary income fell during the Reagan administration and rose under Clinton, with the net effect being a decline from 24 percent to 15 percent in the top capital gains rate and from 70 percent to 35 percent in the top income tax rate.[28] These shifts in capital gains and top income tax rates clearly reflect the differing ideological orientations of the Democratic and Republican administrations, the changing revenue needs of the federal government, and a general trend toward lower and less progressive taxes consistent with the preferences of the well-off.

Cutting or eliminating the inheritance tax was also quite popular among the affluent, but even poor respondents were, on balance, in favor of this change. The "strange appeal of estate tax repeal" among middle- and lower-income Americans has received considerable attention.[29] Whether one attributes this support to public misperceptions or false consciousness, or to a belief that it is unjust to limit people's ability to pass on their fairly earned assets to their children, broad opposition to the estate tax appears to have characterized public attitudes since at least the 1930s.[30] (I revisit the issue of false consciousness in chapter 7 when I discuss the income and estate tax cuts under G. W. Bush.)

The federal estate tax underwent a number of changes in the decades under study, almost all of which reduced the taxes owed by inheritors. The Economic Recovery Act of 1981 tripled the exemption subject to taxes and reduced the top estate tax rate from 70 percent to 50 percent; the Taxpayer Protection Act of 1997 further increased the exemption level from $600,000 to $1,000,000 and created a new exclusion for family-owned businesses; and, most important, the Economic Growth and Tax Relief Reconciliation Act of 2001 phased out the federal estate tax entirely by 2009.[31] During this period there were also some minor changes that served to increase the estate tax (or, more accurately, to delay scheduled decreases in the top estate tax rate). On balance, however, the period since the early 1980s was marked by repeated weakening of the estate tax, consistent with the preferences of higher-income Americans.[32]

The only proposal to raise taxes that did not generate opposition across all income groups concerns federal gasoline or energy taxes. Although poor people, who are hit hardest by gas (and most other excise or consumption) taxes, were solidly opposed, the affluent were evenly split. During the years under study, federal gas tax increased substantially: from only four cents per gallon in 1981 to about eighteen cents beginning in 1993, although this is still very low by international standards.[33]

On most tax proposals that generated significant differences in preference across income groups, then, policy was more consistent with high-income preferences (cutting capital gains taxes, cutting the estate tax, cutting the top marginal income tax rate, and increasing gasoline taxes). The one exception to this rule is proposals for replacing the graduated income tax with a flat tax that would eliminate deductions and apply a single rate to all taxpayers.[34] Across the decades examined, modest majorities of well-off Americans favored the flat tax and modest majorities of the poor opposed it, with median income Americans evenly split. The failure of flat-tax proposals to gain traction in Washington is a consequence of ideological opposition among lawmakers (primarily Democrats) who favor progressive taxes on equity grounds and powerful interests that benefit from exemptions in the current tax system that would be lost under most such proposals (for example, home mortgage interest, which benefits the homebuilding and real estate industries; charitable donations, which benefit universities, hospitals, churches, and other nonprofit organizations; and payroll tax exemptions, which businesses of all kinds favor).

Nontax economic policies that generate preference gaps between low- and high-income Americans often reflect the greater attraction of the free market to the affluent (who, arguably, benefit most from the relative lack of government regulation in the United States). The well-off generally opposed proposals to increase government regulation of the oil and gas industry, opposed increases in unemployment benefits, and were only modestly supportive of efforts to increase corporate regulation outside of the post-Enron period. In contrast, poor and middle-income Americans were considerably more enthusiastic toward government regulation. In a 1985 survey three-quarters of poor and middle-income Americans supported a requirement that employers give a year's notice to employees before closing down the place where they work, while two-thirds thought the federal government should create a government-owned and operated oil corporation "to keep the private oil companies honest" (majorities of the affluent opposed both these ideas). Extending or expanding unemployment benefits was also popular among the poor and middle class but often opposed by the well-off. Americans at all income levels strongly favored raising the minimum wage, but, unlike the affluent, the poor were nearly unanimous on this question.

In considering the failure of widely (if not equally) supported economic policies like tightening corporate regulation or raising the minimum wage, it is important to remember that the preferences of Americans at the 90th income percentile may differ from those of the truly rich. I cannot reliably estimate the preferences of the tiny sliver of the public at the very top of the income distribution, but it seems plausible that this small but influential group holds distinctive positions on some economic policies such as business regulation and tax policy. In my concluding chapter I revisit this distinction between the merely affluent and the truly rich.

In sum, we would expect greater representational equality in the economic sphere to result in a higher minimum wage, more generous unemployment benefits, stricter corporate regulation (including the oil and gas industries in particular), and a more progressive personal tax regime in general. Some of these policies are favored by a majority of Americans at the 90th income percentile as well, but not with sufficient enthusiasm to overcome opposition from business and other interests.

SOCIAL WELFARE

Patterns of responsiveness in the social welfare domain are somewhat distinct from the other three policy domains examined, especially for middle- and low-income Americans. As table 4.3 shows, social welfare is the only policy area in which the decline in responsiveness to middle-income Americans (as their preferences diverge from those of the affluent) is negligible. The interaction of policy preference and preference divergence for the 50th income percentile ranges from –0.42 to –0.46 for the other three domains but is only –0.13 (and not significantly different from zero) for social welfare policies. A similar pattern is evident for the 10th income percentile, where the decline in responsiveness as preferences across income groups diverge is also far weaker than in the other three policy domains.

Social welfare policy during the decades under study was most consistent with public preferences on Medicare and Social Security (which were enhanced or sustained despite budgetary pressures) and the Clinton administration's welfare reforms. In contrast, government policy did not reflect the substantial public support for health care reform. Perhaps surprisingly, preferences across income groups differed more on modifying the universal policies of Medicare and Social Security (as well as health care) than on means-tested welfare per se (i.e., cash assistance programs like Temporary Assistance for Needy Families, or TANF, and its predecessor, Aid for Families with Dependent Children), programs strongly tied to income.

The top panel of table 4.7 shows that most policy preferences on welfare reform do not in fact differ much across income groups. Americans of all income levels strongly support work requirements for welfare re-

Table 4.7 Social Welfare Issue Preferences

Between 45% and 55%	0
Over 55% or under 45%	+/–1
Over 60% or under 40%	+/–2
Over 65% or under 35%	+/–3
Over 75% or under 25%	+/–4
Over 85% or under 15%	+/–5

	Income Percentile			Difference
	10th	50th	90th	(90th – 10th)
Welfare reform				
Work requirements	+4	+4	+3	–1
Job training for welfare recipients	+5	+5	+5	0
Child care for welfare recipients who work	+5	+5	+5	0
Time limits	+1	+3	+3	+2
No extra money for extra kids	0	0	+1	+1
Cut total spending on welfare	+1	+3	+4	+3
Health care				
Tax-funded national health care	+3	+3	+1	–2
Employer mandates	+4	+3	+2	–2
Clinton plan	+3	+2	+1	–2
Medical savings accounts	–3	–2	0	+3
Social Security reform				
Government investment of Soc. Sec. money in stocks	–3	–2	0	+3
Individuals control own stock accounts	0	+2	+3	+3
Change Soc. Sec. rules to discourage early retirement	–2	0	+1	+3
Medicare reform				
Encourage recipients to move to HMOs	–1	+1	+1	+2
Raise premiums/deductibles for Medicare beneficiaries	–3	–1	0	+3
Cut overall Medicare spending	–4	–3	–2	+2
Add a prescription drug benefit to Medicare	+5	+5	+4	–1
Education				
Federal grants and loans to college students	+4	+4	+4	0
School vouchers	–1	0	+1	+2
Other social welfare issues				
Federal unpaid family leave law	+3	+3	+3	0
Cut public works spending	–2	0	+1	+3

cipients and favor increasing job-training opportunities and child care resources for people on welfare. Americans across the income spectrum shared similar (split) opinions on the question of ending additional payments to women who have additional children while on welfare. Middle- and upper-income respondents did express more support for time limits on welfare receipt and were more inclined to want overall welfare spending cut than were low-income respondents. In sum, preferences on welfare reform display a surprising degree of consensus across income groups, a consensus that has characterized public attitudes toward welfare for many decades.[35]

In contrast to the clearly redistributive means-tested welfare programs referenced in the top panel of table 4.7, preferences on universal programs like national health insurance, Social Security, and Medicare show larger preference gaps across income levels. As the second panel shows, the poor are strongly supportive of federal government involvement in health care, whether it is in the form of a tax-funded national health plan, employer mandates, or the Clinton health reform proposal, while the affluent express weak support for each of these policies.[36] Despite the strong support from low- and middle-income Americans and the strenuous efforts of the Clinton administration in 1993 and 1994, these sorts of broad expansions of the federal government's role in health care were not adopted during the decades under study. Studies have pointed to numerous obstacles to health care reform in the United States, including doctors and hospitals, insurance companies, unions, employers, and political gridlock.[37] To this list we can add the lack of enthusiasm among affluent Americans.

Social Security and Medicare are the two most expensive social programs in the United States, accounting for over half of all federal social spending.[38] As table 4.7 shows, affluent Americans are more supportive of market-oriented reforms to both Social Security and Medicare, such as shifting Social Security toward individual stock accounts and encouraging Medicare beneficiaries to join health maintenance organizations (HMOs). The affluent are also more willing to consider changes in these programs that would reduce the benefits they provide (like raising the age at which full Social Security benefits are available or raising premiums and deductibles for Medicare recipients).

Despite the growing costs of Social Security and Medicare, changes to both programs since the early 1980s have been fairly modest. The Social Security reform bill of 1983 increased the retirement age for full benefits from 65 to 67 (to be phased in over the first two decades of the twenty-first century) and made a portion of Social Security benefits subject to income tax for higher-income beneficiaries (about 10 percent of all beneficiaries at the time).[39] Cost savings in Medicare have come primarily at the expense of health care providers (although these savings may translate into poorer service for Medicare beneficiaries), with the most substantial cuts occurring in the early 1980s and late 1990s.[40]

In economic terms the most significant change to the Medicare program over the past few decades was not a cutback but rather the addition of a prescription drug benefit (Medicare Part D) in 2003. Although many people criticized the legislation as a "giveaway" to pharmaceutical companies and a bad deal for American taxpayers, the principle of government-provided prescription drug coverage for Medicare recipients was quite popular across all income levels (although slightly less so for the most affluent Americans).

In sum, the lack of significant change in the core middle-class social welfare programs—Social Security and Medicare—is consistent with the strong support for these highly salient programs among low- and middle-income Americans. Small changes to the Social Security retirement age and efforts to encourage Medicare beneficiaries to join HMOs were more consistent with the preferences of the well-off. But the failure of Social Security privatization, the increase in overall Medicare spending, the addition of drug benefits for Medicare recipients, and the lack of change in the portion of Medicare costs paid by government are all consistent with the preferences of low- and middle-income Americans.[41] This pattern of policy responsiveness on Medicare and Social Security, along with other policy issues discussed below, contributes to the distinctive nature of the social welfare domain revealed in table 4.3 and figure 4.2.

The majority of questions on education policy in my dataset concern either school vouchers for K–12 education or federal financial assistance to college students.[42] College assistance was uniformly popular across income levels while school vouchers, which would help parents pay for private-school education, were opposed by the poor and favored by the affluent. Although it is hard to identify the exact mix of considerations that accounts for the greater support for school vouchers among the well-off, this preference is consistent with the stronger appeal to high-income Americans of market solutions across a range of policies. School vouchers, like many market-oriented social policies, are likely to be most beneficial to those with the financial and informational resources to take advantage of them. Similarly, poor Americans may be more likely to oppose vouchers because they are most concerned about the negative impact such programs might have on existing public schools. Despite numerous proposals over the years (and support from affluent Americans), the only federal voucher program ever passed by Congress is an extremely limited experiment available to under two thousand students in Washington, DC.

Finally, government spending on public works like bridges, roads, water, and sewage is more popular among lower- than higher-income Americans.

After a brief drop between 1981 and 1983, federal spending for such projects rose about 40 percent in constant (inflation-adjusted) dollars over the next two decades.[43]

Social Welfare Policy and Representational Inequality

The social welfare domain is the only policy domain examined in which the divergence of preferences across income groups does not lead to a substantial decline in responsiveness to the preferences of less-well-off Americans (table 4.3 and figure 4.2). The account of social welfare policy above identified four well-represented sets of policy questions on which lower-income Americans' preferences were most likely to prevail: Social Security, Medicare, school vouchers, and public works spending. More specifically, compared with the affluent, lower-income Americans are stronger opponents of Social Security and Medicare benefit cuts, tax increases, and privatization proposals; stronger supporters of prescription drug benefits for Medicare recipients; stronger opponents of school vouchers (especially vouchers that could be used to help pay for private schooling); and stronger supporters of public spending for highways, sewer systems, and so on.

For a number of these policies, less-well-off Americans were more supportive of the status quo and the affluent more favorable toward change (in particular, proposals for various market-oriented reforms of Social Security and Medicare and the adoption of school vouchers). In these cases the strong status quo bias documented above benefits the less advantaged.[44] But in other cases the apparent responsiveness to less-well-off Americans reflects the adoption of favored policy changes, not the maintenance of the status quo. The addition of a drug benefit to the Medicare program and the expansion of spending on Medicare, Social Security, and public works all constitute outcomes more consistent with the preferences of lower- than higher-income Americans.

What unites these different policies (and sets them apart from most policies on which lower- and higher-income preferences diverge) is that poor and middle-income Americans have powerful allies that tend to share their preferences on these issues. The AARP, widely viewed as one of the most powerful lobbies in Washington, has been a strong supporter of Social Security and Medicare.[45] In addition to support from the AARP, the Medicare prescription drug benefit that President Bush signed into law in 2003 also had the backing of the pharmaceutical companies and their well-funded lobbyists.[46] The public education lobby, led by the American Federation of Teachers and the National Education Association, is allied with lower-income Americans in opposing school vouchers.

Finally, developers and the construction industry back government spending on public works like bridges and roads, which is more popular among lower- than among higher-income Americans. Just as important, public works can provide a highly visible form of pork-barrel benefits for individual states or districts, and in their reelection campaigns members of Congress frequently tout their ability to secure such funding.[47]

Powerful interest groups happen to share the preferences of less-well-off Americans on these prominent social welfare issues. But the less well-off lack allies on other issues within this domain. For example, lower-income Americans are more supportive of both taxpayer-funded national health care and mandates requiring employers to provide health insurance for their employees. Lower-income Americans also express more support for proposals to expand unemployment benefits (for example, to cover part-time workers) and to increase federal support for public schools in poor neighborhoods.

Of the 399 policy questions in the social welfare domain, about half concern the four issues on which the preferences of the less well-off are more aligned with powerful interest groups than are those of the affluent: Social Security, Medicare, school vouchers, and public works spending. For these issues there is no evidence that the middle class or the poor lose out when their views diverge from those of the well-off. The interactions of preferences and preference divergence (equivalent to those in table 4.3) are -0.08 and 0.08 for the 10th and 50th income percentiles, respectively ($p = 0.34$ and 0.35; see table A4.3 for full regression results). But for the remaining issues in the social welfare domain, where the less well-off lack strong allies, the estimated decline in the influence of the poor and the middle class is substantial and comparable to the declines in other issue domains shown in table 4.3 ($b = -0.53$ and -0.39 for the 10th and 50th income percentiles; $p = 0.02$ and 0.05).

• • •

Chapter 3 revealed a high degree of inequality in government responsiveness to the preferences of more- and less-affluent segments of the American public. This chapter shows that these representational inequalities extend broadly but not uniformly across different substantive policy domains. For the most part the patterns of inequality evident in my overall analysis of policy responsiveness were replicated in each of the issue domains examined, but social welfare issues did constitute a partial exception to this pattern. In particular the subset of social welfare issues on which the most significant interest groups were aligned with the preferences of lower- rather than upper-income Americans were immune from the inequalities evident on other issues.

Even if exceptional, the alignment of interest groups with the preferences of the less affluent raises the question of *why* this alignment takes place on these issues (and whether such alignments can be fostered more broadly). In most cases the confluence of preferences between interest groups and less-well-off Americans on these issues results from a happy coincidence and not from any actual influence exerted by the poor or the middle class. The pharmaceutical lobby and the National Educational Association, for example, pursue policies that benefit their members and that happen to coincide with the preferences of the less advantaged. The AARP, however, as a mass-membership organization, might actually be considered a conduit through which the influence of less-well-off Americans flows.

The next chapter takes up this question as part of a broader examination of the role of organized interest groups in shaping government responsiveness.

CHAPTER 5

Interest Groups and
Democratic Responsiveness

THE ANALYSIS OF SOCIAL WELFARE POLICY in chapter 4 suggests that interest groups can, at least on occasion, influence policy in a direction more compatible with middle- or low-income Americans' preferences than with those of the affluent. But if interest groups can work against the preferences of the affluent on some issues, there is no reason to think they don't work in favor of the preferences of the affluent on other issues. Indeed, if interest groups tend to align more with the preferences of the affluent, the relationship between preferences and policy outcomes for the well-off may reflect not the influence of this economic stratum, but (at least in part) the influence of interest groups instead.

Over the past decades political scientists have variously portrayed organized interest groups as a foundation of popular influence in politics, as the basis of elite domination, and as everything in between.[1] My analyses in this chapter show a strong association between interest group preferences and policy outcomes, roughly equal to the influence of high-income Americans documented in the previous chapters. But interest groups and affluent members of the public appear to shape federal policy making largely independently of each other. That is, interest groups on balance neither raise nor lower the likelihood that affluent Americans' policy preferences will prevail. Nor does the opposition of interest groups account for the lack of responsiveness to the preferences of the poor or middle class. On particular issues, of course, the alignment of organized interests may favor the preferences of more- or less-well-off citizens. But across the full range of issues captured in my dataset, and, for the most part, across each of the separate substantive issue domains I analyze, interest groups' political power constitutes a separate and parallel influence to that of the public. These findings suggest that representational inequality cannot be blamed on the power of organized interests. Particular groups do undermine the interests of the public on specific issues, but on other occasions interest groups align with public preferences (even if those groups are motivated by their own narrow concerns).

INTEREST GROUP ALIGNMENTS AND THE PUBLIC'S POLICY PREFERENCES

Interest group influence over policy making is an important topic in its own right. But my primary concern is with interest groups and the public as potentially interrelated forces. Interest group activity and public preferences might combine to shape policy outcomes in a number of different ways. First, the apparent influence of the public (or affluent members of the public) revealed in previous chapters might instead reflect, at least in part, the power of organized interests. Some scholars, for example, suggest that interest groups sometimes seek to shape policy outcomes by shifting public preferences on a policy issue.[2] Accounts of the campaigns to reform health care or to eliminate the estate tax, for example, often point to the efforts made to sway public opinion by interest groups and the think tanks and public relations firms they support.[3] But other observers are skeptical that interest groups can shift public preferences even on these high-profile, heavily lobbied issues.[4] For such skeptics, interest groups are more likely to succeed in raising the salience of an issue than in swaying public preferences.[5]

To the extent that interest groups do manage to shift the public's policy preferences, what appears to be the public's independent influence over policy outcomes should rightly be attributed to interest groups instead. Reestimating the preference/policy link while taking interest group alignments into account will shed light on the importance of this mechanism in generating the associations between public preferences and policy outcomes reported in chapters 3 and 4.

Interest groups' efforts to sway public opinion on issues like health care or tax reform might contribute to an association between public preferences and interest group alignments. But such a correlation could arise for other reasons as well. On some issues the public and the dominant groups might have compatible interests apart from any attempt to influence public opinion. For example, the health care and education lobbies favor greater government spending on health care and education, a preference frequently shared by majorities of the public. On other issues, the public's perceived interests and the interests of organized lobbying groups are usually at odds. American citizens are typically supportive of strong environmental regulation, while interest groups tend to align in opposition to strong environmental safeguards.

My data do not allow me to parse out the various factors that generate positive or negative associations between interest group alignments and public preferences. But they do allow me to use multivariate analyses to assess the overall impact that such associations have on the apparent influence exerted by each of these two sets of actors. Most important, my measure of interest group alignments allows me to test the possibility that policy responsiveness as estimated in previous chapters is biased owing to the omitted impact of interest groups on policy outcomes.

A second way in which interest groups might complicate the link between public preferences and government policy is by shaping the conditions under which the public's influence over policy outcomes is larger or smaller. In particular we might expect the public's influence to be greater when interest groups are least engaged in shaping policy, or when opposing interest groups cancel each other out. To assess this possibility, I use my interest group alignment data to measure not the direction of interest group preferences on a given policy but the extent to which interest groups are neutral (or unengaged) rather than aligned on one side of the issue or the other.

Yet a third possible relationship between interest groups and public preferences is that these two influences over policy outcomes interact to reinforce each other. As noted above, some scholars argue that interest groups are less likely to shift public attitudes than they are to publicize and mobilize existing opinion when it coincides with their policy objectives.[6] From this perspective public opinion is a resource that interest groups can draw on when the public's preferences happen to coincide with the group's position. Interest groups, by this understanding, are not simply more likely to prevail when their views align with the public's preferences; they can actually leverage public opinion to exert greater influence than they would otherwise have. Interest groups and the public, in other words, can serve as force multipliers for each other, forming a whole greater than the sum of its parts when their preferences coincide. In the analyses below, this dynamic is captured by including in my models an interaction between the Interest Group Alignment Index and my measures of public preferences.

Finally, interest groups and ordinary citizens might simply influence government policy independently of each other. In that case estimates of policy responsiveness would be unaffected by whether or not we take interest groups into account. Yet even if these two influences operated independently, interest groups might help to explain those cases in which policy outcomes diverge from the patterns expected based on public preferences alone. As we saw in chapter 4, some policies with strong support among high-income Americans were not adopted while some policies that were strongly opposed by high-income Americans were adopted (and in some cases these exceptions pushed policy outcomes more into line with the preferences of lower-income groups). The parallel and independent influence of interest groups and the public would not change our understanding of Americans' ability to influence policy outcomes, but it could help to account for the specific patterns of policies that are adopted.

Measuring Interest Group Alignments

To assess the role of interest groups in explaining representational inequality, more systematic information on interest groups' policy alignments and the relationship of those alignments to the preferences of the public is needed. Identifying the interest groups relevant to any specific policy issue is difficult, and assessing the relative power of interest groups aligned on different sides of an issue is even more so. Perhaps the most ambitious effort along these lines is the Advocacy and Public Policymaking project by Baumgartner and colleagues.[7] These researchers closely examined ninety-eight policy issues selected at random from issues identified in interviews with Washington lobbyists. Based on hundreds of additional interviews and a wide range of archival material, Baumgartner et al. identified the interest groups active on each issue, the lobbying expenditures by those groups, the number of former government officials employed by each group as lobbyists, the campaign contributions of each group in the current and prior election cycles, the groups' membership size, the overall financial resources of each group involved in lobbying on that issue, and the number of active advocates on each side of the issue among officials in the legislative and executive branches. From these data they constructed an index of the relative resource advantage enjoyed by the interest groups on one side of a policy issue compared with the groups advocating other positions on that issue.

Because Baumgartner et al. selected their issues to represent the full set of policy issues that lobbyists were engaged with at the time of their interviews, they included many fairly narrow or obscure issues.[8] In contrast, my dataset based on national survey questions includes only those issues that were of sufficiently broad interest to attract a survey organization to pose a question about it to the American public. Consequently, I cannot link the Advocacy and Public Policymaking dataset with my measures of policy preferences and outcomes. However, the extensive data on interest group activity collected by Baumgartner et al. are helpful to me by validating a less sophisticated but less labor-intensive technique for gauging interest group influence on an issue: counting the number of powerful interest groups that favor and oppose a given policy or proposed policy change.

No list of "powerful interest groups in Washington" could hope to be definitive, but a plausible place to start is the "Power 25" list of lobbying organizations produced by *Fortune* magazine. Every few years since 1997, *Fortune* has surveyed Washington insiders (including members of Congress, congressional staff, White House aides, and lobbyists themselves), asking them to rate the influence of dozens of different lobbying organizations. Baumgartner et al. found that their index of relative interest group resources was strongly related to the difference in the number of Power 25 groups identified with each side of their policy issues.[9]

The basis for my own coding of interest group involvement, then, is based on an expanded version of *Fortune*'s Power 25 list. I began by combining the Power 25 lists from surveys conducted during both the Clinton and the G. W. Bush administrations (since the perceived power of different interest groups may be influenced by changes in partisan control of government). I then added to this combined list the ten industries with the highest lobbying expenditures (that were not already represented in the Power 25 list) based on lobbying disclosure data compiled by opensecrets .org. (Industries that exert most of their lobbying efforts directly rather than through industry-wide organizations tend not to appear in the Power 25 list. For example, financial and investment firms, oil companies, and telecommunications companies all spend heavily on lobbying but not through industry-wide organizations.) This resulted in the expanded list of forty-three interest groups shown in table A5.1.

The list of forty-three interest groups described above is clearly a crude approximation of the interest group environment. First, *Fortune* began its Power 25 survey only in 1997, and my public preference and policy data extend back to the early 1980s. Second, groups that happen to be on the winning side of an issue are likely to be perceived as more powerful regardless of how much influence they may have actually had over the outcome of that issue. Finally, a simple count of the number of groups on each side of an issue ignores the variation in power or influence even among these most influential groups.

Despite these shortcomings, the strong association of the Power 25 group count and the far more sophisticated relative resource index constructed by Baumgartner et al. gives some confidence that a simple interest group count will shed light on the dynamics of policy formation. In addition, while the number of interest groups in Washington has grown over the decades, the proportion of those groups representing different sorts of interests appears to have been fairly stable.[10]

My extended Power 25 index of interest group alignment is constructed as follows. For each policy question, I used the extended list of forty-three interest groups and industries shown in table A5.1 to identify organizations with a possible interest in the policy question. Then I used a variety of print and online resources to assess whether each of these potentially relevant groups took a public stand on the relevant policy issue (these resources included congressional testimony, interest groups' web sites, interest groups' congressional voting scorecards, news accounts, and descriptions of interest group activity from *Congressional Quarterly*). If the policy change under consideration tapped a core concern of an organization, that group was coded as being strongly favorable or unfavorable toward the policy change. If a group took a position on an issue that was not a core focus of the organization, the group was coded as being somewhat favorable or unfavorable toward the issue.[11] After repeating this exercise for each of the interest groups or industries identified as potentially relevant to the policy issue, I constructed an index of the net interest group alignment according to the following formula:

$$\text{Net Interest Group Alignment} = \ln(\text{StFav} + (0.5 * \text{SwFav}) + 1) - \ln(\text{StOpp} + (0.5 * \text{SwOpp}) + 1),$$

where StFav is the number of interest groups or industries coded as strongly favoring the proposed policy change, SwFav is the number of interest groups or industries coded as somewhat favoring the proposed policy change, StOpp is the number of interest groups or industries coded as strongly opposing the proposed policy change, and SwOpp is the number of interest groups or industries coded as somewhat opposing the proposed policy change. The natural log of the sum of interest groups on each side of the policy issue is taken to reflect the diminishing marginal impact of an additional group (e.g., the difference between zero and one groups on one side of an issue is expected to be larger than the difference between ten and eleven groups), and one is added to the interest group count on each side of an issue so that the log of the sum of interest groups will equal zero when there are no groups on that side of the issue.

I made one adjustment to my interest group alignment scores to reflect the unusual case of abortion policy. On abortion issues only two interest groups appear on the Power 25 list—the Christian Coalition and the National Right to Life Committee—and they are both opposed to abortion. But other indicators of lobbying activity on abortion issues suggest that abortion rights groups such as Planned Parenthood and NARAL have devoted more resources to influencing federal policy than have antiabortion groups. Over the past decade, for example, abortion rights groups have donated over seventeen million dollars to federal candidates and political parties compared with about six million dollars for antiabortion groups.[12] Baumgartner et al.'s analysis of interest groups involved in the fight over late-term abortion restrictions during the G. W. Bush administration also reflect the liberal interest group advantage on abortion. Baumgartner et al. found ten groups actively engaged in fighting new restrictions and four groups actively working to pass late-term abortion restrictions.

More important, the combined interest groups favoring abortion rights had three times the resources as those pushing for abortion restrictions.[13]

None of the ten individual interest groups that Baumgartner et al. found to be active in opposing late-term abortion restrictions was named as among the most influential lobbying organizations in any of *Fortune*'s Power 25 surveys. Nevertheless, to better reflect the interest group environment on abortion, I have added three phantom abortion rights groups to my list so that the interest group alignment on abortion issues consists of two antiabortion groups and three abortion rights groups.[14] My aim is to roughly capture the combined influence of the larger number of minor interest groups on the liberal side of abortion issues with the three liberal phantom groups.

THE DISTRIBUTION OF INTEREST GROUP ALIGNMENTS

Across all the proposed policy changes in my dataset, an average of 3.8 interest groups from the expanded Power 25 list were coded as taking a position in support or opposition.[15] Of these interest group positions, slightly more were coded as being only somewhat rather than strongly favorable or unfavorable toward the proposed policy change. Counting the somewhat favorable/unfavorable positions as half an interest group and the strongly favorable/unfavorable positions as a full interest group (as explained above), the average number of interest groups involved per proposed policy change was 2.8 (bottom row of table 5.1).

Of course some of the proposed policy changes in my dataset elicited no interest group involvement (at least among the forty-three powerful groups included in my list), while others elicited involvement from a large number of groups. As table 5.1 shows, interest groups were absent from involvement on almost one-quarter of the policy questions I collected. Among the policy issues coded as not having any interest group involvement were questions about foreign military engagements such as aiding the Nicaraguan Contras or intervening in Bosnia, antiterror policies like allowing the FBI to infiltrate suspected terrorist groups, and some domestic economic and social welfare issues including increasing the child tax deduction and placing time limits on welfare receipt.

Of the proposed policy changes that did engage interest groups from my list, most had interest groups involved on only one side of the issue. About one-third of all policy questions had interest groups in opposition but none in favor, while about one-fifth had interest groups in favor of the proposed change but none opposed. Many of these issues may have had less powerful interest groups—which don't appear on my expanded Power 25 list—on the opposing side. Even so, a complete absence of or-

Table 5.1 Distribution of Interest Group Alignments

	Number of Proposed Policy Changes	Percent of Proposed Policy Changes	Mean Number of Interest Groups
No interest groups	422	23.7	0
Only interest group support	365	20.5	2.3
Only interest group opposition	585	32.9	2.1
Both support and opposition	407	22.9	7.3
All proposed policy changes	1779	100.0	2.8

The mean number of interest groups reflects the number of interests groups coded as strongly favoring or opposing a proposed policy change plus one-half times the number of interest groups coded as somewhat favoring or opposing that change.

ganized interest group activity on one side of an issue does not appear to be unusual. Baumgartner et al. coded a far wider range of interest groups for their analysis, including groups with less influence and fewer resources than those on my expanded Power 25 list. Of the ninety-eight issues they examined, 28 percent had either no interest groups defending the status quo or no interest groups lobbying for change.[16]

Questions in my dataset that elicited only interest group opposition included a range of tax and economic policy issues, such as instituting a national sales or value-added tax, taxing employee health benefits, raising income tax rates, imposing trade sanctions on Russia, cutting farm subsidies, strengthening corporate regulation, and reducing Medicare payments to health care providers. In addition, proposals to strengthen gun control elicited only interest group opposition (again, limited to the forty-three groups and industries on my expanded Power 25 list). In contrast, interest group support but no interest group opposition was found for Bush's tax cuts, aid to Russia and the former Soviet Union, relaxing clean air standards, restricting Japanese imports, cutting personal income tax rates, increasing federal college assistance, and adding a prescription drug benefit to Medicare.

The 23 percent of proposed policy changes that involved powerful interest groups on both sides included numerous issues on which business and labor organizations took opposite sides, including corporate and labor regulation, trade policy, and taxation. Interest groups also lined up on opposite sides of Medicare and Social Security privatization proposals. (The AARP opposed privatization of each, while the Health Insurance Association of America supported Medicare privatization and securities and investment companies supported Social Security privatization.) Health care policy also elicited opposing interest group alignments, with employer health insurance mandates favored by unions and opposed by a number of employer organizations, and medical malpractice reform favored by the American Medical Association and health insurers and opposed by the Association of Trial Lawyers. Finally, abortion law pitted the Christian Coalition and the National Right to Life Committee on one side against numerous smaller abortion rights groups (as explained above).

On issues where interest groups were found on both sides, almost one-third had equal numbers of interest groups on each side, while about half had at least twice as many interest groups on one side as the other. The rather imbalanced nature of interest group alignments on the issues in my dataset may reflect in part the large number of employer and industry groups on my expanded Power 25 list (nineteen industry or employer groups are represented compared with only four unions). In addition my proposed policy changes tended to exclude the sort of narrow policy issues that pit one industry against another. Tariffs on specific goods, for example, typically benefit one set of American industries and harm others. While these sorts of battles have significant consequences for the industries involved (and sometimes for American workers and consumers as well), they are not likely to be asked about in national public opinion surveys. In contrast the much broader questions about trade policy that are represented in my dataset are less likely to engage equal numbers of interest groups on each side.

Of the 1,357 proposed policy changes on which at least one interest group was coded as favoring or opposing, the balance of interest group alignment was on the side of policy change only 36 percent of the time, with the net interest group alignment opposed to policy change 55 percent of the time (interest groups were evenly balanced on the remaining 9 percent of policy questions). In contrast, a majority of the public supported 59 percent of these proposed policy changes. Since the proposed policy changes in my data are far more popular with the public than with interest groups, the survey agenda that my data represent is clearly not tilted toward interest groups. On the contrary the ability of interest groups to influence the set of issues that reach public discussion (at least as indicated by those asked about in national surveys) appears quite limited.[17]

The survey agenda of proposed policy changes is on balance not favorable toward interest groups, and the resulting overrepresentation of interest groups in opposition to the proposed policy changes contributes to the status quo bias we first encountered in chapter 3. As I show below, organized interests and the public constitute parallel simultaneous influences on policy outcomes. Consequently interest groups' tilt toward existing policies and away from proposed changes serves to reinforce the status quo (along with the structural features of American democracy discussed above).

INTEREST GROUP ALIGNMENTS AND POLICY OUTCOMES

Figure 5.1 shows the relationship between the Net Interest Group Alignment Index described above and the probability of a proposed policy change being adopted. When there are no interest groups involved, or when opposing interest groups are equally balanced (in either case a score of 0 on the Net Interest Group Alignment Index), about 35 percent of proposed policy changes are adopted. The slope downward and to the left from the zero point (reflecting increased opposition among interest groups) is steeper and more consistent than the slope upward and to the right, suggesting that interest groups are more effective at blocking changes they oppose than they are at securing adoption of changes they support. As the figure indicates, strong interest group opposition is associated with

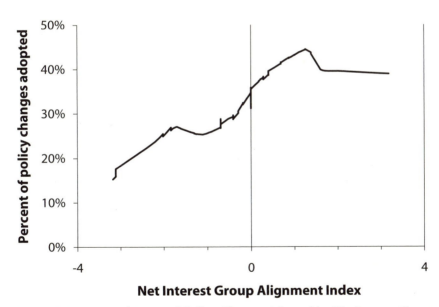

Net Interest Group Alignment Index

Figure 5.1. Percent of Proposed Policy Changes Adopted by Net Interest Group Alignment. The Net Interest Group Alignment Index is the log of one plus the number of interest groups supporting the proposed policy change minus the log of one plus the number of interest groups opposing the policy change. For example, a score of about 2 on the Net Interest Group Alignment Index would result from six interest groups in favor and no interest groups opposed. (See text for further discussion.) Curve is smoothed with Lowess.

a 10- to 20-point decline in the probability of adoption (compared with interest group neutrality), while strong support is associated with a 5- to 10-point increase.

Scholars have long recognized the advantaged position of groups working to maintain the status quo in a political system with multiple veto points, supermajority requirements, and so on.[18] The greater ability to thwart undesired policy changes than to advance desired changes reflected in figure 5.1 is also consistent with the analyses of Baumgartner et al., who found policy outcomes to be about twice as strongly related to their index of interest group resources for groups trying to defend the status quo as for groups attempting to achieve policy change.[19] This pattern may be strengthened by the strategic decisions of interest groups to allocate their resources were they can have the largest impact. If policy change is difficult to bring about but (comparatively) easy to prevent, interest groups may focus more of their efforts on preventing changes they oppose than on advocating changes they favor. If so, the asymmetrical impact of interest groups on policy outcomes would be further strengthened.

When the Net Interest Group Alignment Index is used as a predictor of policy change in a logistic regression model parallel to that used to assess the impact of public preferences in previous chapters, it reveals a fairly strong relationship to policy outcomes with a logistic regression coefficient of 0.36 (s.e. $= 0.05$; $p < 0.001$). A difference in interest group alignment score from one standard deviation below the mean to one standard deviation above the mean (approximately equivalent to the difference between a proposed change with two interest groups strongly opposed and one with two interest groups strongly in favor) raises the predicted probability of the policy being adopted from 0.25 to 0.41. For purposes of comparison, the same two-standard-deviation difference in preferences of the 90th income percentile is associated with a shift in probability of adoption from 0.23 to 0.44. A larger difference of plus/minus two standard deviations (roughly equivalent to six interest groups strongly in favor or strongly opposed) raises the probability of policy adoption from 0.19 to 0.50 (with the analogous difference in the preferences of affluent Americans resulting in a change in predicted probability of adoption from 0.15 to 0.56).

The comparisons above suggest that fairly extreme differences of either interest group alignment or preferences among the affluent when considered separately are each associated with sizable differences in the probability of a proposed policy outcome being adopted (I assess the impact of these two factors considered simultaneously in a variety of multivariate models below). If my measure of interest group alignments took a broader array of interest groups into account, it is possible that these comparisons might suggest a stronger role for interest groups in comparison to well-off members of the public. In addition my sample of proposed policy changes underrepresents the many obscure issues that fly under the radar of public awareness but may attract considerable attention from particular interest groups. On these sorts of issues, whatever influence the public has is likely to arise through the anticipation of possible public response should a policy maker's actions on the obscure issue come to light (e.g., if raised by an opponent in the next election).[20] There can be no single, definitive estimate of the influence of interest groups over policy outcomes— if only because there is no definitive set of interest groups or of possible policy changes to analyze—but the results based on my extended Power 25 list clearly demonstrate a strong association between interest group alignments and policy outcomes. In the following sections I use the Net Interest Group Alignment Index to examine how accounting for the role of interest groups changes our understanding of the link between the public's preferences and government policy.

INTEREST GROUPS AS AN OMITTED VARIABLE

To the extent that interest groups are successful in shaping public preferences, or if interest group alignments and public preferences are systematically related for other reasons, the estimates of policy responsiveness reported in the previous chapters would be biased. Interest groups are of course only one potential influence on policy outcomes the omission of which might bias my estimates of the preference/policy link. Other potential influences include the preferences of lawmakers themselves and of the small group of extremely wealthy politically engaged individuals like billionaires George Soros and Richard Scaife. Neither of these latter influences is easily assessed, and I leave consideration of their roles to chapter 8.

Any potential influence on policy outcomes might bias the estimate of policy responsiveness if that omitted influence both shapes the outcome being examined, and is correlated with the predictor of interest—in this case, the public's policy preferences.[21] Moreover an omitted variable could bias the estimate of the predictor of interest in either a positive or negative direction. Thus the apparent association of preferences and policy outcomes might be stronger or weaker depending on the direction of the correlation between interest group alignments and the preferences of Americans at different income levels. If interest groups and some subset of citizens tend on average to prefer the same policies, then at least some of the apparent influence of those citizens might in fact be due to the power of interest groups. On the other hand, if interest groups and a subset of Americans tend on average to prefer different policies, then the influence of these Americans over policy may be suppressed. In this case the failure to take interest groups into account would lead to an underestimation of the ability of this set of citizens to shape policy outcomes.

We might expect interest group alignments to coincide more closely with the preferences of the affluent than with those of lower-income Americans. First, the more economically advantaged are more likely to belong to organizations that seek to influence government policy.[22] Second, most observers view the distribution of interest group power in Washington to be slanted strongly toward business and away from the citizen and labor groups that might advance the preferences of poor and middle-class Americans.[23] While some scholars argue that the rise of citizen groups in the 1960s and 1970s has changed the complexion of the interest group environment, these more recent additions to the interest group universe tend to focus on social issues or postmaterialist concerns like gay rights or environmental protection.[24] Affluent Americans tend to prioritize these issues more highly than the less well-off and often hold more liberal views than lower-income Americans (see chapter 4). Finally, even those citizen advocacy organizations focused on helping less-privileged groups tend to focus on the interests and concerns of their more advantaged members.[25]

Despite these expectations, the Net Interest Group Alignment Index is unrelated to the policy preferences of the public at any income level, with nonsignificant correlations between 0.02 and 0.04 for the 10th, 50th, and 90th income percentiles. Given this lack of overall association between interest group alignments and public preferences, it is not surprising that controlling for the Net Interest Group Alignment Index does not affect the estimated responsiveness of policy to the preferences of any income group. The top half of table 5.2 shows the estimated impact of policy preferences and interest group alignments on policy outcomes for the 10th, 50th and 90th income percentiles, with all predictors standardized for easier comparison. When public preferences are examined alone, the impact of a one-standard-deviation difference ranges from 0.30 for the 10th income percentile to 0.49 for the 90th percentile. When the Net Interest Group Alignment Index is added to the logistic regression, these estimates are essentially unchanged, ranging from 0.29 to 0.49. In comparison the estimated impact of a one-standard-deviation difference in interest group alignment is 0.35 to 0.36 and is unaffected by controls for any of the income groups' preferences.[26]

The bottom half of table 5.2 shows the same analysis but restricted to the 723 proposed policy changes for which the 10th and 90th income percentiles differ by at least 10 percentage points and the 322 proposed policy changes for which the 50th and 90th percentiles differ by at least that amount. The only hint that interest groups might be biasing the estimates of policy responsiveness is for the 90th income percentile on those issues where the 50th and 90th percentiles differ (adding the Net Interest

Table 5.2   Interest Group Alignment and Public Preferences as Predictors of Policy Outcomes

	Income Percentile		
	10th	50th	90th
Model 1			
Preferences for the indicated income percentile	.30 (.05)***	.38 (.05)***	.49 (.05)***
Model 2			
Preferences for the indicated income percentile	.29 (.05)***	.38 (.05)***	.49 (.05)***
Interest group alignments	.35 (.05)***	.36 (.05)***	.36 (.05)***

	10th vs. 90th Percentiles		50th vs. 90th Percentiles	
	10th	90th	50th	90th
Model 1				
Preferences for the indicated income percentile	.02 (.09)	.46 (.10)***	−.01 (.14)	.47 (.18)**
Model 2				
Preferences for the indicated income percentile	.01 (.09)	.48 (.10)***	−.05 (.14)	.38 (.18)*
Interest group alignments	.34 (.08)***	.36 (.08)***	.44 (.13)***	.40 (.13)**

Table shows logistic regression coefficients with standard errors in parentheses. Dependent variable is policy outcome coded 1 if the proposed policy change took place within four years of the survey date and 0 if it did not. The income groups' preferences are the logits of the imputed percentage of respondents favoring the proposed policy change at each income level. The interest group alignment coding is explained in the text. All predictors are standardized. N is 1,779 for the analyses in the top half of the table, 723 for the comparison of 10th and 90th percentiles, and 322 for comparison of the 50th and 90th percentiles.
$*p < .05; **p < .01; ***p < .001$

Group Alignment Index to the model lowers the estimate for the preferences of the 90th percentile from 0.47 to 0.38). Yet even here the change is modest and falls below conventional levels of statistical significance.[27]

INTEREST GROUP ENGAGEMENT AND POLICY RESPONSIVENESS

Even if interest groups are not important as an omitted variable in estimating the preference/policy link, they might shape that link in a different way. As suggested above, interest groups might serve to specify the conditions under which affluent Americans are more and less influential in shaping federal policy. In particular we might imagine that well-off members of the public wield the greatest influence over policy outcomes when interest groups are unengaged with an issue and that the greater the degree of interest group engagement, the less influence even the most well-off members of the public can exert.

This model of the relationship between interest groups and public opinion predicts not merely that outcomes fit less well with public preferences when interest groups are involved, but that the influence of the public actually declines under these circumstances. If this understanding is correct, the strength of the preference/policy link should decline as the engagement of interest groups on an issue increases. To assess this hypothesis, I estimate a model that includes a nondirectional measure of the degree of interest group engagement, my usual measures of public preferences, and the interaction of the two. Adapting the operationalization of the Net Interest Group Alignment Index described above, the Interest Group Engagement Index is as defined as ln(StFav + StOpp + 0.5*SwFav + 0.5*SwOpp + 1), where StFav is the number of interest groups coded as strongly favoring the proposed policy change, StOpp is the number of interest groups coded as strongly opposing the proposed policy change, SwFav is the number of interest groups coded as somewhat favoring the proposed policy change, and SwOpp is the number of interest groups coded as somewhat opposing the proposed policy change. The Interest Group Engagement Index ranges from 0 when no interest groups are coded as having a position on the proposed policy change to a theoretical maximum of 3.8 when all forty-three interest groups are coded as having a strong position on the issue. (The actual maximum score on the Interest Group Engagement Index is about 3.2, equivalent to twenty-four interest groups coded as taking strong positions on an issue.)

The results from the model described above are presented in table 5.3. The interaction of preferences and interest group engagement is in the expected direction for the 10th and 50th income percentiles, but neither of the coefficients is statistically distinguishable from zero. The interaction of the Interest Group Engagement Index with the preferences of the 90th income percentile is in the opposite direction from that expected, but once again not statistically distinguishable from zero. In short there is no evidence that the degree of interest group engagement on an issue either enhances or detracts from the public's ability to influence policy outcomes.

The bottom half of table 5.3 repeats the analyses in the top half but restricts the model to those proposed policy changes on which preferences

Table 5.3 Interest Group Engagement and Public Preferences as Predictors of Policy Outcomes

	Income Percentile		
	10th	50th	90th
Preferences for the indicated income percentile	.29 (.05)***	.37 (.05)***	.50 (.06)***
Interest group engagement	−.09 (.05)	−.09 (.05)	−.09 (.05)
Interaction of preferences and interest group engagement	−.05 (.05)	−.05 (.06)	.04 (.06)

	10th vs. 90th Percentiles		50th vs. 90th Percentiles	
	10th	90th	50th	90th
Preferences for the indicated income percentile	.03 (.09)	.46 (.10)***	.00 (.16)	.38 (.19)*
Interest group engagement	−.02 (.08)	−.05 (.08)	.24 (.12)*	.23 (.12)
Interaction of preferences and interest group engagement	−.11 (.09)	.02 (.09)	−.14 (.14)	.16 (.18)

Table shows logistic regression coefficients with standard errors in parentheses. Dependent variable is policy outcome coded 1 if the proposed policy change took place within four years of the survey date and 0 if it did not. The income groups' preferences are the logits of the imputed percentage of respondents favoring the proposed policy change at each income level. The interest group engagement coding is explained in the text. Preferences and the Interest Group Engagement Index are standardized and then mean-centered before the interaction terms are computed. The bottom half of the table shows analyses limited to polices on which the indicated income levels diverged by more than 10 percentage points. N is 1,779 for the analyses in the top half of the table, 723 for the 10th vs. 90th percentiles, and 322 for the 50th vs. 90th percentiles.

among the 10th and 90th income percentiles or the 50th and 90th income percentiles diverge by more than 10 percentage points. The nonsignificant interaction terms indicate that the link between preferences and policy outcomes remains strong among the most affluent Americans at any level of interest group engagement, while policy responsiveness is essentially zero for those at the 10th or 50th income percentiles when their preferences diverge from the preferences of those at the 90th.

INTEREST GROUPS AND PUBLIC PREFERENCES
AS FORCE MULTIPLIERS

Interest group alignments do not appear to serve as an omitted variable biasing the estimates of public influence over policy outcomes, nor does interest group engagement seem to enhance or undermine the policy influence of affluent Americans. A third possibility is that interest groups and public opinion might interact to reinforce each other beyond the simple combination of their separate influence. If so, each of these potential influences would serve as a force multiplier for the other.

To assess this possibility, table 5.4 shows the same model of policy outcomes used in table 5.3 but with the Interest Group Alignment Index in place of the measure of Interest Group Engagement. If the power of interest groups to shape policy is enhanced when interest group alignments and public preferences coincide, the interaction term in these analyses will be positive. In fact, however, the interactions as shown in table 5.4 are consistently small and statistically indistinguishable from zero. This is true for all income percentiles and for all proposed policy changes (top half of the table) as well as for proposed changes on which the 10th and 90th or 50th and 90th income percentiles diverge (bottom half of the table).

The lack of interaction between interest group alignments and public preferences does not mean that each of these influences over policy is irrelevant to the prospects of the other. When interest groups share the public's preferences, the likelihood that outcomes will reflect public preferences is increased (just as the likelihood that outcomes will reflect interest group alignments is greater when the public shares interest groups' positions). But each of these two forces shapes policy independently of the other. This parallel influence over policy outcomes is illustrated graphically in figure 5.2, which shows the predicted probability of a proposed change being adopted based on the model of policy outcomes in the top right cell of table 5.4 (that is, including all 1,779 proposed changes and allowing for the possibility of an interaction between the Interest Group Alignment Index and the preferences of Americans at the 90th income percentile).

The front (white) and back (black) rows of figure 5.2 show how policy outcomes relate to the preferences of the 90th income percentile when interest groups are strongly opposed or strongly in favor of the proposed policy change. The probability of policy change is, of course, much higher when interest groups support the change, but in either case the preferences of affluent Americans matter: when interest groups strongly oppose, the likelihood of a change being adopted rises from 0.10 to 0.34 (a factor

Table 5.4 Interest Group Alignment, Public Preferences, and Their Interaction as Predictors of Policy Outcomes

	Income Percentile		
	10th	50th	90th
Preferences for the indicated income percentile	.28 (.05)***	.38 (.05)***	.48 (.06)***
Interest group alignment	.35 (.06)***	.36 (.06)***	.35 (.06)***
Interaction of preferences and interest group alignment	.05 (.06)	.02 (.06)	.04 (.06)

	10th vs. 90th Percentiles		50th vs. 90th Percentiles	
	10th	90th	50th	90th
Preferences for the indicated income percentile	.00 (.09)	.47 (.10)***	−.06 (.15)	.36 (.18)
Interest group	.36 (.09)***	.36 (.09)***	.43 (.13)**	.41 (.13)**
Interaction of preferences and interest group alignment	.04 (.10)	.05 (.09)	−.09 (.15)	.12 (.19)

Table shows logistic regression coefficients with standard errors in parentheses. Dependent variable is policy outcome coded 1 if the proposed policy change took place within four years of the survey date and 0 if it did not. The income groups' preferences are the logits of the imputed percentage of respondents favoring the proposed policy change at each income level. The interest group alignment coding is explained in the text. Preferences and the Interest Group Alignment Index are standardized and then mean-centered before the interaction terms are computed. Bottom half of the table shows analyses limited to policies on which the indicated income levels diverged by more than 10 percentage points. N is 1,779 for the analyses in the top half of the table, 723 for the 10th vs. 90th percentiles, and 322 for the 50th vs. 90th percentiles.

of 3.4) as support among well-off Americans increases; when interest groups are strongly in favor, the likelihood of change rises from 0.23 to 0.75 (a factor of 3.3) as support among the affluent rises. Thus strong agreement among interest groups in favor of or in opposition to a proposed change does not undermine the influence of affluent Americans. Finally, the middle (gray) bars in figure 5.2 show that the impact of high-income Americans' preferences is only slightly higher when interest groups are not aligned on either side of an issue. When the Net Interest Group

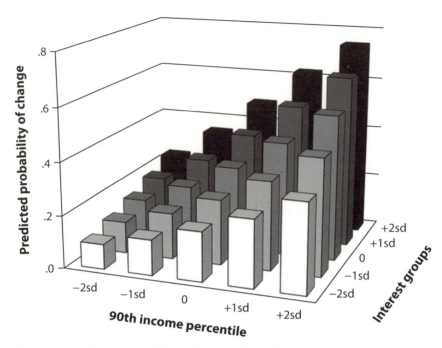

Figure 5.2. Predicted Probability of Policy Change by Interest Group Alignments, Preferences of the 90th Income Percentile, and Their Interaction. Figure shows results of the model of policy change in the top right cell of table 5.4. Policy preferences at the 90th income percentile and the Net Interest Group Alignment Index are standardized (with axis labels reflecting standard deviations from the mean). Far left corner shows that the probability of a proposed change being adopted is 0.10 if support at the 90th income percentile and the Net Interest Group Alignment Index are both 2 standard deviations below the mean. Far right corner shows that the probability of policy change is 0.75 if both are 2 standard deviations above the mean. See text and table 5.4 for details.

Alignment Index is zero, the probability of policy change increases from 0.15 to 0.55, a factor of 3.7.

The patterns shown in the front and back rows of the figure are consistent with Mark Smith's findings that public opinion strongly influences government policy making when business interests are united on one side of a policy or the other.[28] But the gray columns in the middle row suggest that public influence is just as strong (if not stronger) when interest groups are divided or unengaged. Smith argued that we should expect public influence to be greatest on issues where business is unified. But because he restricted his analyses to issues on which business interests were united, it is impossible to know whether he would have found equal or greater public influence if he had conducted similar analyses of issues on which business was divided.[29]

My analyses also differ from Smith's in examining how policy outcomes reflect the varying preferences of *both* public opinion and interest group alignments, while Smith focuses on the impact of public attitudes without taking variation in business preferences into account.[30] Turning again to figure 5.2, we can compare the impact of public preferences at any given level of interest group alignment with the impact of interest groups at any given level of public support or opposition. The leftmost set of columns, for example, shows the increase in the probability of a policy being adopted as support among interest groups rises for those policies to which well-off Americans are strongly opposed. The impact of interest groups at specific levels of public support ranges from a factor of 2.3 (when affluent Americans are strongly opposed) to 2.6 (when the affluent are evenly divided) to 2.2 (when affluent Americans are strong supporters). The somewhat smaller impact of interest groups relative to affluent Americans (whose preferences are associated with differences in policy outcomes by factors of 3.3 to 3.7, as reported above) reflects the somewhat smaller coefficient for interest groups in the logistic regression reported in the top right cell of table 5.4.

Given the difficulties involved in identifying definitive sets of policy issues and interest groups, it would be unwise to put too much stock in the specific estimates reflected in table 5.4 and figure 5.2. But the general results are quite clear and consistent across a wide range of alternative models reported in tables 5.2, 5.3, and 5.4: both interest group alignments and affluent Americans' preferences are strongly related to policy outcomes, and each of these forces appears to operate largely independently of the other. As a consequence the representational inequalities revealed in previous chapters are essentially unaffected by interest groups' influence over policy outcomes. Representational inequality was found consistently and with little variation whether I controlled for interest group alignments (table 5.2), for level of interest group engagement (table 5.3), or for the interaction of interest groups alignments and public preferences (table 5.4).

INTEREST GROUP ALIGNMENTS AND PUBLIC PREFERENCES ACROSS ISSUE DOMAINS

As indicated above, the Net Interest Group Alignment Index is uncorrelated with the public's policy preferences at any income level. But this lack of an overall association masks offsetting associations in different issue

Table 5.5 Correlations between Public Preferences and the Net Interest Group Alignment Index

| | N | All Respondents | Income Percentile | | |
			10th	50th	90th
Economic and tax	355	.27***	.21***	.25***	.32***
Social welfare	359	.42***	.41***	.41***	.40***
Foreign policy	219	−.13	−.21**	−.14*	−.01
Moral and religious	144	.21**	.32***	.22**	.07
Gun control	99	−.53***	−.46***	−.51***	−.60***
Environment	55	−.72***	−.73***	−.71***	−.68***

Includes only questions on which interest groups took a stand.
$*p < .05; **p < .01; ***p < .001$

areas. Table 5.5 shows the correlations between interest groups and public preferences for the four substantive policy domains examined in the previous chapter as well as for gun control and environmental policy (issue areas with too few policy questions to support the kinds of analyses reported in chapter 4). For the public as a whole, interest group alignments are positively related to public preferences on economic, social welfare, and moral issues, and negatively (and more strongly) related on gun control and the environment. Although the strongest of these relationships are negative (for gun control and environmental policy), the number of proposed policy changes on issues with positive associations is far greater, leading to the overall lack of correlation between public preferences and interest group alignments reported above.

The correlations in table 5.5 also help to explain why interest groups are not more strongly aligned with the preferences of the well-off than with those of the poor or middle class. First, on economic and tax policy (where we might expect the intersection of interest group alignments and preferences of the affluent to be greatest), we do find interest groups to be somewhat more closely aligned with the preferences of the well-off than of the poor, but the difference is small and the correlations are quite modest at all income levels.

The lack of a stronger association between interest group positions and the preferences of the affluent on economic issues stems from the countervailing effects of offsetting issues. On the one hand, interest groups and affluent Americans tend to agree on reducing corporate regulation, cutting capital gains taxes, cutting corporate income taxes, and opposing oil and gas price controls. But on the other hand, interest groups tended to be more aligned with the preferences of the poor in opposing federal budget cuts and in supporting a range of government spending for health care, farmers, mass transit, highway construction, and federal revenue sharing with the states. In short, interest groups tended to align more with the affluent on cutting taxes but more with the poor on maintaining or increasing government spending. The consequence, as reflected in table 5.5, is that the relationship between public preferences on economic policy and the Net Interest Group Alignment Index is weak at all income levels and only modestly stronger for those at the top of the income distribution than it is for those at the bottom.

The association between interest group alignments and public preferences on social welfare issues is somewhat stronger than it is on economic issues and essentially equal across all income levels. In part this reflects those issues like federal education aid which are strongly supported by Americans at all income levels and by interest groups like universities, the National Education Association, and the National Governors' Association. But the similar overall associations across income levels also reflect the fact that on some issues in the social welfare domain, interest group alignments coincide more with higher-income preferences and on other issues they coincide more with lower-income preferences. For example, the roles of the AARP and elements of the health care industry in defending Social Security and Medicare tend to coincide with the preferences of the middle class and poor, while the role of many of these same health care interests in supporting market-based health care (including market-oriented reforms to Medicare) tend to coincide more with the preferences of the affluent. Overall then, social welfare policies favored by interest groups tend also to elicit support from the public, although the specific bases for these overlapping preferences differ somewhat by income level.

Preferences on foreign policy issues are negatively related to interest group alignments for the poor and unrelated for the affluent. Poor Americans tend to oppose free-trade agreements, foreign economic aid (especially to the former Soviet Union), and military spending (especially major weapons systems), all of which find support from both interest groups and well-off members of the public. But Americans at all income levels differed from interest groups on other foreign policy issues such as trade sanctions against Russia and Poland in the early 1980s (which the public supported) and military aid for U.S. allies (which the public generally opposed).[31]

Interest group alignments are positively associated with public preferences on moral issues, but only for low- and middle-income Americans. As noted above, interest groups active on abortion policy tend to tilt toward the abortion rights side of the debate and hence are more consistent with the views of the affluent. But interest group alignments on other moral and religious issues such as gay rights and stem cell research tend strongly in the other direction and are more in line with the conservative preferences of lower-income Americans on these issues.

Finally, public preferences on gun control and environmental policy are strongly opposed to interest group alignments. The only interest group from my expanded Power 25 list active on gun control is the National Rifle Association. Since Americans at all income levels tend to support proposals to strengthen gun control, interest groups and public preferences tend strongly to conflict in this policy area. However, lower-income Americans do tend to be slightly less enthusiastic about some aspects of gun control (e.g., banning assault weapons) than those with higher incomes, so the negative correlations between preferences and interest group alignments on gun control are somewhat weaker for low- than for high-income Americans.

On environmental issues Americans at all income levels were opposed to relaxing auto pollution standards (as proposed in the early 1980s), a policy supported by the automobile and oil companies, the National Association of Manufacturers, and the AFL-CIO. Similarly, opening up more federal lands for commercial use was supported by the National Association of Manufacturers, the Chamber of Commerce, and the oil and electric industries but opposed strongly by the public. Essentially the same pattern (with most of the same interest groups) was found with regard to easing environmental standards for electrical generating plants and for the disposal of hazardous waste, and on relaxing pollution standards in national parks. Similarly ratification of the Kyoto Accord on global climate control was supported by about 70 percent of Americans at all income levels but opposed by interest groups. In short, interest groups and the American public typically fell on opposite sides of the various efforts by industry groups and Republican administrations to weaken federal environmental protections. Although the number of proposed policy changes in the environmental domain was small compared with the other domains shown in table 5.5, the negative relationship between public preferences and interest group alignments was quite strong, thus working to offset the weaker but positive associations in the other policy domains.

Most of the correlations between the public's preferences and interest groups alignments within specific issue domains shown in table 5.5 are fairly modest. Yet in some domains for some income levels, the correlations are high enough that taking interest groups into account might change our estimates of the impact of public preferences on policy outcomes.

INTEREST GROUPS, THE PUBLIC, AND POLICY OUTCOMES ACROSS ISSUE DOMAINS

As shown in table 5.6, adding the Net Interest Group Alignment Index to the logistic regressions estimating the impact of preferences on policy outcomes across the various policy domains does little to change those estimates. For the four major policy domains examined in chapter 4, the largest change occurs on social welfare issues, where adding interest group alignments to the equations reduces the apparent impact of public preferences by about 0.12 (starting from initial estimates of 0.38, 0.50, and 0.57 for the 10th, 50th, and 90th income percentiles, respectively). On economic and tax policies the apparent impact of public preferences diminishes by about 0.07 (from initial estimates of 0.50, 0.57, and 0.83), while even less change is evident in the estimates of public influence over foreign policy and moral/religious issues. In sum, the estimates of policy responsiveness change only modestly when the Net Interest Group Alignment Index is added to the model. Moreover the inequality across income levels remains and is in fact slightly larger when taking interest groups into account.

Gun control differs from the other four issue domains in table 5.6 not only in its specificity, but in that interest group alignments are negatively correlated with public preferences at all income levels (table 5.5). As noted above, the one powerful interest group active on gun issues is the National Rifle Association, and it is quite consistent in opposing any tightening of gun laws. The public, on the other hand, has favored most proposals to strengthen gun laws at the federal level, though to different degrees depending on the nature of the proposed policy change. Consequently interest groups (or *group,* in this case) and the public tend to push policy in opposite directions on gun control. Since neither force is completely successful in dominating the other, the result is that both the public and the gun lobby are somewhat more influential in shaping gun laws than it would appear if both factors are not considered simultaneously. Working in opposite directions, these two predictors constitute suppressor variables for each other, resulting in underestimates of the power of both when the other is not taken into account.

Model 1 in the bottom section of table 5.6 shows the estimated influence of low-, middle-, and high-income Americans over gun policy without taking interest groups into account. Unlike the other policy domains in table 5.6, adding the Net Interest Group Alignment Index to the model modestly increases the association between public preferences and policy outcomes for the most affluent Americans (and even more modestly for the middle class). The estimates of interest group influence in this domain

Table 5.6 Interest Group Alignment and Public Preferences as Predictors of Policy Outcomes by Policy Domain

	10th Percentile		50th Percentile		90th Percentile	
	Public Preferences	Interest Groups	Public Preferences	Interest Groups	Public Preferences	Interest Groups
Economic and tax						
Model 1	.50 (.12)***		.57 (.12)***		.83 (.14)***	
Model 2	.43 (.12)***	.24 (.08)**	.50 (.13)***	.22 (.08)**	.76 (.14)***	.16 (.09)
Difference	-.07 (.03)*		-.07 (.03)*		-.07 (.04)	
Social welfare						
Model 1	.38 (.11)***		.50 (.11)***		.57 (.12)***	
Model 2	.26 (.11)*	.48 (.17)**	.39 (.12)**	.42 (.17)*	.45 (.13)***	.41 (.17)*
Difference	-.12 (.05)*		-.11 (.05)*		-.12 (.05)*	
Foreign policy						
Model 1	.37 (.11)***		.55 (.11)***		.76 (.12)***	
Model 2	.41 (.11)***	.56 (.19)**	.59 (.12)***	.57 (.19)**	.77 (.12)***	.50 (.19)**
Difference	.04 (.02)*		.04 (.02)*		.01 (.02)	
Moral and religious						
Model 1	.75 (.24)**		.85 (.24)***		1.04 (.26)***	
Model 2	.70 (.24)**	.24 (.35)	.82 (.25)**	.34 (.35)	1.03 (.27)***	.48 (.35)
Difference	-.05 (.07)		-.03 (.04)		-.01 (.03)	
Gun control						
Model 1	.46 (.27)		.59 (.28)*		.89 (.31)**	
Model 2	.47 (.30)	.08 (.88)	.66 (.32)*	.43 (.91)	1.13 (.36)**	1.58 (1.10)
Difference	.01 (.18)		.07 (.17)		.24 (.30)	

Table shows logistic regression coefficients with standard errors in parentheses. Dependent variable is policy outcome coded 1 if the proposed policy change took place within four years of the survey date and 0 if it did not. The income groups' preferences are the logits of the imputed percentage of respondents favoring the proposed policy change at each income level. The interest group alignment coding is explained in the text. All predictors are standardized. N is 389 for economic and tax, 399 for social welfare, 428 for foreign policy, 161 for moral, and 99 for gun control. Bootstrap standard errors are shown for the differences in coefficients for public preferences across corresponding models 1 and 2.
*p < .05; **p < .01; ***p < .001

are more strongly affected by the inclusion of public preferences. The influence of the gun lobby appears weak when controlling for the preferences of the poor ($b = 0.08$) but appears much stronger when controlling for the preferences of the well-off ($b = 1.58$). Affluent Americans serve as a powerful influence pushing gun control policy in a more liberal direction. When this influence is taken into account, the power of the gun lobby in limiting the impact of the public's pro–gun control preferences becomes apparent. Despite the large difference in coefficients for the impact of interest groups in these equations, the small number of gun control questions in my dataset prevents the resulting coefficients for interest groups from reaching statistical significance.

In sum, tables 5.2 and 5.6 show that taking interest groups into account in estimating the strength of the preference/policy link does not alter these relationships substantially. The size of the coefficients for the preferences of the 10th through 90th income percentiles differs little when the Net Interest Group Alignment Index is added to the models, and the pattern of stronger associations between preferences and policy outcomes for the well-off is, if anything, slightly stronger when controlling for interest group alignments.

INTEREST GROUP INFLUENCE OVER POLICY MAKING

My central focus in this book is the responsiveness of policy makers to the preferences of the public, and my concern with interest groups stems primarily from the role they might play in shaping that responsiveness. But the Net Interest Group Alignment Index also allows me to examine the power of interest groups to shape policy across the various issue domains. As a bit of a digression from my analysis of responsiveness to public preferences, then, I take advantage of the results reported in table 5.6 to briefly examine the variation in the interest group/policy link across issue domains.

The best estimates of the influence of interest groups over policy outcomes come from the regressions in which the preferences of the 90th income percentile are also included as predictors.[32] The rightmost column in table 5.6 shows the association between policy outcomes and the Net Interest Group Alignment Index for each of the substantive domains examined. Surprisingly, perhaps, economic and tax policy stands out as the domain in which interest groups have the least sway over policy outcomes, and (less surprisingly, perhaps) gun control the domain in which interest groups are most influential.

Looking at the proposed changes in the realm of economic and tax policy, we find that interest groups prevailed on some proposals and were defeated on others (as the lack of a significant association between the interest group index and policy outcomes would suggest). Both capital gains and income tax rates for high earners declined over the decades under study, consistent with the preferences of the large number of business- and financial-sector interest groups.[33] Interest groups also favored cutting or eliminating the estate tax, which was reduced in stages over the 1980s and 1990s and then phased out entirely (if temporarily) as part of the Bush tax cuts of 2001.[34] Finally, proposals to adopt a federal sales or value-added tax raised during the early 1980s and again in the mid-1990s never gained traction, consistent with the strong opposition among businesses and unions alike.[35]

In contrast, interest groups lost out on many economic and tax policies during the decades examined. For example, many attempts to reduce government regulation of business were defeated.[36] At the same time new business regulations were adopted, including a series of corporate oversight laws in the wake of the Enron scandal, family-leave policy enacted under Clinton, and federal regulation of electricity pricing under G. W. Bush. Business tax policies changed in a variety of largely offsetting ways over the period under study, with lower statutory rates but the imposition of the alternative minimum tax. As a consequence the effective average corporate tax rate fluctuated between 25 and 30 percent throughout the period and showed no overall trend from 1981 through 2004.[37] With a mix of policy victories and defeats, the overall relationship between interest group alignments and policy outcomes on economic and tax issues was quite weak.

By far the strongest association between interest group alignments and policy outcomes concerns gun control. Two factors probably contribute to this strong association. First, the interest groups engaged on this issue are extremely imbalanced in opposition to gun control. Between 1990 and 2008, for example, pro–gun control groups contributed $1.8 million to parties and candidates at the federal level while anti–gun control groups contributed $21.4 million (these figures include numerous groups that do not appear on my expanded Power 25 list). Similarly, pro–gun control groups spent less than one-fifth the amount on lobbying that their anti–gun control opponents spent.[38]

In addition to the imbalanced resources among interest groups on either side of the gun control issue, the success of the NRA and other opponents of gun control reflects the largely defensive nature of their lobbying efforts. The vast majority of proposed changes to gun laws in my dataset are proposals to strengthen rather than weaken existing regulations. Success in blocking most of these proposed changes reflects in part the difficulty of bringing about policy change compared to maintaining the status quo. Finally, the strong association of the Net Interest Group Alignment

Index with policy outcomes on gun control may reflect policy makers' perception that their pro–gun control constituents, while numerous, lack the passion for the issue that opponents of gun control possess. If so, the measure of pro–gun control sentiments of the public may miss out on an important factor working to deter stronger gun laws, and this missing factor may be picked up by the anti–gun control stance of interest groups. With the data at hand it is impossible to distinguish what role this asymmetry in the strength or salience of gun control preferences among the public might play in shaping federal gun policy.

The strong positive associations of policy preferences with both affluent Americans and the gun control lobby shown in the bottom section of table 5.6 may seem odd, given the strong negative correlation between these two influences shown in table 5.5 ($r = -0.60$). But remember that the coefficients in table 5.6 are estimates of the *influence* of each of these two forces over policy outcomes. The two large positive coefficients suggest that for any given level of public support (among high-income Americans), interest group alignment is strongly related to policy outcomes, and for any given level of interest group alignment, support among the well-off is strongly related to policy outcomes as well. In fact these two powerful forces arguably came to somewhat of a draw on gun policy over the decades of the 1980s, 1990s, and early 2000s. Many popular proposals to strengthen gun laws were defeated, including proposals to register all handguns, to limit the number of guns that could be purchased in a month, to require trigger locks, to close the gun show loophole for background checks, and to require licenses or permits to own a gun. On the other hand, virtually all actual changes to federal laws during this period strengthened gun controls. The Law Enforcement Officers Protection Act of 1986 banned so-called cop-killer bullets, the Undetectable Firearms Act for 1988 banned nonmetallic guns, the 1990 Crime Control Act banned assault weapons, and the 1993 Brady Bill instituted a five-day waiting period for gun purchases.[39]

Gun control legislation seems to represent a policy arena in which powerful opposing forces have produced something of a deadlock. Gun policy has clearly been less restrictive than public preferences at any income level would support. But the preferences of (affluent) Americans have sometimes prevailed over the well-financed NRA and the passion of the anti–gun control minority. The existence of these two opposing forces has served to keep each other in check and resulted in only incremental changes to federal gun control legislation over the past few decades.

INTEREST GROUP ALIGNMENTS AND SPECIFIC
POLICY OUTCOMES

Despite their clear importance in shaping federal policy, interest groups do not appear to alter the impact of public preferences on policy outcomes. Neither the degree of support or opposition to a proposed policy among interest groups nor the extent to which interest groups are engaged on an issue significantly alters the patterns of responsiveness to the public that previous chapters revealed.

Yet even if interest groups operate independently of the public as influences on policy makers, the alignment of interest groups on particular issues may account for exceptions to the patterns of policy outcomes that would be expected based on public preferences alone. That is, even if interest groups sometimes work to push policy toward outcomes favored by the affluent (or the poor) and sometimes work to push policy away from those outcomes, knowing the specific policies that fall into each of these categories may help us understand some of the specifics of government policy making that do not fit the broad overall patterns. I suggested in chapter 4, for example, that a number of specific policy outcomes in the social welfare domain that were more consistent with the preferences of middle- and low-income Americans could be accounted for by the alignment of interest groups on those issues. To be clear, this does not mean that interest groups were *more likely* to align with the preferences of lower- than higher-income Americans in this domain; table 5.5 shows this not to be the case. But it does mean that a subset of issues exists on which interest groups do help to account for outcomes more favorable to the less well-off (just as another subset exists in which interest group alignments favor the affluent).

Focusing on instances in which interest groups appear to have moved policy away from the preferences of the affluent, I find seventy-two proposed policy changes in my dataset that were favored by interest groups but opposed by at least two-thirds of affluent Americans; of these, only sixteen were adopted. Most of the policies adopted over the strong objections of the well-off were also opposed by Americans with more modest incomes. In 1992, for example, the affluent and the poor were united in opposition to proposed U.S. loan guarantees to Israel. The American Israel Public Affairs Committee (AIPAC) was the only interest group engaged on this question and came out strongly in favor of the loan guarantees (which were adopted with solid congressional and White House support). Another case in which interest groups prevailed over strong public sentiments concerned an aspect of G. W. Bush's faith-based initiative. While the general notion of allowing religious organizations to receive government funding to provide social services was popular, strong majorities of

Americans at all income levels believed that organizations receiving government funds for this purpose should not be allowed to restrict their hiring to people who share their religious beliefs. But interest groups like the Christian Coalition favored allowing religious organizations this ability to hire as they pleased, and President Bush established this policy as federal law by executive order in 2002.

While interest groups sometimes contribute to the adoption of policies strongly opposed by the well-off, there are far more cases where interest groups contribute to the failure of proposed changes that the affluent strongly support. Some of the failed policy proposals that the well-off supported were also favored by Americans at lower income levels. But other proposed policy changes resembled those discussed in chapter 4 in which interest groups and less-well-off Americans were aligned against the preferences of the affluent. Proposals to cut spending on Medicaid during the early years of the Reagan administration, for example, were strongly opposed by poor Americans and by health care interest groups as well as the National Governors' Association. Despite the support of high-income Americans, Congress refused to go along with the proposed cuts. Similarly, efforts to cut Social Security spending by changing the inflation indexing or raising the retirement age generally received strong support from the well-off but were strongly opposed by the poor. The major interest group involved with Social Security and related policies, the AARP, aligned with lower-income Americans on these proposals, and most (though not all) were defeated (see chapter 4). Other policies favored by the affluent and opposed by both interest groups and low-income Americans included school vouchers, consumer energy or BTU taxes, restrictions on Japanese imports during the 1980s, and proposals to abolish government farm subsidies or price supports. With few exceptions during the decades under study, these policies were not adopted. As this fairly disparate list of policies suggests, there are a variety of issues on which interest group alignments led to outcomes more congenial to middle- or low-income Americans than to the affluent. But as a proportion of all proposed policy changes on which preferences across income groups diverge, such issues are the exception not the rule.

Even if the balance of interest group alignments only occasionally works to the benefit of the less well-off, particular interest groups may serve this function consistently (even while other interest groups simultaneously work against the preferences of the less advantaged). To better understand the potential of interest groups to advance the needs and preferences of low- and middle-income Americans, in the next section I look not at the balance of interest groups on a given issue or within a particular policy domain but at the specific interest groups on my expanded Power 25 list. Keeping in mind that my forty-three interest groups constitute a very limited (although important) subset of the vastly larger interest group universe, my aim is to at least offer some insight into the potential of interest groups to address the imbalance in policy responsiveness to the preferences of more- and less-advantaged Americans.

Individual Interest Groups and the Public's Policy Preferences

Insight into the potential power of interest groups to redress the inequalities in Americans' influence over government policy may be gained by examining the existing cases in which interest groups appear to push policy in a direction favorable to the less well-off. A congruence of preferences between interest groups and lower-income Americans might arise for three reasons. First, a group might adopt a position for reasons unconnected with the needs or preferences of the poor. For example, if the American Hospital Association helps obtain increased government funding for teaching hospitals, the least well-off members of the public may benefit most (since they are more likely to lack health insurance and rely on uncompensated care from large urban hospitals). In this (hypothetical) case, the AHA would have no particular concern with helping to meet the needs or promote the policy preferences of the less well-off; this confluence of preferences between an interest group and the disadvantaged is merely a happy coincidence.

In other cases, however, interest groups appear to serve as conduits of influence for members of the public. The clearest such cases concern mass-membership organizations that exist to advance some particular set of policy goals and recruit members and attract donations on the basis of those goals. Citizens groups like the Sierra Club, the American Civil Liberties Union, and the National Rifle Association are examples of groups that serve as mechanisms through which like-minded members of the public exert influence over government policy.[40] To the extent that policy stances of such citizens groups reflect the preferences of poor or middle-class Americans, they offer a potential avenue of influence to counter the power exerted by more affluent Americans.

Finally, some interest groups that are not primarily mechanisms for the expression of their members' policy preferences might nevertheless have an ideological commitment to benefit the less advantaged. In her book *Affirmative Advocacy*, for example, Dara Strolovitch examines a wide range of interest groups working to benefit the less well-off, including low-wage workers, women, immigrants, older people, racial, ethnic, and sexual minorities, and so on.[41] Some of these organizations are citizens groups of the type described above. But others are funded through grants and donations, through commercial activities, or through the dues of members who join for reasons other than political advocacy. In these latter categories are labor unions (which workers in unionized businesses often have no choice but to join) and organizations like the AARP which attract members largely on the basis of the "selective incentives" they provide.[42] While most of the forty million members of the AARP may agree with most of the organization's policy positions, AARP membership brings with it a wide range of services and discounts on everything from health insurance to hotels. Moreover, membership dues make up a small part of the AARP's income (with the majority coming from licensing agreements for AARP-branded health plans, life insurance, financial planning, and so on).[43] Because members join for largely nonideological reasons, and because the AARP does not rely on dues to fund its operations, the extent to which the group's positions are constrained by and reflective of its members' policy preferences is much weaker than it is for pure mass-membership advocacy groups like the Sierra Club or the ACLU.

To what extent, then, do the interest groups that tend to align with the preferences of low- or middle-income Americans plausibly reflect the *influence* of the less advantaged over government policy, and to what extent are these congruent preferences merely happy coincidences that arise from interests groups' pursuit of their own agendas? The correlations between the positions coded for each of the forty-three interest groups on my expanded Power 25 list and the preferences of Americans at the 10th, 50th, and 90th income percentiles are shown in table 5.7.[44] The associations shown offer some useful insights into the dynamics of interest groups vis-à-vis the preferences of lower- and higher-income Americans, and I discuss some of these general patterns below. But it is important to keep in mind that these data provide a very partial account of the full constellation of organized groups working to shape federal policy, and that my set of proposed policy changes excludes most of the narrow and typically obscure issues that constitute much of government policy making. I also leave for future studies the analysis of alliances among interest groups—alliances that might, at least under the right circumstances, allow less-powerful interest groups to leverage their resources in ways that might advance the preferences of the less well-off.[45]

The top section of table 5.7 shows the four "pure" mass-membership advocacy organizations among the groups on my list. The policy positions of the Christian Coalition and the National Right to Life Committee are positively related to the preferences of the poor and negatively related to the preferences of the affluent. But none of these associations is especially strong, suggesting only a modest tendency for the preferences of the poor

Table 5.7 Correlations between Public Preferences and Interest Group Positions

	N	10th	50th	90th
		Income Percentile		
Mass membership advocacy organizations				
Christian Coalition	211	.19**	.04	−.15*
National Right to Life Committee	95	.21*	.04	−.24*
National Rifle Association	143	−.24**	−.23**	−.28***
American Israel Public Affairs Committee	99	−.12	−.24*	−.24*
Unions				
AFL-CIO	301	.42***	.38***	.14*
American Federation of State, County, and Municipal Employees	134	.38***	.33***	.12
International Brotherhood of Teamsters	154	.40***	.38***	.21**
United Auto Workers	173	.53***	.48***	.24**
Other organizations that tend to side with the poor				
AARP	301	.52***	.50***	.41***
National Governors' Association	85	.58***	.46***	.39***
Universities	26	.63***	.57**	.37
National Education Association	118	.48***	.41***	.34***
Organizations that tend to side with the affluent				
American Hospital Association	136	.14	.15	.27**
National Federation of Independent Business	245	−.09	−.02	.21***
Securities and investment companies	275	−.10	−.02	.18**
Organizations that tend to side against the poor				
Chamber of Commerce	392	−.20***	−.19***	−.03
National Association of Manufacturers	280	−.33***	−.34***	−.20***
Health Insurance Association	152	−.26***	−.17*	−.10
National Restaurant Association	105	−.39***	−.31***	−.19
Telephone companies	134	−.28***	−.28***	−.07
American Farm Bureau Federation	212	−.20**	−.18**	−.02
Computer software and hardware	159	−.18*	−.17*	.01
Automobile companies	202	−.29***	−.31***	−.17*
Defense contractors	232	−.35***	−.36***	−.23***
Electric companies	194	−.37***	−.38***	−.27***

Table 5.7 (continued)

		Income Percentile		
	N	10th	50th	90th
Other organizations				
Airlines	180	−.13	−.15*	.00
American Bankers Association	171	−.12	−.10	.01
American Council of Life Insurance	87	−.15	−.14	−.10
American Medical Association	127	.09	.06	.16
Association of Trial Lawyers	70	.02	−.11	−.08
Credit Union National Association	82	−.11	−.08	−.08
Independent Insurance Agents of America	96	−.02	−.08	.01
Motion Picture Association of America	57	−.20	−.27*	−.18
National Association of Broadcasters	69	−.29*	−.29*	−.20
National Association of Home Builders	174	.05	.05	.12
National Association of Realtors	128	.05	.08	.13
National Beer Wholesalers Association	170	−.13	−.09	.05
Oil companies	216	−.37***	−.40***	−.33***
Pharmaceutical Research and Manufacturers	159	−.04	−.02	.07
Recording Industry Association	105	−.05	−.04	.02

*p < .05; **p < .01; ***p < .001
N indicates the number of proposed policy changes in dataset on which each organization took a position. Excludes the American Legion and Veterans of Foreign Wars, which took positions on fewer than twenty of the proposed policy changes.

to coincide with the positions of these two interest groups, and at best a modest tendency for policy to align more closely with the preferences of the poor as a result of these groups' efforts.

The strongest positive associations between interest groups' positions and the preferences of the less well-off are shown in the next two sections of table 5.7. The four unions in my expanded Power 25 list show consistently strong tendencies to share the preferences of low- and middle-income Americans, with much weaker (but still positive) associations with the preferences of the affluent. Unions tended to side with the poor and the middle class in opposing free-trade policies and cuts in capital gains and corporate income taxes, and in supporting increases in the minimum wage and the right to strike for groups like firefighters, police officers, and college teachers. Some of these favored changes were supported at lower levels by the affluent (like raising the minimum wage), while others had majorities of the well-off and the poor on opposite sides (like teachers' right to strike).

Based on unions' strong tendency to share the preferences of the less well-off and the large number of policy areas they are engaged in (the AFL-CIO in particular took positions on a large number of issues), unions would appear to be among the most promising interest group bases for strengthening the policy influence of America's poor and middle class. Optimism in this regard must be tempered, however, by the steep decline in private-sector unionization rates over the past sixty years. In addition unions tend to be active on issues on which other powerful interest groups are aligned on the other side. Of the 1,357 proposed policy changes in my dataset on which at least one interest group took a position, interest groups were found on both sides of the issue only 30 percent of the time. In contrast, among the 311 proposed changes on which at least one union took a stand, interest groups were found on both sides 77 percent of the time. Because unions tend to be opposed by other interest groups far more frequently than the average for all interest groups, they are less likely to be able to prevail. Of course poor and middle-class Americans would be even less likely to find their preferences reflected in federal policy were it not for unions' lobbying efforts. Other scholars have examined the obstacles and successes of unions' political efforts in considerable detail.[46] My data are consistent with much of this literature in suggesting both that unions are among the most important forces moving federal policy in a direction desired by the less well-off and that unions' success in these efforts is likely to be fairly limited.

The third section of table 5.7 lists the four remaining interest groups that show strong positive associations with the preferences of the less well-off. The positions of the AARP in support of Medicare and Social Security are often consistent with the preferences of Americans at all income levels, but when preferences diverge (for example, over various market-oriented reforms to these programs), the AARP tends to reflect the desires of those with low and moderate incomes. The considerable power attributed to the AARP as an advocacy organization suggests its important role in maintaining and strengthening government benefits for older Americans, but the exact basis for that power is difficult to discern. The AARP has a large membership and enormous financial resources, but it also advocates positions that strong majorities of the public tend to favor.[47] This rather unique combination of characteristics (and the extent to which the AARP's income derives from its commercial activities) suggests that it cannot serve as a viable model for expanding the role of interest groups in giving a voice to lower-income Americans.

The other three interest groups in this section of table 5.7—universities, the National Governors' Association, and the National Education Association—took positions on relatively few policy issues compared with the interest organizations discussed above. Universities (which share with low- and middle-income Americans their strong support for increasing federal assistance to college students) are engaged on only 26 of my 1,779 proposed policy changes. Of these three organizations, only the National Governors' Association might be viewed as a mechanism of middle- or lower-class influence over federal policy. To the extent that the policy preferences of America's governors reflect their desire to advance the interests of their constituents (either from an ideological commitment or to improve their political prospects), the National Governors' Association lobbying might be an avenue through which less-affluent Americans' preferences help shape federal policy. On the other hand, given the absence of responsiveness of federal policy to the preferences of low- and middle-income Americans, it seems likely that governors too would favor the preferences of their more affluent constituents. If so, the congruence between the NGA's positions and the preferences of the less well-off should be attributed not to the influence of middle-class constituents but to the economic benefits states gain from federal spending on public works and programs like Medicaid and TANF.

The remainder of the interest groups in table 5.7 are business organizations, divided into three sections. The first consists of the few business groups whose positions tend to reflect the preferences of the well-off (although none of these associations is particularly strong). The second set is those business organizations whose positions tend to conflict with the preferences of the poor and whose relationship with the preferences of the affluent are less negative or indistinguishable from zero. Finally, at the bottom of the table are those business groups that took positions that were more or less equally strongly (and negatively) related to the preferences of Americans across the income spectrum (or unrelated to preferences at any income level).

Of the twenty-eight business organizations in the bottom three sections of table 5.7, none has positive and statistically significant associations with the preferences of either poor or middle-income Americans (in contrast, about a dozen of the correlations with each of these two income groups are negative and significant).

In sum, the diverse universe of organized interests (represented in a very partial way in table 5.7) does include groups seeking to promote the preferences of less-well-off Americans. Unfortunately for those concerned about representational inequality, these groups tend to be narrowly focused, disproportionately opposed by other organized interests, and/or declining in size and strength. Still the broader picture as reflected in the statistical analyses presented above is that interest groups sometimes enhance and sometimes diminish the likelihood that low- and middle-income Americans will see their preferences reflected in government policy. As earlier chapters indicated, only affluent Americans appear to have substantial influence over federal policy. This chapter shows that the influence of these citizens, and the lack of influence of the less well-off, cannot be attributed to the operation of interest groups.

Pluralist accounts of interest groups from the 1950s and 1960s often stressed the positive function of organized interests in facilitating popular representation and giving ordinary citizens a voice in government.[48] Pluralism's critics, on the other hand, have tended to focus on the advantages that groups with money and well-defined, narrow interests enjoy.[49] Rather than facilitating responsiveness to the public, these critics argue, the interest group system embodies and perpetuates inequality. Neither of these extreme depictions is consistent with my findings. Organized interests do sometimes push government policy in a direction favored by the public as a whole or by one or another economic subgroup of the public, just as they sometimes push policy in a direction the public opposes. But the interest group system, at least as captured by my coding of the most influential interest groups, appears on balance to neither facilitate nor undermine the public's influence over government policy.

• • •

The findings from previous chapters showing that low- and middle-income Americans lack influence over federal policy are robust to the inclusion of interest groups in the analyses. Neither the direction of interest group alignments nor the extent of interest group engagement significantly alters the patterns of policy responsiveness to Americans at different income levels. While interest groups clearly influence federal policy, they do so independently of the public. Affluent Americans and interest groups both shape federal policy, at times pushing policy in the same direction and at other times in opposite directions. The affluent are more likely to see their preferences reflected in policy outcomes if the balance of interest groups on an issue share those preferences, but the extent to which the affluent move policy in one direction or another is independent of interest groups.

The more detailed analysis of particular issues and interest groups in the final sections of this chapter revealed a variety of specific instances in which interest groups helped move policy in a direction favored more by lower- than by upper-income groups. But these analyses also suggested that such instances are infrequent and often reflect idiosyncratic circumstances—either interest groups that share the preferences of the poor by happy coincidence or the unique case of the AARP, which cannot serve as a general model of interest group advocacy for the needs of the less advantaged.

The liberal citizens groups that some scholars have identified as a counterbalance to the influence of business organizations did not appear on my expanded Power 25 list of interest groups. The Washington insiders *Fortune* surveyed did not view groups like the Sierra Club, the Children's Defense Fund, and the Union of Concerned Scientists as being among the most powerful interest organizations. Taking a wider range of interest groups into account might have altered some of my findings. But the strong correlation between the Power 25 list of interest groups and the broader index of interest group resources constructed by Baumgartner et al. suggests that my story would have likely been much the same even if I had done so.[50]

At any rate, the liberal citizens groups missing from my expanded Power 25 list are not a likely source of influence for low- and middle-income Americans since such groups are more likely to promote the preferences of the more affluent members of the public. As noted above, Berry argues that the liberal citizens groups that emerged over the past decades have focused on postmaterialist issues like civil liberties, consumer protection, and the environment—issues on which Americans at different income levels tend to agree or on which the affluent tend to hold more liberal positions.[51] Even interest groups that explicitly take as their mission addressing the needs of the disadvantaged tend to focus their attention on issues of concern to their least disadvantaged members.[52]

Unions emerged as the interest groups with the most consistent and widespread tendency to share the policy preferences of low- and middle-income Americans. While unions historically have played a central role in obtaining many of the social and economic policies of greatest benefit to these income groups, unions now represent only 12 percent of private-sector workers (down from 36 percent in the 1940s), and their political power has clearly declined.[53] (The lack of union power was perhaps most clearly evidenced by the 1993 passage of NAFTA over strong union opposition and while Democrats controlled both Congress and the White House.)

The good news, such as it is, is that interest groups as a whole do not appear to exacerbate the inequality in policy responsiveness documented in earlier chapters. But neither do they appear to hold much promise for redressing those inequalities in the future.

CHAPTER 6

Parties, Elections, and Democratic Responsiveness

IN THE PREVIOUS CHAPTER I argued that neither the cynical view that interest groups undermine democracy nor the sanguine view that they serve as channels for popular control of government is consistent with my data. Taken as a whole, interest groups neither enhance nor undermine the influence of the public over policy outcomes or consistently shift policy in a direction more congenial to the affluent or the poor. (This is not to deny that interest groups powerfully shape federal policy or that they sometimes push important policies in a direction that one or another subgroup of Americans finds more or less desirable.)

In this chapter I turn my attention to political parties and the elections in which they compete. Like interest groups, political parties are sometimes viewed by observers as a key mechanism of democratic governance and sometimes as an obstacle to popular control. Parties are complex entities with multiple functions. They organize activity within legislatures, field candidates in elections, mobilize and inform the public, embody a wide range of official and unofficial organizations, and operate simultaneously (and sometimes with very different political orientations) in different places and at local, state, and national levels. There is a large literature on the nature of parties in the government, parties as organizations, and parties in the electorate. My particular concern here is with the role of parties in facilitating (or frustrating) the public's influence over government policy, and I will focus on a key distinction between the conception of parties as vote maximizers and the conception of parties as policy maximizers.

One scholarly tradition, most clearly articulated by Anthony Downs, views parties as coalitions of office-seeking politicians whose overarching concern is getting elected and fending off challengers.[1] From this perspective parties are motivated by the desire to obtain and retain control of government, and parties (and the politicians who guide them) adopt policies designed to maximize their appeal to voters. Elections in turn are viewed as the mechanism through which parties' policy commitments are brought in line with the public's preferences. This view of parties is complicated by politicians' need to appeal to both copartisans in primary elections and their constituents more broadly in general elections. It is also complicated by the importance of money and organizational resources in running a successful campaign and the concentration of these resources in the hands of a small number of well-placed groups and individuals. As a result, the conception of parties as election-oriented vote maximizers is not inconsistent with substantial inequality in the segments of the public to which parties and individual politicians are most responsive.

An alternative understanding of political parties sees them as the creatures not of office-seeking politicians but of policy-seeking activists and interest groups.[2] From this perspective, parties in America have evolved from largely independent organizations run by professional politicians and power brokers to captives of "intense policy demanders" who view control of government (or influence over policy making more generally) as a means to an end. Parties, by this account, respond to public preferences to the extent that they must do so to obtain or retain power. But once in power, parties seek to maximize the policy gains for the organized interests, affluent campaign donors, and other policy demanders that form their base of support.

In this chapter I explore patterns of responsiveness and representational inequality as they relate to the four-year federal election cycle, to the length of time one party has held the presidency, and to Democratic versus Republican Party control of government. In chapter 7 I examine the strength of the in-party's dominance and the patterns of policy making across presidential administrations. In each case I find that parties behave more like policy maximizers than vote maximizers, responding to the preferences of the public (and disproportionately to the most affluent segment of the public) when necessary but pursuing their own policy agendas when they can. I show, for example, that policies adopted during presidential election years are more consistent with the preferences of Americans at all income levels compared with policies adopted during other years of the quadrennial election cycle. (Although even in presidential election years, policy responsiveness is substantially stronger for the highest-income Americans.) In a similar vein I show in chapter 7 that the dominance of one party or the other is associated with a lack of responsiveness as the party pursues its own policy agenda, while the heightened political competition that characterizes evenly divided control of Congress is associated with greater responsiveness to the preferences of the public and lower levels of representational inequality.

These and the other analyses in chapters 6 and 7 suggest that American democracy works, at least in the sense that electoral competition generates policy outcomes more responsive to the preferences of the public and (under some limited circumstances) more equally responsive to poor, middle-class, and affluent Americans. But the circumstances that generate these democratically desirable outcomes are infrequent, and the policies that result are more likely to be undone over time.

In this chapter I examine three aspects of political context that might shape policy responsiveness. First, I assess the role of impending elections in strengthening democratic responsiveness and lessening representational inequality. Elections can influence representatives' behavior, and therefore policy responsiveness, through either anticipation or replacement. In the first case the desire for reelection might encourage incumbent representatives to pursue policies popular with their constituents.[3] In the second case elections might serve to replace incumbent representatives who fail to pursue popular policies (or who pursue unpopular policies) with new officeholders whose behavior is more consistent with their constituents' policy preferences.[4] Anticipation should boost responsiveness most in the preelection period since political actors' most recent activities are likely to be the most salient to voters. Replacement should boost responsiveness most following elections in which a new partisan regime is voted into power since the new policies favored by the newly elected leaders will be closer to the public's preferences than those they replace.

Previous scholars have found strong evidence that the link between public preferences and representatives' votes or presidents' policy proposals is stronger during election years than other years, and this pattern may be especially pronounced during presidential election years when both voter turnout and public attention to politics is highest.[5] My analyses show that this pattern of electoral responsiveness holds for policy outcomes as well.

We might expect elections to be particularly important in shaping responsiveness to the less well-off. Under ordinary circumstances, whatever influence poor Americans have over politics is confined primarily to voting, while the affluent are more likely to engage in diverse forms of political activity. Contacting elected representatives, belonging to or participating in organized interest groups, donating money to parties, candidates, or political causes, and even participating in political protests all have greater upward economic biases than voting has.[6] In addition, the least well-off are most likely to be intermittently attentive to politics, tuning in when elections (especially presidential elections) are near and paying little attention otherwise. Consequently officeholders' incentives to pursue the preferences of the affluent are less tied to the electoral cycle than are their incentives to pursue the preferences of the poor. Of course middle-class and affluent Americans also vote (and in somewhat higher proportions than the poor), and campaign donations are concentrated—not surprisingly—during campaign periods. So officeholders have more incentives to appeal to all income levels when elections are near. Still, since the influence of less-affluent Americans is more completely tied to their voting, the election-induced cyclical nature of responsiveness might be greater with regard to lower- than higher-income Americans.

A second way in which elections might shape policy outcomes (and policy responsiveness) is by replacing the officeholders themselves. The replacement of individual legislators who retire or are voted out of office is unlikely to have a substantial impact on policy outcomes, but partisan change in control of the presidency or Congress may. When a new party comes into power in Washington, we would expect the policies it adopts to be more consistent with the public's desires than are those of the party it replaces. But as a party's time in power lengthens, the consistency between preferences and policies is likely to diminish. This pattern might emerge for three distinct reasons. First, as elucidated by Keith Krehbiel's "pivotal politics" theory, when a new party comes into power, the policy status quo is no longer consistent with the in-party's favored policies.[7] The resulting shift in presidential or congressional preferences thus opens up a new set of policies that might achieve sufficient support to be passed by Congress and signed into law. Thus, Krehbiel argues, the flurry of policy making identified with presidential honeymoons should be attributed not to a new president's high popularity or to public enthusiasm about a change in partisan regime, but to the newly emergent disjuncture between the policy status quo and the preferences of the party in power. Change in partisan control, from this perspective, is important not because the parties themselves shape policy outcomes, but because a change in partisan control results in changes in the preferences of the pivotal political actors (such as the president and the sixtieth senator whose vote is needed to override a filibuster).

Expanding on Krehbiel's theory, we might expect that of the set of policies the new party prefers to the status quo, some are more popular with the public and others less so. The subset of policies that are preferred by both the party in power and the public are the most likely to be adopted, while those policies that are supported by the new majority party but not by the public are more likely to be blocked by the minority party. A new partisan regime will therefore be most likely to pursue the low-hanging fruit contained in this subset of popular policies and most likely to succeed in implementing those policy changes. As time goes on, however, the remaining set of popular policies consistent with the in-party's preferences diminishes, and policy adoption is likely to diminish in quantity and in consistency with the public's preferences.

Pivotal politics theory suggests that after an initial flurry of policy making, a new partisan regime will reach the point where any policies that it prefers to the status quo have been implemented and the amount of new policy making will decline dramatically. A somewhat different understanding of the dynamics of government policy making is reflected in the macro-polity perspective of Robert Erikson, Michael MacKuen, and James Stimson.[8] From this perspective, policies become less consistent with public preferences over time because the party in power continues to pursue its preferred policies but in doing so moves existing policy too far in its favored direction. According to these authors, when Democrats are in power, federal policy tends to move further and further leftward over time, while Republicans move policy more and more in a rightward direction. At first the shift in policy that accompanies a change in party control works to bring policy more in line with public preferences (since the previous regime moved policy too far in its own preferred direction). But the longer a party is in power, the greater the gap between the public's preferences and existing policy grows. By this account the public acts as a thermostat calling for more conservative policies when the in-party has pushed policy too far in a liberal direction and for more liberal policies when the in-party has pushed policy too far in a conservative direction.[9]

Both the pivotal politics and macro-polity/thermostat theories predict a decline over time in policy responsiveness once a new party gains control of the government even in the absence of any shift in the preferences of the public. But shifts in public preferences can also contribute to a decline in the preference/policy link in the years after a new partisan regime is established. One basis for shifts in public preferences is changing conditions. For example, when crime increased during the 1960s, the Republican Party's "tough on crime" orientation became more appealing to the public, contributing to Richard Nixon's victory over Hubert Humphrey in 1968.[10] Similarly, as conditions in Iraq deteriorated over time, the popularity of G. W. Bush's foreign policy declined, leading to the Democratic takeover of Congress in 2006. A new party coming into power on the basis of the perceived failures of the previous regime will almost by definition pursue policies more in line with the public's preferences. Once these policy changes are made, however, the new in-party may or may not be able to retain its advantage in the public's mind (depending on the success of its policies and whether the issues that it rode into power continue to be salient).

In sum, we have multiple reasons to expect that government policy will most closely align with the public's preferences after a shift in partisan control, but previous research provides little relevant empirical evidence one way or the other. Legislative productivity does not seem to be clearly related to changes in party control or the length of time a party has held power,[11] and analyses of the public as thermostat have not looked at shifts in partisan control per se.[12] As I show below, policy responsiveness is indeed highest during the first congressional session after a shift in partisan control of the presidency. Relative to other time periods, a new partisan presidential regime appears particularly beneficial to high-income Americans whose preferences are most strongly reflected in policies adopted during these early years after a change in presidential control. As one party's continuous control of the presidency lengthens over time, the preference/policy link becomes uniformly low for all income levels. Thus regime change has an arguably prodemocratic consequence in boosting responsiveness to the well-off, but a clearly antidemocratic consequence in exacerbating representational inequality.

A third aspect of parties and elections that might be expected to influence representational inequality is the degree of Republican versus Democratic control over the federal government. Democrats have long been identified as the party of the working class, and less-well-off Americans continue to identify as Democrats in larger numbers than the affluent. In a 2004 survey 53 percent of respondents at the 10th income percentile identified as Democrats compared with 45 percent of those at the 90th percentile, while Republican identifiers were more numerous among high-income than among low-income respondents by 48 percent to 36 percent.[13] We might therefore expect policy to be more consistent with the preferences of the least well-off during periods of Democratic control and more consistent with the preferences of the affluent when Republicans are in power.

Scholars have found patterns consistent with this expectation, at least for a small number of policies with clear and strongly differential impacts on low- versus high-income Americans. For example, Larry Bartels finds a strong impact of partisan control on the minimum wage (with the minimum wage keeping pace with inflation during Democratic administrations but declining during Republican administrations).[14] On the other hand, there are reasons to think this pattern of partisan policy making linking Democrats with the preferences of the less well-off and Republicans with the economically advantaged may be somewhat limited. First, the traditional policy orientations of the parties tend to align the Democrats with the preferences of lower-income Americans only on economic and social welfare issues (on which both tend to be more liberal) but align the Republicans with the preferences of the less well-off on issues like abortion and gay rights (on which both tend to be more conservative). Second, affluent Americans are more supportive of the shift toward antiregulatory, free-market, and free-trade policies, which has characterized national policy making over the past few decades during both Democratic and Republican administrations (with important deregulation of transportation, finance, and telecommunications under presidents Carter and Clinton and landmark free-trade legislation under Clinton). On many regulatory and market-oriented economic issues, then, the policy orientations of the two parties have become much more similar, if not indistinguishable. Finally, with the federal government's multiple veto points and the Senate's supermajority requirement to overcome a filibuster, even unified party control requires some degree of compromise with the opposing party. In short, the simple association of Republican Party control with policies favored by the well-off is not likely to describe patterns of federal policy making very fully.

EXPANDING AND RESTRUCTURING THE PREFERENCE/POLICY DATASET

As described in chapter 2, the core of my data consists of survey questions posed between 1981 and 2002, with a four-year coding window used to determine whether or not the proposed policy change was adopted. These data have two important limitations for studying change in policy responsiveness over time. First, the four-year coding window is too long to reflect changes in political conditions like the partisan control of Congress or the year in the quadrennial federal election cycle.

In light of this concern, I restructured the data used in previous chapters as follows. I treat each calendar year as a separate observation. If a policy is not adopted in the same year that the survey question is asked, the outcome for that year is coded 0 and the policy is considered to remain on the agenda for the next calendar year. If the policy is also not adopted in the second year (i.e., the calendar year following the year in which the question was asked), the observation for that second year is also coded 0. Policies are not considered to remain on the agenda beyond the second year, and any of the original proposed policy changes that were adopted in the third or fourth years are dropped from the dataset (this eliminates about 6 percent of the proposed policy changes and about 19 percent of the changes that had originally been coded as being adopted within the four-year window). If a policy was adopted in the second year, the observation for that year is coded 1, and if a policy was adopted in the same year the question was asked, the outcome for that year is coded 1 and there is no observation for that proposed policy change for the following year. Thus most proposed policy changes generate two observations (either 0/0 or 0/1, for the first and second years, respectively), while policies adopted in the first year generate only a single observation (see table 6.1). To better reflect the distribution of items on the survey agenda in my original sample, I then reweight the restructured data so that observations reflecting policies adopted in the first year (which generate a single case in the restructured data) are weighted at 1.0 and observations that were adopted in the second year or not adopted in either year (which in either case would generate two separate observations in the restructured data) are weighted at 0.5. Consequently all the original survey questions that remain in the dataset (i.e., all those except questions ad-

Table 6.1 Restructuring the Dataset to Create Two Annual Observations from Each Policy Question

Proposed Change Adopted in Same Year Survey Question Was Asked?	Proposed Change Adopted in Following Year?	First Observation		Second Observation	
		Outcome Code	Weight	Outcome Code	Weight
No	No	0	0.5	0	0.5
No	Yes	0	0.5	1	0.5
Yes	Missing	1	1.0	Missing	Missing

opted in years three or four) are weighted equally, irrespective of whether and when they were adopted.

A second limitation of my core dataset consisting of questions posed between 1981 and 2002 is the lack of variation in partisan control. The president's party controlled both houses of Congress for only two of the twenty-two years in this period (1993 and 1994—the first two years of Bill Clinton's first term).[15] Moreover Clinton came into office with only 43 percent of the popular vote, and the Democrats lost ten seats in the House of Representatives in the 1992 election. For these and other reasons,[16] many of the Democrats' liberal policy reform efforts were either compromised (the Don't Ask, Don't Tell policy on gay people in the military) or defeated (health care reform).[17] Consequently even this brief period of unified government may not reveal much about the impact of complete partisan control on policy outcomes.

To capture periods of stronger unified party control of the federal government, I supplement my 1981–2002 dataset with survey questions asked during 1964–68 and 2005–06. The 1964 election was a landslide victory for President Johnson, and during the 1964–68 period the Democrats held between sixty-four and sixty-eight Senate seats and strong majorities in the House of Representatives. In addition, labor unions were still near their historical peak of private-sector membership and economic inequality was low relative to recent decades.[18] All these factors might plausibly be thought to contribute to greater responsiveness to the preferences of the less well-off, and therefore I chose these years in the mid-1960s as the period during the past half-century that might be expected to result in the greatest degree of representational equality.[19]

In addition to 1964–68, I supplement my core dataset with survey questions asked in 2005 and 2006. These first two years of the second G. W. Bush administration constitute the period of strongest Republican control of the federal government in the postwar period. Although far weaker than the overwhelming Democratic majorities of the mid-1960s, the Republicans did hold the presidency along with a ten-seat advantage in the Senate and a thirty-seat advantage in the House during these two years.

COERCED RESPONSIVENESS AND THE ELECTORAL CYCLE

To assess the impact of electoral proximity on policy responsiveness, I divide my restructured data into policies that were on the agenda during presidential election years, congressional election years, and years in which no federal elections took place, and I restrict the data to presidential administrations with complete data for at least one full electoral cycle.[20]

In most respects the characteristics of the policy agenda across the different years of the electoral cycle hardly change at all: average favorability varies from 53 percent to 55 percent, the proportion of proposed policy changes with lopsided support or opposition varies from 49 percent to 53 percent, and the proportion of proposed changes on which the 10th and 90th income percentiles diverge by more than 10 percentage points varies from 41 percent to 43 percent (none of these differences approaches statistical significance). The differences in responsiveness across the different years of the electoral cycle, then, do not result from variations in the kinds of proposed policy changes that are prominent on the public agenda.

Casual commentary on Washington gridlock suggests that the parties might become less willing to compromise during election years, resulting in less legislation as the out-party works to prevent the majority party from claiming credit for any legislative achievements. My data do fit this pattern, but the differences in the probability of a proposed change being adopted across years of the electoral cycle are quite small. Of the policies on the agenda in my restructured data, 34 percent were adopted in an average nonelection year, compared with 29 percent in a congressional election year and 30 percent in a presidential election year.

Previous studies based on representatives' voting patterns or presidents' policy proposals have found electoral proximity to strengthen policy responsiveness to the public as a whole. My data reflect this pattern, but only for presidential election years. As the top left cell of table 6.2 shows, policy responsiveness in nonelection and congressional election years is 0.35 compared with 0.65 during presidential election years. The analyses reported in table 6.2 also show that the electoral cycle has differential impacts on responsiveness to more- and less-well-off Americans. While the tendency for responsiveness to be greatest in presidential election years holds for all income levels, this pattern is somewhat stronger for the

Table 6.2 Policy Responsiveness and the Federal Election Cycle

	N	All	Income Percentile		
			10th	50th	90th
Nonelection years	844	.35*** (.09)	.20* (.09)	.31*** (.09)	.48*** (.09)
Congressional election years	440	.35** (.13)	.28* (.13)	.31** (.12)	.39** (.12)
Presidential election years	360	.65*** (.17)	.51*** (.16)	.60*** (.16)	.75*** (.17)

	10th vs. 90th Income Percentiles			50th vs. 90th Income Percentiles		
	N	10th	90th	N	50th	90th
Nonelection years	362	−.02 (.14)	.50 (.16)**	400	.02 (.14)	.39 (.16)*
Congressional election years	183	−.16 (.22)	.20 (.22)	216	.25 (.20)	.40 (.23)
Presidential election years	154	.54 (.25)*	1.25 (.35)***	176	.63 (.24)**	.95 (.28)***

Table shows logistic regression coefficients (with standard errors in parentheses). Policy preference measured by the log of the odds ratio of the imputed percentage supporting the proposed policy change at each income level. Bottom half of the table shows policies on which the preferences of the 10th and 90th income percentiles diverge by at least 10 percentage points and the 50th and 90th percentiles by at least 5 percentage points. Analyses are weighted to reflect the distribution of proposed policy changes before restructuring for annual analysis. All the analyses include fixed effects for the four policy domains examined in chapter 4.
$*p < .05; **p < .01; ***p < .001$

poor and middle class, and there is less of a drop-off in responsiveness in nonelection years for Americans at the top of the income distribution.

These patterns of differential responsiveness by income are clearest in the bottom half of table 6.2 (and figure 6.1), which repeats the analyses for those proposed changes on which preferences of the affluent diverge from those of the poor or middle class. Responsiveness to the poor and middle class appears to be completely absent during nonelection years. Congressional elections years show similar lack of responsiveness to the poor and a weak (and nonsignificant) suggestion of responsiveness to the middle class. In contrast the association of preferences and policy outcomes during presidential election years is substantial (and statistically significant) for both these groups. As we might expect, responsiveness to affluent Americans is stronger than responsiveness to the less well-off during all parts of the electoral cycle. But because the only solid evidence

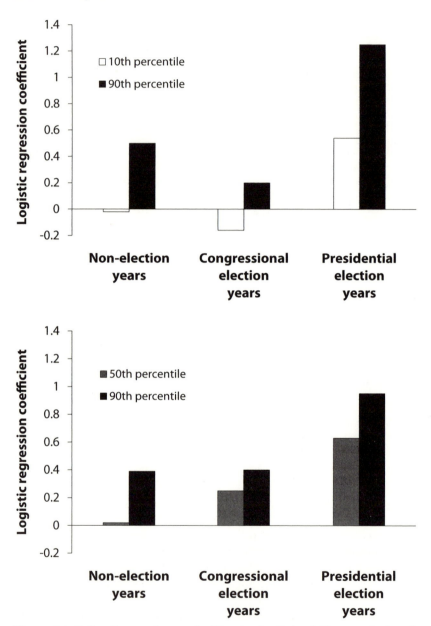

Figure 6.1. Policy Responsiveness by Year in the Federal Election Cycle When Preferences across Income Levels Diverge. Figure shows logistic regression estimates reflecting the strength of the preference/policy link during different years in the quadrennial federal election cycle. See table 6.2 for regression results.

of representation of the poor and middle class concerns presidential election years, these periods reflect the greatest degree of representational equality.

Based on the findings reported in table 6.2, it appears that the electoral pressures on policy makers to respond to the preferences of the public are most important in shaping the representation of less-well-off Americans. It is vital to stress that this is not because elections make policy makers more responsive to the middle class (or the poor) than to the affluent in absolute terms; in every year of the election cycle, policy responsiveness is strongest for the well-off and weakest for the poor. But the degree of representational inequality is lower in election years when democratic pressures are greatest. In a study that so consistently finds the political playing field to be tilted strongly toward the well-off, this evidence of democracy at work is an encouraging sign.

The most plausible explanation for the increase in responsiveness during presidential election years is that citizens' attention to politics typically rises and falls along with the electoral cycle, while other sources of influence over policy makers tend to be more constant over time. Interest groups and party leaders are in a position to monitor legislators' behavior between elections, and legislators' own policy preferences are likely to play a steady role in shaping their actions (net of other factors that do change over time). Elections thus serve democracy by inducing policy makers to take actions that they would otherwise prefer not to take.[21]

If this view of policy makers as coerced by impending elections is correct, then we might expect policies adopted during election years to fare less well over time than policies adopted in other years. Most studies of federal policy making (including my own) neglect the durability of programs once adopted.[22] However, an extensive dataset compiled by Christopher Berry, Barry Burden, and William Howell can be used to assess the durability of programs adopted in different years.[23] Examining federal domestic programs adopted over a three-decade period, Berry, Burden, and Howell find that the funding for programs adopted during presidential election years was more likely to be cut over time compared to programs adopted during other years of the federal election cycle.[24]

This understanding of the political system as both responding to electoral pressure and undermining that responsiveness when pressure abates is less consistent with models of parties as vote maximizers[25] and more consist with the view of parties as policy maximizers seeking to implement their favored policies.[26] From the latter perspective, parties view political power as a means to achieve their policy goals, and voters' approval as a means to achieve political power. When conditions permit, the party's associated activists, donors, and interest groups dictate policy, with officeholders and other party elites attempting to gauge the degree of autonomy from popular preferences they can safely adopt. As we'll see below, this view of parties as policy maximizers rather than vote maximizers is consistent with other patterns of policy responsiveness over time.

Electoral pressures do not eliminate inequality in policy responsiveness, but they do appear to at least partially offset the tendency for policy makers to respond to the preferences of the affluent and ignore those of the middle class and the poor. At the same time, the rather dismaying obverse to this coin is the complete lack of responsiveness to the middle class and the poor during nonelection years. A government that responds to the majority of its citizens only when elections are imminent falls far short of what most would consider a minimum standard of democracy, and all the more so if the policies adopted during these periods of coerced responsiveness are more likely to be eroded over time.

DECLINING RESPONSIVENESS AND PARTISAN REGIME LENGTH

Electoral pressures appear to suppress the antidemocratic urges of policy-maximizing parties in the run-up to high-visibility elections. A more drastic democratic remedy to policy making that strays too far from the public's preferences is to "throw the bums out." I look next at the role of electoral replacement, and in particular at how a new presidential partisan regime responds to the policy preferences of the poor, the middle class, and the affluent. The anticipation of elections, as shown above, appears to increase responsiveness to Americans at all income levels. In contrast, I find that the increased responsiveness associated with a new partisan regime appears to benefit only the affluent. If a new regime first picks the low-hanging fruit of policies on which party preferences and public preferences coincide, it is not the public as a whole whose preferences matter but only those affluent citizens at the top of the income distribution.

Policy shifts—and therefore shifts in the strength of the preference/policy link—might result from changes in partisan control of either the presidency or Congress. The expected impact of a partisan change in the presidency, however, is much clearer than a change in congressional majority. That is because the president is a solitary actor while the Congress consists of multiple actors in two separate institutions with complex systems of control over legislative activity. In the Senate, minority party members must be accommodated to overcome a filibuster, and in both houses, the more conservative Democrats and more liberal Republicans can prevent the majority party from enacting its preferred policies unless that party has an unusually large seat advantage. As an expedient, if imperfect simplification, I therefore identify partisan regimes solely by the party of the president and examine the change in responsiveness to public preferences during periods after control of the presidency switches from one party to the other.

To assess changes in responsiveness as the amount of time a political party has held the presidency grows, I model policy outcomes as a function of public preferences, the number of continuous Congresses that the current president's party has held the presidency, and the interaction of these two predictors. An initial analysis using dummy variables suggests that responsiveness declines the most in absolute terms between the first and second Congresses that a new party holds the presidency, with continuing but less dramatic declines over time.[27] This pattern suggest that the measure of the number of Congresses a party has held the presidency should be logged, and goodness-of-fit tests confirm that a logged indicator performs better than either a linear measure or exponential transformation.

Table 6.3 shows the estimated responsiveness from the model described above. As expected, policy responsiveness for all income levels is strongest during the first Congress of a new presidential party and declines over time (all the analyses of partisan regime length control for presidential election year). By the third Congress after a new party gains control of the presidency, responsiveness is about half the level it was during the first Congress. In the early Congresses of a new presidential partisan regime, the preference/policy link is stronger for affluent Americans than for the less well-off, but it also declines more steeply such that responsiveness to all income levels is uniformly low when a party has held the presidency for a substantial period.

To better gauge the influence of more- and less-well-off Americans, I repeat these analyses restricting the sample to policies on which preferences of the 10th and 90th income percentiles diverge by at least 10 percentage points and those on which the 50th and 90th percentiles diverge by at least 5 points (bottom half of table 6.3). Consistent with previous analyses, eliminating those policies that show little difference across income has little impact on policy responsiveness for the affluent but a substantial impact on the middle class and the poor (figure 6.2). The top panel of figure 6.2 shows essentially no responsiveness to the preferences of the 10th income percentile even in the first Congress of a new presidential regime. The bottom panel shows some responsiveness to middle-income Americans, while the decline in responsiveness is again steeper for the affluent. As a result, representational inequality is greatest during the early Congresses when responsiveness to both the middle class and the affluent is highest, but the decline in inequality is of little benefit to middle-income Americans since it is accompanied by a decline in responsiveness to their preferences as well.

Table 6.3   Policy Responsiveness and the Length of the Presidential Partisan Regime

	All	Income Percentile		
		10th	50th	90th
Preference	.66 (.11)***	.50 (.11)***	.61 (.10)***	.76 (.11)***
Congress number	−.30 (.11)**	−.36 (.11)***	−.30 (.11)**	−.25 (.11)*
Preference * Congress number	−.28 (.11)**	−.18 (.10)	−.26 (.10)**	−.34 (.10)***

	10th vs. 90th Income Percentiles		50th vs. 90th Income Percentiles	
	10th	90th	50th	90th
Preference	.10 (.15)	.77 (.17)***	.35 (.14)*	.76 (.17)***
Congress number	−.63 (.16)***	−.47 (.17)**	−.54 (.15)***	−.44 (.16)**
Preference * Congress number	.01 (.17)	−.40 (.18)*	−.14 (.17)	−.38 (.19)*

Table shows logistic regression coefficients (with standard errors in parentheses). Congress number refers to the number of continuous Congresses the current president's party has held control of the presidency. Policy preference measured by the log of the odds ratio of the imputed percentage supporting the proposed policy change at each income level. Bottom half of the table shows policies on which the preferences of the 10th and 90th income percentiles diverge by at least 10 percentage points and the 50th and 90th percentiles by at least 5 percentage points. Analyses are weighted to reflect the distribution of proposed policy changes before restructuring for annual analysis. All the analyses include controls for presidential election year and fixed effects for the four policy domains examined in chapter 4. Full regression results appear in table A6.5.
$*p < .05; **p < .01; ***p < .001$

The patterns of responsiveness revealed by these analyses of partisan regime duration suggest a very different set of mechanisms from those implied by the analyses of the presidential election cycle reported above. While the latter appear to reflect the coercive power of voters to shape the behavior of incumbent officials, the higher responsiveness during the first Congresses of a new regime suggest the importance of electoral replacement in shaping government policy to match the preferences of the (affluent) public. Past research has found both the conversion (or coercion) of incumbent legislators and the replacement of legislators during elections to be important in generating responsiveness to public preferences.[28] While hardly definitive, the results from these two sets of analyses of my data suggest that impending elections may be somewhat more important in generating responsiveness to the least well-off (table 6.2), while both electoral anticipation and electoral replacement enhance policy

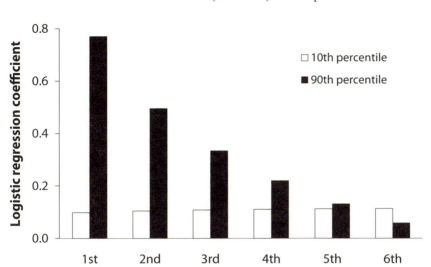

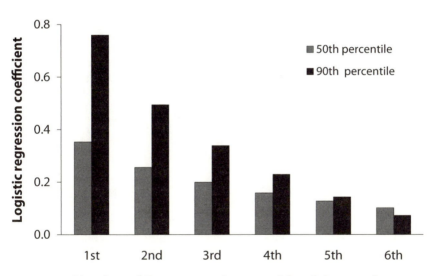

Figure 6.2. Policy Responsiveness by Length of Partisan Regime When Preferences across Income Levels Diverge. Figures show logistic regression estimates reflecting the strength of the preference/policy link during each successive Congress that a president's party holds the presidency (that is, the first through sixth Congresses after control of the presidency changes from one party to the other). See tables 6.3 and A6.1 for regression results.

responsiveness for middle-class and, especially, affluent Americans (table 6.3 and figure 6.2).

PARTISAN CONTROL

Although the American party system has traditionally been viewed as rooted less in economic class than are many European democracies, the Democratic Party is still associated with unions and the working class and the Republican Party with business interests and the affluent.[29] As I show below, downwardly redistributive policies like increases in the minimum wage or tax reforms that increase the progressivity of the tax code are more common when Democrats control the national government, and upwardly redistributive policies like reductions in the estate tax are more common under Republican rule. But the broader expectation that the preferences of low- or middle-income Americans would be reflected more strongly in policy outcomes under Democratic than Republican control is not met. My data show the expected pattern of partisan responsiveness on social welfare issues only, and even there the party differences are modest. For moral/religious issues, foreign policy, and economic issues, responsiveness to all income levels is higher under Republican than under Democratic control. I discuss below the specific policy issues that account for these partisan patterns. Of particular note, two factors explain the absence of the expected association between Democratic Party control and policy responsiveness to the poor. First, redistributive policies account for only a portion of the economic and social welfare policy issues (and a small minority of all policy issues) in my dataset; and second, preferences on these redistributive policies are often similar for poor and affluent Americans.

As described above, my expanded dataset includes seven years of unified Democratic control (under Johnson and Clinton) and two years of unified Republican control (under G. W. Bush). Consequently, most of the policy outcomes in my data took place during various constellations of divided government. To assess the influence of partisan control in a way that reflects more than the few years of unified government in my data, I constructed a 0-to-1 scale indicating the degree to which the Democratic or Republican Party controlled the federal government, with the presidency accorded one-half point and each house of Congress one-quarter point. High scores on this scale reflect a greater degree of Republican control such that unified Democratic control is scored 0, unified Republican control 1, and divided control between 0.25 and 0.75 depending on which institutions were controlled by which party (the eight periods of partisan

Table 6.4 Party Control Score

Years in Which Policy Questions Were Asked	President	House of Representatives	Senate	Party Control Score
1964–68	Johnson	Democrats	Democrats	0.00
1981–86	Reagan	Democrats	Republicans	0.75
1987–88	Reagan	Democrats	Democrats	0.50
1989–92	G.H.W. Bush	Democrats	Democrats	0.50
1993–94	Clinton	Democrats	Democrats	0.00
1995–2000	Clinton	Republicans	Republicans	0.50
2001–02	G. W. Bush	Republicans	Democrats[*]	0.75
2005–06	G. W. Bush	Republicans	Republicans	1.00

[*]From late January through late May 2001, the Senate was split 50/50 with Vice President Cheney casting the deciding vote. In late May Jim Jeffords left the Republican Party, giving the Democrats effective control of the Senate. My data are not fine-grained enough to distinguish these months in early 2001, so I code Democratic control of the Senate for all of the 107th Congress (2001–02).

control in my data and the resulting scale scores for each are shown in table 6.4).

As table 6.4 shows, assessments of the impact of Democratic versus Republican Party control hinge on the difference between the seven years of unified Democratic control (1964–68 under Johnson and 1993–94 under Clinton) and the ten years of Republican control (1981–86 under Reagan and 2001–02 and 2005–06 under G. W. Bush). For the remaining twelve years in my dataset, control of the federal government was evenly divided, with either a Democratic president and Republican Congress (1995–2000) or a Republican president and Democratic Congress (1987–1992). Thus even with my more nuanced scale of party control, the number of distinct periods is quite limited. We must therefore be alert to the possibility that at least some of the partisan patterns my data reveal will reflect not enduring characteristics of Democratic and Republican control, but the idiosyncrasies of the particular administrations and Congresses examined.

It is also important to keep in mind that my scale of Republican Party control—like any similar summary measure—is a substantial simplification of the factors that shape the parties' influence over federal policy making. A more complete assessment would require consideration of the

size of the partisan majority, the supermajority requirement to end a filibuster in the Senate, and the degree of ideological cohesion within each
party (an ideologically diverse party with a slim majority of seats would
not be able to exert as much control over the legislative process as a more
ideologically homogeneous party with the same size majority). But given
the ongoing debates among political scientists about the degree of party
influence in the House and Senate and the role of partisan seat advantage
in shaping that influence, the uncertainties surrounding a more nuanced
measure of partisan control would be considerable.[30]

The model I use to assess the variation in responsiveness by degree
of Republican Party control is to regress policy outcome on the public's
policy preference, the degree of Republican control, and the interaction
of these two predictors. The dataset used for these analyses consists of
the restructured annual measures of proposed policy changes described
at the beginning of this chapter. The coefficients from these equations
(run separately for different subsets of policies and levels of income) are
then used to calculate the strength of the preference/policy link under maximum Democratic control and maximum Republican control. I use the
labels "maximum control" rather than "unified control" to reflect the
fact that these estimates are based on the full array of partisan configura-
tions in my data, not just the nine years of unified control. As such they
constitute the predicted levels of responsiveness under the assumption
that whatever difference it might make to have one party or the other
exert greater sway over national policy making, that difference will be
greater according to the *degree* to which the Congress and presidency are
in that party's hands.

The top panel of table 6.5 shows the associations of preferences and
policy outcomes from four logistic regressions (one for each income category; the full regression results that produced these estimates are reported
in table A6.2). Policy responsiveness is strongest for the affluent whether
Democrats or Republicans dominate the policy-making institutions of
the national government, but some subtle partisan differences in representational inequality are evident in these results. In comparing responsiveness to the affluent and the poor, inequality appears to be somewhat
greater under Republican than Democratic control, while inequality between the affluent and the middle class appears somewhat stronger under
Democratic control. These patterns across income groups appear more
clearly in the bottom panel of table 6.5 and in figure 6.3, where the analyses are restricted to policies on which preferences across income groups
diverge.

A stronger and more consistent pattern evident across all the cells in
table 6.5 is the greater responsiveness to the preferences of all income
levels under Republican than under Democratic control. In the top panel,

Table 6.5   Policy Responsiveness and Partisan Control

	N	Income Percentile			
		All	10th	50th	90th
All policies					
Maximum Republican control	2229	.56**	.42**	.52**	.60**
Maximum Democratic control		.25**	.22	.20*	.31**

When Preferences across Income Levels Diverge

	10th vs. 90th Income Percentiles			50th vs. 90th Income Percentiles		
	N	10th	90th	N	50th	90th
All policies						
Maximum Republican control	922	.27*	.69**	1055	.56**	.72**
Maximum Democratic control		.08	.26		.09	.42*

Table shows logistic regression coefficients (or differences in logistic regression coefficients) indicating the association between preferences and policy outcomes. Significance levels based on bootstrap confidence intervals. Policy preference measured by the log of the odds ratio of the imputed percentage supporting the proposed policy change at each income level. Analyses are weighted to reflect the distribution of proposed policy changes before restructuring for annual analysis and to give proposed changes on the agenda in each calendar year equal weight. The analyses include fixed effects for the four policy domains in chapter 4. Analyses in bottom half are restricted to policies on which the preferences of the 10th and 90th income percentiles diverge by at least 10 percentage points or the 50th and 90th percentiles diverge by at least 5 percentage points. Full regression results appear in table A6.2.
*$p < .05$; **$p < .01$; ***$p < .001$

which includes all the proposed changes in my restructured dataset, the preference/policy link is over twice as strong under maximum Republican control as it is under maximum Democratic control. The difference in responsiveness under Republican and Democratic control is somewhat larger for affluent and middle-class Americans than for the poor (for whom the partisan difference does not reach statistical significance).

As noted above, any analysis of partisan control over a limited number of decades runs the risk of attributing to the parties differences that are in fact idiosyncratic to the particular administrations and political conditions associated with the periods of Democratic or Republican control examined. Thus we might wonder how much of the partisan differences shown in table 6.5 are a function of the particular periods of strong party control represented in my data. Repeating the analyses reported in the top row of the table but excluding data from the G. W. Bush years shows a similar pattern: the preference/policy link under maximum Republican control is about twice as strong as under maximum Democratic control. On the other hand, removing the Johnson years from the data does reduce

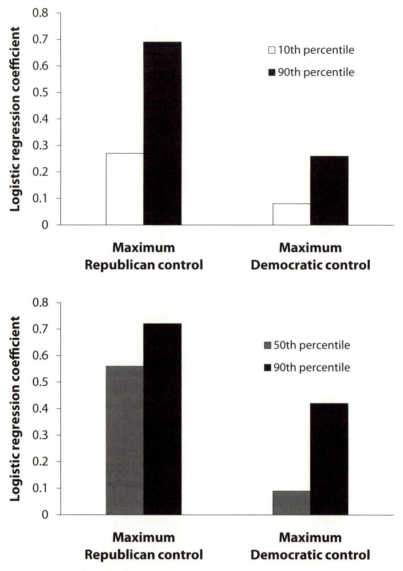

Figure 6.3. Policy Responsiveness under Maximum Republican or Democratic Party Control When Preferences across Income Levels Diverge. Figures show logistic regression estimates reflecting the strength of the preference/policy link. See tables 6.5 and A6.2 for regression results.

the partisan difference; excluding data from the 1960s increases the predicted association of preferences and policies under full Democratic control from 0.25 to 0.40—much closer to the estimated association under full Republican control.

Excluding these two extreme periods of partisan control, then, suggests that the basic pattern of results based on the full dataset are not a reflection of the idiosyncrasies of the Bush years but are somewhat dependent on the low level of responsiveness under President Johnson (a topic I explore in chapter 7). Yet even with the Johnson years removed from the data, policy responsiveness remains slightly (although nonsignificantly) stronger under Republican than under Democratic Party control.[31]

To elucidate the substantive policy issues that give rise to the partisan differences in representation shown in table 6.5, table 6.6 shows the same estimates of responsiveness under maximum Republican and Democratic control separately for each of the four broad policy domains examined in chapter 4. The first column of table 6.6 reveals that public preferences and government policy are more tightly aligned under Republican control in all policy domains except social welfare. The specific policies that account for the partisan differences in the economic, foreign policy, and social welfare domains appear for the most part to reflect not the idiosyncrasies of particular administrations but the enduring policy orientations of the two parties. Within the economic policy domain the stronger preference/policy link under Republican control reflects the popularity of income and inheritance tax cuts under Reagan and G. W. Bush as well as most of the antiregulatory policies adopted under Reagan and the unpopularity of the 1993 Clinton tax increase (adopted under unified Democratic control), and the unpopularity of the Johnson administration's income tax surcharge to help pay for the Vietnam War.

Whether Americans at any given income level are wise to oppose tax increases and support tax cuts is a complicated question that I take up briefly in chapter 8. But the fact remains that, wise or not, the public almost uniformly displays antitax preferences tempered only slightly by variations in the distributional character of the proposed tax changes in my dataset. Of those tax changes in my dataset that occurred when one or the other party disproportionately controlled federal policy making, most of the significant tax increases took place during periods of Democratic control (1968 and 1993), and most of the tax cuts during periods of Republican control (1981, 1986, 2001, and 2003).[32]

In the social welfare policy domain responsiveness to public preferences across all income levels combined is similar under Republican and Democratic Party control. But the patterns of responsiveness for Americans at different income levels vary considerably. Under maximum Republican control the preference/policy link is weakest for the poor and

Table 6.6 Policy Responsiveness and Partisan Control by Policy Domain

		Income Percentile		
	N	10th	50th	90th
Economic policy				
Maximum Republican control	482	.96**	.91**	1.16**
Maximum Democratic control		.02	.07	.05
Social welfare				
Maximum Republican control	454	.10	.29	.41*
Maximum Democratic control		.32*	.20	.15
Foreign policy				
Maximum Republican control	613	.31*	.52**	.60**
Maximum Democratic control		.13	.07	.31*
Moral/religious issues				
Maximum Republican control	146	1.48*	1.42**	1.61**
Maximum Democratic control		.19	.53	.76

Table shows logistic regression coefficients (or differences in logistic regression coefficients) indicating the association between preferences and policy outcomes. Significance levels based on bootstrap confidence intervals. Policy preference measured by the log of the odds ratio of the imputed percentage supporting the proposed policy change at each income level. Analyses are weighted to reflect the distribution of proposed policy changes before restructuring for annual analysis and to give proposed changes on the agenda in each calendar year equal weight. Full regression results appear in table A6.3.
*$p < .05$; **$p < .01$

strongest for the affluent, while under Democratic control this association is reversed. These patterns reflect the traditional association of the Democratic Party with the welfare state (broadly understood to include not just antipoverty programs but pensions, health care, education, and spending on public works of all sorts). Although none of the individual partisan comparisons in the social welfare domain reaches statistical significance, the greater responsiveness to the well-off under Republican control in contrast with the greater responsiveness to the poor when the Democrats hold sway in Washington is significantly different at $p < 0.05$.

In the foreign policy domain responsiveness to public preferences is higher under Republican than under Democratic control, although this difference is only statistically significant for middle-income Americans. The patterns of inequality in foreign policy are slightly different depending on the party in power. Under Republican control the largest difference concerns the lower responsiveness to the poor than to the other two income groups, while under Democratic control it is the greater responsiveness to the affluent that differs from the rest. These distinct patterns reflect the kinds of issues that divide the poor from the middle class and affluent, on the one hand, and the affluent from the middle class and the poor, on the other.

In the foreign policy domain poor Americans were distinctive in supporting proposed policies after 9/11 that singled out Arabs or Muslims (e.g., for more intensive security checks at airports or requiring American Muslims to carry a special ID card) or that impinged on citizens' privacy by allowing the government to monitor the telephone calls and e-mails of ordinary Americans on a regular basis. Since these policies were rejected (for the most part) under Republican control, the middle class and affluent (majorities of whom opposed all these proposed policies) fared better with regard to policies related to the war on terror. In contrast affluent Americans were distinctive from others in their support for NAFTA and other free-trade policies adopted during the Clinton administration, as well as Clinton's efforts to reduce the size of the U.S. Armed Forces and increase aid to the countries of the former Soviet Union.[33] Consequently Republican policies tended to reflect the preferences of both the middle class and the affluent more than the poor, while policies adopted under Democratic control tended to align (albeit weakly) with the affluent and not with either of the other two groups.

While the patterns of foreign policy preferences across income groups differed for the issues outlined above, the broader pattern of responsiveness in the foreign policy domain is the consistently stronger preference/policy link under Republican than under Democratic control at all income levels. This pattern reflects the broad popularity of the Reagan administration's prodefense policies (including the substantial expansion of defense spending, the Strategic Defense Initiative antimissile program, and the deployment of new nuclear missiles in Europe) as well as support for the Afghan and Iraq wars, which was strong during most of the first six years of G. W. Bush's tenure.

In the moral/religious issues domain the higher level of responsiveness during Republican Party control partly reflects the timing of these proposed policy changes and in all likelihood is not indicative of the consistent policy orientations of the two parties over the past couple of decades (especially with regard to high-income Americans, who tend to hold preferences in this domain that are more consistent with the Democratic Party's liberal leanings).[34]

Although my data extend back to the mid-1960s, religious-based moral issues were not strongly politicized during the early postwar decades and did not constitute a significant part of the survey agenda of proposed policy changes (or the government agenda of actual policy changes) until the 1990s. In my dataset of proposed policy changes, religious/moral issues constituted less than 2 percent of all proposed changes during the Johnson, Reagan, and G.H.W. Bush administrations, increasing to 6 percent under Clinton and 9 percent under G. W. Bush. This appears to reflect not just a change in the behavior of survey organizations, but the paucity of attention to these issues at the federal level prior to the 1990s (despite the strong association of President Reagan with the Moral Majority and other elements of the religious Right). As an independent indicator of federal policy makers' attention to moral/religious issues, consider the number of abortion votes in the House of Representatives each year. During Reagan's terms in office, for example, abortion votes in the House occurred less than twice per year. This increased to about four votes per year under G.H.W. Bush and eleven per year in the first years of Clinton's presidency.[35]

Given the lack of religious/moral issues in my dataset prior to the Clinton years, the partisan differences in responsiveness in this domain primarily reflect the contrast between the first two years of Clinton's presidency (with unified Democratic Party control) and the years of Republican control under G. W. Bush. During the early Clinton years, the most prominent moral/religious issue concerned gays in the military (on which Americans were split); under Bush, the most prominent moral/religious issues concerned Bush's faith-based social service initiative and the debate over federal funding for stem cell research. Americans at all income levels strongly supported the faith-based initiative, while the compromise position on stem cell research taken by the Bush administration was arguably more consistent with the ambivalent views expressed by lower- and middle-income Americans than with the views of the well-off (see chapter 4).

Although abortion policy received more attention than any other single moral/religious issue represented in my dataset, gay rights (including service in the military), stem cell research, and federal funding for religious organizations that provide social services were the most prominent issues during the periods of strong party control. Consequently the higher level of policy responsiveness in this domain during Republican control reflects in large measure the ambivalence of the public toward Clinton's efforts to revise the military's policy on homosexuals and the popularity of Bush's high-profile faith-based initiative. If abortion had been a more prominent issue on the federal agenda during the periods of strong party control in my dataset, we might have found a different pattern of responsiveness, especially for the affluent, who tend to share the Democratic Party's more pro-choice position on abortion.[36]

Among the American public, Democratic identifiers have outnumbered Republican identifiers consistently since at least the 1930s. It is therefore surprising to find that policies adopted during periods of greater Republican control are generally more consistent with public preferences than those adopted during periods of strong Democratic control. As an independent check on this finding, I analyzed the American National Election

Study's 7-point issue scales on which respondents are asked to place themselves and both major political parties. Combining the seventy-two partisan comparisons from all available data from 1970 through 2008, I found that respondents placed themselves closer to their perceptions of the Republican Party's position on fifty-seven occasions and closer to the Democratic Party's on fifteen occasions.[37]

If policies adopted during periods of Republican control of the national government are more consistent with the preferences of the public at all income levels and in most policy domains, how, one might wonder, have the Democrats managed to maintain their viability as a national political party? One factor may be the strong appeal of and high importance attached to Social Security and Medicare. Although these two programs do figure prominently in my dataset, their salience to voters may exceed their representation on the survey agenda, and the long-standing perception of the Democratic Party's support for these two programs may help cement voters' attachment to the Democrats. More broadly the overall Republican advantage on policy issues that is reflected in tables 6.5 and 6.6 is partially offset by the perception that the Democrats are the party of the middle class or the "common man" and the Republicans the party of business. This perception is, of course, rooted in part in the specific policies that the two parties tend to endorse (including their respective orientations toward Medicare and Social Security). But the image of the Democrats as the party of the working class goes beyond a set of policy positions and constitutes a perception of the kinds of people who identify as Democrats and the kinds of people whose interests the party represents.

In their examination of the nature of partisan attachment, Donald Green, Bradley Palmquist, and Eric Schickler argue that citizens ask themselves two questions: "What kinds of social groups come to mind as I think about Democrats, Republicans, and Independents? [And] Which assemblage of groups (if any) best describes me?"[38] While the bases of party attachment surely vary from person to person, these more social as opposed to policy-based foundations of partisan attachment do appear to play a central role in shaping party identification (and consequently voting), as Green, Palmquist, and Schickler show.

Reflecting the diverse considerations that drive partisan attachments, the bases of partisan attraction appear to differ for the two major political parties, with the appeal of the Democratic Party depending more on its perceived social composition and the appeal of the Republican Party more on its issue positions. The different basis of attraction to the two major political parties can be seen in survey questions that ask respondents what they like about each party. The American National Election Study has been asking this open-ended question in the same format since

1972. When asked "Is there anything in particular you like about the Democratic Party? [If so] What is that?" only 32 percent of respondents mentioned any policy or philosophy of governing while 42 percent mentioned a connection between the party and a social group. In response to this same question asked about the Republicans, 56 percent mentioned a policy or philosophy of governing and only 6 percent a social group.[39]

In addition to its more favorable social group associations, the Democratic Party may benefit from the better economic performance under its stewardship, at least in the postwar years. The state of the national economy is a powerful determinant of congressional and presidential voting,[40] and economic growth has been stronger for Americans at all levels of the economic distribution under Democratic than under Republican presidents.[41]

As shown above, policies adopted during periods of greater Republican control appear to be more consistent with the preferences of the poor than those adopted under stronger Democratic Party control. But this finding should not be understood to mean that Republican policies are necessarily better for the poor. People are sometimes bad judges of their own interests, and poor Americans—like those of every economic position— sometimes support policies that they recognize to conflict with their material interests but that they value for other reasons (fairness, patriotism, humanitarian concern, etc.).

The greater consistency of poor Americans' preferences with policies adopted under Republican control should also not be understood as indicating that Republican policies are more likely to redistribute resources toward the less advantaged than Democratic policies. About 11 percent of the proposed policy changes in my dataset can be clearly classified as downwardly redistributive, including proposals to raise the minimum wage, protect the right to strike, expand federal college assistance, lower taxes for low-income Americans or raise taxes for those with high incomes, and protect or expand government support for health care. An additional 8 percent of proposed policy changes can be classified as upwardly redistributive, including proposals to restrict welfare benefits in various ways, reduce inheritance, capital gains, or income taxes imposed on the affluent, cut federal spending on means-tested health care or education benefits, and restructure Medicare or Social Security in ways that would make those programs less beneficial to the poor.

As expected, poor Americans were more supportive of policy changes that would redistribute resources downward and affluent Americans were more supportive of changes that would redistribute resources upward, but the differences were fairly modest. On average, downwardly redistributive policies were supported by 65 percent of respondents at the 10th income percentile and 58 percent of respondents at the 90th percentile, while upwardly redistributive policies received support from 41 percent of the poor and 49 percent of the affluent. The modest size of these differences attests to the popularity of many downwardly redistributive policies, including the minimum wage, federal support for education and health care, and means-tested benefits that are not viewed as substitutes for employment (for example, child care, job training, medical care, legal aid, and housing assistance). In addition some upwardly redistributive policies receive strong support even from the least well-off. Majorities of poor people, for example, favored imposing work requirements and time limits on welfare recipients, eliminating the inheritance tax, cutting capital gains tax rates, and giving employers a stronger voice on the National Labor Relations Board.

The public's preferences on redistributive policies are not as strongly differentiated by income as one might expect. But the impact of partisan control over the adoption of upwardly and downwardly redistributive policies is quite strong. The probability of a policy being adopted that would redistribute resources toward the least well-off was twice as high during periods of maximum Democratic than of maximum Republican control (0.31 versus 0.15, $p < 0.04$), with even larger partisan differences apparent for policy changes that would redistribute resources toward the most affluent (0.07 during periods of maximum Democratic control versus 0.39 under maximum Republican control, $p < 0.03$; see table A6.4). On redistributive issues policy outcomes depend greatly on which party controls the government in Washington, but redistributive issues constitute fewer than one in five of the proposed policy changes in my dataset, and preferences on redistributive issues are not dramatically different for low- and high-income Americans. As a consequence Democratic Party control does not have the positive impact on policy responsiveness for less-advantaged Americans that income-based patterns of partisan identification might lead one to expect. As table 6.6 shows, policies in the social welfare domain adopted under Democratic control are more consistent with the preferences of the poor than those adopted while Republicans held power in Washington, but the same is not true for the other policy domains I examined. Nor is there any consistent tendency for representational inequality to be lower under periods of Democratic control.

These findings may be disappointing to those who look to the Democratic Party as the ally of the disadvantaged. In some respects the Democratic Party has indeed served this function, and this is reflected in the pattern of partisan responsiveness in the social welfare domain shown above. But in other domains policies adopted under Republican control appear to be more consistent with the preferences of all income groups than are those adopted during periods dominated by the Democratic Party. Observers on the left might view some of these popular Republican policies as inconsistent with the true interests of poor or middle-class Americans and attribute the public's support to false consciousness of one form or another (an issue I take up in chapter 8). In other cases left-leaning observers might be inclined to view the Democratic Party as having abandoned the disadvantaged out of either political expediency or misplaced enthusiasm for free-market reforms that disproportionately benefit the well-off. And in some cases—like abortion or gay rights—the traditional liberal policy orientations of the Democratic Party are more closely aligned with the preferences of higher-income Americans. In sum, partisan control does affect policy responsiveness, but not in the ways most observers would expect. Downwardly redistributive policies were much more likely to be adopted during periods of Democratic control, but these are only a small subset of all federal policies, and in other respects the policies adopted under Republican control were more consistent with the preferences expressed by affluent and poor Americans alike.

• • •

In the analyses of contextual changes discussed above, I have examined each of the three hypothesized factors separately. The electoral cycle, the length of time the presidency was held by the same party, and the degree to which the Democratic rather than Republican Party controlled the national government all shaped representation. These three significant moderators of responsiveness cannot simply be combined into a single statistical model because the subsets of the data and the weighting schemes I used differ across the analyses.[42] Still, the two excluded predictors can be added to each of these analyses to provide some gauge of the sensitivity of the results to multivariate controls.

Table 6.7 shows the relevant interaction terms for each of the three significant influences on responsiveness from the original analyses and those same coefficients when the other two predictors (and their interactions with preferences) are added to the logistic equations (full results in table A6.5). The results show that each of these three factors moderates the impact of preferences on policy outcomes independently of the others. There are no substantial changes in the estimated coefficients when the controls are added. The largest changes that do emerge in the multivariate analyses concern the election cycle (in the top two rows of table 6.7) and suggest that the apparent impact of presidential election year as an influence on policy responsiveness is strengthened by taking partisan control and partisan regime length into account.

Chapter 4 showed that representational inequality is spread broadly, if not exactly equally, across the different domains of federal government policy. Chapter 5 showed that interest groups, while important in shap-

Table 6.7   Multivariate Analyses of Policy Responsiveness

		Income Percentile		
	All	10th	50th	90th
Presidential election year	.30 (.18)*	.28 (.17)*	.29 (.17)*	.30 (.19)
(with control variables)	.43 (.19)*	.38 (.18)*	.40 (.18)*	.45 (.20)**
Partisan regime length	−.28 (.10)**	−.21 (.10)*	−.24 (.10)*	−.35 (.10)***
(with control variables)	−.27 (.11)**	−.21 (.10)*	−.23 (.10)*	−.35 (.10)***
Partisan control	.31 (.18)*	.20 (.17)	.32 (.17)*	.28 (.18)
(with control variables)	.27 (.18)	.18 (.17)	.29 (.17)*	.23 (.18)

Table reports the interaction of preferences with the three indicated influences on policy responsiveness. Control variables consist of each of the other two influences on responsiveness shown in this table and their interactions with preferences. Full results appear in table A6.5.
*$p < .05$; **$p < .01$; ***$p < .001$ (one-tailed tests)

ing policy outcomes, do not account for the broad patterns of representational inequality documented in chapters 3 and 4. In contrast, this chapter showed significant differences in responsiveness and in representational inequality as a function of political conditions. First, impending elections enhance responsiveness toward the preferences of all income levels, but most importantly for poor and middle-income Americans for whom there is little evidence of responsiveness in nonelection years. Second, new partisan presidential regimes display significantly greater responsiveness to the preferences of the affluent but not of the middle class or the poor. Finally, policy responsiveness is stronger for Americans at all income levels when the Republican Party holds the reins of government, with the one exception of poor people's preferences on social welfare issues. At the same time I found that upwardly redistributive policies are far more common during periods of strong Republican control, while policies that redistribute resources to the less advantage are far more likely to be adopted when Democrats control Congress and the White House.

This strong link between party control and redistributive policies underscores the conception of parties as policy maximizers. Activist groups, major donors, and interest organizations aligned with each party help shape the party's agenda, while the preferences of broad groups of constituents—even affluent ones—appear to shape policy outcomes only under limited conditions, such as impending presidential elections or changes in partisan regime.

Large-scale democracy is inconceivable without elections, and most observers view political parties as equally essential to the democratic control of national governments. But parties have their own policy agendas, and elections appear to be only modestly successful at aligning policy outcomes with the preferences of the public. As we'll see in the next chapter, when one party gains strong control of the levers of government, the preferences of the public—including its most affluent segments—are least likely to be reflected in policy outcomes.

CHAPTER 7

Democratic Responsiveness across Time

AMERICAN POLITICS HAS CHANGED in important ways over the decades covered by my data. The parties today are more polarized than they were in the 1960s, the media environment through which citizens experience elections and learn about officeholders' actions has changed dramatically, the partisan division of Congress has become markedly more equal, political campaigns have become vastly more expensive, and economic conditions have shifted as income and wealth have become increasingly concentrated at the top of the distribution. It would be surprising if these and other changes in political and economic conditions had no impact on the responsiveness of policy makers to public preferences.

The analyses of change over time in this chapter do reveal an important general trend: the strengthening of policy responsiveness for affluent Americans. But they also strongly reinforce the notion that short-term political circumstances are critical in shaping the degree to which government policy reflects the preferences of the governed, especially for nonaffluent Americans. In the following pages I examine broad temporal changes in responsiveness to different income groups over the forty years my dataset covers, I look in more detail at the nature of representation during different presidential administrations, and I examine the impact on responsiveness of changes in gridlock and majority-party seat advantage.

Contrary to my expectations, my results show that the strong Democratic Party control during the Johnson years did not coincide with high responsiveness to the less well-off. Instead this period—like the period of strong Republican control in 2005 and 2006—was characterized by extremely low levels of responsiveness to all income levels. During these periods the parties behaved like policy maximizers, pursuing their own policy agendas in apparent indifference to the preferences of the public. (Of course some of the policies the Democrats pursued under Johnson and the Republicans under G. W. Bush in 2005–06 benefited and were supported by lower- and higher-income Americans, respectively, but these were counterbalanced by other policies that these constituencies opposed.)

Also contrary to my expectations, I found that the highest level of responsiveness to the preferences of low-, middle-, and high-income Americans alike came during the early years of G. W. Bush's presidency. Although Bush was in many ways a polarizing figure (an observation I'll return to below), his first years in office were characterized by unusually popular policy outcomes in comparison with earlier (or later) years. During Bush's first term, when Congress was closely divided, the parties compromised on a number of broadly popular policies (like the No Child Left Behind education reforms, the Medicare drug benefit, Bush's faith-based initiative, and, somewhat more controversially, the Bush tax cuts). Just as we saw in chapter 6 that impending elections boost responsiveness to less-well-off Americans, I show here that high levels of political competition in the form of an evenly divided Congress have this same beneficial effect. In contrast the low level of responsiveness during 2005 and 2006, when the Republicans enjoyed strong and unified control of the government, shows that political conditions, rather than the predilections of particular political actors, are most important in accounting for changes in representation.

Finally, legislative gridlock appears, somewhat perversely, to be associated with higher levels of responsiveness to public preferences. As I discuss below, polarization and the gridlock it produces reduce the amount of policy making in a given period of time and thereby limit the extent to which the public's desires for policy change are realized. But at the same time, polarization and gridlock serve as filter mechanisms that work to block unpopular policy changes (which the minority party is able to obstruct) but not popular policy changes (which the minority party would pay a political price for opposing). Thus two politically desirable qualities—facilitating policy change and ensuring that policy outcomes conform to public preferences—are in opposition to each other.

Changes in Political Context

A number of scholars have suggested that government responsiveness to public preferences in the United States may have declined over the past decades. Lawrence Jacobs and Robert Shapiro nicely summarize a series of changes in the national political context that they hypothesize might reduce the incentives or ability of representatives to purse the policies most favored by the public.[1] First, they argue, increased partisan polarization makes it more costly for parties to compromise on broadly popular centrist policies because their activists and core constituents have become more ideologically extreme. Second, the increased independence of individual members of Congress makes the efforts of party leaders to respond to public preferences (in order to enhance their party's reputation with the public) less effective. Third, the growth of the incumbency advantage has made many members less worried about reelection and therefore less sensitive to their constituents' preferences. Fourth, the proliferation of interest groups has increased the pressure on politicians to pursue policies that may not comport with public desires. Finally, the prevalence of divided party control of Congress and the White House during the post–World War II period, in combination with partisan polarization and individualistic behavior of members of Congress, has resulted in the neglect of centrist public opinion as politicians fight over their conflicting policy objectives.

While scholarly attention has tended to focus on perceived or hypothesized *declines* in policy responsiveness over time, some observers note reasons to expect an *increase* in the association of public preferences and government policies. Paul Quirk, for example, argues that the rise of opinionated news coverage and the increase in issue-oriented campaign advertising have enhanced voters' ability to cast policy-based votes (consequently increasing the incentives for officeholders to pursue popular policies).[2] In addition, Quirk argues, the declining size of congressional majorities and greater likelihood that control of Congress could change hands at the next election increase the incentives for politicians to pander to public preferences and for party leaders to moderate their own policy aspirations to better reflect the public's desires.

Another factor that might be thought to have increased policy responsiveness over the past decades is the greater use of polling by officeholders, candidates, and parties.[3] Better measures of the public's views allow politicians to identify policies (or aspects of policies) that are consistent with public preferences, thus expanding opportunities to bolster their support among the public. Equally important, better measures of public preferences provide advantages to challengers and minority parties as well. Not only does a clearer understanding of the public's policy preferences allow policy makers to cater to those preferences should they so choose, but it also enhances the ability of opposing politicians to exact a cost when policy makers pursue policies that conflict with the public's preferences.

Better survey data not only enhance politicians' abilities to shape policy to conform to public preferences (and opposition candidates' abilities to exact a cost if incumbents fail to do so) but also allows politicians to better craft their communications to generate public support for policies that officeholders already favor.[4] The increased use of surveys allows officeholders to more effectively pursue either of these strategies, depending on the circumstances. When appealing to the public's existing preferences becomes more important (for example, during preelection periods), richer survey data enhance the ability of incumbents to gain voters' support. But when incentives to please the public are less pressing, policy makers may be more inclined to use survey data to try to influence public preferences. (Of course efforts to shape public preferences rarely come only from one side in a policy debate. Thus the enhanced ability of officeholders to influence the public is counterbalanced by the enhanced ability of their political opponents to do the same.)

Empirical studies of government responsiveness to public preferences point to a weaker preference/policy link during the 1980s and 1990s than in earlier decades. Alan Monroe found a decrease in the proportion of government policies that were consistent with majority preferences from 63 percent to 55 percent between 1960–79 and 1980–93.[5] Consistent with these findings, Jacobs and Shapiro report that their preliminary study found a decline in the correspondence between public opinion and policy during the 1980s and 1990s relative to earlier periods, at least on the issues of crime, welfare, health care, and Social Security.[6]

While previous studies suggest a decline in policy responsiveness to the public as a whole, my interest extends beyond this issue to the question of whether responsiveness to more- and less-advantaged Americans has become more equal or less equal. Americans at different economic levels differentially supply various kinds of valued resources to politicians. For lower-income Americans, these resources consist primarily of votes, while high-income Americans also contribute money. Thus any change over time in the relative value attached to money over votes will tend to shift policy responsiveness in the direction of the better-off. Of course a chief benefit of campaign donations lies in their utility in obtaining votes by funding campaign activities like advertising and voter mobilization. (Campaign donations do provide other advantages to candidates, such as scaring off potential challengers and the opportunity to enhance political influence by redirecting resources to other candidates.) Thus the short-term trade-off between maximizing votes (by appealing to the broadest number of likely voters) and maximizing campaign donations (by appealing to the wealthy) must also be understood as a longer-run trade-off between directly increasing votes through popular policy making and indirectly increasing votes through greater campaign spending.

Two related trends in electoral campaigns suggest that money may have become more important over time in comparison with other factors. First, campaigns for federal office have become significantly more expensive. Most of the money to fund these campaigns comes from individual contributions,[7] and the vast majority of individual contributions come from Americans at the top of the income distribution. One study based on self-reported donations, for example, found that a majority of all campaign dollars from individual donors were given by Americans in the top 9 percent of the income distribution, and of these, almost two-thirds of the money came from the top 3 percent.[8] Another study, based on actual donor lists filed with the Federal Election Commission, found that four-fifths of donors who gave $200 or more to congressional candidates in 1996 had incomes in the top 10 percent of all Americans.[9]

Related to the growing cost of attaining (or retaining) political office is the shift toward more professionalized, media-based, candidate-centered campaigns.[10] This shift itself has been reflected in and exacerbated by a variety of social and political changes, including the decline of party machines,[11] the changing nature of American civic life from fellowship groups involving face-to-face interactions to advocacy organizations in which membership consists primarily of check writing,[12] and the change from party volunteers going door to door mobilizing voters to the use of commercial phone banks, direct mail, and television advertising.[13] All these changes have served to increase the importance of money in absolute terms and relative to other campaign resources (like party support or the mobilization activities of unions, churches, and other voluntary organizations). As money becomes more critical to winning elections, pleasing the people who can supply that money naturally becomes more important to office seekers and officeholders.

Of course elected representatives rarely acknowledge that government policy is bent to fit the preferences of campaign donors (at least not while they still hold office), but they do complain frequently about the increased demands of fund-raising.[14] Senator Robert Byrd, with decades of experience in the Senate, said in a debate on election financing that "The incessant money chase that currently permeates every crevice of our political system is like an unending circular marathon."[15] Debate continues in the scholarly literature over the impact of campaign contributions, lobbying, and other resource-based efforts to influence policy makers. I briefly discuss these issues in chapter 8, but for now I simply note that officeholders and office seekers are quite open about the burden of raising money, and that individuals and organizations that spend money on political pursuits do so in the expectation that their efforts will help shape policy outcomes, whether by shifting policy makers' behavior or by empowering those policy makers who already share their preferences.

The influence of increased campaign expenditures on representation is likely to have been exacerbated by the concomitant increase in economic inequality over the past decades. The share of income accruing to the top 10 percent of the income distribution in the United States increased from about one-third in the mid-1960s to one-half by 2007, while the share of income going to the top 1 percent of Americans doubled during this period.[16] If campaign donations over this period also became more concentrated in the upper reaches of the income distribution, the disproportionate influence of the affluent would likely be even further enhanced. These changes in the income distribution suggest an additional possibility, which

I take up in chapter 8: the apparent influence of Americans at the 90th income percentile may in fact reflect the tendency of people at this income level to share the preferences of the far more affluent Americans at the 99th (or the 99.9th) income percentile.

Previous research generates firm expectations for some of the following analyses of change over time in policy responsiveness, but in many cases a lack of empirical evidence or countervailing theoretical considerations provide little guidance for what to expect. Moreover, enhanced responsiveness of individual representatives need not translate into a stronger association between eventual policy outcomes and the preferences of the public as a whole. The policy-making process is a complex one, and members of Congress have reelection constituencies that are distinct from both their state or district constituents as a whole and from the national electorate.[17] In addition the trade-off discussed above between money and votes implies that even electoral pressures to maximize votes might work against representational equality if politicians are less interested in directly appealing to the majority of voters by advancing favored policies and more interested in appealing to potential campaign donors and interest groups. In short, the way various incentives play out in terms of policy responsiveness are complex and uncertain. I return to these theoretical considerations toward the end of the chapter after taking a look at the actual patterns of responsiveness and their associations with the hypothesized conditions outlined above.

INCREASES IN POLICY RESPONSIVENESS OVER TIME

As discussed above, scholars have identified a variety of contextual changes in the political environment that might have led to either a strengthening or a weakening of policy responsiveness over the past decades. To assess change over time in policy makers' responsiveness to the public, I use my expanded dataset with policy changes proposed in 1964–68, 1981–2002, and 2005–06, with a four-year window during which a proposed change can be adopted. I begin by looking at the broad patterns of change over time based on linear and quadratic time trends, and then examine the more detailed (and illuminating differences across individual presidential administrations.

Analyses of the preference/policy link using a linear time trend show a clear and strong increase in responsiveness between the 1960s and the 2000s for all income levels (table A7.1). But statistical tests indicate that changes in responsiveness over time were not linear for poor and middle-income Americans.[18] For these groups there was little apparent difference between the mid-1960s and the early 1980s, but a clear upward trend be-

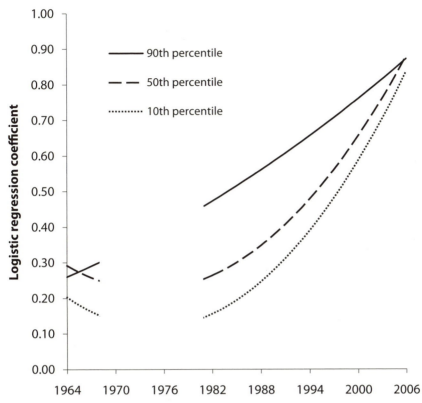

Figure 7.1. Time Trends in Policy Responsiveness. Based on the second panel of table A7.1.

tween the early 1980s and 2006. The pattern of responsiveness to low-, middle-, and high-income Americans based on the analyses that include both linear and nonlinear time trends is shown in figure 7.1 (and in table A7.1). While all income groups show stronger responsiveness at the end of the period, only the affluent show steady increases in the preference/ policy link across these four decades.

A more detailed view of the change in responsiveness over time is available by separating out each of the five presidents represented in my data. Table 7.1 and figure 7.2 show changes in responsiveness similar to the pattern shown in figure 7.1. Responsiveness to the preferences of all income levels was very low during the Johnson years; responsiveness during the Reagan, G.H.W. Bush, and Clinton years was substantially higher for the affluent and somewhat less so for the middle class and the poor; and responsiveness to all income levels was quite high during G. W. Bush's tenure.

Table 7.1   Policy Responsiveness by President by Income Percentile

| | N | Income Percentile | | | |
		All	10th	50th	90th
Johnson	225	.21 (.14)	.17 (.13)	.20 (.13)	.20 (.14)
Reagan	524	.40 (.11)***	.21 (.10)*	.38 (.10)***	.52 (.10)***
G.H.W. Bush	134	.29 (.23)	.29 (.24)	.16 (.22)	.50 (.24)*
Clinton	807	.37 (.09)***	.24 (.08)**	.32 (.08)***	.51 (.09)***
G. W. Bush	497	1.03 (.13)***	.94 (.12)***	.95 (.12)***	1.00 (.13)***

Analyses based on the annual restructured dataset with policy questions from 1964–68, 1981–2002, 2005–06. Table shows logistic regression coefficients (with standard errors in parentheses). Dependent variable is policy outcome coded 1 if the proposed policy change took place in the calendar year in question and 0 if it did not. Predictors are the logit of the imputed percentage of respondents at a given income level favoring the proposed policy change. All analyses include fixed effects for the four policy domains examined in chapter 4.
$*p < .05$; $**p < .01$; $***p < .001$

As usual, patterns of responsiveness across income levels are clearer when restricting the analyses to proposed policy changes for which preferences across income groups diverged. Figure 7.3 (based on the bottom section of table A7.1) shows these patterns using the quadratic model of change over time. The steady growth in responsiveness to the preferences

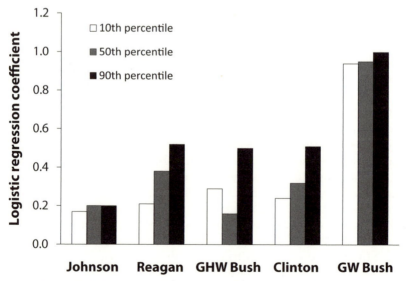

Figure 7.2. Policy Responsiveness by President. Based on table 7.1.

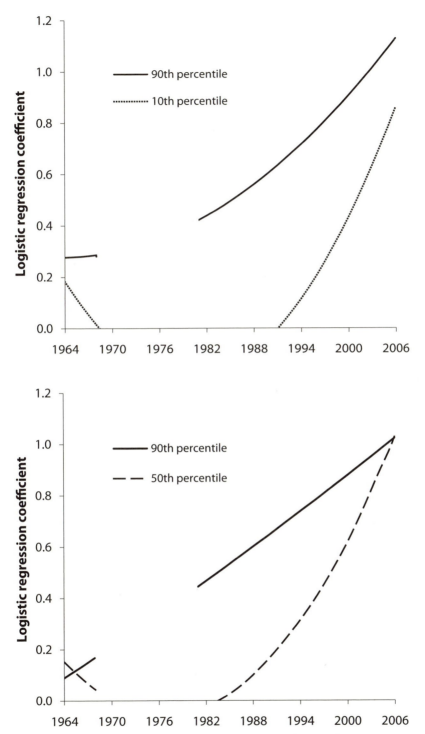

Figure 7.3. Time Trends in Policy Responsiveness When Preferences across Income Levels Diverge. Based on the bottom panel of table A7.1.

Table 7.2 Policy Responsiveness by President When Preferences across Income Levels Diverge

	10th vs. 90th Income Percentiles			50th vs. 90th Income Percentiles		
	N	10th	90th	N	50th	90th
Johnson	102	.13 (.22)	.10 (.24)	102	−.03 (.23)	−.05 (.25)
Reagan	226	−.14 (.16)	.48 (.17)**	244	.20 (.16)	.54 (.19)**
Clinton	319	.02 (.15)	.66 (.17)***	393	.18 (.13)	.62 (.16)***
G. W. Bush	191	.79 (.21)***	1.11 (.24)***	229	1.07 (.21)***	1.20 (.23)***

Analyses based on the annual restructured dataset with policy questions from 1964–68, 1981–2002, 2005–06. Table shows logistic regression coefficients (with standard errors in parentheses). Dependent variable is policy outcome coded 1 if the proposed policy change took place in the calendar year in question and 0 if it did not. Predictors are the logit of the imputed percentage of respondents at a given income level favoring the proposed policy change. Includes only cases where the 10th and 90th income percentiles differ by over 10 percentage points and the 50th and 90th income percentiles differ by over 5 percentage points. All analyses include fixed effects for the four policy domains examined in chapter 4.
$*p < .05$; $**p < .01$; $***p < .001$

of the affluent is still evident in this figure, but the concentration of change in responsiveness for the other income groups in the most recent years is even starker. Most strikingly, these models suggest that even on policies where preferences diverged, representational inequality was quite low toward the end of the period my data cover. (These analyses also indicate that representational inequality was low during the earliest years in my dataset, but that is because responsiveness was itself very low with regard to all income levels.)

The pattern in figure 7.3 is replicated in the analyses of individual presidents found in table 7.2 and figure 7.4. When preferences across income groups diverged, responsiveness to the preferences of the poor and middle class was negligible during the Johnson, Reagan, and Clinton administrations, but strong during the G. W. Bush administration. (Restricting the analysis to proposed changes on which preferences across income levels diverged results in too few questions from the G.H.W. Bush years to permit meaningful estimates.) In contrast responsiveness to the affluent on these policies grew steadily over time, consistent with the results of the nonlinear time trend analyses shown above.

Before exploring the changing political conditions that might explain these patterns of responsiveness across time and income levels, I look briefly at the characteristics of the proposed policy changes that were on the agenda during each of the five presidents in my dataset. Table 7.3 shows some key characteristics of the proposed policy changes on the survey agenda during each president's tenure in office. For the most part

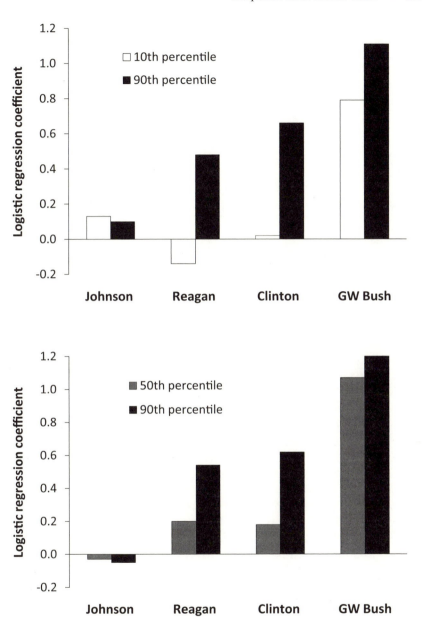

Figure 7.4. Policy Responsiveness by President When Preferences across Income Levels Diverge. Based on table 7.2.

Table 7.3   Characteristics of Proposed Policy Changes by President

	N	Percent Lopsided	Percent Divergent	Percent Favored*	Percent Adopted*	Percent Adopted (excluding 1st Congress)*
Johnson	225	.52	.45	.43	.31	.31
Reagan	524	.48	.43	.52	.37	.39
G.H.W. Bush	134	.53	.46	.58	.20	.20
Clinton	810	.47	.39	.57	.26	.21
G. W. Bush	497	.48	.38	.56	.28	.16

Percent lopsided shows the percentage of questions in each policy domain for which at least two-thirds of the respondents either favor or oppose the proposed change; percent divergent shows the percentage of questions for which preferences of the 10th and 90th income percentiles diverge by more than 10 percentage points.
* Difference across presidents significant at $p < .001$.

the nature of these policies remained remarkably constant over the four decades examined. The first column of the table shows that the percentage of proposed changes that were lopsided (i.e., that were strongly favored or strongly opposed) varied within a narrow range from 47 to 53 percent. Similarly the percentage of proposed policy changes that elicited a difference in preferences between the 10th and the 90th income percentiles of more than 10 percentage points varied only modestly, from 38 to 46 percent. The average favorability of the proposed policy changes was somewhat lower under Johnson than under any of the other presidents I examined. (On average, 43 percent of respondents favored the proposed policy changes under Johnson compared with 52 to 58 percent for the other four presidents.) This could be due in part to changes in the practices of survey organizations but more likely relates to the Johnson administration's strong influence over the public agenda and the disconnect between Johnson administration policies and the preferences of the public, which I discuss below. Finally, the percentage of proposed changes that were adopted varied somewhat, with the lowest adoption rate under G.H.W. Bush (20 percent) and the highest under Reagan (37 percent).

In light of the expectation that shifts in partisan control increase the amount of new policy activity (as discussed in chapter 6 and below), the last column of table 7.3 shows the percent of proposed policy changes adopted under each president after excluding the first year of a new partisan presidential regime (i.e., excluding 1981, 1993, and 2001). This adjustment reveals a clear pattern of decline over time in the proportion of proposed policy changes that were adopted. I explore this trend in more depth when I examine the role of polarization and gridlock in shaping policy responsiveness.

Based on the similarity of proposed policy changes across presidential administrations shown in table 7.3, it appears that the substantial shifts in responsiveness over time shown in figures 7.1–7.4 cannot be attributed to shifts in the nature of the policy agenda, at least as it is reflected in the proposed policy changes captured in my data. The only substantial change over time revealed in table 7.3 concerns not the policy agenda per se, but rather the response of policy makers to that agenda (i.e., the likelihood of a proposed policy change being adopted).

In the remainder of this chapter I first explore the broad changes in political and economic conditions that have been suggested as influences on representation and which might help to account for the steady increase in responsiveness to well-off Americans. I then look in more detail at the Johnson and G. W. Bush administrations in an effort to understand the specific conditions that led, respectively, to the uniformly low and uniformly high levels of responsiveness shown in the figures and tables above.

CHANGES IN THE POLITICAL AND ECONOMIC ENVIRONMENT

The increase in responsiveness to the affluent over the decades examined lends plausibility to some of the hypothesized influences over representation discussed above and appears to undermine others. In the following pages I focus on those hypothesized changes consistent with the increase in responsiveness to well-off Americans. For some of these factors, consistent measures across the relevant time period are available, making them amenable to quantitative assessment. In particular I analyze the impact on representation of the increase in partisan polarization and gridlock and the decline in the size of the majority party's seat advantage in Congress. On the other hand, I am much less able to statistically evaluate the impact of politicians' increased use of surveys, changes in the media environment, the rise in economic inequality, and the growing cost of political campaigns. For these latter factors either we lack consistent quantitative measures for the relevant time period or the trends over time are so steady as to be indistinguishable from each other. Despite these data limitations I begin with a brief review of these difficult-to-assess factors before turning to my analyses of gridlock and the size of the congressional majority.

Over the past decades the use of surveys in all walks of life has grown. News media, marketing firms, health care organizations, and even professional sports teams have made increasing use of surveys.[19] Not surprisingly politicians appear to have followed suit. But despite some scholarly attention to politicians' use of surveys,[20] the only systematic data available concern the use of polls by presidents or presidential candidates; no data appear to have been collected regarding survey use by political parties or by legislative incumbents or candidates.[21] While the scholars who have explored politicians' use of surveys agree that polling has increased over time, no quantitative measures of the extent of polling are available.

Politicians' responsiveness to the public's issue preferences is also hypothesized to reflect the extent to which citizens pay attention to political issues and base their votes on issue considerations at election time. Paul Quirk suggests that changes in the media environment, such as the rise of opinionated news on cable television, may have contributed to a richer information environment.[22] Other scholars have suggested that increases in campaign advertising may have played a similar role. Consistent with these claims, analyses of the reasons survey respondents give for preferring one presidential or congressional candidate over another do reveal an increase in policy focus over time. Examining data from 1952 through 2000, Lynn Vavreck, Martin Cohen, and I found an increase in the proportion of policy-related reasons respondents gave for their presidential vote preference (as opposed to the candidates' character, their partisan ties, their perceived social group affiliations, or other considerations).[23] We also found a shift in the predictors of respondents' presidential vote choice toward policy-based considerations and away from character-based considerations over this time period. Similar analyses of the reasons survey respondents offer for liking or disliking congressional candidates (available only from 1978 thorough 2000) show similar trends.[24]

A third factor that is consistent with the observed increase in responsiveness to the affluent is the rise in campaign expenditures and candidates' consequent need for ever-increasing resources to mount competitive campaigns. As shown in figure 7.5, campaign spending in both House and Senate races has been growing steadily since the Federal Election Commission began collecting data in 1974. With congressional races, on average, four times as expensive in 2006 as they were in 1974 (adjusted for inflation), the pressure on politicians to please their campaign donors is likely to have increased.

The growth of economic inequality is another factor plausibly related to changes in representation, but difficult to assess. Figure 7.6 shows the share of all family income in the United States that went to the top 10 percent and top 1 percent of the income distribution. Family income inequality in the United States held more or less steady from the mid-1960s to the early 1980s and then began to climb. With brief dips in the late 1980s and early 2000s, income inequality has continued to rise. In 1981 the top 10 percent of American families received about 35 percent of all

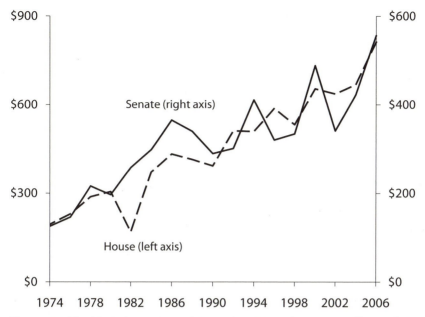

Figure 7.5. Total U.S. Congressional Campaign Expenditures (in millions of 2010 dollars). Total primary and general election campaign expenditures for Democratic and Republican House and Senate candidates, 1974–2006, based on Federal Election Commission data. Source: Campaign Finance Institute.

income; by 2006 the top decile was receiving almost half of all income. Incomes grew even more dramatically for the top 1 percent of all families. Over this same quarter-century, the income of the top 1 percent of families grew from about 10 percent of all income to about 23 percent. This pattern suggests that the growth in income inequality might play some role in explaining increases in responsiveness to the affluent during the 1980s and beyond, but not the increase between the 1960s and the 1980s.

Some of the influences discussed above (and in chapter 6) might be expected to influence responsiveness in a tight, short-term fashion. For example, the strength of the preference/policy link appears to respond to the annual changes of the federal election cycle. Other influences, however, are not likely to work in such a short-term manner. Increases in economic inequality or the growing use of surveys by politicians might shape responsiveness, but we would not expect this association, if it exists, to follow the short-term fluctuations in economic inequality or survey use from year to year. A lack of a short-term relationship does not necessarily make these factors less important in shaping responsiveness over the long haul, but it does make their effects more difficult to detect. Since many of the hypothesized factors discussed above have grown steadily

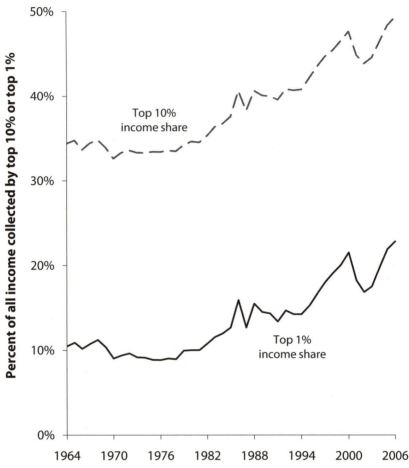

Figure 7.6. Income Inequality in the United States. Source: Piketty and Saez (2011).

over time, it is impossible to statistically disentangle their effects. Both a lack of data, then, and a lack of short-term variation or reasonable expectation of short-term influence make these possible influences on representation poor candidates for quantitative analysis.

POLARIZATION AND GRIDLOCK

Another factor hypothesized to influence government responsiveness is partisan polarization and the resulting gridlock in government policy making that accompanies it.[25] Polarized parties with highly divergent policy preferences, scholars argue, are less likely to compromise and more likely to expend their efforts blocking each other's policy initiatives. This policy gridlock in turn prevents government from successfully addressing the issues of concern to the public.

While the relationship between partisan polarization and policy gridlock is well established,[26] the connection between gridlock and responsiveness is more complex than often recognized. If responsiveness is understood as meaning simply the quantity of new policy (or important new policy) adopted during a given period of time, or the quantity of new policy relative to the size of the issue agenda, gridlock and responsiveness are necessarily inversely related. But if we understand responsiveness as I have been using it—to refer to the fit between government policies and public preferences—the implications of gridlock for responsiveness are more complex. In particular, we might expect that the difficulty of adopting new policies during periods of high gridlock means that only those policies with the strongest political support are likely to be adopted. When the pressure on lawmakers to adopt a new policy is great enough, neither party will want to be seen as standing in the way. Thus high levels of gridlock may result in less new policy being adopted, but those policies that do make it through the "gridlock filter" are likely to be especially popular. In other words, by inhibiting the adoption of unpopular policies even more than popular policies, gridlock may result in less getting done, but also in a stronger association between public preferences and policy outcomes. In this way gridlock acts as a selection mechanism, permitting the adoption of those new policies that both parties fear opposing but inhibiting the adoption of less popular policy changes.

The most comprehensive quantitative analysis of gridlock is Sarah Binder's *Stalemate: Causes and Consequences of Legislative Gridlock*. Binder expands on David Mayhew's seminal study of legislative productivity by examining not just the number of important laws adopted during a given Congress, but also the number of important issues on the public agenda that the government failed to address.[27] Using *New York Times* editorials as the basis for assembling a list of the systemic agenda items before Congress, Binder is able to provide a denominator for assessing federal government productivity at any given time.

My data, based on the survey agenda of proposed policy changes, provides an alternative measure of federal government productivity (or gridlock) based on the proportion of proposed policy changes that were adopted in any given year. Binder's data cover the twenty-seven Congresses between 1947 and 2000, while my data include the thirty-one years between 1964 and 2006. Our data overlap for thirteen Congresses (twenty-six years). For these overlapping years, both datasets show increased gridlock over time, and the correlation between our measures is 0.55.[28]

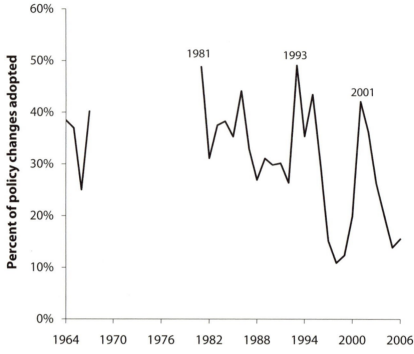

Figure 7.7. Change over Time in Percentage of Proposed Policy Changes Adopted. Partisan control of the presidency changed hands in 1981, 1993, and 2001.

My annual measure of the proportion of proposed policy changes adopted is shown in figure 7.7. This figure reveals both the general decline over time in the percent adopted and the strong upticks in legislative productivity when partisan control of the presidency changed hands in 1981, 1993, and 2001. My concern, of course, is not with gridlock per se, but with its impact on representation. I therefore add gridlock (i.e., the percentage of proposed changes not adopted in a given year) and the interaction of gridlock and policy preferences to my model of policy outcomes.

The results of this analysis (shown in table A7.2) indicate that policy responsiveness is no weaker or stronger during periods when gridlock is high than at other periods for any income level. But the relationship between gridlock and responsiveness to public preferences is complicated by the role of partisan regime change. We saw in chapter 6 that when the presidency changes partisan hands, responsiveness increases with the emergence of a new set of policies favored by both the public and the new party in power. Thus shifts in partisan control have a positive direct impact on responsiveness. But if gridlock also has a positive impact on responsive-

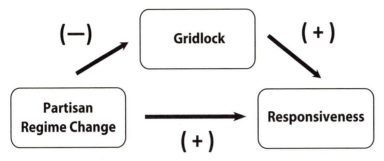

Figure 7.8. Relationship of Partisan Regime Change and Gridlock as Influences on Policy Responsiveness

ness, then shifts in partisan control—by reducing gridlock—will produce an offsetting negative impact on responsiveness. This understanding of the offsetting effects of partisan regime change is illustrated in figure 7.8 and implies that we must control for regime change to accurately estimate the impact of gridlock on policy responsiveness. The second set of analyses in table A7.2 does exactly that by using both gridlock and partisan change of the presidency (and their interactions with public preferences) as predictors of policy outcomes.

Taking partisan change into account reveals that higher levels of gridlock are associated with higher levels of responsiveness (with statistically significant interaction coefficients for the 50th and 90th income percentiles). Net of partisan change, periods of higher gridlock produce less policy change, but the changes that are adopted are more consistent with public preferences (relative to those not adopted) than is the case during periods when gridlock is lower. Figure 7.9 shows the estimated strength of policy responsiveness for low-, middle-, and high-income Americans when gridlock (measured as described above) is at its lowest and highest points. In each case policy outcomes are tied more closely to public preferences during periods when a smaller portion of the proposed policy changes are adopted.

This finding suggests that gridlock may have both positive and negative impacts on the relationship between public preferences and government policy. On the one hand, gridlock undermines the government's ability to respond to public concerns. But gridlock appears to be even more powerful in undermining the adoption of *unpopular* policies since the minority party will have little incentive to cooperate with the majority in adopting such changes. In contrast, standing in the way of proposed policy changes that the public strongly supports will exact a political cost. Consequently gridlock has a selection effect on policy by preventing less popular policies from being adopted.

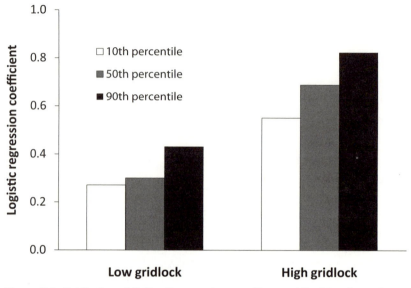

Figure 7.9. Gridlock and Policy Responsiveness. "Low gridlock" reflects the average proportion of proposed policy changes adopted in the three years in which gridlock was lowest; "high gridlock," the three years in which gridlock was highest. Details in table A7.2.

Figure 7.10 shows the analogous results for the impact of gridlock on the preference/policy link when the analysis is restricted to policies on which preferences across income levels diverge (details in table A7.2). This figure shows the dramatically higher level of responsiveness to the preferences of the middle class and the affluent when gridlock is high than when gridlock is low. But the poor benefit quite modestly, with very low levels of responsiveness under either condition. Like the emergence of a new partisan regime, it appears that the impact of gridlock on enhancing responsiveness to the public is beneficial primarily for the affluent and the middle class. Of course responsiveness here must be understood in the particular way I have been using this term throughout: the extent to which the public's favorability toward a given policy change is associated with the likelihood of that change being adopted. Periods of low gridlock (and high levels of policy adoption) might bring about more of the changes popular with one or another segment of the public. But these periods also bring about more unpopular changes; so much so in fact that, on average, policy outcomes during low gridlock periods are substantially less consistent with the preferences of the affluent and the middle class (with little difference for the poor, who enjoy little responsiveness whether gridlock is low or high).

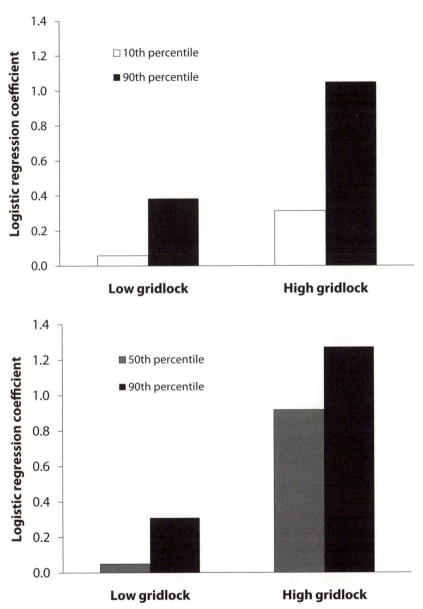

Figure 7.10. Gridlock and Policy Responsiveness When Preferences across Income Levels Diverge. "Low gridlock" reflects the average proportion of proposed policy changes adopted in the three years in which gridlock was lowest; "high gridlock," the three years in which gridlock was highest. Includes only cases where the 10th and 90th income percentiles differ by over 10 percentage points and the 50th and 90th income percentiles differ by over 5 percentage points. Details in table A7.2.

While the policies adopted during periods of greater gridlock are more consistent with the preferences of middle-class and affluent Americans, this enhanced responsiveness comes at a cost in terms of the breadth of issues that the government addresses. Whether political polarization and the gridlock induced by the "setting of faction against faction" is on balance beneficial will depend, in part, on how one views the status quo at a given time. Clearly too much gridlock is dysfunctional, but these findings suggest that too few constraints on the party in power also produces a democratic deficit, resulting in policy that bears little resemblance to the preferences of the public.

Majority-Party Seat Advantage and Uncertainty of Congressional Control

Even political parties that are strongly motivated to enact their preferred policies will temper their efforts when their continued control of the government would be threatened or their prospects for gaining control of the government imperiled. The stronger congressional majorities in earlier decades helped to insulate the majority party from such pressures. When there was little prospect of a change in control of Congress, parties had less incentive to pursue popular centrist policies and more incentive to please the activists, interest groups, and others that compose their base. The decline in majority party size, as Paul Quirk notes, by more frequently throwing control of Congress up for grabs at the next election, may have led both parties to temper their policy pursuits over time and enhance their responsiveness to the public.[29]

Figure 7.11 shows the decline in the size of the partisan seat advantage in Congress over the period covered by my responsiveness data. The strong Democratic majorities during the Johnson years appear on the left side of the figure. In contrast, the majority party advantage was fairly small in the early 1980s (as the first Reagan election brought Republicans control of the Senate and a closer partisan division in the House) and extremely small in the late 1990s and early 2000s, with the first Congress under G. W. Bush being the most extreme case.

I assess the impact of majority-party seat advantage on responsiveness with separate measures of the difference in seats held by the majority and minority parties in the House and Senate.[30] Using the interaction of public preferences with the size of the seat advantage in each chamber, I can estimate the impact of majority-party power on the strength of the preference/policy link. These results are reported in table A7.3 and shown graphically in figure 7.12. Seat advantage in the House of Representatives is not strongly (or significantly) related to strength of responsiveness, but

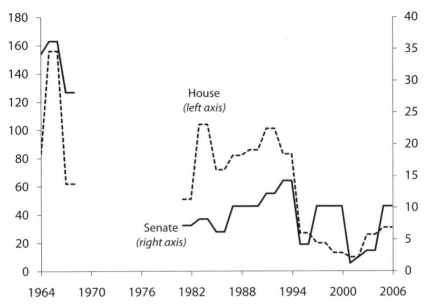

Figure 7.11. Size of the Majority Party Seat Advantage, 1964–2006. Figure shows the difference in seats held by the majority and minority parties for the House of Representatives (left axis) and the Senate (right axis).

seat advantage in the Senate is. The larger the size of the Senate seat advantage, the weaker the link between public preferences and policy outcomes. Indeed, as figure 7.12 shows, policy responsiveness shrinks to zero for all income levels when the majority party has a dominant seat advantage in the Senate.

The impact of Senate seat advantage when preferences across income levels diverge is show in figure 7.13. Reminiscent of the analyses of gridlock above, responsiveness to the poor is minimal under any condition, and majority-party dominance is therefore most consequential to the middle class and the affluent. When the Senate is most evenly divided (and seat advantage at its lowest point), responsiveness is high for the affluent and only modestly lower for the middle class. But when the majority party has a more dominant position, policy outcomes bear no relationship to the preferences of Americans at any income level. We saw in chapter 6 that impending elections induce policy makers to hew more closely to the public's preferences. In the analysis of majority-party seat advantage, we again see patterns of policy making consistent with the conception of parties as policy maximizers. When one party has the legislative clout to pursue its preferred agenda, policy outcomes bear no relationship to public preferences, but when party strength in the Senate is more even, and

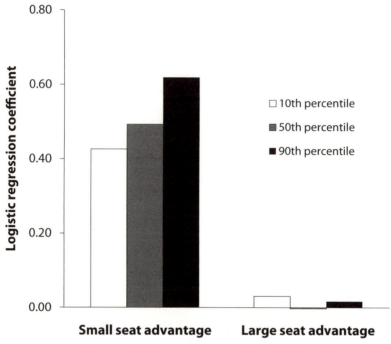

Figure 7.12. Majority Party Seat Advantage in the Senate and Policy Responsiveness. "Small seat advantage" is two seats and "large seat advantage" is thirty-two seats; these are equivalent to the average seat advantages of the first G. W. Bush administration and the Johnson administration, respectively. Details in table A7.3.

partisan control after the next election more uncertain, policy responsiveness is strong, at least for the middle class and the affluent.

The greater impact of Senate seat advantage compared with the House of Representatives may be due to the greater prospect of change in control of the Senate during the time period covered by my data. Control of the House changed hands only twice between 1964 and 2007, while control of the Senate switched parties six times. Of course the possibility of a change in control of Congress is only one reason why a large seat advantage may be associated with lower levels of responsiveness. At least during periods of strong partisan polarization (and accompanying gridlock), a small seat advantage for the majority party may mean that only policies that appeal to centrist members of its own party can be passed. Moreover the filibuster threat in the Senate means that much legislation requires the implicit support of at least sixty members to be passed. Under such conditions the smaller the majority party's seat advantage, the less able the party is to adopt policies that please its core supporters unless the public strongly favors those policies.

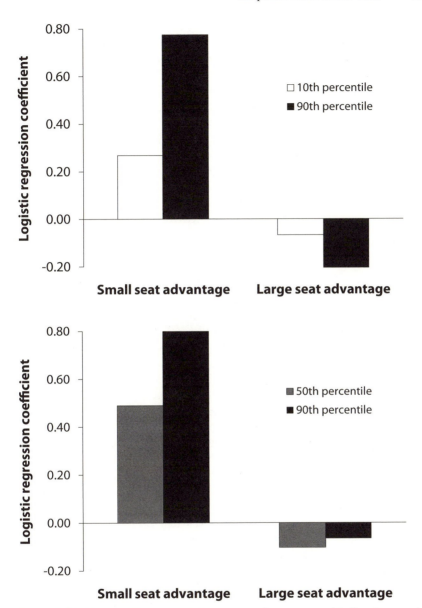

Figure 7.13. Majority Party Seat Advantage in the Senate and Policy Responsiveness When Preferences across Income Levels Diverge. "Small seat advantage" is two seats and "large seat advantage" is thirty-two seats; these are equivalent to the average seat advantages of the first G. W. Bush administration and the Johnson administration, respectively. Includes only cases where the 10th and 90th income percentiles differ by over 10 percentage points and the 50th and 90th income percentiles differ by over 5 percentage points. Details in table A7.3.

Gridlock operates like a filter, thwarting the majority party's efforts to achieve its noncentrist policy goals. A small majority-party seat advantage can operate in much the same way, by necessitating bipartisan cooperation and consideration of the preferences of centrist party members. But a small seat advantage can also create positive incentives for politicians to pursue popular policies. By generating uncertainty about control over Congress after the next election, a closely divided legislature raises the political stakes and induces both parties to resist the demands of their activist supporters and appeal to centrist voters instead. Moreover while a large seat advantage might reduce gridlock, gridlock is a consequence of numerous other factors as well.[31] In practical terms, gridlock and majority-party seat advantage are correlated at only -0.12 in my data, and, as we'll see shortly, these two measures appear to have independent influences on responsiveness.[32]

CHANGING CONDITIONS AND CHANGING RESPONSIVENESS

Before turning to a more substantive examination of the two extreme periods in my dataset—the Johnson and G. W. Bush administrations—I assess how well the influences on responsiveness identified in this and the previous chapter explain the patterns of change over time shown in figures 7.1–7.4. The most significant change for poor and middle-class Americans is the dramatic increase in responsiveness under Bush in comparison to all his predecessors. For the affluent, responsiveness was also high under Bush and low under Johnson but increased over the intervening years during the presidencies of Reagan, G.H.W. Bush, and Clinton. For the affluent, then, the Johnson and G. W. Bush presidencies constitute the extremities of low and high levels of responsiveness, respectively.

To estimate the extent to which the characteristics of the political environment discussed in chapters 6 and 7 account for the uniquely low and uniquely high levels of responsiveness under Johnson and Bush, I add indicator variables for each of those administrations, and interactions of those indicator variables with public preferences, to my logistic regression analyses of the preference/policy link. The observed differences in responsiveness during the Johnson and Bush administrations (relative to the other three presidents in my dataset) is shown in the top two lines of table 7.4 and at the top of figure 7.14 (details in table A7.4). As the analyses at the beginning of this chapter would lead one to expect, policy responsiveness was significantly higher under G. W. Bush for all income levels in comparison with Reagan, G.H.W. Bush, and Clinton (as shown in the top line of table 7.4 and the three rightward-pointing bars at the top of figure 7.14). In contrast responsiveness under Johnson was lower

Table 7.4 Policy Responsiveness under G. W. Bush and Johnson by Income Percentile (in Comparison with Reagan, G.H.W. Bush, and Clinton)

	Income Percentile		
	10th	50th	90th
Preference * G. W. Bush	.60 (.14)***	.55 (.14)***	.47 (.15)**
Preference * Johnson	−.07 (.19)	−.22 (.19)	−.44 (.19)*
Controlling for presidential regime length, Democratic/ Republican Party control, and year in the election cycle			
Preference * G. W. Bush	.64 (.18)***	.50 (.17)**	.46 (.18)*
Preference * Johnson	−.21 (.24)	−.20 (.24)	−.54 (.25)*
Controlling for Senate seat advantage, gridlock, and years in which the president's party changed hands			
Preference * G. W. Bush	.37 (.20)	.30 (.20)	.23 (.21)
Preference * Johnson	.41 (.52)	.31 (.49)	−.14 (.51)

Table shows the interaction coefficients from nine logistic regressions in which Presidents Johnson and G. W. Bush are included as indicator variables and all predicators are interacted with policy preferences (with standard errors in parentheses). Main effects of all predictors and fixed effects for the four policy domains examined in chapter 4 are included in all analyses. N is 2,229. Details appear in table A7.4.
*$p <.05$; **$p < .01$; ***$p < .001$

than under the three comparison presidents (as shown in the second line of table 7.4 and the three leftward-pointing bars in figure 7.14), a difference that was modest (and nonsignificant) for low- and middle-income Americans, but strong and significant for the affluent.

In the second section of table 7.4, I add the three moderators of responsiveness that emerged from my analyses in chapter 6 (details in table A7.4). Although regime length, partisan control, and year in the quadrennial election cycle are all related to responsiveness, none of these factors shifts consistently over time, and I did not expect them to explain either the low level of responsiveness under Johnson or the high level under Bush. The results in table 7.4 confirm this expectation. Adding these predictors (and their interactions with preferences) to my analyses does not appreciably change the interaction coefficients for either Johnson or Bush.

Greater success in accounting for the change in responsiveness over time is shown in the bottom sections of table 7.4 and figure 7.14, where I include the size of the Senate seat majority, my measure of gridlock based on the proportion of proposed changes adopted in a given year, and an

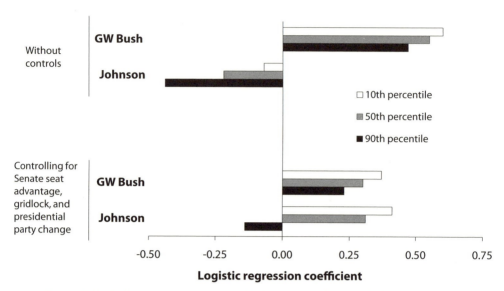

Figure 7.14. Policy Responsiveness under Johnson and G. W. Bush (in Comparison with Reagan, G.H.W. Bush, and Clinton). Figure shows the extent to which responsiveness under G. W. Bush and Johnson was higher or lower than responsiveness under the remaining three presidents in the dataset. Details in table A7.4.

indicator variable for years in which control of the White House changed partisan hands.[33] For poor Americans these factors appear to account for about two-fifths of the uniquely high level of responsiveness under Bush (reducing the interaction coefficient from 0.60 to 0.37); for middle- and upper-income Americans these factors reduce the estimated influence of the Bush years by about half (from 0.55 to 0.30 and from 0.47 to 0.23, respectively). In interpreting the three models in table 7.4, it is important to keep in mind that the introduction of explanatory factors such as seat advantage or gridlock does not mean that the resulting estimates of changes in responsiveness represent the real differences between responsiveness under Bush (or Johnson) and other presidents. The coefficients shown in the top model of the table are the real differences in representation (or at least my best estimate of them based on the available data). The changes in the estimated impact of these presidential administrations when controls are added simply show how much of the observed differences can be attributed to the systematic factors introduced into the analysis. These factors, then, can account for a portion of the uniquely high responsiveness under Bush but leave unexplained a fair amount of the increased responsiveness under Bush as well.

In contrast to the case for Bush, the three factors included in the bottom section of table 7.4 appear to do an excellent job of accounting for the distinctively low level of responsiveness during the Johnson years. For affluent Americans the interaction between policy preferences and the indictor for the Johnson years is -0.44 (second line of table 7.4), but this difference in responsiveness diminishes to only -0.14 when seat advantage, gridlock, and change of presidential partisan regime are added to the model. With multiple interactions in the model and a limited number of policy questions from the Johnson years, this estimate is subject to considerable uncertainty. But as our best guess as to what responsiveness during the Johnson administration would have looked like absent the Democrats' huge seat advantage in Congress and the relatively low level of gridlock during this period, the analysis suggests that responsiveness to the affluent would have been very similar to responsiveness during the years that Reagan, G.H.W. Bush, and Clinton held office. For poor and middle-income Americans, the analysis suggests that net of the controls introduced in the bottom sections of table 7.4 and figure 7.14, responsiveness under Johnson might have been higher than under his three immediate successors (by 0.41 and 0.31, respectively), and equal to that under G. W. Bush (although the uncertainty around this estimate is also very large).

Given the limitations of the available data and the inherent difficulty in explaining changes over time in any outcome influenced by multiple and intertwined factors, it would be foolish to expect the quantitative analysis of responsiveness to account for all the observed variation in representation over the past few decades. Further, not all influences on responsiveness emerge from the lawlike operation of measurable conditions; politics, like other aspects of human affairs, reflects in part the idiosyncrasies of individual actors and their responses to the circumstances in which they find themselves.

In the following sections I look in more depth at policy making during the Johnson and G. W. Bush administrations in order to better understand the substantive manifestations of the patterns of responsiveness documented above, and to gain additional insight into the idiosyncratic factors that contributed to those patterns.

LACK OF POLICY RESPONSIVENESS UNDER PRESIDENT JOHNSON

The low association between public preferences and policy outcomes during the Johnson administration is not a reflection of the Vietnam War or foreign policy more generally. When foreign policy questions are excluded from the analysis of responsiveness under Johnson, the size of the preference/policy association (shown in table 7.1) actually decreases slightly from 0.21 to 0.19.

On the domestic side the Johnson administration is remembered for landmark legislation including the 1964 and 1965 civil rights bills, the war on poverty, the establishment of Medicare and Medicaid, significant immigration reform, and a substantial expansion of federal aid to education. Some of these programs were indeed quite popular. Medicare and federal aid to education were strongly favored by low- and middle-income Americans and only modestly less so by the affluent. Public support for civil rights legislation grew during the early 1960s, and most of the civil rights bills from the Johnson years had solid public support by the time they were passed (support shared more or less equally across the income spectrum).

But the majority of Americans were opposed to many of the other domestic programs of the Johnson years. The Great Society and the war on poverty were not responses to an upwelling of public concern for the disadvantaged or a desire to expand the role of government in addressing social needs. If anything, public support for government activism appears to have been declining during the early to mid-1960s.[34] During the Johnson administration strong majorities at all income levels opposed increased spending on aid to cities, on low-income housing, and on welfare or relief payments. Even more unpopular was the loosening of immigration laws in 1965, opposed by 90 percent of poor Americans and about three-quarters of the affluent and middle class. Johnson's escalation of the war in Vietnam grew less popular over time (although even fewer Americans favored a U.S. withdrawal from Vietnam), and strong majorities at all levels opposed the Vietnam War income tax surcharge adopted in 1968. In short, the policies pursued by the Johnson administration spanned a wide range of popularity, from strong public support to strong public opposition, and this was as true for Americans at the bottom of the income distribution as it was for those at the top. Core middle-class domestic programs like Medicare and aid to education were broadly favored (albeit with less enthusiasm from the affluent), while other policies like immigration reform and the war on poverty were opposed by a majority of Americans at all income levels.

An unusual constellation of factors gave the Johnson administration and its congressional allies an uncommon degree of autonomy to pursue (and achieve) their policy goals. The president accumulated political capital first as the heir to John Kennedy's legislative program and then through his overwhelming victory over Barry Goldwater in the 1964 election. In addition Johnson displayed unusual skill in marshaling congressional support not only from Democrats but from Senate Republicans as well— an achievement that rested not only on the president's particular political skills and his background in the Senate, but also on the less polarized nature of the parties in Congress in that era.[35]

The unique political circumstances of the Johnson years help to shed light on the representational consequences of strong partisan control. The expectation that the constellation of political conditions during Johnson's tenure in office would bring strong responsiveness to the preferences of the less well-off is clearly wrong. Instead the Democrats' large majority in Congress, the relatively strong power of labor unions,[36] the more limited demands of campaign fund-raising during that era,[37] and the smaller number of organized interest groups[38] appear to have given the administration and its allies in Congress relative independence from both popular and political pressures.

Circumstances during the mid-1960s, and the Johnson administration's response to those circumstances, are consistent with the pattern we have seen repeatedly: when political pressure is high, owing to an impending election or to uncertainty about continued control of the government, policy is more responsive to the preferences of the public overall, including the less advantaged. But absent this pressure, policy makers tend to respond only to the preferences of the affluent or, in more extreme cases, only to the party's core constituents and policy-demanding groups, irrespective of the preferences of low- and high-income Americans alike.

Of course relative political independence is not complete independence, and even with overwhelming Democratic majorities in the House and Senate, the Johnson administration was unable to achieve all its policy goals. For one thing, the large number of conservative southern Democrats in Congress often meant that Johnson needed the support of some Republicans to overcome the filibuster threat in the Senate (especially, but not only, on civil rights issues). Moreover concern over rising inflation and a growing federal budget deficit led many Democrats to oppose further government spending and undermined the president's efforts to further expand social welfare legislation. Yet, tellingly, the decline in the ability of the Johnson administration to further pursue its social welfare agenda does not appear to have contributed to the overall lack of association between public preferences and government policy during these years. For example, Johnson tried but failed to expand Medicare to include children and prenatal coverage. While this failure appears to have been rooted more in the perceived fiscal stress produced by the expanding war in Vietnam than in concerns about public opposition, a majority of middle-income Americans and two-thirds of those at the 90th income percentile opposed Kiddycare—as this proposal was christened.[39]

The patterns of responsiveness (and nonresponsiveness) revealed in this and the previous chapters fit well with the conception of parties as policy maximizers. When parties are most insulated from political pressure, the policies they adopt are least constrained by the preferences of the public—

even the affluent members of the public. When constraint exists, policy shows a stronger connection to public preferences, but with a decided tilt toward the well-off. And only when political pressures are greatest—when an election looms, when gridlock is strong, or when control of Congress is uncertain—does a preference/policy link emerge for less-advantaged Americans.

Responsiveness under President G. W. Bush

At the other end of the spectrum, both in time and in political circumstances, we find high levels of responsiveness to public preferences during the tenure of George W. Bush. This uniformly strong relationship with public preferences across the income levels is especially surprising given that many viewed Bush as an unusually divisive president. Although Bush ran for office as a "compassionate conservative" and claimed to be "a uniter not a divider," many observers, especially on the left, dismissed this rhetoric as empty posturing and saw Bush's policy agenda as catering to the Republican base rather than seeking middle ground on broadly popular policies.[40]

Survey data on presidential job approval can provide some insight into how united or divided the public was in its views of Bush. This task is complicated, however, by the twin considerations of the September 11 attacks, which unified the country around the president, and the disputed nature of the 2000 election, which divided Democrats and Republicans, who viewed the postelection legal battle and Supreme Court decision in very different terms.[41] There is, of course, no way to eliminate these factors from the public's evaluation of President Bush. The best I can do is to examine public sentiments prior to September 11, 2001, but as far from the date of the election as possible. Using surveys of presidential approval from July and August of Bush's first year in office and comparing the public's perceptions of Bush with surveys from the same time period for previous presidents shows that evaluations of Bush were indeed the most divided along partisan lines of the four presidents examined (top panel of figure 7.15). But the partisan disagreement over Bush's performance in office was not mirrored in divergent views across the income spectrum. As the bottom panel of the figure shows, Bush was in fact the least polarizing by income of the four presidents examined. These analyses of presidential approval only reflect the public's views early in each administration, but they do provide some independent evidence that the lack of income-based inequality in responsiveness during the G. W. Bush administration shown in figures 7.1–7.4 plausibly reflects the nature of policy responsiveness during those years. However polarized Democrats

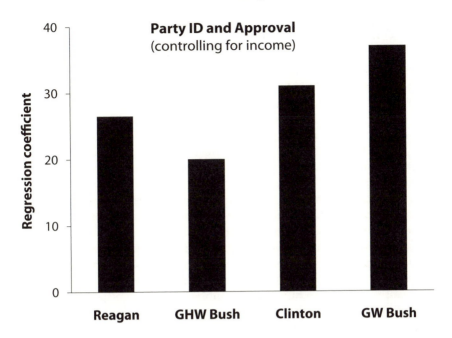

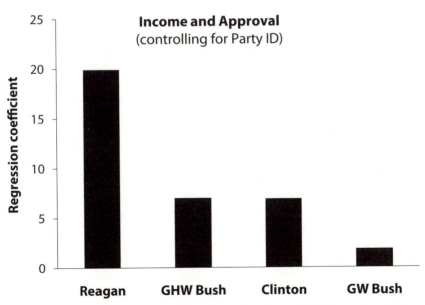

Figure 7.15. Association of Presidential Job Approval with Respondents' Party Identification and Income during July/August of First Year in Office. Based on Harris surveys of presidential approval taken during July and August of each president's first year in office.

and Republicans may have been in their views of Bush, the overall evaluations of high- and low-income Americans were remarkably alike.

What policies account for the high level of responsiveness to affluent and poor alike during the Bush years? In part this responsiveness is due to the generally high level of approval for the Afghan and Iraq wars and the Bush administration's antiterror policies. But these are only a small part of the picture, and responsiveness outside the foreign policy domain looks similar. Indeed, eliminating all foreign policy questions from the analyses reported in table 7.1 reduces the estimated preference/policy link for Bush from 1.03 to 0.84, still quite strong in comparison with previous presidents.

Of the domestic policies adopted during the Bush administration, the clearest examples of popular initiatives that appealed to Americans at all income levels are the Medicare drug benefit, the No Child Left Behind education reforms (a long-standing Democratic agenda item on which Bush partnered with Senator Ted Kennedy), and Bush's faith-based social services initiative. The changes adopted to federal regulations on funding stem cell research also fit well with public sentiments, especially for the less well-off (see chapter 4).

Finally, the income tax cuts and estate tax repeal adopted in 2001 and 2003, while clearly providing the largest benefits to those at the top of the income distribution, were nevertheless supported by majorities of Americans at all income levels. For example, in a pair of survey questions asked just before and just after passage of the 2001 income tax cuts, 55 percent of respondents at the 10th income percentile expressed support, rising to about 68 percent of those at the 90th percentile.[42] Subsequent questions about whether the tax cuts should be made permanent elicited even higher levels of support among those at all income levels. Still larger proportions of Americans expressed support for eliminating the estate tax, a change favored by 68 percent of those at the bottom of the income distribution and 79 percent of those at the top.[43] The reason for the strong support for these tax cuts among those who stood to benefit least has generated considerable discussion.[44] I'll return to this question shortly.

This brief description of the most prominent broadly popular domestic policies adopted under Bush helps account for the content of the strong preference/policy link reported above, but not the cause. Some of the explanation can be attributed to the systemic factors addressed in table 7.4. Congress was more closely divided as Bush came into office than at any time in the previous half-century. Republicans held a mere nine-seat majority in the House, and the Senate was evenly divided (with Vice President Cheney casting the deciding vote) until Jim Jeffords abandoned the Republican Party, giving the Democrats (in combination with the two independent senators, Jeffords and Bernie Sanders) an advantage of fifty-one to forty-nine. Adding to the tenuous nature of Republican control, the Republican Party lost seats in both houses of Congress in the 2000 election, Bush took office having won fewer popular votes than his Democratic presidential opponent, and the protracted struggle over the Florida recount led many Democrats to view Bush's claim to the presidency as illegitimate.

With control of the national government so tenuous, both parties had reason to dampen their efforts to achieve their core goals and direct their activity toward appealing to as broad a swath of voters as possible. A tenuous grip on power can be expected to induce any political actor to prioritize election-enhancing positions at the expense of ideological commitments. But Bush and his White House team was by many accounts uncommonly focused on political considerations at the expense of a clear policy agenda. This is not to say that the Bush administration did not have a policy agenda, but rather that the agenda was influenced strongly by what they perceived the political consequences of pursuing those policies would be. Of course every administration (indeed every political actor) needs to balance electoral considerations against its own preferred policy commitments. But circumstances and individual inclinations lead some administrations to place more emphasis on one side of this continuum or the other.

The strong role played by political considerations in the Bush White House was reflected in the centrality of political strategist Karl Rove in the development of administration policy. Rove established the White House Office of Strategic Initiatives as part of an effort to elevate the place of long-term political strategy in the daily development of government policy.[45] "The object," Rove told Washington Post reporter Dana Milbank, "is to have a strategic framework ... which is brought down to each office by the participants. Everybody in the White House has a role in long-term planning and a seat at the table so they buy into the process."[46]

The keen focus on political strategy to the neglect of policy by the Bush administration was most forcefully (and colorfully) conveyed by John DiIulio, the first director of Bush's faith-based initiative. "There is no precedent in any modern White House for what is going on in this one: a complete lack of a policy apparatus. What you've got is everything—and I mean everything—being run by the political arm. It's the reign of the Mayberry Machiavellis."[47]

To some extent, the centrist policy initiatives of the early Bush years were determined even before Bush gained office. In the historically close 2000 election (in which Florida and its large elderly population were to play a central role), Bush sought centrist voters' support by promising a Medicare drug benefit and education reform.[48] Moreover, as governor, Bush had a history of bipartisan engagement, necessitated by the Demo-

Table 7.5 Policy Responsiveness under G. W. Bush in 2001–02 vs. 2005–06 by Income Percentile

	N	All	Income Percentile		
			10th	50th	90th
All policies					
2001–02	251	.99 (.19)***	.91 (.19)***	.90 (.18)***	1.01 (.19)***
2005–06	188	.22 (.30)	.09 (.28)	.25 (.29)	.23 (.29)
Excluding defense and terrorism					
2001–02	193	.68 (.22)**	.61 (.21)***	.59 (.21)**	.74 (.22)***
2005–06	147	−.09 (.34)	−.03 (.31)	−.07 (.32)	−.17 (.33)

Analyses based on the annual restructured dataset with policy questions from 1964–68, 1981–2002, 2005–06. Table shows logistic regression coefficients (with standard errors in parentheses). Dependent variable is policy outcome coded 1 if the proposed policy change took place in the calendar year in question and 0 if it did not. Preference is the logit of the imputed percentage of respondents at a given income level favoring the proposed policy change. All analyses include fixed effects for the four policy domains examined in chapter 4.
$*p < .05; **p < .01; ***p < .001$

cratic control of the Texas legislature.[49] Bush's centrist posture may have been a product of his circumstances in Texas, the close nature of the 2000 presidential election, and the conditions under which Bush took office. But this centrist orientation produced broadly popular policies in education, health care, tax reform, stem cell research, and the administration's faith-based initiative to fund social services through religious institutions.

Some leverage on the extent to which the unusually strong responsiveness to public preferences under Bush was a consequence of political circumstances as opposed to the personal inclinations and priorities of the president and his administration can be gained by comparing the early years of the Bush presidency, when Congress was evenly divided and party control was split (with the Democrats holding a razor-thin majority in the Senate and Republicans a slim majority in the House), with 2005–06, when the Republicans held solid control of both houses of Congress and as well as the presidency.

Table 7.5 shows responsiveness under Bush divided into the two periods from which my survey questions on proposed policy changes were drawn. The top two rows of the table compare the preference/policy link for 2001 and 2002 with 2005 and 2006 (using my annual restructured data so that only policies adopted during calendar years 2001, 2002, 2005, or 2006 count as adopted). Although the number of cases in each time period is limited, the difference in responsiveness is dramatic. Across all income levels, responsiveness during the earlier period of divided and uncertain partisan control was far higher than during the later period of strong Republican power. Since some of this difference could be due to the declining popularity of the Iraq War, I reestimated these coefficients after excluding all questions about the military, the Iraq and Afghanistan wars, and antiterror policy. The number of cases is, of course, even smaller, but the pattern is the same. As the bottom section of table 7.5 shows, excluding these issues modestly reduces the preference/policy link during both 2001–02 and 2005–06, leaving the gap in responsiveness between these two periods intact.

The contrast between high levels of responsiveness during 2001–02 and low levels during 2005–06 is consistent with the independent analysis of the Bush administration by Lawrence Jacobs and Robert Shapiro.[50] Jacobs and Shapiro indentified ninety-three key votes in Congress between 2001 and 2006 that they were able to clearly identify as congruent or noncongruent with public preferences. Of these, fully 74 (80%) were in accord with majority preferences. But like my analyses, they found that the proportion of incongruent policies grew over time. During 2001 and 2002 only 13 percent of these votes ran counter to public preferences, but the proportion of incongruent votes doubled to 26 percent during 2005 and 2006. Jacobs and Shapiro associate this shift with the Republican congressional gains in the 2002 election. "From 2003 through 2006," they write, "when the Republicans enjoyed majorities in the House and Senate, there was a notable increase in legislative actions that were neither congruent nor clear with respect to policy content and public opinion."[51]

Individual officeholders clearly shape political strategies and define policy priorities. But the circumstances in which those individuals find themselves appear to matter even more. When Republicans gained unified control of the federal government for the first time in over half a century, policy responsiveness to the public plummeted. Neither affluent nor other Americans appear to have had any more influence over policy making during 2005–06 than they did during the height of Democratic Party control in the mid-1960s.

PUBLIC SUPPORT FOR THE BUSH TAX CUTS

Many on the left viewed the Bush tax cuts as a triumph of manipulation and misinformation or, somewhat less dramatically, as a sad illustration of the public's inability to identify its own best interests. I briefly discussed the repeal of the estate tax in chapter 1, arguing that considerations of equity and fairness, rather than economic self-interest, appeared to dominate the public's consideration of the estate tax.[52] Whether this focus on considerations of fairness (and neglect of self-interest) is itself a product of elite manipulation or false consciousness is a difficult question, but there is no reason to accept the legitimacy of non-self-interested considerations among affluent supporters of the estate tax (like Warren Buffett or George Soros) and deny the legitimacy of non-self-interested considerations among the less well-off. Perhaps a clearer understanding of the workings of the estate tax or a more sophisticated view of the ways in which society makes the accumulation of wealth by individuals possible would have led some Americans to shift their preferences. But the public has long opposed the estate tax, and there is no clear evidence that that opposition is misplaced or a product of elite manipulation.[53]

In contrast to the estate tax, there is little principled opposition to the income tax as such. Consequently we can be more confident in focusing on the economic consequences alone as we assess the bases for public support. The income tax cuts passed in 2001 and 2003 were widely seen (especially by those on the left) as contrary to the interests of most of the public and especially of low-income Americans. The Bush tax cuts were structured to provide some benefit to Americans at all income levels, but the savings that accrued to the most affluent Americans were substantial while the savings for those with low incomes were quite small. The total tax reduction for the top 1 percent of the income distribution was nearly as great as that for the entire bottom 60 percent, and the average savings for families in the top 1 percent were almost 1,000 times as great as the savings for families in the bottom income quintile.[54] Yet despite this strong upward tilt to the tax reductions, support for both the 2001 and the 2003 tax cuts was surprisingly strong among low-income, as well as high-income, Americans. When asked in a 2004 survey, those with low incomes were more likely to say they hadn't thought about the Bush tax cuts. But among those expressing an opinion, 51 percent of respondents in the bottom income quintile favored the tax cuts, compared with 59 percent of those in the top quintile.[55]

Political observers wondered why tax cuts so strongly unequal in their benefits did not generate similarly unequal levels of popular support. One possibility is that the supporters of the tax cut were simply uninformed (or misinformed) about the distribution of benefits it entailed. But surveys taken at the time indicated that majorities of the public perceived a strong upward tilt to the Bush tax cut proposals.[56] Three-quarters of respondents, for example, said, "The wealthy will benefit more from the tax cut than the middle class," and when asked, "Who do you think would benefit most?" 63 percent said rich people, 31 percent middle-income people, and 5 percent said poor people. Nor did most Americans feel that the proposed tax cuts would have a large impact on them, or on the average taxpayer. Only 40 percent said that "the average taxpayer will get substantial tax relief" if the proposed cuts were adopted, only 29 percent thought they personally would get "substantial tax relief," and only 7 percent thought their own taxes would "go down a lot."[57]

For the most part, then, public support for the Bush tax cuts did not seem to rest on Americans' overly rosy expectation of the benefits they could expect or a lack of understanding of the upward tilt of those benefits toward the most affluent taxpayers. Given the public's rather modest expectations for tax relief, it is not surprising that surveys showed a preference for more progressive tax reform. "Public opinion was clearly and consistently hostile to the top-heavy skew of the Bush tax cuts," write Jacob Hacker and Paul Pierson.[58] For example, when asked whether the "rich should get a bigger tax cut because they pay more in taxes," or whether "everyone should get the same level of tax cut," 70 percent of voters chose the latter.

To the extent that Americans supported the Bush tax cuts, it was despite these perceived shortcomings and their modest expectations for reductions in their own tax burdens. One reason for the public's support may have been that the modest tax reductions enjoyed by low-income Americans was more significant to them than observers (who typically had far higher incomes) recognized. In dollar amounts the tax savings enjoyed by low-income Americans were very modest, but as a percentage of their total incomes, Americans in the bottom fifth of the income distribution benefited more than those in any other income quintile. According to a Congressional Budget Office study, the $283 average savings for tax filers in the lowest income quintile represented 1.9 percent of their pretax income (which averaged about $15,000).[59] In comparison tax savings for the second, third, fourth, and top income quintiles were, respectively, 1.8, 1.3. 1.1, and 1.3 percent of their pretax income.[60] Only at the very top of the income distribution did the tax savings as a percentage of income exceed that for the bottom quintile: the top 1 percent of earners enjoyed a 2.6-percentage-point reduction in their federal income taxes. From this perspective, the support for the Bush tax cuts from lower-income Americans is not especially surprising. The direct impact of the tax cuts on lower-income families' finances was larger relative to their incomes than it was for most Americans. Consistent with this understanding, Larry Bartels shows that support for the Bush tax cuts was related to Americans' perceptions of their own tax burdens, but not to their views about the tax burdens of the rich or the poor, about government waste, or about preferences for more or less government spending.[61]

But direct impacts on taxpayers' finances are only one consequence of tax cuts. If the public was overly focused on the impact of tax reform on their own tax burdens but failed to take any longer term consequences of the tax cuts into account, then their self-interested calculations may have been misguided. In particular, if Americans failed to recognize the

likelihood that tax cuts would reduce government services that they valued (like spending on education or health care), increase the federal debt,
or lead to offsetting increases in state or local taxes, then their support
for cutting taxes might have conflicted with their own material interests
more broadly understood.

It is hard to assess how realistic or unrealistic the public's expectations
for the consequences of the tax cuts was. In surveys fielded during 2001
(a period of federal budget surpluses) about half of the American public
thought it was possible to enact the proposed tax cut without increasing
the federal deficit, or cutting spending on Social Security, education, or
health care.[62] There may have been some plausibility to this rather rosy
outlook during 2001, but the subsequent return to federal budget deficits,
the additional tax cuts adopted in 2003, and the huge new expenditures
devoted to the wars in Afghanistan and Iraq made federal fiscal conditions much gloomier by the middle of the decade. Perhaps reflecting these
changes, support for the Bush tax cuts did decline somewhat, from about
71 percent to about 60 percent between 2002 and 2004.[63]

What can we conclude about false consciousness and elite manipulation from this brief exploration of the Bush tax cuts? First, the public
does not appear to have been wildly misinformed about the nature of the
tax cuts or unrealistic about the level of tax reduction they could expect.
On the other hand, public perceptions may have been unrealistic in ap-
preciating the longer-term impact of the lost revenue on government
services they value and on other taxes they pay. Yet these longer-term
consequences are difficult to assess and even more difficult to predict in
advance. As John Zaller points out, "unrealistic" public demands for both
more government services and lower taxes may reflect a sensible inclination to pressure government to provide the greatest benefits at the lowest
cost.[64] Zaller compares these "inconsistent" demands with consumers' desires for the highest quality goods at the lowest possible prices. "In many
cases," he writes, "pressuring politicians to do the impossible could serve
the public's interests as well as any feasible alternative."[65]

• • •

The findings in this chapter provide three broad insights into the nature
of policy responsiveness over the past decades. First, they reinforce the
understanding of political parties as policy maximizers. When majority-
party control is strong and gridlock is low, policy outcomes are weakly
related to the preferences of affluent Americans and unrelated to the preferences of the less well-off. When political pressure is present (in the form
of an impending election or uncertain control of government), policy
makers respond to the preferences of the affluent and, when that pressure

is sufficient, to the preferences of the public more broadly. But left to their own devices, political parties pursue the policies that their core activists and policy-demanding groups desire.

Second, there has been a steady increase in responsiveness to the affluent that is only partially explained by the decline in Senate seat advantage and the increase in gridlock. How much each of the other hypothesized factors may have contributed to this increased responsiveness is hard to tell. The growth of economic inequality, the rising cost of political campaigns, the changing nature of the media environment, and politicians' increased use of surveys may all have played a part by intensifying candidates' need for money, by concentrating the supply of that money even further in the hands of the affluent, and by enhancing the role of policy considerations in elections. Whatever combination of factors is at work, the steady strengthening of policy responsiveness for affluent Americans has not been accompanied by a similar increase in responsiveness to the less well-off. The strong responsiveness and low level of representational inequality of the early G. W. Bush years were short-lived, and the apparently positive time trend in responsiveness for the middle class and the poor shown in figure 7.3 turned out to be a function of the unique political conditions during this brief period.

Finally, the results in this and the previous chapter underscore the importance of political circumstances in determining the strength of representation and the equality of policy responsiveness. When circumstances align, policy adheres more closely to the preferences of the public, and more equally to the preferences of both low- and high-income Americans. Alas, circumstances do not appear to align in this way very often. Under ordinary conditions responsiveness, when it occurs at all, is strongly tilted toward the preferences of the affluent. Still, the importance of political circumstances suggests that despite its ubiquitous nature, representational inequality is not inevitable, and political reforms might have at least some prospect of boosting responsiveness to the preferences of the less well-off.

CHAPTER 8

Money and American Politics

POLITICAL EQUALITY IS A CENTRAL TENET OF DEMOCRACY. But it remains a guiding principle, not a description of any existing democratic society. Given the many inequalities among citizens not only in economic resources but also in time, knowledge, and interest in social and political affairs, it would be unrealistic to expect equal influence over policy making. Still, the extent and nature of representational inequalities reflect the degree of democracy in a given society, and when inequalities in political influence become too large, democracy shades into oligarchy (rule by the few) or plutocracy (rule by the wealthy).

The patterns of responsiveness found in previous chapters often corresponded more closely to a plutocracy than to a democracy. We saw in chapter 3 that when preferences across income groups diverged, only the most affluent appeared to influence policy outcomes. Chapter 4 revealed that this representational inequality was spread widely across policy domains, with a strong tilt toward high-income Americans on economic issues, foreign policy, and moral/religious issues, and only modestly greater equality of responsiveness to the middle class and the poor in the social welfare domain. Chapter 5 showed that even this partial exception to the dominance of the affluent was accounted for by the fortuitous confluence of preferences between middle-class citizens and powerful interest groups on issues like health care, education, and Social Security.

This bleak assessment of the state of American democracy was tempered somewhat by findings in chapters 6 and 7 suggesting that under the right circumstances, representational inequalities are reduced, if never fully eliminated. An impending presidential election, a closely divided Congress, and a high level of policy gridlock are all associated with greater equality in responsiveness to the public. None of these conditions is associated with particularly strong responsiveness to the poor, and responsiveness to the affluent always exceeds responsiveness to the middle class. Moreover, strong party dominance reduces policy responsiveness to all income levels, as parties reward the activists and interest groups that form their base of support. Nonetheless the degree of representational inequality does vary depending on political circumstances, giving some hope that political reforms might help to broaden the responsiveness of policy makers to Americans at all economic levels.

What kinds of political reforms are likely to be most efficacious depends, at least in part, on the mechanisms that produce unequal policy responsiveness to begin with. In this concluding chapter I therefore explore the role of money in politics in an effort to better account for the outsize influence of affluent Americans, and to identify the means by which representational inequality might be reduced.

THE MILLIONAIRES CLUB

By one recent calculation 44 percent of the members of the U.S. Congress are millionaires.[1] More prosaically, *all* members of Congress, by dint of their congressional salaries alone, are solidly in the top decile of the American income distribution.[2] Perhaps one reason public policy tends to reflect the preferences of the affluent, then, is simply that policy makers who are themselves affluent pursue policies that reflect their personal values and interests.

If representatives were fully constrained by the desires of their constituents, party leaders, interest groups, and campaign donors, then their personal preferences and interests would have no independent impact on their activities. Even under this extreme scenario, we would still expect to find a match between members' personal views and their congressional voting since members with more liberal personal views would be more likely to be elected from liberal districts and those with more conservative views from conservative districts. More likely, of course, members of Congress have some degree of leeway in their voting, and consequently their personal interests and preferences are likely to exert at least some influence over their behavior as senators or representatives.

As the extreme scenario suggests, disentangling the personal preferences of members of Congress from the other influences that might affect their behavior is difficult. We have no reliable way to measure representatives' personal preferences unaffected by the demands of their constituents, campaign donors, and so on. Most scholars who have examined this question have attempted to assess the role of personal preferences by identifying some personal characteristic that is plausibly related to members' preferences or interests. For example, members' personal wealth might be associated with their preferences on economic policy, members' use of tobacco might be associated with their preferences on tobacco legislation, and whether members have children in public schools might be associated with their preferences on school funding or voucher programs. These associations might arise either through the anticipated impact of the relevant policies on the members' well-being or through the values and orientations that are reflected in and shaped by members' choices (e.g., to smoke cigarettes or to send their children to public rather than private schools). But members with certain characteristics are likely to come from states or districts that share those characteristics, with wealthier members coming, on average, from wealthier jurisdictions, members who smoke coming from areas in which more constituents smoke and the tobacco industry has a larger presence, and so on. Thus any effort to isolate the impact of personal characteristics must take these correlated district characteristics into account.

Studies using this approach have found evidence that the personal characteristics of legislators are sometimes related to their behavior in Congress. For example, Ebonya Washington finds that U.S. legislators who have more daughters tend to have more feminist voting records as judged by the National Organization for Women and the American Association of University Women (holding other factors, including their total number of children, constant).[3] Similarly, Barry Burden finds that U.S. House members who smoke have more "pro-tobacco" voting records (holding constant the presence or absence of the tobacco industry in the representative's district among other factors), and that Democratic members with children in public schools are more likely to vote in opposition to school voucher plans.[4]

Each of the above examples relies on the variation among members of Congress in the relevant personal characteristics—some members have more female children and others fewer, some smoke while others don't, and some have children in public schools. But as mentioned above, *all* members of Congress are in the top decile of family income. It is impossible, therefore, to address the question of whether being in the top income decile influences members' voting by comparing the records of more- or less-affluent members of Congress. Nevertheless, there are other comparisons that might shed some light on the question. First, although all U.S. senators and representatives are in the top income decile, some are far more affluent than others. If personal economic interests (or the political outlooks associated with them) influence congressional voting behavior, we might be able to discern a pattern by comparing members with more or less outside income (i.e., in addition to their congressional salaries) or members with higher or lower net worth. Second, members of Congress came from different class backgrounds before they entered politics. While their economic status and economic interests might have changed over time, their prepolitical careers might have lasting influence over their outlooks and voting tendencies. If so, we might conclude that the tendency for representatives to come from more privileged backgrounds might shape the policies they pursue after they enter Congress.

Although the U.S. Senate is often viewed as a "millionaires club," there is substantial variation in the income and assets of senators and House members. In 2008, 18 members of Congress reported more than $200,000 from their own or their spouse's outside income, while 142 members reported no outside income at all.[5] With regard to wealth, 14 senators and 38 House members reported net assets above $10 million in 2008, while 9 senators and 142 representatives reported less than $250,000 in assets.

Nicholas Carnes examined both the outside incomes and net worth of U.S. senators and representatives.[6] Using a variety of measures of congressional voting on economic issues, including scorecards compiled by the Chamber of Commerce and the AFL-CIO, Carnes finds no association between members' voting records and their outside income or wealth. Some of the richest members of Congress are economic conservatives (like Darrell Issa, R-CA, with an estimated net worth of about $251 million, or Vernon Buchanan, R-FL, at $143 million), but others are economic liberals (like Herb Kohl, D-WI, with $214 million in assets, or John Kerry, D-MA, with $208 million). While there might be specific votes on which members' personal economic interests exert an influence, broad measures of congressional economic voting like those complied by the Chamber of Commerce or the AFL-CIO show no association with members' financial status.

In addition to representatives' current financial status, Carnes also examined representatives' professional histories before they entered Congress.[7] Carnes finds that, unlike contemporaneous economic status, previous professional histories are related to members' congressional voting records. Depending on the voting measure used, Carnes reports substantial differences between representatives from the most "conservative professions" (like business owners or skilled professionals) and the most "liberal professions" (like manual laborers or service industry workers). The differences between these extreme occupation groups range from about 25 to 50 percent of the range in the economic voting scales Carnes employs.

As suggested above, some of this difference may result from the kinds of states or districts that the representatives were elected from rather than any independent influence of their occupational backgrounds; if business owners tend to get elected to Congress from conservative districts and service workers from liberal districts, then the association between their voting records and the their previous occupations may be spurious. To test for this possibility, Carnes adds a wide range of control variables to his analyses, including district characteristics like median income, percent union, partisan identification, and political ideology. These controls reduce the apparent association of professional background and congressional voting, but they do not eliminate it. Representatives with the most and least conservative former occupations differ by about 14 to 20 percent of the economic voting scales once these other factors are taken into account.

Taken together the analyses described above suggest that legislators' personal interests and preferences can shape their congressional voting, but that concern over the growing wealth of members of Congress is probably misplaced. At least in terms of economic policy broadly conceived, liberals and conservatives are equally likely to be found among Congress's wealthiest members and among those with the fewest resources. It's impossible to say with any confidence whether U.S. representatives would behave differently if their salaries put them in the middle of the U.S. income distribution rather than toward the top. But it does appear that the substantial existing differences in economic status among members of Congress are not related to broad patterns of voting on economic policy.

In contrast the association between previous occupation and congressional voting does suggest that at least some of the representational inequality found in previous chapters might result from the class composition of Congress. As Carnes shows, representatives with different occupational backgrounds who are elected from similar districts vote differently. A Congress composed of more members from modest backgrounds might therefore be expected to adopt policies at least somewhat more consistent with the preferences and interests of poor and middle-class Americans.

Yet the class bias of Congress does not vary over the short term, while policy responsiveness to the affluent does. As chapters 6 and 7 showed, it is not only responsiveness to the poor and the middle class but also to the well-off that varies across the electoral cycle and over periods of greater and lesser partisan competition. Since the impetus to adopt policies favored by well-off Americans depends on fluctuating political pressures, the (essentially unchanging) personal preferences of elected representatives can, at most, explain a small part of the representational inequalities documented in the previous chapters.

A Congress that looks more like America in terms of wealth or occupational background may have other advantages. Proponents of descriptive representation argue, for example, that social and demographic similarity between constituents and their representatives can serve to heighten political interest and engagement and to enhance support for the political system.[8] But holding a working-class occupation before entering Congress is no guarantee that a member will favor economically liberal policies. The real challenge for those who would like to see federal policy more equally reflective of the preferences of all Americans is to elect representatives (from any background) who share those preferences and to create more powerful incentives for members of Congress to advance the interests and respond to the desires of all their constituents, regardless of income.

INCOME AND POLITICAL ENGAGEMENT

If the affluent status of elected representatives cannot explain the patterns of representational inequality documented in previous chapters, what does account for the consistently stronger association of preferences and policies for affluent than for poor or middle-class Americans?

The most straightforward explanation for representational inequality is that high-income Americans are more likely to vote, more likely to volunteer in campaigns, and more likely to make political donations (and to make larger donations) than are less-well-off citizens. All these political activities increase with income but as figure 8.1 shows, they do so in different ways. It is low-income Americans who are distinctive in their lower rates of voting and volunteering while the differences between middle-income and affluent Americans are modest. But when it comes to campaign donations, it is high-income American who stand out.

Political donations, then, but not voting or volunteering, resembles the pattern of representational inequality we saw in earlier chapters: under typical circumstances, the middle class has no more sway than the poor when their preferences diverge from those of the affluent.

The fit between political donations and representation suggested by figure 8.1—and the lack of fit with voter turnout or volunteering—is also consistent with Larry Bartels's analysis of Senators' roll-call voting.[9] Bartels considers three aspects of political engagement, all of which are more characteristic of higher-income Americans: voter turnout, respondents' contact with their senators (or their office), and respondents' knowledge of the Senate candidates in their state's most recent election. These three factors, he concludes, can account for only a small part of the disparities in senators' responsiveness to their low-, middle-, and high-income constituents. Bartels finds more support for the notion that senators are responsive to their affluent constituents because they supply the money that fuels the political system. But this evidence is indirect (since the surveys Bartels analyzes do not include data on individual respondents' donations) and not always consistent with the patterns of representational inequality Bartels finds.[10]

Of course money is not the only valued commodity in politics. Groups that can mobilize large numbers of volunteers (like labor and religious organizations) may exert a policy influence that competes with that of the affluent, at least on particular issues at particular times. In addition we saw in chapter 6 that policy makers appeal directly to less-affluent voters during presidential election years. Nevertheless electoral campaigns require money, and more and more of it over time. While the evidence here is circumstantial, the associated patterns of policy influence and political contributions offer at least one highly plausible explanation for the

Self-reported turnout

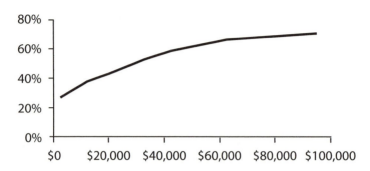

Percent working in a political campaign

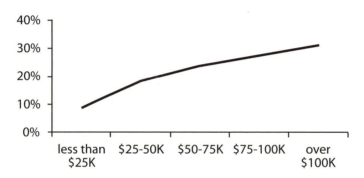

Average political donation

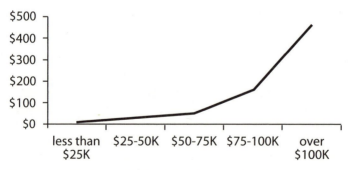

Figure 8.1. Forms of Political Involvement by Income. Sources: Self-reported turnout from the 2000 Current Population Survey; percent working in a political campaign and average political donation from the 1988 American Citizen Participation Study (Verba, Schlozman, and Brady, 1995).

inequality of policy responsiveness to different economic strata found repeatedly in the previous chapters.

The Merely Affluent and the Truly Rich

The analyses in the previous chapters contrasted the preferences of the 90th income percentile with less-well-off Americans and showed that the preferences of the well-off group are much more likely to be reflected in policy outcomes than are those of less-affluent citizens. But we might wonder whether the thirty million Americans in the top income decile are really shaping political outcomes or whether the stronger association we observe arises from the confluence of their preferences with a much smaller and more affluent circle that wields true influence over government policy. Even if the merely affluent do exert influence over political outcomes consistent with findings reported in previous chapters, the truly rich may dominate on those issues that most strongly affect their collective interests. As Jeffrey Winters and Benjamin Page point out, moneyed interests may dominate policy making on particular issues like corporate regulation or the tax treatment of investment income, while a (somewhat) broader set of Americans shape outcomes on other issues.[11]

As shown above, Americans at the 90th income percentile donate much more money to political campaigns than middle-income Americans do. But the citizens who make the most substantial contributions to politicians and political organizations are typically far more affluent still. During the 2004 election cycle, for example, insurance magnate Peter Lewis and investor George Soros each gave over $23 million dollars to Democratic candidates and organizations.[12] On the conservative side, Texas homebuilder Robert Perry (known for bankrolling the "Swift Boat Veterans for Truth" attacks on John Kerry in 2004) recently donated $7 million to one of Karl Rove's Republican advocacy groups,[13] while the Koch brothers have spent at least $100 million supporting conservative causes over the years.[14] Wealthy supporters contribute to both Democratic and Republican causes, but donations from this elite economic stratum tend to tilt strongly Republican. In the most recent election cycle, for example, over three-quarters of the money from the fifty largest individual donors to independent spending groups working to influence the election was from conservatives.[15]

Data on many aspects of political donations are plentiful, thanks to federal reporting requirements. But many kinds of political donations fall outside these requirements, and even when donations are reported we typically have no way of knowing the donors' incomes or other characteristics. Survey studies that ask respondents whether and how much they contributed to political candidates or organizations provide the best indication of the sources of political money, but such studies rarely include respondents with very high incomes (and often use broad income categories that make it impossible to identify any such respondents who might be included). For example, the results shown in the bottom panel of figure 8.1 are based on a 1990 survey in which the top income category included everyone with family incomes above $125,000.[16] Despite this limitation, the extremely top-heavy nature of campaign contributions is clear: the majority of the money that respondents reported donating came from Americans in the top 9 percent of the income distribution, and of these donations, almost two-thirds of the money came from the top 3 percent.[17]

Another study that sheds light on the contribution activity of very affluent Americans focused on people who gave at least $200 to one or more congressional candidates in 1996 (the threshold requiring the donation be reported to the Federal Election Commission in that year).[18] Even among these highly engaged (and affluent) individuals, most of the money donated came from the most affluent donors. About one-third of all reported donations to congressional candidates came from respondents with family incomes above a half-million dollars (an income level attained by less than one-quarter of one percent of American families), and over 60 percent of this money came from people with incomes above $250,000 (a level attained by less than one percent of the population in 1996).[19]

Campaign donations are only one form of political contribution. Individuals hoping to influence policy making can also give money to parties, PACs, independent expenditure groups, and lobbying organizations. Some of these forms of political donations also have individual limits and reporting requirements (e.g., donations to political parties and PACs), but these limits are higher than those for individual candidate donations. Owing to higher or nonexistent donation limits, the source of funds flowing through these other channels is even more biased toward upper-income Americans than are direct campaign donations.[20]

In sum, if political money explains the greater influence over policy enjoyed by affluent Americans, then we might expect the truly wealthy to be even more influential. To the extent that the preferences of Americans at the 90th percentile coincide with those at the 99th or the 99.9th percentiles, the apparent influence of the merely affluent might actually reflect the influence of a much smaller number of truly rich.

We know little about the policy preferences of very wealthy Americans for the same reasons we know little about their political donations: there are relatively few of them, and polling organizations usually do a poor job of identifying them even when they are included in survey samples. In an effort to overcome these twin obstacles, Benjamin Page and Cari Hennessy combined multiple years of data from the General Social Survey.[21] Based on three years of data from the late 1970s in which very high income earners were distinguished, they were able to identify 132 respondents with incomes in the top 4 percent of the distribution. Page and Hennessy assess the policy preferences for this group and compare them with the top one-third of the income distribution and with the remainder of the survey respondents. For most of the policy issues they examine, the top 4 percent express preferences that are similar to those of the top one-third (and consequently differ in a similar fashion from those of the bottom two-thirds of the income distribution). On many issues, however, the top 4 percent are more extreme in their views. For example, these highest-income respondents are considerably more favorable toward abortion rights, less supportive of spending to protect the environment, and more likely to say that the United States should take an active part in world affairs in comparison to the top one-third of the income distribution. They are also considerably more likely to identify as Republicans.

Unfortunately these General Social Survey data lack questions about policies where one might expect to find the largest preference differences among very high earners (e.g., on business regulation or tax policy). A clearer picture of the range of attitudes among America's most affluent citizens will require surveys specifically targeted at this population. Benjamin Page and Larry Bartels are currently conducting a pilot study to gauge the feasibility of such a survey. If they succeed in interviewing sufficient numbers of very high income Americans, we may be able to assess empirically the extent to which the preferences of the truly rich differ from those of the merely well-off and, by extension, the extent to which the influence of the truly rich accounts for the responsiveness to the 90th income percentile that I have documented in this book.

MONEY AND POLITICAL OUTCOMES

Money, it is said, is the mother's milk of politics. But as many a losing candidate can attest, money is no guarantee of victory. In 2008 Mitt Romney spent $107 million in an effort to secure the Republican nomination but was out of the running by February.[22] And in Alaska's Republican Senate primary in 2010, the little-known lawyer Joe Miller upset incumbent Lisa Murkowski despite Murkowski's 20-to-1 fund-raising advantage.[23] Referenda too sometimes defy the spending advantage of one side or the other. In Ohio payday lenders spent $16 million in an effort to overturn new lending restrictions imposed by the legislature, while their opponents managed to raise only $266,000 to keep the restrictions alive.[24] Voters rejected the referendum by 64 percent to 36 percent.

Lobbying government for favorable policies also requires money, and enormous sums are spent every year on lobbying by corporations, unions, professional organizations, and single-issue groups like the National Rifle Association and the AARP. Over thirteen thousand registered lobbyists spent almost $3.5 billion in 2009 alone.[25] But here as well, more money does not necessarily translate into favorable policy outcomes. For example, the banking lobby, "one of the most powerful, well-connected, and politically savvy actors in national politics," has fought for years to constrain the growth of credit unions.[26] But credit unions' small-town, mom-and-pop image has served them well, and they have consistently prevailed over the American Bankers Association and its well-funded PAC. (Credit unions are, of course, only one minor issue among the many consequential policies on which banks have lobbied. As government response to the economic crisis that began in 2008 reveals, the banking lobby's powerful reputation is well deserved indeed.)

Money does not guarantee victory in elections or policy battles, but that doesn't mean money is irrelevant to these outcomes. A substantial body of research has attempted to assess the connection between campaign spending or lobbying activity and election or policy outcomes. This effort is complicated by the endogenous nature of spending. For example, incumbent politicians raise and spend more money if they anticipate a closer reelection race. Consequently it may appear that the more money an incumbent raises, the lower his or her vote share turns out to be. Analyses of the impact of lobbying and interest group donations on congressional voting face similarly challenging obstacles. Interest groups may attempt to sway members' votes or other activities on the issues they care about, but they might also adopt a strategy of rewarding their friends. In the first case we might expect to see individual members' votes shifting in response to interest group efforts, but in the second case we would find no such relationship.

These and other complexities in the relationship between money and political outcomes have contributed to the still murky picture of money's influence in politics. With regard to election outcomes, what is clear is that some basic (and probably growing) level of funding is necessary to compete successfully as a primary or general election candidate. While this basic funding level may be low for local and even some statewide offices, the funding threshold for viability in federal elections clearly excludes many candidates from realistic contention (and gives a decided advantage in this regard to candidates wealthy enough to fund their own campaigns). Affluent contributors consequently serve as a political filter mechanism; without the support of a sufficient core of well-off contributors, a prospective candidate has little chance of mounting a competitive campaign.

Beyond this threshold, the importance of money to election outcomes is less clear. A number of studies have shown that spending by challengers in congressional races has a larger impact in terms of votes-per-dollar than spending by incumbents.[27] How large this difference appears, and whether spending by incumbents appears to matter at all, seems to depend heavily on the methodology used.[28]

Studies of presidential campaign spending are much less common, perhaps because there are so few presidential contests available to study. One recent study of presidential contests by Larry Bartels finds a considerable effect of spending on presidential vote choice.[29] Holding constant the state of the economy and the length of time the incumbent party had held the presidency, each $1 per voter advantage in total campaign spending was associated with almost 4 percentage points greater probability of voting for the better-funded candidate among voters who were otherwise equally inclined toward both candidates. In the fourteen elections Bartels examined (1952–2004), the Republican presidential candidate always outspent the Democratic candidate, with the difference ranging from extremely little (in 1952, 1956, and 1960) to about $2 per voter (in 1972, 1980, and 1984). Consequently unequal campaign spending boosted Republican vote share in each one of these fourteen elections, and according to Bartels's calculations enough to swing the outcome to Richard Nixon in 1968 and George W. Bush in 2000.

Research on the impact of money on policy outcomes is also somewhat unsettled, in part because so many studies focus only on short-term associations. Results from the numerous studies that have looked at PAC contributions and congressional roll-call voting are mixed. For example, Stephen Ansolabehere, John de Figueiredo, and James Snyder examined forty such studies, finding that campaign contributions had no statistically discernable effects in three out of four cases.[30] On the other hand, Thomas Stratmann assessed these same forty studies and concluded that even though the results of many of the individual studies were not statistically compelling, the combined evidence that campaign contributions affect congressional voting was extremely strong.[31] In addition studies that look at specific votes and donation patterns do frequently find associations in the expected direction. In their study of trade legislation, for example, Robert Baldwin and Christopher Magee find that contributions from labor and business groups influenced representatives' votes on NAFTA and the Uruguay round of the GATT, but not on the 1994 vote to renew most-favored nation status for China.[32]

As this brief account suggests, analyses of the short-term associations between PAC donations and roll-call voting come to differing conclusions. But some scholars argue that this is not where we should expect to find evidence of the influence of money over policy outcomes to begin with. First, most interest organizations (as well as individual donors and activists) build long-term relationships with representatives. From this perspective, political donations are not part of a quid pro quo in which money is exchanged for particular votes, but part of the long-term cultivation of a relationship in which campaign donations and other forms of support to legislators help an interest organization maintain access to and a favorable disposition from those representatives. As James Snyder suggests in an article titled "Long Term Investing in Politicians," "a contributor cannot simply buy a congressman's vote on an important bill with a $5,000 campaign donation. Large donations over several elections, however, together with intelligent, informative discussions about matters of concern to the contributor, may eventually yield considerable benefits."[33]

"Long-term investing" helps ensure that representatives favorably inclined toward a donors' preferred policies will remain in Congress (and remain favorably inclined). In addition the actions that such investors seek go beyond roll-call votes. Indeed, congressional scholars often note the importance of representatives' activities that take place behind the scenes, shaping the congressional agenda and determining which policy options get roll-call votes and which do not. In describing congressional wrangling over the massive tax reforms of the Reagan years, for example, Douglas Arnold writes that "virtually all of the relevant decisions were made early in the legislative process, behind closed doors, and without recorded votes."[34]

For obvious reasons congressional roll-call votes are easier to analyze than members' behind-the-scenes activities. One study that did collect data on such activities combined committee markup records and interviews with congressional staff to indentify six activities that members might engage in to advance a particular policy, such as negotiating with other members or offering amendments during committee markup.[35] The authors find solid evidence that PAC contributions are related to these sorts of activities, noting that interest groups' goals are to shape not only the direction of legislators' policy preferences, but the vigor with which they pursue those policies.

In sum, the role of money in politics is complex and far from completely understood. Popular impressions of a Congress for sale to the highest bidder, or an electoral system in which money is the singular key to victory, are grossly oversimplified. But it would be equally naive to think that the "mother's milk of politics" is of little importance.

Concerns about the distorting role of money in shaping government policy and election outcomes tend to focus on organized interest groups. But most of the money raised by candidates and political parties comes from individual donors. During the four congressional elections between

2002 and 2008, for, example, contributions from individuals constituted about 53 percent of the campaign money raised by House candidates and about 66 percent of that raised by Senate candidates (compared with 35 percent and 17 percent from PACs, with the remainder coming from the parties or the candidates themselves).[36]

Individual campaign donors are a distinctive subset of the American population. Donors tend to be older than average, male, highly educated, with high incomes and high levels of political interest, and more strongly partisan than other Americans.[37] Of the various predictors of individuals' political donations, however, income stands out as by far the strongest.[38] Thus any effort to strengthen the influence of less-affluent Americans over federal policy must address the highly skewed sources of individual campaign donations.

CAMPAIGN FINANCE REFORM

Recognizing the potentially corrupting influence of money in elections, federal legislation beginning in the early twentieth century sought to restrict corporate and individual contributions, require disclosures, and limit overall campaign spending by candidates for federal office. But these regulations were largely ineffective owing to a variety of loopholes and a lack of enforcement provisions. The 1971 Federal Election Campaign Act and the 1974 amendments that established the Federal Election Commission mark the beginning of serious campaign finance regulation at the federal level. These laws required reporting of campaign contributions and expenditures, established PACs as regulated vehicles through which corporations, unions, and interest organizations could raise and donate money, provided for federal financing of presidential election campaigns, and established limits on contributions and expenditures for candidates for all federal offices.

Since the mid-1970s federal campaign finance regulations have been in more or less constant flux owing to a series of Supreme Court decisions and new legislation. The most important recent changes to federal campaign finance laws are the 2002 Bipartisan Campaign Reform Act (also known as McCain-Feingold) and the Supreme Court's 2010 *Citizens United* decision invalidating certain restrictions on expenditures by third parties like corporations or unions. The overall impact of the many changes over the previous decades is hard to assess. Spending by outside organizations like the anti-Kerry Swift Boat Veterans for Truth, Karl Rove's American Crossroads, and Moveon.org has clearly become more important, but these expenditures are difficult to trace, and the legal form the organizations takes varies almost from one election to the next. One clear trend in congressional elections is a shift in the source of individual donations toward larger gifts. Between the 2000 and 2008 election cycles, the proportion of all individual contributions that came from people who donated at least $1,000 to House candidates grew from 24 to 35 percent, while the proportion from people who donated less than $200 fell from 15 to 8 percent. Thousand-dollar donors accounted for 28 percent of the money raised by Senate candidates in 2000 and 40 percent in 2008, with money from under-$200 donors falling from 17 to 14 percent of the total.

Presidential elections, with higher visibility and public interest, tend to draw larger numbers of small donations, although even in this case the dollars contributed by large donors swamp those from the far more numerous smaller donations. In 2004 Kerry and Bush received, respectively, 20 and 26 percent of their campaign donations in small (i.e., under $200) contributions, compared with 56 and 60 percent from contributors giving at least $1,000. In 2008 John McCain's fundraising followed a similar pattern, with 21 and 60 percent of his individual contribution dollars coming in the form of small and large contributions, respectively. But Barack Obama did raise a somewhat larger proportion of his money in small gifts: under-$200 donors accounted for 30 percent of Obama's individual donations, while contributions over $1,000 accounted for 43 percent. Clearly the Internet has helped make the collection of small political donations easier, and perhaps the 2008 Obama campaign reflects a trend in this direction. If so, this would be a welcome development for those concerned about representational inequality since larger donations tend to come from more affluent donors.[39]

There is some reason to hope that campaign finance reforms that shift the sources of campaign money away from interest groups and large donors might have a democratizing impact on federal policy making. But many observers frustrated over the continued ability of moneyed interests to dominate political life have likened campaign finance regulation to squeezing a balloon—if you squeeze in one place the balloon simply pops out in another. Money, it is thought, will find its way into politics no matter what obstacles are thrown in its way. Campaign finance reform also faces the prospect of scrutiny by an increasingly unsympathetic Supreme Court. The Court's equation of spending and speech, recently affirmed and extended in the 2010 *Citizens United* decision, undercuts campaign reform efforts that seek to limit spending in some way.

Since policies that limit campaign spending risk Court censure, some reformers have focused on proposals to equalize political influence by increasing campaign spending from sources other than affluent individuals and organized interest groups. A variety of state and federal public financing programs take this approach, including the existing but threatened matching-funds program for presidential campaigns.[40] Among the most intriguing suggestions along these lines is the "voting with dollars" proposal advanced by Bruce Ackerman and Ian Ayres.[41] Under this proposal all eligible voters would be given publicly funded vouchers, which could be used to make donations to federal candidates of their choice (they propose $25 for presidential campaigns, $15 for Senate campaigns, and $10 for House campaigns). Any unspent money would disappear and could not be rolled over to the next election or used for any other purpose. Depending on the level of funding, such a system might provide the majority of contributions in federal elections and would pressure candidates to address the issues and promote the policies of concern to the greatest number of voters. (Similarly, incumbents seeking reelection would have greater incentives to pursue policies consistent with the preferences of the majority of voters—who under this system would also be the source of the majority of campaign contributions).[42]

One way to assess the impact of potential changes in the way campaigns are funded is to look to the states, which have adopted a much wider range of campaign finance regimes than has the federal government. For example, contributions to candidates for governor or state legislature are limited to only $200 in Colorado, while candidates in New York can accept $10,000 from individual donors, and thirteen states currently place no limits at all on the size of individuals' contributions. Similarly large variation exists in states' limits on campaign contributions by corporations, labor unions, PACs, and political parties.[43]

A small research literature on the impact of state campaign finance laws suggests that such regulations do have the potential to shape electoral outcomes and perhaps state policy as well. For example, Kihong Eom and Donald Gross find that contribution limits can reduce gubernatorial incumbents' typical fund-raising advantage over their challengers, and Thomas Stratmann and Francisco Aparicio-Castillo show that such limits bolster challengers' competitiveness in state legislative elections as well.[44] The competitiveness of state legislative races is also enhanced when states adopt public financing.[45] Finally, Timothy Besley and Anne Case show that restrictions on corporate contributions result in higher voter turnout and larger numbers of Democrats and women in state legislatures.[46]

None of this research on state campaign finance laws examines the impact of these regulations on the strength of policy responsiveness or representational inequality.[47] But these studies suggest two ways in which campaign finance reform might enhance representation. First, by shifting the source of political contributions away from the most affluent (through contribution limits or public financing), campaign finance reform might help equalize responsiveness to more- and less-well-off citizens. At the same time these reforms might enhance representation through their impact on electoral competitiveness. The findings in chapter 7 showed the powerful impact of partisan competition and electoral uncertainty in shaping policy responsiveness at the national level. If the enhanced electoral competition associated with state campaign finance reforms has a similar impact on state policy, then the fifty "laboratories of democracy" may help point the way toward more effective campaign reforms at the national level as well.

Enhancing Democratic Responsiveness

As suggested above, campaign reforms that reduce the importance of money in elections or shift the sources of that money toward less-affluent donors may help to equalize responsiveness both directly (by reducing the incentives for politicians to appeal to affluent constituents) and indirectly (by increasing electoral competitiveness and thereby increasing the incentives for politicians to appeal to all voters). Other policies that increase electoral competitiveness similarly promise to improve representational equality. Gerrymandering, for example, is often used to generate safe seats for incumbents and consequently uncompetitive elections. Research suggests that the trend toward nonpartisan redistricting of state and federal election districts will result in more competitive elections and in legislatures that more closely match the partisan distribution of the electorate.[48] Other policies that reduce the incumbency advantage and enhance electoral completion include nonpartisan get-out-the-vote drives. In one intriguing recent study, Costas Panagopoulos and Donald Green broadcast nonpartisan radio ads in randomly chosen cities with mayoral elections.[49] The ads reminded citizens of the upcoming election date, encouraged them to vote, and stated the names of the mayoral candidates. The cities that received these ads had substantially more competitive elections than the control cities in which no such ads were broadcast.

Critics of American democracy have long called for efforts to increase electoral competitiveness, and a multitude of reforms have been suggested (and occasionally implemented) at the state and national levels.[50] My findings suggest that strong party control reduces responsiveness to any subset of the public, but that political pressures from impending elections or uncertain control over the legislature enhances responsiveness to both well-off and middle-class Americans. Reforms that increase electoral competition are not likely to be popular among incumbents, but to the extent that such reforms can be achieved, the political system may become at least somewhat more responsive to the preferences of all citizens.

In addition to reducing politicians' reliance on affluent campaign donors and enhancing the competitiveness of elections, a third route toward bringing public policy more into line with the preferences of all Americans lies in taking advantage of policies that are supported by affluent and poor alike. This approach has sometimes taken the form of "targeting within universalism" on the theory that universal programs like Social Security or Medicare will garner broader support than policies that restrict their benefits to the disadvantaged.[51] As we saw in chapter 4, however, some means-tested programs garner strong support across the income spectrum, and some market-oriented reforms to universal programs are much more popular among the affluent than among the less well-off.

The set of policies that are strongly favored across the income spectrum but especially beneficial to the least well-off include support services like child care and job training for welfare recipients, increases in the minimum wage, and spending for education.[52] In some of these cases (like the minimum wage), the poor show more enthusiasm than the affluent. But even so, strong majorities of Americans at the 90th income percentile favored increasing the minimum wage in each of the fifteen separate questions in my dataset.[53] These sorts of policies provide opportunities not only to shift government policy in a direction favored by the less advantaged, but to advance their economic interests at a time when the balance of political and economic forces is pushing strongly in the opposite direction.

Finally, redressing the imbalance in political influence will be difficult if the trend toward increased economic inequality continues unabated. The share of all income received by the top 10 percent of U.S. families grew from about one-third in the 1950s and 1960s to almost one-half today.[54] Much of these gains, moreover, have gone to the very top of the income distribution. Including capital gains as well as earned income, the share of income going to the top 1 percent of earners has grown from about 9 percent in 1974 to over 23 percent.[55] A huge economics literature has explored the causes of growing income inequality in the United States and other countries, and factors such as globalization, technological development, and increased returns to education are typically identified as important contributors. But government policy clearly plays an important role as well, especially with regard to the concentration of income and wealth at the very top of the distribution.[56] Moreover how such forces play out in any given society depends heavily on the policy choices that society makes. For example, tax and transfer policies in most advanced democracies have become more downwardly redistributive over the past decades, helping to reduce the growth in economic inequality, but in the

United States these policies have become less downwardly redistributive, thereby exacerbating the growth of income inequality instead.[57]

The relative importance of the various political forces and policy choices that have contributed to rising inequality in the United States are difficult to discern. Larry Bartels shows the dramatically different trajectories of posttax inequality during the past three decades under Democratic presidents (essentially unchanged) and Republican presidents (dramatically increased), but the specific policies that account for this difference are unclear.[58] Jacob Hacker and Paul Pierson focus on the extreme income growth enjoyed by the very highest earners.[59] Hacker and Pierson argue that tax policies, corporate governance arrangements, financial deregulation, and labor relations have all contributed to the growth of a "winner-take-all" society.

The political and economic causes of increased economic inequality are still much debated.[60] Whatever their cause, their effect can only be to exacerbate representational inequality. As resources flow toward the already most advantaged Americans, their ability to use those resources to shape policy increases. Of course rich Americans hold diverse preferences, just as the poor and the middle class do. But despite some prominent liberal counterexamples, rich Americans tend to support the economic policies from which they have so greatly benefited. This raises the disturbing prospect of a vicious cycle in which growing economic and political inequality are mutually reinforcing.

Economic inequality has been increasing in the United States for roughly the past three decades. As the analyses in the previous chapter showed, responsiveness to the affluent also grew over this period, while responsiveness to the poor and the middle class depended on the proximity of a presidential election or the unusual political circumstances of the early G. W. Bush years. Yet the importance of political conditions in shaping responsiveness means that our political destiny is not predetermined. The obstacles to enhancing representational equality in America are considerable, both because political reform is always hard to achieve and because economic resources and the political influence that accompanies them continue to shift toward the already advantaged. But the costs of not doing so are considerable as well. The poor and the middle class are already far more likely than the affluent to feel that their preferences and interests are ignored by government policy makers.[61] Further concentration of political influence among the country's affluent threatens both the perception and the reality of a shared political community so central to the health of even the modestly democratic republic we currently enjoy.

Appendix

As explained in chapter 3, using the same survey questions to gauge the preferences of respondents at different income levels can produce correlated measurement errors. One indication that my preference measures do indeed contain correlated errors is the implausible coefficients that result when multiple preference measures are included in the same prediction equation. The first column of table A3.3 shows the coefficients from three bivariate ordinary least squares (OLS) regressions using the preferences of the 10th, 50th, and 90th income percentiles, respectively. (Unlike logistic regression, OLS regression can be estimated from a variance/covariance matrix; the technique of correcting correlated errors by deflating the covariances among predictors can therefore be applied to OLS but not to logistic regression.) These coefficients tell the same story as the logistic coefficients in table 3.1: a modestly stronger link between preferences and policy for those at higher income levels.

The second column of table A3.3 shows the results when all three preference measures are included simultaneously. In this multivariate analysis, the estimates for the preferences of the 10th and 50th percentiles become negative (suggesting, implausibly, that net of other income groups' preferences, greater support for a policy change among the poor and the middle class leads to a lower probability of that change being adopted). Also, implausibly, the estimated impact of the preferences of the well-off increases from 0.51 to 1.01 when the preferences of the 10th and 50th percentiles are added.

In his investigation of the sources of "wrong signs" in regression analysis, Christopher Achen shows that when predictors with correlated measurement errors are included simultaneously in the same equation, the coefficients for the predictors with the weakest true relationship to the outcome being measured (in my analyses, the coefficients for the lowest income level) may be unreliable and even incorrectly signed.[1] As Achen and others indicate, when error covariances among predictors can be estimated, a variety of techniques exist to compensate for them and produce unbiased estimates.[2] Estimating error covariances, however, requires multiple independent measures of the same underlying concept or attitude. Multiple measures can plausibly be identified only for the subset of my data where I have alternative survey questions from different organizations or with different wordings that tap the same underlying policy change. As explained in chapter 2, the 1,779 questions in my dataset include 387 questions with at least one alternative version relating to essentially the

Table A3.1   Policy Responsiveness by Size of Preference Gap across Income Percentiles

	10th vs. 90th Income Percentiles		50th vs. 90th Income Percentiles	
Size of Preference Gap	10th	90th	50th	90th
Less than 5 points				
Logit coefficient (s.e.)	.54 (.09)	.54 (.09)	.48 (.07)	.50 (.07)
Intercept	−1.01 (.11)	−1.02 (.11)	−.93 (.08)	−.95 (.08)
N	600	600	936	936
Log likelihood	718	717	1140	1133
Likelihood ratio χ^2	$\chi^2(1) = 40$	$\chi^2(1) = 42$	$\chi^2(1) = 55$	$\chi^2(1) = 60$
	$p < .001$	$p < .001$	$p < .001$	$p < .001$
Between 5 and 10 points				
Logit coefficient (s.e.)	.41 (.11)	.52 (.11)	.33 (.10)	.51 (.12)
Intercept	−.92 (.11)	−.99 (.12)	−.78 (.10)	−.84 (.10)
N	456	456	521	521
Log likelihood	552	541	653	643
Likelihood ratio χ^2	$\chi^2(1) = 16$	$\chi^2(1) = 26$	$\chi^2(1) = 10$	$\chi^2(1) = 21$
	$p < .001$	$p < .001$	$p = .001$	$p < .001$
Greater than 10 points				
Logit coefficient (s.e.)	.02 (.09)	.46 (.10)	−.01 (.14)	.47 (.18)
Intercept	−.65 (.08)	−.77 (.09)	−.80 (.12)	−.86 (.13)
N	723	723	322	322
Log likelihood	931	908	399	392
Likelihood ratio χ^2	$\chi^2(1) = 0.3$	$\chi^2(1) = 23$	$\chi^2(1) = .01$	$\chi^2(1) = 6.9$
	$p = .85$	$p < .001$	$p = .93$	$p = .009$

Full results for table 3.2 and figure 3.5.

same potential policy change. These 387 questions form 116 sets with exactly two alternative versions, 25 sets with three alternative versions, and 20 sets with four or more alternative versions. The questions within each of these 161 sets are all from the same calendar year and refer to identical or nearly identical proposed policy changes (see table 2.2 for examples).

If there were no correlated error in these preference measures, the covariance of preferences across different income groups on the same version of a proposed policy change would (on average) equal the covariance of preferences across those income groups on alternative versions. Consequently the difference between the same-version covariances and the alternate-version covariances provides an estimate of the magnitude of the error covariance. Calculating these covariances for the associations between preferences for the 10th and 90th, the 50th and 90th, and the

Table A3.2 Policy Responsiveness by Income Percentile When Preferences Diverge

	When 10th and 90th Income Percentiles Diverge		When 30th and 90th Income Percentiles Diverge		When 50th and 90th Income Percentiles Diverge		When 70th and 90th Income Percentiles Diverge	
	10th	90th	30th	90th	50th	90th	70th	90th
Logit coefficient	.02	.46***	-.09	.41**	-.01	.47**	.16	.46**
(Standard error)	(.09)	(.10)	(.11)	(.14)	(.14)	(.18)	(.14)	(.18)
Intercept	-.65	-.77	-.78	-.85	-.80	-.86	-.76	-.81
N	723	723	481	481	322	322	344	344
-2 Log likelihood	931	892	598	590	399	392	431	426
Likelihood ratio χ^2	$\chi^2(1) = 0.3$ $p = .85$	$\chi^2(1) = 23$ $p < .001$	$\chi^2(1) = 0.7$ $p = .41$	$\chi^2(1) = 8.9$ $p = .003$	$\chi^2(1) = 0.1$ $p = .93$	$\chi^2(1) = 6.9$ $p = .009$	$\chi^2(1) = 1.2$ $p = .28$	$\chi^2(1) = 6.9$ $p = .01$

Cases consist of survey questions about proposed policy changes asked between 1981 and 2002. The dependent variable is policy outcome coded 1 if the proposed policy change took place within four years of the survey date and 0 if it did not. The predictors are the logits of the imputed percentage of respondents at a given income percentile favoring the proposed policy change. Comparisons for the 10th, 30th, and 50th percentiles included policies for which preferences diverge from the 90th percentile by more than 10 percentage points; the comparison for the 70th percentile includes policies for which preferences diverge from the 90th percentile by more than 6 percentage points.
**$p < .01$; ***$p < .001$

Table A3.3   Alternative Estimates of Policy Responsiveness by Income Percentile

| Income Percentile | Ordinary Least Squares Regression | | | Marginal Impact Based on Bivariate Logistic Regressions When Preference Gap Is > .10 | |
	Bivariate	Multivariate	Deflated Multivariate	10th vs. 90th Percentiles	50th vs. 90th Percentiles
10th	.31 (.05)***	−.21 (.15)	−.10 (.09)	.02	
50th	.39 (.05)***	−.33 (.22)	.08 (.10)		−.01
90th	.51 (.05)***	1.01 (.16)***	.51 (.09)***	.44***	.45***

Predictors for the OLS analyses are the imputed percentage of respondents at a given income percentile favoring the proposed policy change. Dependent variable is policy outcome coded 1 if the proposed policy change took place within four years of the survey date and 0 if it did not. The coefficients in the first column are from three separate OLS regressions. The coefficients in the third column are from a multivariate regression in which the covariance matrix was deflated to correct for correlated measurement error among the predictors, as explained in the appendix. The marginal impacts in the last two columns are based on the logistic regressions for policies in which preferences for the indicated income percentiles diverged by more than 10 percentage points (bottom row of table A3.1) and are estimated at the mean of the dependent variable. N is 1,779 for all OLS regressions, 723 for the 10th vs. 90th income percentile logistic regressions, and 322 for the 50th vs. 90th logistic regressions.
*** p < .001

10th and 50th income percentiles revealed that error covariance accounted for 19, 17, and 14 percent of the observed covariance of the preference measures, respectively. With these estimates of error covariance in hand, I adjusted the three covariances representing the associations of the preferences of the 10th, 50th, and 90th income percentiles in the covariance matrix that produced the regression coefficients in the second column of table A3.3 to remove that portion attributable to correlated error. I then used the deflated covariance matrix as the basis for the regression that produced the coefficients reported in the third column of the table.

Deflating the covariance matrix used in the multivariate analysis eliminates the symptoms of correlated error. The third column shows weak and nonsignificant coefficients for the 10th and 50th income percentiles and a coefficient of 0.51 for the 90th percentile, indicating no decline in the preference/policy link for the well-off when the preferences of the other income levels are taken into account. The estimated impact for the 10th income percentile is still negative, but the coefficients for both the 10th and 50th percentiles are substantially reduced, and neither is statistically distinguishable from zero.

Finally, the last two columns of the table show results based on the logistic regressions reported in the bottom row of table 3.2 (that is, the association of preferences and policy outcomes for the 10th, 50th, and 90th income percentiles when preferences across the indicated income groups diverge by more than 10 percentage points). To make these estimates comparable to the OLS estimates discussed above, I calculate the marginal impact of each predictor at the mean of the dependent variable. Reflecting the results shown in table 3.2, policy responsiveness for the 10th and 50th income percentiles is essentially zero. The estimates for the 90th percentile indicate that a 1-percentage-point difference in support for a policy change is associated with a 0.44- or 0.45-point difference in the probability of that change being adopted (on issues where the preferences of the affluent diverge from those of the poor or middle class, respectively).

The multivariate OLS estimates based on a deflated covariance matrix parallel the analogous estimates from bivariate logistic analyses when the data are restricted to questions on which preferences across income levels diverge. But this reassuring conclusion rests on the assumption that the set of multiple-measure items I use in estimating the error covariance is representative of my data as a whole. Of particular concern in this regard is the possibility that the proposed policy changes for which I could identify multiple survey questions might represent more prominent issues. If so, respondents might have stronger or more-stable attitudes on these questions, and as a result their responses might contain less measurement error in general and be less susceptible to the influence of question wording, survey timing, and so on than would be true for the remainder of the questions in my dataset.

To assess the similarity of questions with multiple versions to those without, I compare the 1,392 questions with single versions to the 232 question with two versions, and the 155 questions with three or four versions. These comparisons show that neither the average support for the policy changes nor (more important) the level of opinionation differs significantly across these three groups of questions. On average, 58 percent of survey respondents favored proposed changes that had only single preference measures compared with 59 and 57 percent of changes with two and three or four measures, respectively. The percentage of respondents answering "Don't know" for the three groups was 4.9 percent for single-version questions, 5.1 percent for two-version questions, and 6.4 percent for three- and four-version questions. Since my concern was that policy changes with larger numbers of questions might be more salient to respondents, the slightly larger percentage of "Don't know" responses to these questions is reassuring.

Finally, additional confirmation that the number of different versions of preference questions about a given policy change is not associated with systematic differences in the error structure of those questions comes from the estimated reliabilities of items with two, three, or four versions. Since reliability estimates require at least two alternative measures, I cannot compare the multiple-measure policies with the single-measure policies. However, estimated item reliabilities are 0.79, 0.82, and 0.77 for questions from two-item, three-item, and four-item groups, suggesting that the preference measures of policy changes with larger numbers of items do not differ systematically from those with fewer items (at least among questions with two or more alternative measures).

A variety of evidence, then, suggests that the subset of multiple-item policy proposals resembles the single-item proposals in ways that would be most likely to influence their error structures and hence the size of the error covariances of preference measures across different income levels. This provides some confidence in applying the error covariance estimates from the 387 questions with multiple measures to the dataset overall. This does not mean, however, that the error structures of *all* subsets of policy preferences are likely to be the same. For example, as suggested above, questions about more salient or familiar issues might generate stronger opinions and more-stable (and less-error-prone) responses. Consequently the adjustments to the preference covariance across income levels that are appropriate for the dataset as a whole might not be appropriate for subsets of questions on different substantive topics or asked during different time periods (e.g., during election versus nonelection years).

The inability to apply these same error covariance estimates to the variety of policy subsets I examine in the following chapters severely limits the usefulness of the covariance deflation approach to dealing with correlated measurement error. But as table A3.3 shows, at least for the dataset as a whole, multivariate analyses with deflated covariances produce the same substantive findings as restricting my analysis to questions with large preference gaps across income levels.

My analyses of the different substantive policy domains in chapter 4, of interest groups in chapter 5, and of changes over time or across political conditions in chapters 6 and 7 will rely, therefore, on some variation of the approach used for table 3.2 based on the size of the preference gap across income levels.

Table A3.4   Policy Responsiveness When Preferences across Income or
Education Levels Diverge

	Education Percentile		
	10th	50th	90th
10th income percentile			
Policy preference	.13 (.07)	.20 (.07)	.27 (.08)
Intercept	−.70 (.07)	−.72 (.07)	−.74 (.07)
Log likelihood	1334	1331	1326
Likelihood ratio χ^2	$\chi^2(1) = 3.9$	$\chi^2(1) = 7.4$	$\chi^2(1) = 12.1$
Significance	$p < .05$	$p < .01$	$p = .001$
50th income percentile			
Policy preference	.28 (.07)	.32 (.07)	.39 (.08)
Intercept	−.74 (.07)	−.76 (.07)	−.78 (.07)
Log likelihood	1324	1320	1313
Likelihood ratio χ^2	$\chi^2(1) = 13.8$	$\chi^2(1) = 18.3$	$\chi^2(1) = 25.3$
Significance	$p < .001$	$p < .001$	$p < .001$
90th income percentile			
Policy preference	.41 (.08)	.40 (.07)	.48 (.07)
Intercept	−.79 (.07)	−.81 (.07)	−.83 (.07)
Log likelihood	1302	1301	1294
Likelihood ratio χ^2	$\chi^2(1) = 31.1$	$\chi^2(1) = 32.4$	$\chi^2(1) = 44.1$
Significance	$p < .001$	$p < .001$	$p < .001$

Full results for figure 3.9. Table reports nine separate logistic regressions. Dependent
variable is policy outcome coded 1 if the proposed policy change took place within four
years of the survey date and 0 if it did not. Predictors are the logits of the imputed
percentage of respondents at a given combination of income and education percentiles
favoring the proposed policy change. Analysis is restricted to the 1,050 questions on
which preferences diverged by at least 10 percentage points between the 10th and 90th
income percentiles or the 10th and 90th education percentiles.

Table A4.1 Policy Responsiveness by Policy Domain by Income Percentile

	Foreign Policy/ National Security	Social Welfare	Policy Economic	Religious Issues
10th income percentile				
Logit coefficient	.37	.39	.51	.76
(Standard error)	(.11)	(.11)	(.12)	(.24)
Intercept	.14	−1.40	−.74	−1.55
Log likelihood	578	410	491	165
Likelihood ratio χ^2	$\chi^2(1) = 12.2$	$\chi^2(1) = 13.7$	$\chi^2(1) = 17.8$	$\chi^2(1) = 11.0$
Significance	$p < .001$	$p < .001$	$p < .001$	$p = .001$
50th income percentile				
Logit coefficient	.54	.49	.55	.83
(Standard error)	(.11)	(.11)	(.12)	(.24)
Intercept	.12	−1.51	−.81	−1.56
Log likelihood	564	403	487	162
Likelihood ratio χ^2	$\chi^2(1) = 26.5$	$\chi^2(1) = 20.7$	$\chi^2(1) = 22.2$	$\chi^2(1) = 13.7$
Significance	$p < .001$	$p < .001$	$p < .001$	$p < .001$
90th income percentile				
Logit coefficient	.77	.58	.84	1.05
(Standard error)	(.10)	(.13)	(.14)	(.26)
Intercept	.10	−1.58	−.90	−1.66
Log likelihood	542	401	468	157
Likelihood ratio χ^2	$\chi^2(1) = 48.0$	$\chi^2(1) = 22.7$	$\chi^2(1) = 41.7$	$\chi^2(1) = 18.9$
Significance	$p < .001$	$p < .001$	$p < .001$	$p < .001$
N	428	399	389	161

Cases consist of survey questions about proposed policy changes asked between 1981 and 2002. Dependent variable is policy outcome coded 1 if the proposed policy change took place within four years of the survey date and 0 if it did not. Predictors are the logits of the percentage of respondents favoring the proposed policy change.

Table A4.2   Policy Preference, Preference Divergence, and Their Interaction as Predictors of
Policy Outcome by Policy Domain by Income Percentile

	Foreign Policy/ National Security	Social Welfare	Economic Policy	Religious Issues
10th income percentile				
Policy preference	−1.51 (.65)	−.42 (.45)	−.74 (.69)	−1.70 (1.16)
Preference divergence	.03 (.18)	.27 (.22)	.09 (.21)	.53 (.44)
Interaction	−.62 (.22)	−.26 (.14)	−.43 (.24)	−.79 (.38)
Intercept	.18 (.54)	−.67 (.61)	−.48 (.60)	−.01 (1.26)
Log likelihood	569	406	488	160
Likelihood ratio χ²	χ²(1) = 21.7	χ²(1) = 17.5	χ²(1) = 21.7	χ²(1) = 16.3
Significance	$p < .001$	$p < .001$	$p < .001$	$p = .001$
50th income percentile				
Policy preference	−.76 (.66)	.08 (.47)	−.75 (.66)	−.61 (1.06)
Preference divergence	.04 (.18)	.22 (.22)	.10 (.22)	.34 (.40)
Interaction	−.42 (.22)	−.13 (.14)	−.45 (.23)	−.46 (.33)
Intercept	.22 (.54)	−.88 (.64)	−.55 (.64)	−.58 (1.15)
Log likelihood	560	402	482	160
Likelihood ratio χ²	χ²(1) = 30.7	χ²(1) = 22.0	χ²(1) = 27.2	χ²(1) = 15.8
Significance	$p < .001$	$p < .001$	$p < .001$	$p = .001$
90th income percentile				
Policy preference	.59 (.66)	.52 (.54)	−.36 (.72)	.22 (1.09)
Preference divergence	.01 (.18)	.14 (.22)	.01 (.21)	.30 (.41)
Interaction	−.06 (.21)	−.03 (.16)	−.16 (.24)	−.27 (.34)
Intercept	.12 (.55)	−1.18 (.65)	−.87 (.63)	−.77 (1.19)
Log likelihood	542	400	467	156
Likelihood ratio χ²	χ²(1) = 48.1	χ²(1) = 23.2	χ²(1) = 42.3	χ²(1) = 19.7
Significance	$p < .001$	$p < .001$	$p < .001$	$p < .001$
N	428	399	389	161

Cases consist of survey questions about proposed policy changes asked between 1981 and 2002.
Dependent variable is policy outcome coded 1 if the proposed policy change took place within four
years of the survey date and 0 if it did not. Policy preference is the logit of the percentage of respondents
favoring the proposed policy change; preference divergence is the log of the mean absolute difference
between the 10th and 50th and the 50th and 90th income percentiles.

Table A4.3 Social Welfare Policy Preferences, Preference Divergence, and Their
Interaction by Income by Interest Group Alignment

	Social Welfare Policies on Which Interest Groups Align with Lower-Income Americans	Remaining Social Welfare Policies
10th income percentile		
Policy preference	.28 (.64)	−1.44 (.77)
Preference divergence	.49 (.33)	.24 (.31)
Interaction	−.08 (.20)	−.53 (.23)
Intercept	−.11 (.91)	−.60 (.89)
Log likelihood	168	233
Likelihood ratio χ^2	11.1	$\chi^2(1) = 9.8$
Significance	$p < .02$	$p < .02$
50th income percentile		
Policy preference	.82 (.66)	−.82 (.79)
Preference divergence	.39 (.32)	.26 (.34)
Interaction	.08 (.19)	−.39 (.24)
Intercept	−.43 (.90)	−.67 (1.00)
Log likelihood	166	231
Likelihood ratio χ^2	12.9	$\chi^2(1) = 11.7$
Significance	$p < .01$	$p < .01$
90th income percentile		
Policy preference	1.54 (.88)	−.15 (.79)
Preference divergence	.27 (.32)	.12 (.33)
Interaction	.25 (.24)	−.22 (.23)
Intercept	−.85 (.90)	−1.17 (.98)
Log likelihood	166	230
Likelihood ratio χ^2	13.1	$\chi^2(1) = 12.0$
Significance	$p < .01$	$p < .01$
N	184	215

Cases consist of survey questions about proposed policy changes asked between 1981 and
2002. The first column shows results for Social Security, Medicare, school vouchers, and
public works spending. Dependent variable is policy outcome coded 1 if the proposed
policy change took place within four years of the survey date and 0 if it did not. Policy
preference is the logit of the percentage of respondents favoring the proposed policy
change; preference divergence is the log of the mean absolute difference between the
10th and 50th and the 50th and 90th income percentiles. Standard errors in parentheses.

Table A5.1   Expanded Power 25 List of Interest Groups in Washington, DC

Lobbying organizations based on Fortune's *Power 25 surveys*

1   AARP
2   National Rifle Association
3   National Federation of Independent Business
4   American Israel Public Affairs Committee
5   AFL-CIO
6   Association of Trial Lawyers
7   Chamber of Commerce
8   American Medical Association
9   National Association of Manufacturers
10   National Association of Realtors
11   National Right to Life Committee
12   National Education Association
13   National Association of Home Builders
14   American Farm Bureau Federation
15   National Beer Wholesalers Association
16   Motion Picture Association of America
17   National Restaurant Association
18   National Association of Broadcasters
19   American Bankers Association
20   American Hospital Association
21   National Governors' Association
22   Health Insurance Association
23   Christian Coalition
24   International Brotherhood of Teamsters
25   Credit Union National Association
26   Recording Industry Association
27   American Federation of State, County, and Municipal Employees
28   Pharmaceutical Research and Manufacturers
29   Veterans of Foreign Wars of the U.S.
30   Independent Insurance Agents of America
31   American Council of Life Insurance
32   American Legion
33   United Auto Workers

Industries with highest lobbying expenditures not represented above

1   Electric companies
2   Computer software and hardware
3   Universities
4   Oil companies
5   Telephone companies
6   Automobile companies
7   Securities and investment companies
8   Airlines
9   Defense contractors
10   Tobacco companies

Lobbying organizations include all organizations listed at least once on *Fortune* magazine's Power 25 surveys from 1997 through 2001. Organizations are listed above in order of their average Power 25 ranking or by their lobbying expenditures between 1988 and 1992 as reported by opensecrets.org, although these distinctions among organizations were not used in the interest group alignment scores. See text for the formula used to compute interest group alignment scores.

Table A6.1 Policy Responsiveness and Length of Presidential Partisan Regime

All policies	All	Income Percentile		
		10th	50th	90th
Policy preference	.66 (.11)	.50 (.11)	.61 (.10)	.76 (.11)
Economic policy	.39 (.17)	.38 (.17)	.36 (.17)	.43 (.18)
Religious/moral	−.01 (.27)	−.05 (.27)	−.01 (.27)	.02 (.27)
Foreign policy	1.13 (.16)	1.08 (.16)	1.11 (.16)	1.17 (.16)
Social welfare	−.34 (.20)	−.34 (.20)	−.35 (.20)	−.32 (.20)
Preference * Congress number	−.28 (.11)	−.18 (.10)	−.26 (.10)	−.34 (.10)
Congress number	−.30 (.11)	−.36 (.11)	−.30 (.11)	−.25 (.11)
Election year	−.15 (.15)	−.16 (.15)	−.16 (.15)	−.15 (.15)
Preference * election year	−.09 (.15)	−.10 (.14)	−.09 (.14)	−.05 (.15)
Intercept	−1.65 (.16)	−1.54 (.16)	−1.63 (.16)	−1.76 (.17)
Log likelihood	2018	2038	2022	1998
Likelihood ratio χ^2	$\chi^2(9) = 168.7$	$\chi^2(9) = 148.4$	$\chi^2(9) = 164.7$	$\chi^2(9) = 188.1$
Significance	$p < .001$	$p < .001$	$p < .001$	$p < .001$
N	2230	2230	2230	2230

Table A6.1   (continued)

All policies	10th vs. 90th Income Percentiles		50th vs. 90th Income Percentiles	
	10th	90th	50th	90th
Policy preference	.10 (.15)	.77 (.17)	.35 (.14)	.76 (.17)
Economic policy	.51 (.28)	.56 (.28)	.46 (.26)	.58 (.27)
Religious/moral	.05 (.39)	.14 (.39)	−.01 (.36)	.06 (.37)
Foreign policy	1.24 (.26)	1.39 (.27)	1.21 (.25)	1.34 (.26)
Social welfare	.03 (.29)	−.00 (.30)	−.26 (.29)	−.22 (.30)
Preference * Congress number	.01 (.17)	−.40 (.18)	−.14 (.17)	−.38 (.19)
Congress number	−.63 (.16)	−.47 (.17)	−.54 (.15)	−.44 (.16)
Election year	.05 (.25)	−.03 (.27)	.09 (.25)	.03 (.26)
Preference * election year	.23 (.26)	.29 (.31)	.23 (.26)	.38 (.29)
Intercept	−1.42 (.24)	−1.72 (.26)	−1.54 (.23)	−1.76 (.25)
Log likelihood	877	847	965	942
Likelihood ratio χ^2	$\chi^2(9) = 63.3$	$\chi^2(9) = 92.9$	$\chi^2(9) = 78.6$	$\chi^2(9) = 101.6$
Significance	$p < .001$	$p < .001$	$p < .001$	$p < .001$
N	926	926	1046	1046

Full results for table 6.3 and figure 6.2.

Table A6.2 Policy Responsiveness and Partisan Control

	All	Income Percentile		
		10th	50th	90th
Policy preference	.25 (.11)	.22 (.10)	.20 (.10)	.31 (.11)
Economic policy	.43 (.17)	.41 (.17)	.41 (.17)	.48 (.17)
Religious/moral	.03 (.27)	−.02 (.27)	.03 (.27)	.06 (.27)
Foreign policy	1.13 (.16)	1.08 (.16)	1.11 (.16)	1.18 (.16)
Social welfare	−.33 (.20)	−.33 (.20)	−.34 (.20)	−.30 (.20)
Preference * Republican control	.31 (.18)	−.20 (.17)	.32 (.17)	.28 (.18)
Republican control	.10 (.19)	.16 (.19)	.10 (.19)	.08 (.19)
Intercept	−2.03 (.16)	−1.99 (.15)	−2.01 (.15)	−2.08 (.16)
Log likelihood	2046	2063	2049	2030
Likelihood ratio χ^2	$\chi^2(7) = 140.6$	$\chi^2(7) = 122.8$	$\chi^2(7) = 137.0$	$\chi^2(7) = 156.7$
Significance	$p < .001$	$p < .001$	$p < .001$	$p < .001$
N	2229	2229	2229	2229

When Preferences across Income Levels Diverge

	10th vs. 90th Income Percentiles		50th vs. 90th Income Percentiles	
	10th	90th	50th	90th
Policy preference	.08 (.17)	.26 (.20)	.09 (.17)	.42 (.20)
Economic policy	.41 (.29)	.51 (.29)	.39 (.27)	.52 (.27)
Religious/moral	.08 (.42)	.20 (.42)	−.09 (.41)	−.05 (.41)
Foreign policy	1.28 (.27)	1.49 (.28)	1.26 (.25)	1.40 (.26)
Social welfare	.13 (.30)	.18 (.31)	−.19 (.30)	−.13 (.30)
Preference * Republican control	.20 (.30)	.43 (.34)	.47 (.29)	.30 (.35)
Republican control	.23 (.28)	.06 (.29)	−.19 (.27)	−.19 (.28)
Intercept	−1.42 (.24)	−2.23 (.27)	−1.91 (.25)	−2.02 (.26)
Log likelihood	857	837	956	940
Likelihood ratio χ^2	$\chi^2(7) = 42.8$	$\chi^2(7) = 62.7$	$\chi^2(7) = 63.5$	$\chi^2(7) = 79.2$
Significance	$p < .001$	$p < .001$	$p < .001$	$p < .001$
N	922	922	1055	1055

Full results for table 6.5 and figure 6.3.

Table A6.3   Policy Responsiveness and Partisan Control by Policy Domain

| Economic policy | All | Income Percentile | | |
		10th	50th	90th
Policy preference	.05 (.27)	.02 (.27)	.07(.25)	.05 (.28)
Preference * Republican control	1.02 (.46)	.94 (.45)	.85 (.42)	1.11 (.47)
Republican control	.83 (.49)	.94 (.48)	.85 (.49)	.80 (.49)
Intercept	−2.12 (.31)	−2.12 (.30)	−2.12 (.31)	−2.12 (.30)
Log likelihood	443	447	447	439
Likelihood ratio χ^2	$\chi^2(3) = 33.2$	$\chi^2(3) = 29.2$	$\chi^2(3) = 29.7$	$\chi^2(3) = 37.2$
Significance	$p < .001$	$p < .001$	$p < .001$	$p < .001$
N	482	482	482	482

Social welfare	All	10th	50th	90th
Policy preference	.23 (.22)	.32 (.21)	.20 (.21)	.15 (.23)
Preference * Republican control	.05 (.43)	−.21 (.41)	.09 (.41)	.26 (.45)
Republican control	−.53 (.52)	−.38 (.51)	−.55 (.52)	−.64 (.52)
Intercept	−1.98 (.27)	−2.03 (.28)	−1.98 (.27)	−1.96 (.26)
Log likelihood	302	302	302	302
Likelihood ratio χ^2	$\chi^2(3) = 4.23$	$\chi^2(3) = 4.34$	$\chi^2(3) = 4.29$	$\chi^2(3) = 4.15$
Significance	$p = .238$	$p = .227$	$p = .232$	$p = .246$
N	454	454	454	454

(continued)

Table A6.3   (continued)

Foreign policy	All	Income Percentile		
		10th	50th	90th
Policy preference	.15 (.19)	.13 (.20)	.07 (.18)	.31 (.19)
Preference * Republican control	.37 (.31)	.18 (.31)	.45 (.29)	.29 (.31)
Republican control	.54 (.29)	.57 (.28)	.55 (.29)	.53 (.29)
Intercept	−1.13 (.18)	−1.12 (.18)	−1.14 (.18)	−1.14 (.18)
Log likelihood	739	748	739	727
Likelihood ratio χ^2	$\chi^2(3) = 21.1$	$\chi^2(3) = 11.7$	$\chi^2(3) = 20.3$	$\chi^2(3) = 32.7$
Significance	$p < .001$	$p < .01$	$p < .001$	$p < .001$
N	613	613	613	613

Moral/religious issues	All	10th	50th	90th
Policy preference	.58 (.73)	.19 (.71)	.53 (.71)	.76 (.65)
Preference * Republican control	1.03 (1.35)	1.29 (1.33)	.89 (1.28)	.86 (1.28)
Republican control	−2.45 (1.13)	−2.54 (1.08)	−2.39 (1.10)	−2.31 (1.16)
Intercept	−1.11 (.57)	−.95 (.54)	−1.08 (.57)	−1.25 (.59)
Log likelihood	104	108	105	102
Likelihood ratio χ^2	$\chi^2(3) = 16.1$	$\chi^2(3) = 12.7$	$\chi^2(3) = 15.4$	$\chi^2(3) = 17.9$
Significance	$p = .001$	$p < .01$	$p < .01$	$p < .001$
N	146	146	146	146

Full results for table 6.6.

Table A6.4   Policy Responsiveness by Direction of
Redistributive Policies by Partisan Control

Downwardly redistributive policy	.94 (.31)
Upwardly redistributive policy	−.87 (.59)
Economic policy	.27 (.18)
Religious/moral	−.02 (.27)
Foreign policy	1.00 (.15)
Social welfare	−.54 (.22)
Downward * Republican control	−1.21 (.57)
Upward * Republican control	1.86 (.83)
Republican control	.32 (.20)
Intercept	−1.97 (.16)
Log likelihood	2090
Likelihood ratio χ^2	$\chi^2(9) = 104.1$
Significance	$p < .001$
N	2237

Table shows logistic regression coefficients. Dependent variable is
policy outcome coded 1 if the proposed policy change took place
within four years of the survey date and 0 if it did not. Predictors are
indicator variables for whether the policy is upwardly or downwardly
redistributive, partisan control, the interaction of the redistributive
indicators and partisan control, and fixed effects for the four policy
domains examined in chapter 4.

Table A6.5   Multivariate Analyses of Policy Responsiveness

		Income Percentile		
	All	10th	50th	90th
Partisan control				
Preference	.25 (.11)	.22 (.10)	.21 (.10)	.31 (.11)
Economic policy	.43 (.17)	.41 (.17)	.41 (.17)	.48 (.17)
Religious/moral	.03 (.27)	−.02 (.27)	.03 (.27)	.06 (.27)
Foreign policy	1.13 (.16)	1.08 (.16)	1.11 (.16)	1.18 (.16)
Social welfare	−.33 (.20)	−.33 (.20)	−.34 (.20)	−.30 (.20)
Republican control	.10 (.19)	.16 (.19)	.10 (.19)	.08 (.19)
Preference * Republican control	.31 (.18)	.20 (.17)	.32 (.17)	.28 (.18)
Intercept	−2.03 (.16)	−1.99 (.15)	−2.01 (.15)	−2.08 (.16)
Log likelihood	2046	2063	2049	2030
Likelihood ratio χ^2	$\chi^2(7) = 140.6$	$\chi2(7) = 122.8$	$\chi^2(7) = 137.0$	$\chi^2(7) = 156.7$
Significance	$p < .001$	$p < .001$	$p < .001$	$p < .001$
N	2230	2230	2230	2230
Partisan control (+ controls)				
Preference	.52 (.15)	.41 (.14)	.46 (.14)	.64 (.15)
Economic policy	.37 (.17)	.37 (.17)	.35 (.17)	.41 (.18)
Religious/moral	−.02 (.27)	−.06 (.27)	−.02 (.27)	.02 (.27)
Foreign policy	1.11 (.16)	1.07 (.16)	1.10 (.16)	1.16 (.16)
Social welfare	−.35 (.20)	−.34 (.20)	−.36 (.20)	−.34 (.20)
Republican control	.04 (.19)	.08 (.19)	.04 (.19)	.05 (.19)
Preference * Republican control	.27 (.18)	.18 (.17)	.29 (.17)	.23 (.18)
Election year	−.15 (.15)	−.15 (.15)	−.15 (.15)	−.15 (.15)
Preference * election year	−.06 (.15)	−.08 (.14)	−.05 (.14)	−.03 (.15)
Preference * regime length	−.27 (.11)	−.17 (.10)	−.25 (.10)	−.33 (.10)
Regime length	−.31 (.11)	−.37 (.11)	−.32 (.11)	−.26 (.11)
Intercept	−1.66 (.19)	−1.57 (.19)	−1.64 (.19)	−1.77 (.20)
Log likelihood	2015	2036	2018	1996
Likelihood ratio χ^2	$\chi^2(11) = 171.3$	$\chi^2(11) = 149.8$	$\chi^2(11) = 167.9$	$\chi^2(11) = 190.1$
Significance	$p < .001$	$p < .001$	$p < .001$	$p < .001$
N	2230	2230	2230	2230

Table A6.5   (continued)

| | All | Income Percentile | | |
		10th	50th	90th
Partisan regime length				
Preference	.63 (.09)	.48 (.09)	.56 (.09)	.74 (.09)
Economic policy	.60 (.17)	.58 (.17)	.58 (.17)	.65 (.17)
Religious/moral	.23 (.24)	.19 (.24)	.23 (.24)	.27 (.24)
Foreign policy	1.26 (.16)	1.20 (.16)	1.25 (.16)	1.32 (.16)
Social welfare	−.31 (.20)	−.30 (.20)	−.32 (.20)	−.30 (.20)
Preference * regime length	−.28 (.10)	−.21 (.10)	−.24 (.10)	−.35 (.10)
Regime length	−.41 (.11)	−.46 (.10)	−.42 (.11)	−.34 (.11)
Intercept	−1.72 (.15)	−1.60 (.15)	−1.69 (.15)	−1.84 (.16)
Log likelihood	2028	2054	2034	2001
Likelihood ratio χ^2	$\chi^2(7) = 205.5$	$\chi^2(7) = 180.0$	$\chi^2(7) = 200.2$	$\chi^2(7) = 233.0$
Significance	$p < .001$	$p < .001$	$p < .001$	$p < .001$
N	2230	2230	2230	2230
Partisan regime length (+ controls)				
Preference	.51 (.14)	.41 (.13)	.43 (.13)	.67 (.14)
Economic policy	.60 (.17)	.59 (.17)	.59 (.17)	.66 (.17)
Religious/moral	.24 (.24)	.19 (.24)	.24 (.24)	.28 (.24)
Foreign policy	1.26 (.16)	1.21 (.16)	1.25 (.16)	1.33 (.16)
Social welfare	−.31 (.20)	−.30 (.20)	−.32 (.20)	−.30 (.20)
Preference * regime length	−.27 (.11)	−.21 (.10)	−.23 (.10)	−.35 (.10)
Regime length	−.41 (.11)	−.46 (.11)	−.43 (.11)	−.35 (.11)
Republican control	−.23 (.19)	−.20 (.18)	−.25 (.19)	−.21 (.19)
Preference * Republican control	.19 (.18)	.11 (.18)	.23 (.17)	.12 (.18)
Election year	−.06 (.18)	−.05 (.17)	−.05 (.18)	−.06 (.18)
Preference * election year	.07 (.17)	.07 (.16)	.06 (.16)	.09 (.17)
Intercept	−1.59 (.18)	−1.50 (.18)	−1.55 (.18)	−1.73 (.19)
Log likelihood	2015	2052	2031	1999
Likelihood ratio χ^2	$\chi^2(11) = 171.3$	$\chi^2(11) = 181.5$	$\chi^2(11) = 203.1$	$\chi^2(11) = 234.4$
Significance	$p < .001$	$p < .001$	$p < .001$	$p < .001$
N	2230	2230	2230	2230

(continued)

Table A6.5   (continued)

	All	Income Percentile		
		10th	50th	90th
Presidential election year				
Preference	.35 (.08)	.22 (.07)	.31 (.07)	.45 (.07)
Economic policy	.70 (.20)	.68 (.20)	.68 (.20)	.77 (.20)
Religious/moral	.68 (.27)	.65 (.28)	.69 (.28)	.73 (.28)
Foreign policy	1.63 (.20)	1.55 (.19)	1.61 (.19)	1.71 (.20)
Social welfare	−.07 (.23)	−.07 (.22)	−.07 (.23)	−.05 (.23)
Election year	−.67 (.21)	−.62 (.20)	−.66 (.21)	−.69 (.21)
Preference * election year	.30 (.18)	.28 (.17)	.29 (.17)	.30 (.19)
Intercept	−2.03 (.17)	−1.95 (.16)	−2.01 (.16)	−2.12 (.17)
Log likelihood	1529	1546	1532	1510
Likelihood ratio χ^2	$\chi^2(7) = 144.2$	$\chi^2(7) = 127.2$	$\chi^2(7) = 141.4$	$\chi^2(7) = 163.8$
Significance	$p < .001$	$p < .001$	$p < .001$	$p < .001$
N	2230	2230	2230	2230
Presidential election year (+ control variables)				
Preference	.62 (.15)	.50 (.15)	.52 (.14)	.78 (.16)
Economic policy	.47 (.21)	.48 (.21)	.45 (.21)	.55 (.21)
Religious/moral	.65 (.28)	.63 (.28)	.65 (.28)	.71 (.28)
Foreign policy	1.56 (.20)	1.50 (.20)	1.54 (.20)	1.65 (.20)
Social welfare	−.14 (.23)	−.12 (.23)	−.15 (.23)	−.13 (.23)
Election year	−.53 (.21)	−.47 (.20)	−.52 (.21)	−.56 (.22)
Preference * election year	.43 (.19)	.38 (.18)	.40 (.18)	.45 (.20)
Republican control	.67 (.25)	.65 (.24)	.63 (.25)	.73 (.25)
Preference * Republican control	−.05 (.24)	−.22 (.24)	.00 (.22)	−.07 (.24)
Preference * regime length	−.35 (.13)	−.24 (.13)	−.30 (.12)	−.43 (.13)
Regime length	−.53 (.13)	−.57 (.12)	−.54 (.13)	−.47 (.13)
Intercept	−1.87 (.22)	−1.77 (.21)	−1.83 (.21)	−2.04 (.23)
Log likelihood	1488	1508	1492	1464
Likelihood ratio χ^2	$\chi^2(11) = 185.1$	$\chi^2(11) = 165.9$	$\chi^2(11) = 181.0$	$\chi^2(11) = 209.0$
Significance	$p < .001$	$p < .001$	$p < .001$	$p < .001$
N	2230	2230	2230	2230

Full results for table 6.7.

Table A7.1 Linear and Quadratic Time Trends in Policy Responsiveness by Income Percentile

		Income Percentile		
	All	10th	50th	90th
Linear model				
Preference	.23 (.11)*	.10 (.11)	.21 (.11)*	.33 (.12)**
Year	−.90 (.18)***	−.76 (.18)***	−.88 (.18)***	−1.01 (.19)***
Preference * year	.48 (.17)**	.47 (.16)**	.44 (.16)**	.47 (.17)**
Intercept	−.95 (.16)***	−.94 (.16)***	−.95 (.16)***	−.97 (.16)***
N	2245	2245	2245	2245
Quadratic model				
Preference	.29 (.15)	.20 (.14)	.29 (.14)*	.26 (.15)
Year	1.53 (.66)*	1.83 (.66)**	1.56 (.67)*	1.13 (.67)
Year-squared	−2.46 (.64)***	−2.63 (.63)***	−2.48 (.64)***	−2.11 (.64)***
Preference * year	−.38 (.62)	−.67 (.58)	−.56 (.58)	.41 (.62)
Preference * year-squared	1.03 (.60)	1.30 (.57)*	1.14 (.56)*	.20 (.60)
Intercept	−1.30 (.19)***	−1.32 (.19)***	−1.29 (.19)***	−1.30 (.19)***
N	2245	2245	2245	2245

	10th vs. 90th Income Percentiles		50th vs. 90th Income Percentiles	
	10th	90th	50th	90th
Quadratic model				
Preference	.18 (.23)	.27 (.26)	.15 (.25)	.08 (.27)
Year	2.11 (.95)*	1.48 (.99)	1.86 (.93)*	1.26 (.95)
Year-squared	−2.85 (.91)**	−2.61 (96)**	−2.97 (.89)***	−2.51 (.91)**
Preference * year	−2.03 (.94)*	.02 (1.09)	−1.35 (.97)	.84 (1.10)
Preference * year-squared	2.70 (.93)**	.83 (1.05)	2.22 (.92)*	.09 (1.06)
Intercept	−1.06 (.27)***	−1.05 (.29)***	−.98 (.27)***	−1.00 (.28)***
N	932	932	1063	1063

Analyses based on nonrestructured dataset with policy questions from 1964–68, 1981–2002, 2005–06. Table shows logistic regression coefficients (with standard errors in parentheses). Dependent variable is policy outcome coded 1 if the proposed policy change took place in the calendar year in question and 0 if it did not. Preference is the logit of the imputed percentage of respondents at a given income level favoring the proposed policy change. Year is rescaled to range from 0 to 1. In the bottom section, preferences of the 10th and 90th income percentiles differ by more than 10 percentage points and preferences of the 50th and 90th percentiles by more than 5 percentage points. All analyses include fixed effects for the four policy domains examined in chapter 4.
*$p < .05$; **$p < .01$; ***$p < .001$

Table A7.2   Gridlock and Policy Responsiveness by Income Percentile

| | All | Income Percentile | | |
		10th	50th	90th
Preference	.39 (.31)	.28 (.31)	.28 (.29)	.65 (.30)*
Gridlock	−4.52 (.57)***	−4.55 (.57)***	−4.58 (.57)***	−4.31 (.56)***
Preference * gridlock	.09 (.48)	.11 (.48)	.19 (.45)	−.20 (.45)
Intercept	1.04 (.38)**	1.13 (.38)**	1.09 (.38)**	.83 (.38)*
N	2229	2229	2229	2229
Preference	−.37 (.39)	−.24 (.38)	−.40 (.36)	−.33 (.38)
Change in partisan regime	−.15 (.17)	.01 (.16)	−.11 (.16)	−.32 (.18)
Gridlock	−4.78 (.70)***	−4.50 (.69)***	−4.77 (.70)***	−4.88 (.70)***
Preference * regime change	.46 (.14)***	.31 (.14)*	.40 (.13)**	.60 (.15)***
Preference * gridlock	1.12 (.56)*	.80 (.56)	1.11 (.53)*	1.12 (.55)*
Intercept	1.21 (.48)*	1.08 (.47)*	1.22 (.48)*	1.22 (.48)*
N	2229	2229	2229	2229

Table A7.2   (continued)

| | 10th vs. 90th Income Percentiles | | 50th vs. 90th Income Percentiles | |
	10th	90th	50th	90th
Preference	−.34 (.64)	−.83 (.69)	−1.34 (.65)	−1.33 (.73)
Change in partisan regime	.30 (.22)	−.13 (.25)	−.12 (.22)	−.38 (.24)
Gridlock	−3.66 (.97)***	−4.66 (1.06)***	−6.00 (1.07)***	−6.41 (1.08)***
Preference * regime change	.04 (.23)	.74 (.26)**	.27 (.22)	.65 (.26)*
Preference * gridlock	.73 (.94)	1.90 (1.00)	2.48 (.95)**	2.75 (1.06)**
Intercept	.57 (.69)	1.12 (.72)	2.11 (.73)**	2.26 (.72)**
N	992	992	1054	1054

Analyses based on the annual restructured dataset with policy questions from 1964–68, 1981–2002, 2005–06. Table shows logistic regression coefficients (with standard errors in parentheses). Dependent variable is policy outcome coded 1 if the proposed policy change took place in the calendar year in question and 0 if it did not. Preference is the logit of the imputed percentage of respondents at a given income level favoring the proposed policy change. Gridlock is the proportion of proposed policy changes not adopted in the calendar year in question. Partisan regime change is scored 1 for years in which the party of the president changed hands (1981, 1993, 2001) and 0 otherwise. In the bottom section, preferences of the 10th and 90th income percentiles differ by more than 10 percentage points and preferences of the 50th and 90th percentiles by more than five percentage points. All analyses include fixed effects for the four policy domains examined in chapter 4.
$*p < .05; **p < .01; ***p < .001$

Table A7.3 Size of Majority Party Seat Advantage and Policy Responsiveness by Income Percentile

		Income Percentile		
	All	10th	50th	90th
Preference	.50 (.10)***	.39 (.09)***	.46 (.09)***	.58 (.10)***
House seat advantage	.21 (.22)	.13 (.22)	.20 (.22)	.29 (.23)
Preference * House advantage	−.24 (.20)	−.17 (.19)	−.22 (.19)	−.31 (.20)
Intercept	−2.07 (.16)***	−1.97 (.15)***	−2.05 (.16)***	−2.16 (.16)***
N	2229	2229	2229	2229
Preference	.56 (.09)***	.44 (.08)***	.51 (.08)***	.64 (.08)***
Senate seat advantage	−.64 (.23)**	−.70 (.23)**	−.66 (.23)**	−.58 (.23)*
Preference * Senate advantage	−.62 (.20)**	−.46 (.19)*	−.58 (.19)**	−.70 (.20)***
Intercept	−1.79 (.15)***	−1.70 (.15)***	−1.77 (.15)***	−1.88 (.15)***
N	2229	2229	2229	2229
	10th vs. 90th Income Percentiles		50th vs. 90th Income Percentiles	
	10th	90th	50th	90th
Preference	.28 (.14)*	.81 (.16)***	.51 (.14)***	.85 (.16)***
Senate seat advantage	−.96 (.34)**	−.85 (.36)*	−.45 (.33)	−.34 (.33)
Preference * Senate advantage	−.39 (.33)	−1.17 (.37)***	−.69 (.33)*	−1.03 (.37)**
Intercept	−1.70 (.25)***	−2.02 (.27)***	−1.87 (.24)***	−2.08 (.26)***
N	922	922	1054	1054

Analyses based on the annual restructured dataset with policy questions from 1964–68, 1981–2002, 2005–06. Table shows logistic regression coefficients (with standard errors in parentheses). Dependent variable is policy outcome coded 1 if the proposed policy change took place in the calendar year in question and 0 if it did not. Preference is the logit of the imputed percentage of respondents at a given income level favoring the proposed policy change. Seat advantage is rescaled to run from 0 to 1 separately for each house of Congress. In the bottom section, preferences of the 10th and 90th income percentiles differ by more than 10 percentage points and preferences of the 50th and 90th percentiles by more than five percentage points. All analyses include fixed effects for the four policy domains examined in chapter 4.
*$p < .05$; **$p < .01$; ***$p < .001$

Table A7.4 Policy Responsiveness under Johnson and G. W. Bush

| | Income Percentile | | |
	10th	50th	90th
G. W. Bush	−.76 (.17)	−.78 (.17)	−.75 (.18)
Johnson	−.52 (.21)	−.48 (.22)	−.44 (.22)
Preference	.21 (.07)	.30 (.07)	.46 (.07)
Preference * G. W. Bush	.60 (.14)	.55 (.14)	.46 (.15)
Preference * Johnson	−.07 (.19)	−.22 (.19)	−.44 (.19)
Intercept	−1.77 (.13)	−1.84 (.14)	−1.96 (.14)
N	2229	2229	2229

Controlling for regime length, Democratic vs. Republican Party control, and year in the election cycle

| | Income Percentile | | |
	10th	50th	90th
G. W. Bush	−1.00 (.20)	−1.00 (.20)	−1.04 (.20)
Johnson	−.11 (.27)	−.10 (.28)	.07 (.29)
Preference	.51 (.16)	.49 (.15)	.86 (.17)
Preference * G. W. Bush	.64 (.18)	.50 (.17)	.46 (.18)
Preference * Johnson	−.21 (.24)	−.20 (.24)	−.54 (.25)
Preference * regime length	−.17 (.11)	−.21 (.11)	−.28 (.11)
Regime length	−.50 (.12)	−.48 (.12)	−.44 (.12)
Preference * Republican control	−.33 (.28)	−.09 (.26)	−.38 (.29)
Republican control	.34 (.28)	.31 (.29)	.57 (.30)
Election year	−.19 (.17)	−.19 (.18)	−.20 (.18)
Preference * election cycle	.15 (.16)	.11 (.16)	.11 (.16)
Intercept	−1.51 (.20)	−1.56 (.20)	−1.86 (.22)
N	2229	2229	2229

(continued)

Table A7.4 (continued)

Controlling for Senate seat advantage, gridlock, and years in which the president's party changed hands

	Income Percentile		
	10th	50th	90th
G. W. Bush	−.59 (.22)	−.56 (.23)	−.52 (.23)
Johnson	−.40 (.54)	−.44 (.55)	−.33 (.57)
Preference	.10 (.51)	−.07 (.50)	.02 (.53)
Preference * G. W. Bush	.37 (.20)	.30 (.20)	.22 (.21)
Preference * Johnson	.41 (.51)	.31 (.49)	−.14 (.51)
Senate seats	−.25 (.71)	−.16 (.72)	−.30 (.75)
Preference * Senate seats	−.67 (.66)	−.69 (.63)	−.31 (.67)
Gridlock	−3.87 (.88)	−4.14 (.92)	−4.17 (.95)
Preference * gridlock	.36 (.82)	.73 (.81)	.66 (.85)
Preference * regime change	.21 (.21)	.31 (.20)	.48 (.22)
Regime change	.08 (.22)	−.02 (.23)	−.19 (.24)
Intercept	.90 (.56)	1.00 (.58)	.95 (.60)
N	2229	2229	2229

Analyses based on the annual restructured dataset with policy questions from 1964–68, 1981–2002, 2005–06. Table shows logistic regression coefficients (with standard errors in parentheses). Dependent variable is policy outcome coded 1 if the proposed policy change took place in the calendar year in question and 0 if it did not. Preference is the logit of the imputed percentage of respondents at a given income level favoring the proposed policy change. See tables A7.2 and A7.3 for variable descriptions. All analyses include fixed effects for the four policy domains examined in chapter 4.
$^*p < .05; ^{**}p < .01; ^{***}p < .001$

Notes

Chapter 1: Citizen Competence and Democratic Decision Making

1. Berelson, Lazarsfeld, and McPhee, *Voting*, 308.
2. Schumpeter, *Capitalism, Socialism, and Democracy*, 262.
3. Ibid., 273.
4. Ibid., 295.
5. Ibid.; Przeworski, "The Minimalist Conception of Democracy"; Riker, *Liberalism against Populism*.
6. Fiorina, *Retrospective Voting in American National Elections*, 5.
7. Kramer, "Short-Term Fluctuations in U.S. Voting Behavior"; Tufte, *Political Control of the Economy*.
8. Stokes, "Spatial Models of Party Competition."
9. Brody and Sniderman, "Life Space to Polling Place"; Feldman, "Economic Self-Interest and Political-Behavior"; Mutz, "Contextualizing Personal Experience."
10. Wolfers, "Are Voters Rational?"
11. Ibid.; Achen and Bartels, "Blind Retrospection"; Bartels and Achen, "Musical Chairs."
12. Bartels, *Unequal Democracy*.
13. Converse, "The Nature of Belief Systems in Mass Publics," 245.
14. Delli Carpini and Keeter, *What Americans Know about Politics and Why It Matters*, 269.
15. Ibid., 270.
16. Berelson, Lazarsfeld, and McPhee, *Voting*, 311.
17. Ibid., 109.
18. Downs, *An Economic Theory of Democracy*, 233.
19. Carmines and Kuklinski, "Incentives, Opportunities, and the Logic of Public Opinion in American Political Representation"; Gilens and Murakawa, "Elite Cues and Political Decision-Making"; Lau and Redlawsk, *How Voters Decide*; Lau and Redlawsk, "Voting Correctly"; Lupia, "Shortcuts versus Encyclopedias"; Lupia and McCubbins, *The Democratic Dilemma*; Popkin, *The Reasoning Voter*; Sniderman, Brody, and Tetlock, *Reasoning and Choice*; Zaller, *The Nature and Origins of Mass Opinion*.
20. Lupia, "Who Can Persuade?"
21. E.g., Kingdon, *Congressmen's Voting Decisions*.
22. Converse assessed issue public membership by dint of the consistency of responses to the same questions over time. Converse, "The Nature of Belief Systems in Mass Publics," n. 43.
23. Ibid., 246.
24. Gershkoff, "How Issue Interest Can Rescue the American Public"; Iyengar et al., "Selective Exposure to Campaign Communication"; Krosnick, "Government Policy and Citizen Passion."

25. Achen, "Mass Political Attitudes and the Survey Response"; Converse, "Popular Representation and the Distribution of Information"; Miller, "Information, Electorates, and Democracy"; Page and Shapiro, *The Rational Public*.

26. Zaller, *The Nature and Origins of Mass Opinion*; Zaller and Feldman, "A Simple Theory of the Survey Response.".

27. Page and Shapiro, *The Rational Public*.

28. Ibid., 14.

29. Ibid.

30. Owing to lack of sufficient numbers of respondents, Page and Shapiro were unable to analyze other racial or ethnic groups' preferences over time.

31. See Feldman, Huddy, and Marcus, "Going to War," for a fascinating discussion of the role of media, information, and alternative elite voices in shaping preferences during the lead-up to the Iraq War.

32. Bennett, "Toward a Theory of Press-State Relations in the United States"; Page and Shapiro, *The Rational Public*.

33. Canes-Wrone, *Who Leads Whom?*; Mycoff and Pika, *Confrontation and Compromise*.

34. Meyerson, *False Consciousness*; Pines, *Ideology and False Consciousness*.

35. Jacobs and Shapiro, *Politicians Don't Pander*, 322.

36. Bartels, "Unenlightened Self-Interest"; Bartels, *Unequal Democracy*; Graetz and Shapiro, *Death by a Thousand Cuts*.

37. Gershkoff and Kushner, "Shaping Public Opinion"; Kull, Ramsay, and Lewis, "Misperceptions, the Media, and the Iraq War."

38. Gilens, "Political Ignorance and Collective Policy Preferences"; Gilens, *Why Americans Hate Welfare*; Kuklinski et al., "Misinformation and the Currency of Democratic Citizenship."

39. Page and Shapiro, *The Rational Public*, 381.

40. Althaus, *Collective Preferences in Democratic Politics*.

41. With 20 percent of respondents reporting the "wrong" preference, the true 75 percent favoring is reduced by 15 percentage points (75 * 0.20) who are recorded instead as opposing. The true 25 percent who oppose is reduced by 5 percentage points (25 * 0.20) who are recorded instead as favoring. Thus the total percentage recorded as favoring is $75 - 15 + 5 = 65$, and the total percentage recorded as opposing is $25 - 5 + 15 = 35$.

42. To see why a group that appears more centrist than it really is would show a stronger relationship between its preferences and policy outcomes than would otherwise be the case, imagine two groups that favor some set of policies (call them A) by 80 percent and another set of policies (B) by only 20 percent. If the first group's preference are measured without error, that group will have a 60-percentage-point gap in preferences between the two sets of policies. If the second group's preferences are measured with error, it might appear they favor the A policies by 75 percent and the B policies by 25 percent, for a 50-percentage-point gap. In this example the A policies will be more likely to be adopted (since they're much more popular among both groups), but the differences in probability of adoption between the A and B policies will be associated with a 60-percentage-point difference in favorability among the first group and a 50-percentage-point difference among the second group. It would appear, there-

fore, to require a bigger difference in preferences to produce the same change in probability of adoption for the first group than for the second group, or, equivalently, that the association between preferences and policy outcomes is stronger for the second group than for the first.

43. Alwin and Krosnick, "The Reliability of Survey Attitude Measurement."

44. Lupia, "Shortcuts versus Encyclopedias."

45. Fishkin and Luskin, "Bringing Deliberation to the Democratic Dialogue"; Fishkin and Luskin, "Experimenting with a Democratic Ideal"; Luskin and Fishkin, "Deliberative Polling, Public Opinion, and Democracy."

46. See Gilens and Murakawa, "Elite Cues and Political Decision-Making," for an analysis of these results.

47. Converse, "Assessing the Capacity of Mass Electorates."

48. Bartels, "Uninformed Votes."

49. Ibid., table 3.

50. Althaus, *Collective Preferences in Democratic Politics*.

51. As one would expect, individual differences between observed and imputed fully informed preferences were larger than aggregate differences (about 13 percentage points compared with about 6.5). On any given issue, some respondents' expressed preferences were more liberal than their imputed preferences while other respondents' expressed preferences were more conservative, so about half the individual-level difference between observed and imputed preferences canceled out in the aggregate.

52. Smith, "That Which We Call Welfare by Any Other Name Would Smell Sweeter."

53. Schuman and Presser, *Questions and Answers in Attitude Surveys*, 277.

54. Quattrone and Tversky, "Contrasting Rational and Psychological Analyses of Political Choice."

55. Gilens, *Why Americans Hate Welfare*.

56. Schuman and Presser, *Questions and Answers in Attitude Surveys*, 281–83.

57. Druckman, "Political Preference Formation."

58. Quattrone and Tversky, "Contrasting Rational and Psychological Analyses of Political Choice," 728.

59. Druckman, "Political Preference Formation"; Sniderman and Theriault, "The Structure of Political Argument and the Logic of Issue Framing."

60. Graetz and Shapiro, *Death by a Thousand Cuts*.

61. Bartels, *Unequal Democracy*.

62. Butler, "George Lakoff Says Environmentalists Need to Watch Their Language."

63. Villar and Krosnick, "Global Warming vs. Climate Change, Taxes vs. Prices."

64. Druckman, "Political Preference Formation," 683.

65. Bishop, Tuchfarber, and Oldendick, "Opinions on Fictitious Issues."

66. Ninety-one percent of the proposed policy-change questions in my dataset elicited no more than 10 percent "Don't know" responses; 97 percent of the questions elicited no more than 15 percent such responses.

67. Berinsky, *Silent Voices*.

68. Dahl, *Polyarchy*, 1.

69. Dahl, *A Preface to Democratic Theory*, 90.

70. Olson, *The Logic of Collective Action*.

71. Substantial literatures in philosophy and social choice theory consider the difficulties of interpersonal comparisons of utilities (or differences in utilities associated with different states of the world). See, for example, Nozick, "Interpersonal Utility Theory"; Sen, *Collective Choice and Social Welfare*.

72. Arnold, *The Logic of Congressional Action*; Key, *Public Opinion and American Democracy*; Kingdon, *Congressmen's Voting Decisions*; Zaller, "Coming to Grips with V.O. Key's Concept of Latent Opinion."

73. Key, *Public Opinion and American Democracy*.

74. Arnold, *The Logic of Congressional Action*.

75. Page and Shapiro, *The Rational Public*, 65–66.

76. Gilens and Murakawa, "Elite Cues and Political Decision-Making."

77. Key, *Public Opinion and American Democracy*, 263.

78. Langworth, *Churchill by Himself*, 573.

79. Bartels, "Democracy with Attitudes."

80. See Glynn et al., *Public Opinion*, chap. 9; Manza and Cook, "A Democratic Polity?"; and Monroe and Gardner, "Public Policy Linkages," for reviews of this literature.

81. Achen, "Measuring Representation"; Ansolabehere, Snyder, and Stewart, "Candidate Positioning in US House Elections"; Bartels, "Instrumental and 'Quasi-Instrumental' Variables"; Miller and Stokes, "Constituency Influence in Congress"; Stimson, MacKuen, and Erikson, "Dynamic Representation."

82. Page and Shapiro, "Effects of Public Opinion on Policy."

83. Erikson, MacKuen, and Stimson, *The Macro Polity*.

84. Ibid., 316.

85. Monroe, "Consistency between Public Preferences and National Policy Decisions"; Monroe, "Public Opinion and Public Policy, 1980–1993."

86. Monroe, "Public Opinion and Public Policy, 1980–1993."

87. Griffin and Newman, *Minority Report*.

88. Jacobs and Page, "Who Influences US Foreign Policy?"

89. Bartels, "Economic Inequality and Political Representation"; Bartels, *Unequal Democracy*.

90. Bachrach and Baratz, "Decisions and Nondecisions—an Analytical Framework"; Bachrach and Baratz, "Two Faces of Power."

91. E.g., Cox and McCubbins, *Legislative Leviathan*; Cox and McCubbins, *Setting the Agenda*.

92. Hacker and Pierson, "Winner-Take-All Politics."

93. Binder, *Stalemate*.

94. Mayhew, *Divided We Govern*.

95. Arnold, *The Logic of Congressional Action*.

96. Ibid., Fenno, *Home Style*; Kingdon, *Congressmen's Voting Decisions*.

97. Hall and Wayman, "Buying Time."

98. Crespin, "Serving Two Masters."

99. Hutchings, McClerking, and Charles, "Congressional Representation of Black Interests."

100. E.g., Erikson, MacKuen, and Stimson, *The Macro Polity*.
101. Hacker and Pierson, *Winner-Take-All Politics*, 22.

Chapter 2: Data and Methods

1. With the exception of a very limited program available to under two thousand students in Washington, DC.
2. Kingdon, *Agendas, Alternatives, and Public Policies*.
3. Simon, *Models of Discovery*, 157.
4. E.g., Burstein, "Why Estimates of the Impact of Public Opinion on Public Policy Are Too High."
5. E.g., Binder, "The Dynamics of Legislative Gridlock, 1947–96"; Binder, *Stalemate*.
6. About 10 percent of the policy-preference questions in my dataset ask instead whether respondents favor or oppose an existing policy rather than a proposed change. For example, as part of a series of questions on arms sales, respondents were asked whether they favored or opposed selling weapons to Chile, Egypt, and Pakistan. At the time the United States was in fact selling arms to Chile and Egypt but not to Pakistan, so the first two questions asked about support for an existing policy while the latter asked about support for a policy change. When questions asked about support for an existing policy, the policy was redefined as support for change and the percentage favor and opposed were transposed. With regard to Chile, for example, the 80 percent of respondents who expressed opposition to selling weapons were reclassified as favoring a change in policy (i.e., a cessation of weapon sales to Chile), while the policy itself was redefined as "stopping weapon sales to Chile." By treating these sorts of questions in this way, the outcome variable consistently reflects change in current policy and the preference measures consistently reflect the level of support for change in current policy. Of course only questions about current policies that implied specific alternatives could be used. A question asking whether respondents favored or opposed current U.S. policy toward Israel would not be suitable since it doesn't contrast current policy with some specific alternative.
7. E.g., Erikson, MacKuen, and Stimson, *The Macro Polity*; Monroe, "Consistency between Public Preferences and National Policy Decisions"; Monroe, "Public Opinion and Public Policy, 1980–1993"; Page and Shapiro, "Effects of Public Opinion on Policy"; Wlezien, "Patterns of Representation"; Wlezien, "The Public as Thermostat."
8. Burstein, "Why Estimates of the Impact of Public Opinion on Public Policy Are Too High"; Lee, "The Sovereign Status of Survey Data"; Page, "The Semi-Sovereign Public."
9. Burstein, "Why Estimates of the Impact of Public Opinion on Public Policy Are Too High"; Page, "The Semi-Sovereign Public."
10. Roper Organization, April 25–May 2, 1987. I did not include this question in my dataset.
11. Kingdon, *Congressmen's Voting Decisions*, 240.

12. A second, related concern is that many of the surveys most commonly used to assess democratic responsiveness are sponsored by news organizations whose survey agenda may be driven primarily by the issues that are considered newsworthy at any given time. Scott Althaus, for example, found that at least half the questions in the iPOLL database (the most compressive database of survey questions) between 1980 and 2007 came from surveys sponsored by news organizations. But when Althaus compared the topics covered in CBS News/*New York Times* polls with the stories aired on the *CBS Evening News*, he found the survey questions to cover a much broader range of issues and to be essentially unrelated over time to the news agenda. See Althaus and Oats-Sargent, "What Prompts the Pollsters?"

13. These figures are for my primary dataset covering questions asked in 1981–2002 and exclude respondents who answered "Don't know."

14. In addition to income and education, my data contain responses within categories of race, sex, age, partisan identification, ideological self-placement, and region when those are available from the original survey.

15. Most of the survey items that were excluded because they were not dichotomous (favor/oppose) either asked respondents to place themselves on a multipoint scale where each of the endpoints was associated with some policy orientation (like government versus individual responsibility for paying for health care) or gave respondents three rather than two policy options to choose from (like whether spending in some policy area should be increased, decreased, or kept the same). Multipoint-scale items tend to use very broad descriptions of general policy orientations to identify the scale endpoints and thus fail the second criterion of referencing a policy change that is specific enough to be coded with confidence. Spending questions with three response options are typically more specific in nature, and in these cases policy outcomes could be coded with a reasonable degree of confidence. These items present a different difficulty for my purposes: by dividing respondents into three groups, they allow the possibility that no option reflects a majority preference. In such cases even maximally responsive government policy might appear to be unresponsive to the public's preferences. For example, if equal numbers of respondents favored increasing, decreasing, and maintaining spending in some area, the option most consistent with public preferences would seem to be to maintain spending at current levels. But this policy outcome would be coded as consistent with the preferences of only one-third of Americans. In addition it appears that the most common government spending questions provide little leverage in assessing representational inequalities because they generate smaller differences across income levels than is typical for the questions in my dataset. See Gilens, "Preference Gaps and Inequality in Representation"; and Soroka and Wlezien, "On the Limits to Inequality in Representation," for an analysis of this comparison.

16. Page and Shapiro, *The Rational Public.*

17. In fact, support was about 9 percentage points lower in response to the first of these questions when both were asked in 1999.

18. To determine whether a proposed policy change occurred, my research assistants and I relied on a combination of news accounts, government data (for example, on changes in tax rates or arms sales to different countries), *Congressional*

Quarterly's publications and web site, and academic papers detailing U.S. policy in specific areas.

19. Monroe, "Public Opinion and Public Policy, 1980–1993."

20. To perform these calculations, I used the aggregate data reflecting the number of respondents at each income level favoring or opposing each policy proposal to reconstitute the individual-level data. More specifically, I treated each combination of income category by policy preference as a single observation weighted by the number of respondents in that income-by-preference cell. I then used these weighted data as the basis for the logistic regression analyses described in the text.

21. Following Krippendorff, *Content Analysis*, alpha is defined as 1 – (*observed disagreement/expected disagreement*) and computed by $1 - [(2r - 1)(number\ of\ mismatched\ cases)/n_0 n_1]$, where r indicates the number of cases coded and $n0$ and $n1$ indicate the total number of 0 (absent) and 1 (present) codes assigned to that variable by the two coders. The reliability score for this coding is considered adequate by conventional standards. See Riffe, Lacy, and Fico, *Analyzing Media Messages*.

22. The other difference between my reliability estimates and those typically used to assess survey questions is that my data reflect not the responses of hundreds of respondents to two alternative questions, but the average response of all respondents (or of all respondents at specific income levels) to hundreds of survey questions.

23. Alwin and Krosnick, "The Reliability of Survey Attitude Measurement."

24. Page and Shapiro, "Effects of Public Opinion on Policy"; Stimson, MacKuen, and Erikson, "Dynamic Representation."

25. Monroe, "Consistency between Public Preferences and National Policy Decisions"; Monroe, "Public Opinion and Public Policy, 1980–1993"; Monroe, "Public Opinion and Public Policy 1960–1999."

26. These figures represent the proportion supporting the proposed policy change among respondents expressing a preference and the proportion of policies adopted within the four-year coding window I employ.

27. Alternatively, federal legislation can be adopted by overriding a presidential veto with two-thirds vote of both the House and the Senate.

Chapter 3: The Preference/Policy Link

1. In this discussion of electoral incentives, I treat the federal government as a unitary actor responding to the preferences of the public as a whole. In fact our system of government is based on geographic constituencies, and even presidential elections are shaped by state-level considerations as a consequence of the electoral college. This means that electoral incentives depend on the distribution of preferences not only among the public as a whole but among residents of particular states or congressional districts. In the extreme case a policy that a majority of Americans favor may not be favored by a majority of residents in a majority of states or districts (that is, majority support for the policy may be found in fewer than half the states or congressional districts). As a simple illustration,

imagine a polity composed of five equal-sized districts. If strong majorities favor a particular policy in two of the districts and weak majorities oppose the policy in the other three districts, the overall distribution of opinion in the polity may favor the policy, but representatives from only two of the five districts will have constituencies with majority support. In a perfectly responsive political system in which each representative votes according to his or her constituents' preferences, a policy such as this would be defeated despite having overall majority support. If, however, we allow representatives to horse-trade across issues, we would expect that those from districts with weak opposition to the policy might concede to representatives from districts with strong support (since the latter have more to gain from the policy's enactment than the former have to lose). In this case policy outcomes would be brought back in line with majority opinion for the polity as a whole. In the real world, of course, a variety of obstacles stand in the way of efficient bargaining of this sort, even if representatives are inclined to do so.

2. In *The Federalist 10* Madison writes, "If a faction consists of less than a majority … it will be unable to execute and mask its violence under the forms of the Constitution. When a majority is included in a faction, the form of popular government, on the other hand, enables it to sacrifice to its ruling passion or interest both the public good and the rights of other citizens. To secure the public good and private rights against the danger of such a faction, and at the same time to preserve the spirit and the form of popular government, is then the great object to which our inquiries are directed."

3. Unless a presidential veto is overridden by two-thirds majorities in both houses of Congress.

4. Unpopular policies that were nevertheless adopted include various tax increases over the years, loan guarantees or other economic assistance to foreign countries, and sending U.S. troops to Haiti and Bosnia.

5. Most of the approaches other scholars have used to assess the link between public preferences and policy outcomes do not generate data suitable for estimating the status quo bias (e.g., Erikson, MacKuen, and Stimson, *The Macro Polity*; Page and Shapiro, "Effects of Public Opinion on Policy"). Alan Monroe, in his works "Consistency between Public Preferences and National Policy Decisions" and "Public Opinion and Public Policy, 1980–1993," does examine the status quo bias for his data for 1960–93, showing that outcomes are consistent with majority preference about three-quarters of the time when the majority favors the status quo but only half the time when the majority favors policy change. However, Monroe does not report the size of the preference majorities for these two sets of issues, leaving open the possibility that the status quo bias might be larger than this difference would imply (if the size of the majorities on issues where a majority favored change outnumbered, on average, the size of the majorities on issues where the majority favored the status quo) or smaller (if the opposite were true).

6. To provide a sufficient number of policy questions with divergent preferences, the analysis of the 70th versus the 90th income percentiles includes questions on which preferences differ by more than 6 percentage points rather than the 10-percentage-point cut-off used for the other comparisons. We would expect this more inclusive criterion for the 70th percentile analysis in figure 3.6 to slightly increase the estimated impact of the preferences of respondents at the

70th income percentile relative to the analyses of the other income levels in the figure.

7. E.g., Downs, *An Economic Theory of Democracy*; Enelow and Hinich, *The Spatial Theory of Voting*.

8. E.g., Adams, Merrill, and Grofman, *A Unified Theory of Party Competition*; Gerber and Lewis, "Beyond the Median"; Green and Shapiro, *Pathologies of Rational Choice Theory*; Grofman, "Downs and Two-Party Convergence"; McKelvey and Ordeshook, "Information, Electoral Equilibria, and the Democratic Ideal."

9. Lupu and Pontusson, "The Structure of Inequality and the Politics of Redistribution."

10. Specifically I isolate (1) those policies on which preferences of the 10th and 50th income percentiles are within 5 percentage points and both diverge from the 90th percentile by at least 10 percentage points, and (2) those policies on which preferences of the 50th and 90th income percentiles are within 5 percentage points and both diverge from the 10th percentile by at least 10 percentage points.

11. Lupu and Pontusson, "The Structure of Inequality and the Politics of Redistribution," 18.

12. The sources and consequences of measurement error in survey questions have generated a large literature. See, for example, Achen, "Mass Political Attitudes and the Survey Response"; Achen, "Proxy Variables and Incorrect Signs on Regression Coefficients"; Berk, *Regression Analysis*; Brady, "The Perils of Survey Research"; Carmines and Zeller, *Reliability and Validity Assessment*; Converse, "The Nature of Belief Systems in Mass Publics"; Stanley Feldman, "Measuring Issue Preferences"; Green and Citrin, "Measurement Error and the Structure of Attitudes"; Green and Palmquist, "Of Artifacts and Partisan Instability"; Jones and Norrander, "The Reliability of Aggregated Public Opinion Measures"; Krosnick, "The Stability of Political Preferences"; O'Brien, "Correcting Measures of Relationship between Aggregate-Level Variables"; O'Brien, "Correcting Measures of Relationship between Aggregate-Level Variables for Both Unreliability and Correlated Errors"; Wiley and Wiley, "The Estimation of Measurement Error in Panel Data."

13. The consequences of correlated errors depend on whether the errors and the true scores on the variables of interest are correlated in the same or opposite directions.

14. For a discussion of correlated measurement error in aggregated data, see O'Brien, "Correcting Measures of Relationship between Aggregate-Level Variables"; O'Brien, "Correcting Measures of Relationship between Aggregate-Level Variables for Both Unreliability and Correlated Errors."

15. Alwin and Krosnick, "The Reliability of Survey Attitude Measurement."

16. This same phenomenon in which differences across income groups at the individual level disappear when the individual-level data are aggregated can be observed with panel data containing repeated measures of the same survey question posed to the same respondents. For example, Larry Bartels examined a series of policy questions asked of National Election Study panel respondents in 1992, 1994, and 1996. Bartels found substantially more individual-level instability

across survey years among low-income than among middle- or high-income respondents. However, the aggregate preferences for the three income groups were equally stable from one survey year to the next (Bartels, personal communication).

17. While the difference between 4 percent and 8 percent "Don't know" responses for the 10th and 50th income percentiles seems considerable, the politically relevant distinction is between the 92 percent of low-income respondents and the 96 percent of middle- and high-income respondents that express a preference for or against the proposed policy change. Even if the pattern of opinionation across income levels as indicated by "Don't know" responses did fit the pattern of responsiveness to policy preferences, it is hard to imagine that the 4 percent difference could have much impact on the inclination of policy makers to take the preferences of different income groups into account.

18. Sturgis and Smith, "Fictitious Issues Revisited."

19. Bishop, Tuchfarber, and Oldendick, "Opinions on Fictitious Issues."

20. Schuman and Presser, "Public-Opinion and Public Ignorance."

21. Lupia, "Shortcuts versus Encyclopedias"; Lupia and McCubbins, *The Democratic Dilemma*; Popkin, *The Reasoning Voter*; Sniderman, Brody, and Tetlock, *Reasoning and Choice*; Zaller, *The Nature and Origins of Mass Opinion*.

22. Nie, Junn, and Stehlik-Barry, *Education and Democratic Citizenship in America*, 77; Zaller, *The Nature and Origins of Mass Opinion*.

23. Neither of these latter coefficients is statistically distinguishable from their counterparts for low and high income.

24. Because my dataset contains only aggregate rather than individual-level data, calculating the joint relationship of income and education with the policy outcomes was complicated. My data indicate the proportion of respondents favoring each policy change for each level of income and education, but not for the joint distribution of income and education. By basing my imputation equations on a variance/covariance matrix for each policy question, however, I was able to overcome this limitation. My data contain the means and the covariances of each policy outcome with income and with education. The only missing information needed to estimate the desired imputation equations was the covariance of income with education. Using General Social Survey data from the same time period, I calculated the covariance of income and education (after transforming each into percentiles to parallel the measures in my policy-preference dataset). To capture any change over time in the income/education covariance, I calculated this statistic separately for four-year blocks starting with 1980–84. However, this turned out to be unnecessary as the income/education covariance was extremely stable across the twenty-year time period (from 0.031 to 0.033), with no consistent trend.

25. Delli Carpini and Keeter, *What Americans Know about Politics and Why It Matters*.

26. Or at least by the preferences of their most affluent constituents; Bartels, "Economic Inequality and Political Representation"; Bartels, *Unequal Democracy*.

27. Canes-Wrone and Shotts, "The Conditional Nature of Presidential Responsiveness to Public Opinion." Their argument is that this is exactly the condition

under which a president has the greatest incentive to cater to public preferences. If a president's popularity is very high, he or she can safely disregard the public's wishes on most issues and still be confident of reelection, and if a president's popularity is very low, he or she will be unlikely to win reelection regardless of the policies he or she adopts. But if reelection is uncertain, a president's incentive to respond to the public's preferences is greatest.

28. Elling, "Ideological Change in the United States Senate"; Kuklinski, "Representativeness and Elections"; Thomas, "Election Proximity and Senatorial Roll Call Voting."

Chapter 4: Policy Domains and Democratic Responsiveness

1. Wildavsky, "The Two Presidencies."

2. E.g., Kull and Destler, *Misreading the Public*; Page and Bouton, *The Foreign Policy Disconnect*.

3. After Mikhail Gorbachev came to office and introduced far-reaching reforms to the Soviet system in 1986, Reagan administration policy on nuclear arms began to change, and the Strategic Arms Reduction Treaty (START) was eventually signed in 1991. The signing of the treaty, however, cannot be considered a positive example of government response to public preferences both because of the long delay and because of the apparently critical role of altered conditions in bringing about change in U.S. government policy.

4. U.S. Department of Defense, "Missile Defense Agency, FY85–FY07 Historical Funding Chart."

5. Ferguson, *Golden Rule*; U.S. International Trade Commission, *Value of U.S. Imports for Consumption, Duties Collected, and Ratio of Duties to Values 1891–2005*.

6. U.S. Bureau of the Census, *Statistical Abstract*, table 1270, "U.S. Foreign Economic And Military Aid Programs: 1980 to 2005."

7. Page and Barabas, "Foreign Policy Gaps between Citizens and Leaders"; Page and Bouton, *The Foreign Policy Disconnect*; Jacobs and Page, "Who Influences US Foreign Policy?"; Kull and Destler, *Misreading the Public*.

8. As explained in chapter 2, the attitudes on constitutional amendments to ban abortion or permit school prayer shown in table 4.5 are not included in the quantitative analyses.

9. White House, "The Quiet Revolution."

10. Cohen, "Regulation of Broadcast Indecency"; Smith, "V-Chip and TV Ratings."

11. Executive Office of the President, "National Drug Control Strategy, FY 2007 Budget Summary"; U.S. Department of Justice, "Drug Demand Reduction Activities, Report No. 03-12."

12. U.S. Department of Labor, "Drug-Free Workforce Conference."

13. Eddy, "Medical Marijuana."

14. Jones and Boonstra, "Confidential Reproductive Health Services for Minors."

15. Hogan, "The Life of the Abortion Pill in the United States."

16. Fried, "Abortion in the United States."

17. Buckley, "Crucial Steps in Combating the Aids Epidemic."

18. Johnson and Smith, "AIDS."

19. Shimabukuro, "Background and Legal Issues Related to Stem Cell Research."

20. O'Connor, *No Neutral Ground?*; Solinger, *Abortion Wars*.

21. Jelen and Wilcox, "Causes and Consequences of Public Attitudes toward Abortion."

22. Guttmacher Institute, "State Policies in Brief."

23. Planned Parenthood, "History & Successes."

24. Citrin and Green, "The Self-Interest Motive in American Public Opinion"; Page and Jacobs, *Class War?*; Sears and Funk, "The Role of Self-Interest in Social and Political Attitudes."

25. The group targeted for tax increases in these proposals was considerably better off than the 90th income percentile that I use to represent high-income Americans. The relevant questions in my dataset were asked during the early 1990s and referred to families with incomes above $180,000 or $200,000 at a time when the 90th percentile of household income was about $75,000.

26. National Bureau of Economic Research, "Summary Measures of the US Income Tax System, 1960–2005."

27. Congressional Budget Office, "Historical Effective Federal Tax Rates: 1979 to 2003."

28. Burman and Kobes, "Preferential Capital Gains Tax Rates"; Congressional Budget Office, *How Capital Gains Tax Rates Affect Revenues*; U.S. Department of the Treasury, "U.S. Individual Income Tax."

29. Bartels, "Unenlightened Self-Interest"; Bartels, "A Tale of Two Tax Cuts, a Wage Squeeze, and a Tax Credit"; Bartels, *Unequal Democracy*; Graetz and Shapiro, *Death by a Thousand Cuts*.

30. Bartels, *Unequal Democracy*.

31. Luckey, "A History of Federal Estate, Gift, and Generation-Skipping Taxes." When the provisions of the Economic Growth and Tax Relief Reconciliation Act of 2001 expired at the end of 2010, a reinstituted estate tax was adopted with a higher exemption and lower rate than the tax that existed prior to the 2001 reform.

32. Whether reducing or eliminating the estate tax is also in the economic interest of the high-income respondents in my surveys is doubtful. In recent decades a tiny fraction of Americans have paid the estate tax: about 1–2 percent of deceased adults had any estate tax liability in each year between 1981 and 2004 (Chamberlain, Prante, and Fleenor, "Death and Taxes"). Consequently the interest of most Americans at the 90th income percentile would not appear to be well served by eliminating this tax on the very wealthiest citizens.

33. Jackson, "The Federal Excise Tax on Gasoline and the Highway Trust Fund."

34. Flat-tax proposals invariably exempt some amount of income from taxation, thereby generating at least a modestly progressive tax system among taxpayers above the exemption level. Some flat-tax proposals over the years have

retained some of the existing specific deductions and exemptions, while others actually included more than one tax bracket; not all flat-tax proposals are really flat.

35. Gilens, *Why Americans Hate Welfare*; Page and Jacobs, *Class War?*

36. This same general pattern was evident during the debate over the Obama administration's health care reform efforts. For example a July 2009 Gallup survey sponsored by *USA Today*, 73 percent of low-income respondents and 58 percent of high-income respondents with an opinion favored "Congress passing a major health care reform bill this year."

37. Gottschalk, *The Shadow Welfare State*; Hacker, *Health at Risk*; Quadagno, *One Nation, Uninsured*; Skocpol, *Boomerang*.

38. U.S. Bureau of the Census, *Statistical Abstract*.

39. Kollmann, "Social Security."

40. Chaikind et al., "Medicare Provisions in the Medicare, Medicaid, and Schip Benefits Improvement and Protection Act of 2000."

41. The most significant cost increases to Medicare beneficiaries during the 1981–2004 time period were deductibles for inpatient hospital care, which increased from $204 to $876 (roughly equal to the medical inflation rate and about twice the overall rate of inflation), and monthly premiums for Medicare Part B, which increased from $11 to $66 (about 1.5 times the rate of medical inflation). In contrast deductibles for Part B rose only 67 percent across these decades— considerably less than inflation—and Part B coinsurance remained at 20 percent. U.S. Social Security Administration, "Annual Statistical Supplement," table 2.C1.

42. Congress passed the No Child Left Behind Act in 2001, but the first survey question to ask explicitly about this legislation in the Roper Center's iPOLL database is from January 2003 (beyond my December 2002 cutoff for survey questions).

43. Congressional Budget Office, *Trends in Public Spending on Transportation and Water Infrastructure, 1956 to 2004*.

44. These examples run counter to the pattern identified by Jacob Hacker and Paul Pierson in which status quo bias (or the related notion of policy drift) during periods of increasing inequality serves to benefit the affluent (Hacker and Pierson, "Winner-Take-All Politics" ; Hacker and Pierson, *Winner-Take-All Politics*). On the contingent nature of the status quo bias and inequality, see Rigby and Wright, "Whose Statehouse Democracy?"

45. Morris, *The AARP*.

46. Although the AARP had initially opposed many of the bill's provisions (like forbidding Medicare to negotiate for lower drug prices), it eventually came round to supporting the legislation, creating a powerful alliance. Dreyfuss, "The Shocking Story of How AARP Backed the Medicare Bill."

47. District pork-barrel projects and the interest of developers and construction companies frequently come together when these projects benefit specific developers or other commercial interests within a district, which then increase their support for their incumbent representative. That is, the benefit of pork-barrel projects may be less in their direct appeal to voters and more in their appeal to businesses.

Chapter 5: Interest Groups and Democratic Responsiveness

1. Berry, *The Interest Group Society*; Dahl, *Who Governs?*; Lindblom, *Politics and Markets*; Schattschneider, *The Semisovereign People*; Truman, *The Governmental Process*.

2. Schlozman and Tierney, *Organized Interests and American Democracy*; Smith, *American Business and Political Power*.

3. Graetz and Shapiro, *Death by a Thousand Cuts*; Skocpol, *Boomerang*.

4. Bartels, *Unequal Democracy*; Jamieson, "When Harry Met Louise."

5. Kollman, *Outside Lobbying*. Even Mark Smith, who provides some of the key quantitative evidence of the power of business to shape public preferences, comes to a measured conclusion about the ability of organized interests to sway the public, writing, "Given so many forces shaping public opinion, it would certainly be difficult and more likely impossible for business to determine the public's core values and policy preferences.... If business influences but does not dominate public opinion, then much of what the public believes and supports represents an authentic response to competing political ideas, prevailing conditions and circumstances, and historical changes." Smith, *American Business and Political Power*, 213.

6. E.g., Kollman, *Outside Lobbying*.

7. Details on the Advocacy and Public Policymaking project are available at http://lobby.la.psu.edu/ and in Baumgartner et al., *Lobbying and Policy Change*.

8. For example, among the first five issues listed in the Advocacy and Public Policy dataset are the granting of patent extensions to pipeline drugs, government funding of hearing screenings for infants, the imposition of a "risk adjuster" to help limit overpayments by the Health Care Financing Administration, and increasing the Medicare payment schedule for PAP screenings.

9. Correlation = 0.73, $p < 0.001$; Baumgartner et al., *Lobbying and Policy Change*.

10. Schlozman et al., "Who Sings in the Heavenly Chorus?" The high degree of stability of the list of interest groups across the years the *Fortune* Power 25 survey was administered also suggests that changes in the interest group environment in Washington tend to be gradual.

11. One hundred fifty questions were coded independently by a second coder, producing an intercoder reliability of alpha = 0.87.

12. Opensecrets.org, accessed June 18, 2009, http://www.opensecrets.org/industries/indus.php?ind=Q14.

13. Scores on the summary index of interest group resources totaled 1.15 for the ten groups active against new restrictions on late-term abortion compared with 0.39 for the four groups active in favor of new restrictions. The interest group resource index ranges from 0 for the single interest group with the fewest resources to 1 for the interest group with the greatest resources. I am indebted to Beth Leech for generously providing these data. See Baumgartner et al., *Lobbying and Policy Change*, and the project's web site for details.

14. These three unnamed abortion rights groups were coded as taking the opposite position to the National Right to Life Committee on all proposed policy changes on which the NRLC took a position.

15. The following discussion of interest group alignments includes only the 1,779 proposed policy changes eligible for analysis, as explained in chapter 3.

16. Baumgartner et al., *Lobbying and Policy Change*, 60.

17. Whether these issues also appear on the government agenda and are taken up by Congress or the White House is a different matter, of course. This latter question is folded into the analysis of policy adoption and reflected in the associations between interest group alignments and policy outcomes described below.

18. Schattschneider, *The Semisovereign People*; Truman, *The Governmental Process*; Wright, *Interest Groups and Congress*.

19. Baumgartner et al., *Lobbying and Policy Change*, tables 11.6 and 11.7.

20. Arnold, *The Logic of Congressional Action*; Kingdon, *Congressmen's Voting Decisions*.

21. An additional condition for an omitted variable to bias a causal estimate is that the omitted variable be at least partially exogenous to the predictor of interest. If the omitted variable is intervening between the predictor of interest and the outcome, it should be excluded from the equation estimating the causal impact of the predictor of interest. Since interest group alignments are largely exogenous to public preferences, their exclusion might serve to bias the estimated influence of public preferences on policy outcomes.

22. Verba, Schlozman, and E. Brady, *Voice and Equality*.

23. Baumgartner and Leech, *Basic Interests*; Domhoff, *Who Rules America?*; Lowery and Gray, "Bias in the Heavenly Chorus"; Schattschneider, *The Semisovereign People*; Schlozman and Tierney, *Organized Interests and American Democracy*; Schlozman, "Who Sings in the Heavenly Chorus?"; Schlozman et al., "Who Sings in the Heavenly Chorus?"

24. E.g., Berry, *The New Liberalism*.

25. Strolovitch, *Affirmative Advocacy*.

26. With no other predictor in the model, the coefficient for the standardized Net Interest Group Alignment Index is 0.36 (s.e. = 0.05).

27. A bootstrapped standard error for the difference between these two coefficients is 0.045 ($p < 0.07$).

28. Smith, *American Business and Political Power*.

29. In addition to including issues on which interest groups were divided or unengaged, my analyses differ from Smith's in considering a broader range of interest groups (he focused exclusively on business), in using individual policy changes rather than annual averages as the basis for my study, and in differentiating between the preferences of Americans with lower and higher incomes.

30. Smith's analysis uses year-by-year variation in public opinion to predict variation in the extent to which policy making reflects the unified preferences of the business lobby. This design can provide important insights into the *variation* in business success but tells us nothing about the stable factors that determine the mean around which business success varies. In some of his analyses, Smith does include measures of business lobbying behavior, showing, for example, that year-to-year variation in corporate PAC contributions are not significantly related to variation in business success (p. 123). But if PAC contributions (or other measures of business lobbying activity) tend to be fairly steady when aggregated into

annual averages, then the role of business lobbying in shaping policy making will remain hidden.

31. Opposition to trade sanctions against Russia and Poland came from American manufacturing, farming, and oil industries as well as broad business lobbying organizations like the Chamber of Commerce and the National Association of Manufactures. In addition, the American Israel Public Affairs Committee opposed these sanctions. Military aid to U.S. allies was favored by defense contractors.

32. The analyses in chapters 3 and 4 suggest that the association between preferences and policy outcomes at income levels below the 90th percentile are largely spurious owing to the overlap between the preferences of high-income Americans and the preferences of those with lower incomes. Since the preferences of the well-off retain their predictive power even when the preferences of other income levels are controlled for or when the analysis is restricted to policy changes on which preferences across income groups diverge, the preferences of the well-off are an appropriate control when estimating the influence of interest groups over policy outcomes.

33. Burman and Kobes, "Preferential Capital Gains Tax Rates"; Congressional Budget Office, *How Capital Gains Tax Rates Affect Revenues*.

34. See chapter 4 for specifics on the history of estate tax policy.

35. See AFL-CIO, "AFL-CIO Convention Resolution 6," for an example of union opposition to a national sales tax.

36. Defeated efforts to reduce government regulation included eliminating the requirement to provide advance notice before closing a business or factory and reducing the record keeping associated with the Foreign Corrupt Practices Act.

37. Slivinski, "The Corporate Tax Burden."

38. Data from opensecrets.org, accessed July 29, 2009.

39. Carter, *Gun Control in the United States*.

40. Berry, *The New Liberalism*.

41. Strolovitch, *Affirmative Advocacy*.

42. Ainsworth, *Analyzing Interest Groups*; Olson, *The Logic of Collective Action*.

43. AARP, "Aarp Consolidated Financial Statements 2007–2008." For 2007, membership dues accounted for about 21 percent of the AARP's operating revenue, with 59 percent coming from royalties, advertising income from AARP publications, and investments.

44. Table 5.7 excludes the American Legion and Veterans of Foreign Wars, which took positions on fewer than twenty of the proposed policy changes in my dataset.

45. Baumgartner et al., *Lobbying and Policy Change*.

46. E.g., Masters and Delaney, "Organized Labor's Political Scorecard."

47. The AARP spent over $160 million on lobbying over the past decade, behind only the U.S. Chamber of Commerce, the American Medical Association, General Electric, and the American Hospital Association, according to opensecrets.org.

48. Dahl, *Who Governs?*; Truman, *The Governmental Process*.

49. Lindblom, *Politics and Markets*; Olson, *The Logic of Collective Action*; Schattschneider, *The Semisovereign People*.

50. Baumgartner et al., *Lobbying and Policy Change*.

51. Berry, *The New Liberalism*.

52. Strolovitch, *Affirmative Advocacy*.

53. Freeman and Medoff, *What Do Unions Do?*

Chapter 6: Parties, Elections, and Democratic Responsiveness

1. Downs, *An Economic Theory of Democracy*; Mayhew, *Congress*.

2. Cohen et al., *The Party Decides*; Ferguson, *Golden Rule*; Key, *Politics, Parties and Pressure Groups*; Wilson, *The Amateur Democrat*.

3. Mayhew, *Congress*; Arnold, *The Logic of Congressional Action*.

4. Wright and Berkman, "Candidates and Policy in United States Senate Elections."

5. Ahuja, "Electoral Status and Representation in the United-States-Senate"; Canes-Wrone and Shotts, "The Conditional Nature of Presidential Responsiveness to Public Opinion"; Canes-Wrone, *Who Leads Whom?*; Levitt, "How Do Senators Vote?"; Wood and Andersson, "The Dynamics of Senatorial Representation, 1952–1991."

6. Verba, Schlozman, and Brady, *Voice and Equality*. Americans with family incomes below $15,000 in 1990 constituted 19 percent of all survey respondents, 14 percent of all voters, 12 percent of those who had contacted an elected official, and 12 percent of those who reported having taken part in a political protest. Ibid., 194.

7. Krehbiel, *Pivotal Politics*.

8. Erikson, MacKuen, and Stimson, *The Macro Polity*.

9. Wlezien, "The Public as Thermostat."

10. Vavreck, *The Message Matters*.

11. Binder, *Stalemate*; Mayhew, *Divided We Govern*.

12. Erikson, MacKuen, and Stimson, *The Macro Polity*; Wlezien, "The Public as Thermostat." One bit of empirical evidence consistent with the partisan change hypothesis is that net of other predictors, the longer a party has held the presidency, the less likely that party is to prevail in the next presidential election. Bartels and Zaller, "Al Gore and George Bush's Not-So-Excellent Adventure."

13. These data are from the 2004 American National Election Study and include independents who lean toward one party or the other as well as outright partisans.

14. Bartels, *Unequal Democracy*.

15. In addition, by virtue of the vice president's deciding vote in the Senate, the Republicans controlled both houses of Congress during the first few months of 2001 before Jim Jeffords left the Republican Party.

16. See Sundquist, *Back to Gridlock?*

17. The Democrats were successful in passing the Brady gun control bill and the federal unpaid family leave legislation during this period.

18. Hirsch and Macpherson, "Union Membership and Coverage Database from the Current Population Survey"; Saez, "Striking It Richer."

19. I am indebted to Eric Wanner, president of the Russell Sage Foundation, for encouraging me to collect these data and for providing the necessary funding.

20. Thus data from the G. W. Bush presidency are excluded altogether, and data from the 1960s are restricted to 1964–67, providing one complete electoral cycle for President Johnson.

21. Arnold, *The Logic of Congressional Action*; Fenno, *Home Style*. For any given policy change, some representatives would typically support the change even in the absence of an election. But for elected officials as a body, elections appear to induce policy outcomes that would not otherwise have occurred.

22. But see Patashnik, *Reforms at Risk*, for an important exception.

23. Berry, Burden, and Howell, "After Enactment."

24. Howell, personal communication, 2010. Despite being more likely to have their funding cut, programs adopted during presidential election years were no more likely to be entirely killed off by later Congresses (an action that would be more likely to draw the public's attention).

25. For example, Downs, *An Economic Theory of Democracy*.

26. Wilson, *The Amateur Democrat*; Cohen et al., *The Party Decides*; Fiorina and Abrams, *Disconnect*.

27. The only case in my data of a party holding the presidency for more than four consecutive Congresses is the George H. W. Bush administration (which constituted the fifth and sixth Congresses since Reagan took control of the presidency from Carter). Estimates for these Congresses using dummy variables are consequently quite noisy.

28. Brady and Sinclair, "Building Majorities for Policy Changes in the House of Representatives"; Erikson, MacKuen, and Stimson, *The Macro Polity*; Treier, "Explaining Policy Change."

29. Lipset and Rokkan, *Party Systems and Voter Alignments*.

30. E.g., Cox and McCubbins, *Legislative Leviathan*; Cox and McCubbins, *Setting the Agenda*; Krehbiel, *Pivotal Politics*.

31. Removing each presidential administration in turn from the analyses reported in table 6.5 shows that responsiveness to the public overall is always stronger under maximum Republican control than under maximum Democratic control. The partisan differences (corresponding to the third row) are 0.11, 0.42, 0.31, 0.51, and 0.17 when estimated without presidents Johnson, Reagan, G.H.W. Bush, Clinton, and G. W. Bush, respectively.

32. The only exception to this pattern was the 1982 tax increase when the Republicans controlled the White House and the Senate. In addition a large tax cut was passed during the Johnson administration (in February 1964) but did not generate any questions in my survey data from the Johnson years (which covered 1964–68). If my data extended further back in time and had captured questions about this tax cut asked in 1963, responsiveness to public preferences during the Johnson years would have appeared slightly stronger. Two major tax changes took place during periods of evenly divided partisan control: a 1990 tax increase under G.H.W. Bush (and Democratic House and Senate) and a 1997 tax cut under Clinton (and Republican House and Senate). The public may have associated these

changes more with the respective presidents than with the Congresses controlled by the opposite parties, but our assessments of the partisan influences on policy making must take both presidential and congressional actors into account.

33. In addition the affluent were uniquely supportive of dropping government restrictions on selling various goods to Russia during the Johnson administration.

34. While the Republican Party is now associated with a pro-life position on abortion and with religious conservatism more generally, this is a fairly recent phenomenon. During the most of the 1970s and 1980s, Americans who expressed pro-life views were more likely than those who expressed pro-choice views to identify as Democrats; it was not until the late 1980s that these positions reversed. Adams, "Abortion."

35. Ibid.

36. Layman, "'Culture Wars' in the American Party System."

37. The issue scales included government responsibility for jobs and living standards, government spending and services, government involvement in health insurance, spending on defense, the rights of the accused, government help for black people, and liberal/conservative ideology.

38. Green, Palmquist, and Schickler, *Partisan Hearts and Minds*, 8.

39. The figures are from the Cumulative American National Election Study 1948–2004, version of 10/2005, for the 1972 through 2004 survey years (weighted by VCF0009A). The social groups most often mentioned as a reason for liking the Democratic Party are "common man/people/working people" (56 percent of all group mentions), "poor people/needy people/the unemployed" (22 percent), and "white collar workers/salaried people/middle class" (10 percent).

40. Bartels and Zaller, "Al Gore and George Bush's Not-So-Excellent Adventure"; Erikson, "Economic Conditions and the Congressional Vote"; Lewis-Beck and Stegmaier, "Economic Determinants of Electoral Outcomes."

41. Bartels, *Unequal Democracy*; Hibbs, *The American Political Economy*.

42. The analyses of the electoral cycle presented in table 6.2 differ from the other two sets of analyses in using only complete, full four-year cycles from those presidents for which at least one four-year cycle is available. The analyses of length of partisan regime presented in table 6.3 differ from the other two sets of analyses in weighting only for the distribution of proposed policy changes in the original (nonrestructured) data to take account of the duplication of survey questions when the data were restructured to represent year-specific outcomes but not weighted to give proposed changes on the agenda in each calendar year equal weight.

Chapter 7: Democratic Responsiveness across Time

1. Jacobs and Shapiro, *Politicians Don't Pander*.

2. Quirk, "Politicians Do Pander."

3. Druckman and Jacobs, "Presidential Responsiveness to Public Opinion"; Jacobs and Shapiro, "The Rise of Presidential Polling."

4. Jacobs and Shapiro, *Politicians Don't Pander*; Quirk and Hinchliffe, "The Rising Hegemony of Mass Opinion."

5. Monroe, "Public Opinion and Public Policy, 1980–1993."

6. Ibid.; Jacobs and Shapiro, *Politicians Don't Pander*, 4. Less directly related to policy outcomes, Ansolabehere, Snyder, and Stewart, in "Candidate Positioning in US House Elections," found a decline in the association of House members' roll-call voting with the presidential vote in their districts between the early 1970s and the mid-1990s. They suggest that this decline might reflect an increase in the parties' ideological homogeneity and their power in Congress. If so, the same factors that decrease the dyadic link between constituents' preferences and representatives' votes might increase the link between the preferences of the public nationally and the policies that emerge from a supermajoritarian federal government (for reasons discussed below).

7. After individual donations, PACs and candidates themselves are the most important sources of campaign money. Campaign Finance Institute, http://cfinst.org.

8. Verba, Schlozman, and Brady, *Voice and Equality*, 194. Individual donations to candidates provide a limited picture of the flow of money in politics but one on which, thanks to Federal Election Commission reporting requirements, we have good data. These data, however, substantially understate the degree to which the most affluent members of the public finance political campaigns and lobbying. Fund-raising (e.g., by bundling many individual donations) and donations to parties, PACs, and independent expenditure groups have much higher or no donation limits and are therefore attractive alternatives for individuals wishing to contribute larger sums.

9. Green et al., "Individual Congressional Campaign Contributors."

10. Polsby and Wildavsky, *Presidential Elections*.

11. Aldrich, *Why Parties?*; Mayhew, *Placing Parties in American Politics*.

12. Skocpol, *Diminished Democracy*.

13. Ware, *The Breakdown of Democratic Party Organization, 1940–1980*.

14. For some on-the-record exceptions, however, see Makinson, *Speaking Freely*.

15. Breedlove, "Money, Politics, and Government Corruption."

16. Saez, "Striking It Richer."

17. Fenno, *Home Style*.

18. Chi-square tests of model fit indicate that the addition of a quadratic term significantly improves the fit of the model ($p < 0.001$ for the improvement in chi-squares for all income levels).

19. Asher, *Polling and the Public*.

20. For example, Druckman and Jacobs, "Presidential Responsiveness to Public Opinion"; Jacobs and Shapiro, "The Rise of Presidential Polling"; Kernell, *Going Public*.

21. Herbst, *Reading Public Opinion*.

22. Quirk, "Politicians Do Pander."

23. Gilens, Vavreck, and Cohen, "The Mass Media and the Public's Assessments of Presidential Candidates, 1952–2000."

24. Based on my analysis of open-ended congressional candidate likes and dislikes from the American National Election Study.

25. Binder, *Stalemate*; Jacobs and Shapiro, *Politicians Don't Pander*; McCarty, "The Policy Effects of Political Polarization"; McCarty, Poole, and Rosenthal, *Polarized America*.

26. McCarty, "The Policy Effects of Political Polarization."

27. Mayhew, *Divided We Govern*.

28. The correlation of 0.55 refers to Binder's preferred measure of gridlock (labeled "gridlock 4"). The correlations with her other gridlock measures are 0.36, 0.54, 0.61, and 0.57 for gridlock 1, 2, 3, and 5, respectively.

29. Quirk, "Politicians Do Pander."

30. The smallest seat advantage in the House was the Republicans' 9-seat advantage in 2001–02, and the largest was the Democrats' 155-seat advantage in 1965–66. In the Senate the Democrats held a 2-seat advantage in (most of) 2001–02 and 2007–08, and the Republicans a 2-seat advantage in 2003–04. The largest seat advantage in the Senate was the Democrats' 36-seat edge in 1965–66.

31. Binder, *Stalemate*.

32. The correlation between gridlock and the House seat advantage is somewhat higher at –0.32, but, as shown in table A7.3, it is the Senate not House seat advantage size that appears to influence strength of responsiveness.

33. As explained above, analyses of the impact of gridlock on responsiveness need to take into account the countervailing paths through which a change in partisan regime affects representation.

34. Newman and Jacobs, *Who Cares?*; Stimson, *Public Opinion in America*.

35. McCarty, Poole, and Rosenthal, *Polarized America*; Watson and Markman, *Chief of Staff*.

36. At least compared with later years; Masters and Delaney, "Organized Labor's Political Scorecard."

37. Polsby and Wildavsky, *Presidential Elections*.

38. Conway, Green, and Currinder, "Interest Group Money in Elections"; Schlozman and Tierney, *Organized Interests and American Democracy*.

39. Jacobs, "The Medicare Approach."

40. Hacker and Pierson, *Off Center*; Jacobson, *A Divider, Not a Uniter*.

41. In addition to the prolonged dispute over the vote in Florida, the fact that Bush took office having won fewer popular votes nationwide than his opponent added to the sense among many Democrats that Bush lacked a legitimate claim on the presidency.

42. The first of these questions reads, "Do you favor or oppose George W. Bush's 1.6 trillion dollar tax cut for the country over the next ten years?" (CBS News, April 23–25, 2001); and the second, "As you may know, Congress recently passed and President Bush signed a bill that will cut taxes by an estimated $1.35 trillion over 11 years. Do you favor or oppose this tax cut?" (NBC News/*Wall Street Journal*, June 23–25, 2001).

43. "I'd like your opinion of some programs and proposals being discussed in this country today. Please tell me if you strongly favor, favor, oppose, or strongly oppose each one. Eliminating the inheritance tax" (Pew Research Center for the People & the Press, August 24–September 10, 2000).

44. Bartels, *Unequal Democracy*; Graetz and Shapiro, *Death by a Thousand Cuts*; Lupia et al., "Were Bush Tax Cut Supporters 'Simply Ignorant'?"

45. Milbank, "Serious 'Strategery.'"

46. Ibid.

47. DiIulio, "Why Judging George W. Bush Is Never as Easy as It Seems."

48. Hussey and Zaller, "Who Do Parties Represent?"

49. Fortier and Ornstein, "President Bush." The Democrats controlled both houses of the Texas legislature when Bush took office in 1994 but lost control of the Texas Senate in 1996.

50. Jacobs and Shapiro, "Bush's Democratic Ambivalence."

51. This brief description of Jacobs and Shapiro's investigation of policy making during Bush's administration does not do justice to the full complexity of their analysis, which employs additional categories of policy congruence and examines strategies used by Republican leaders to craft (some) legislation in ways that served to minimize public scrutiny. Ibid., 57.

52. Bartels, "A Tale of Two Tax Cuts"; Bartels, *Unequal Democracy*; Graetz and Shapiro, *Death by a Thousand Cuts*.

53. Bartels, *Unequal Democracy*.

54. Congressional Budget Office, *Effective Federal Tax Rates under Current Law, 2001 to 2014*.

55. These figures are from the 2004 American National Election Study. The question asked, "As you may recall, President Bush signed a big tax cut a few years ago. Did you favor or oppose the tax cut, or is this something you haven't thought about?" A similar question from the 2002 American National Election Study found support for the tax cuts at about 60 percent for the bottom quintile and about 66 percent for the top quintile. In a 2001 survey fielded before the first cuts were passed, about 46 percent of those in the bottom quintile and 67 percent of those in the top quintile favored the proposed tax cuts (Associated Press Poll #815Q, April 4–7, 2001).

56. Bartels, *Unequal Democracy*, 172–73.

57. Survey results for the "substantial tax relief" question are cited in ibid., 172. Results for the "go down a lot" question are from Associated Press Poll #815Q, April 4–7, 2001, available from the Roper Center's iPOLL database.

58. Hacker and Pierson, *Off Center*, 51.

59. Congressional Budget Office, *Effective Federal Tax Rates under Current Law, 2001 to 2014*.

60. Since the various provisions of the tax cuts were devised to phase in between 2001 and 2010 and then expire in 2011, their full effect can best be judged by comparing federal tax rates in 2010 with what they would have been in 2010 under the tax laws existing in 2000. The figures in the text reflect this calculation for the federal income tax alone. Considering all federal taxes, the differences in rates for the first to fifth income quintiles are 1.9, 1.7, 1.3, 1.1, and 1.2 percent. Typical tax filers in the bottom quintile did not pay any federal income tax before the Bush tax cuts took effect. But many of these families did receive refundable child and earned-income tax credits, which were expanded as part of the Bush tax reforms. Consequently, average federal income tax for the bottom quintile was reduced from –3.4 percent to –5.2 percent of income, which had the effect of in-

creasing the refunds these families received (or offsetting the federal payroll taxes they owed).

61. Bartels, *Unequal Democracy*, 178.

62. ABC News/*Washington Post* Poll, February 2001. The question read, "As you may know, (George W.) Bush has proposed cutting taxes by one-point-six trillion dollars over 10 years. Do you think this tax cut would or would not leave enough money to keep the federal budget balanced and provide enough money for programs such as Social Security, education, and health care?"

63. Based on data from the American National Election Study surveys cited in Bartels, *Unequal Democracy*, 188.

64. Zaller, "Coming to Grips with V.O. Key's Concept of Latent Opinion."

65. Ibid., 329.

Chapter 8: Money and American Politics

1. Montopoli, "237 Millionaires in Congress."

2. In 2008 rank-and-file members of the House and Senate were paid $169,300, while the 90th percentile of household income was $138,000. Johnson, "Webinar on 2008 Income, Poverty, and Health Insurances Estimates from the Current Population Survey."

3. Washington, "Female Socialization."

4. Burden, *Personal Roots of Representation*. Republican members tend to favor school vouchers regardless of their own children's schooling.

5. Data on assets and incomes of members of Congress are from opensecrets .org.

6. Carnes, "Class and Representation."

7. While other scholars have looked at some aspects of representatives' backgrounds (e.g., Witko and Friedman, "Business Backgrounds and Congressional Behavior"), Carnes collected the most complete data and provides the most sophisticated treatment of the question.

8. E.g., Bobo and Gilliam, "Race, Sociopolitical Participation, and Black Empowerment"; Mansbridge, "Should Blacks Represent Blacks and Women Represent Women?"

9. Bartels, *Unequal Democracy*.

10. Bartels's analysis of Senate roll-call voting and my analysis of policy outcomes both show far stronger associations with the preferences of the affluent than of the poor. Our results differ, however, in that Bartels sometimes finds a robust association between preferences and senators' votes for middle-income Americans (depending on the issue at hand). There are many differences in our data and analyses that might contribute to these contrasting results, including the key difference in the outcomes we seek to explain. As discussed in chapter 1, there are good reasons to expect representatives' roll-call votes to be more closely aligned with their constituents' preferences than are other measures of political outcomes.

11. Winters, *Oligarchy*; Winters and Page, "Oligarchy in the United States?"

12. These data on political donations are from opensecrets.org, accessed July 13, 2011.

13. Lichtblau and Luo, "Big Gifts to G.O.P. Groups Push Donor to New Level."

14. Mayer, "Covert Operations."

15. See http://www.opensecrets.org/outsidespending/summ.php?cycle=2010 &disp=D&type=V, accessed July 13, 2011.

16. Verba, Schlozman, and Brady, *Voice and Equality*.

17. Ibid.

18. Francia et al., *The Financiers of Congressional Elections*.

19. These estimates are approximate given the vagaries of individual memories and reporting, and the uncertainty of the exact amounts of donations that were recorded in broad categories. I am grateful to Lynda Powell for supplying me with data from the 1996 Congressional Campaign Finance Study. See ibid. for details.

20. Of course specific PACs or lobbying organizations may draw relatively more of their resources from less-affluent Americans (e.g., those associated with labor). But funding for these organizations as a whole comes disproportionately from those with the highest incomes.

21. Page and Hennessy, "What Affluent Americans Want from Politics."

22. Campaign spending data from http://www.opensecrets.org/pres08/also rans.php.

23. Faler and Coyne, "Alaska Senator Murkowski Loses Nomination Bid to Tea Party-Backed Miller."

24. "Ohio Voters Cut through Pricey Baloney."

25. This compares with about $5 billion spent during the 2008 election cycle on congressional and presidential primary and general elections. All figures from opensecrets.org.

26. Baumgartner et al., *Lobbying and Policy Change*, 192.

27. Abramowitz, "Explaining Senate Election Outcomes"; Jacobson, "Campaign Spending Effects in US Senate Elections"; Jacobson, "The Effects of Campaign Spending in House Elections."

28. Gerber, "Estimating the Effect of Campaign Spending on Senate Election Outcomes Using Instrumental Variables"; Green and Krasno, "Rebuttal to Jacobson's 'New Evidence for Old Arguments'"; Green and Krasno, "Salvation for the Spendthrift Incumbent."

29. Bartels, *Unequal Democracy*.

30. Ansolabehere, de Figueiredo, and Snyder, "Why Is There So Little Money in US Politics?"

31. Stratmann, "Some Talk." Stratmann reports that the null hypothesis that contributions have no effect on voting could be rejected with 99 percent certainty when weighting each of the forty studies equally, when giving twice the weight to studies that correct for simultaneity of voting and contributions, and when restricting the analyses to only those studies that correct for simultaneity.

32. Baldwin and Magee, "Is Trade Policy for Sale?"

33. Snyder, "Long-Term Investing in Politicians," 17.

34. Arnold, *The Logic of Congressional Action*, 270.

35. Hall and Wayman, "Buying Time."

36. These data are from the Campaign Finance Institute, "Campaign Funding Sources for House and Senate Candidates."

37. Francia et al., *The Financiers of Congressional Elections*; Verba, Schlozman, and Brady, *Voice and Equality*.

38. Verba, Schlozman, and Brady, *Voice and Equality*, 358.

39. Based on self-reported donations during the 1988 election, respondents who made no donations to a candidate, party, or political organization had average incomes of about $34,000 (the 43rd percentile of income at the time). Those reporting donations of under $250 had average incomes of about $52,000 (the 60th percentile), while those reporting donations totaling over $1,000 had incomes of about $134,000 (the 88th percentile). These calculations are from the 1990 Citizen Participation Study. See ibid. for details.

40. In 2008 both eventual major party nominees opted out of the matching-funds program for their primary election campaigns, and Barack Obama also opted out of the program for the general election.

41. Ackerman and Ayres, *Voting with Dollars*.

42. A second major component of Ackerman and Ayres's proposal is the "laundering" of campaign contributions through the Federal Election Commission, which would allow individuals or organizations to make large contributions but would obscure the identity of those contributions such that candidates would have no direct way of knowing their source and contributors would have no way to prove that they donated to one candidate or another.

43. In addition Arizona, Maine, Vermont, and Connecticut have implemented "clean elections" programs that seek to completely replace private sources of campaign donations with public funding.

44. Eom and Gross, "Contribution Limits and Disparity in Contributions between Gubernatorial Candidates"; Stratmann and Aparicio-Castillo, "Competition Policy for Elections."

45. Donnay and Ramsden, "Public Financing of Legislative Elections"; Primo, Milyo, and Groseclose, "State Finance Reform, Competitiveness, and Party Advantage in Gubernatorial Elections."

46. Besley and Case, "Political Institutions and Policy Choices."

47. Rigby and Wright, "Whose Statehouse Democracy?" do examine responsiveness to the preferences of different income levels in states, finding generally higher responsiveness to the affluent, but in somewhat complex patterns that differ across poorer and wealthier states. See also Rigby and Wright, "Political Parties and Representation of the Poor in the American States."

48. Cottrill, "The Effects of Independent Redistricting Commissions on Competition in Congressional Elections."

49. Panagopoulos and Green, "Field Experiments Testing the Impact of Radio Advertisements on Electoral Competition."

50. E.g., Donovan and Bowler, *Reforming the Republic*; McDonald and Samples, *The Marketplace of Democracy*.

51. Skocpol, "Targeting within Universalism."

52. See chapter 4 as well as Gilens, *Why Americans Hate Welfare*; McCall and Kenworthy, "Americans' Social Policy Preferences in the Era of Rising Inequality."

53. Averaged across the fifteen questions, support for increasing the minimum wage was 86 percent among the poor, 81 percent among the middle class, and 71 percent among the affluent.

54. Saez, "Striking It Richer."

55. Piketty and Saez, "Income Inequality in the United States, 1913–1998." Updates are available at Emmanuel Saez's web site at http://elsa.berkeley.edu/~saez/.

56. Hacker and Pierson, *Winner-Take-All Politics*.

57. Hacker, Mettler, and Pinderhughes, "Inequality and Public Policy."

58. Bartels, *Unequal Democracy*.

59. Hacker and Pierson, "Winner-Take-All Politics"; Hacker and Pierson, *Winner-Take-All Politics*; Hacker and Pierson, "Winner-Take-All Politics and Political Science."

60. See, e.g., Campbell, "The Public's Role in Winner-Take-All Politics"; Fligstein, "Politics, the Reorganization of the Economy, and Income Inequality, 1980–2009"; Hochschild, Page, and Stimson, "Perspectives on Unequal Democracy"; Jacobs, "Democracy and Capitalism"; Kenworthy, "Business Political Capacity and the Top-Heavy Rise in Income Inequality."

61. Sixty-two percent of middle-income ($35,000–$65,000 in family income) respondents to the 2000 American National Election Study agreed that "public officials don't care much what people like me think," compared with 36 percent of respondents in the top income decile (over $100,000).

Appendix

1. Achen, "Proxy Variables and Incorrect Signs on Regression Coefficients."

2. Ibid.; O'Brien, "Correcting Measures of Relationship between Aggregate-Level Variables for Both Unreliability and Correlated Errors."

References

AARP. "Aarp Consolidated Financial Statements 2007–2008." http://assets.aarp
.org/www.aarp.org_/articles/aboutaarp/AnnualReports/hq_main.html.

Abramowitz, Alan I. "Explaining Senate Election Outcomes." *American Political Science Review* 82, no. 2 (1988): 385–403.

Achen, Christopher H. "Mass Political Attitudes and the Survey Response." *American Political Science Review* 69, no. 4 (1975): 1218–31.

———. "Measuring Representation." *American Journal of Political Science* 22, no. 3 (1978): 475–510.

———. "Proxy Variables and Incorrect Signs on Regression Coefficients." *Political Methodology* 11, no. 4 (1985): 299–317.

Achen, Christopher H., and Larry M. Bartels. "Blind Retrospection: Electoral Responses to Drought, Flu, and Shark Attacks." Ms., University of California at San Diego, 2004.

Ackerman, Bruce A., and Ian Ayres. *Voting with Dollars: A New Paradigm for Campaign Finance*. New Haven: Yale University Press, 2002.

Adams, Greg D. "Abortion: Evidence of an Issue Evolution." *American Journal of Political Science* 41, no. 3 (1997): 718–37.

Adams, James, Samuel Merrill, and Bernard Grofman. *A Unified Theory of Party Competition: A Cross-National Analysis Integrating Spatial and Behavioral Factors*. Cambridge: Cambridge University Press, 2005.

AFL-CIO. "AFL-CIO Convention Resolution 6." http://www.aflcio.org/aboutus/thisistheaflcio/convention/2001/resolutions/.

Ahuja, Sunil. "Electoral Status and Representation in the United States Senate: Does Temporal Proximity to Election Matter?" *American Politics Quarterly* 22, no. 1 (1994): 104–18.

Ainsworth, Scott H. *Analyzing Interest Groups: Group Influence on People and Policies*. New York: Norton, 2002.

Aldrich, John Herbert. *Why Parties? The Origin and Transformation of Political Parties in America*. Chicago: University of Chicago Press, 1995.

Althaus, Scott L. *Collective Preferences in Democratic Politics: Opinion Surveys and the Will of the People*. New York: Cambridge University Press, 2003.

Althaus, Scott L., and Jennifer Oats-Sargent. "What Prompts the Pollsters? New Agendas, Survey Agendas, and the Uncertain Validity of Policy Responsiveness Research." Paper presented at annual meeting of the Midwest Political Science Association, Chicago, April 2007.

Alwin, Duane F., and Jon A. Krosnick. "The Reliability of Survey Attitude Measurement: The Influence of Question and Respondent Attributes." *Sociological Methods & Research* 20, no. 1 (1991): 139–81.

Ansolabehere, Stephen, John M. de Figueiredo, and James M. Snyder. "Why Is There So Little Money in US Politics?" *Journal of Economic Perspectives* 17, no. 1 (2003): 105–30.

Ansolabehere, Stephen, James M. Snyder, and Charles Stewart, III. "Candidate Positioning in US House Elections." *American Journal of Political Science* 45, no. 1 (2001): 136–59.

Arnold, R. Douglas. *The Logic of Congressional Action*. New Haven: Yale University Press, 1990.

Asher, Herbert B. *Polling and the Public: What Every Citizen Should Know*. 7th ed. Washington, DC: CQ Press, 2007.

Bachrach, Peter, and Morton S. Baratz. "Decisions and Nondecisions—an Analytical Framework." *American Political Science Review* 57, no. 3 (1963): 632–42.

———. "Two Faces of Power." *American Political Science Review* 56, no. 4 (1962): 947–52.

Baldwin, Robert E., and Christopher S. Magee. "Is Trade Policy for Sale? Congressional Voting on Recent Trade Bills." *Public Choice* 105, nos. 1–2 (2000): 79–101.

Bartels, Larry M. "Democracy with Attitudes." In *Electoral Democracy*, edited by Michael B. MacKuen and George Rabinowitz, 48–82. Ann Arbor: University of Michigan Press, 2003.

———. "Economic Inequality and Political Representation." Paper presented at annual meeting of the American Political Science Association, Boston, August 2002.

———. "Instrumental and 'Quasi-Instrumental' Variables." *American Journal of Political Science* 35, no. 3 (1991): 777–800.

———. "A Tale of Two Tax Cuts, a Wage Squeeze, and a Tax Credit." *National Tax Journal* 59, no. 3 (2006): 403–23.

———. Personal communication, May 15, 2007.

———. "Unenlightened Self-Interest: The Strange Appeal of Estate Tax Repeal." *American Prospect* (2004): A17–A19.

———. *Unequal Democracy: The Political Economy of the New Gilded Age*. Princeton: Princeton University Press, 2008.

———. "Uninformed Votes: Information Effects in Presidential Elections." *American Journal of Political Science* 40, no. 1 (1996): 194–230.

Bartels, Larry M., and Christopher H. Achen. "Musical Chairs: Pocketbook Voting and the Limits of Democratic Accountability." Ms., Princeton, NJ, 2004.

Bartels, Larry M., and John Zaller. "Al Gore and George Bush's Not-So-Excellent Adventure—Presidential Vote Models: A Recount." *Ps–Political Science & Politics* 34, no. 1 (2001): 8–20.

Baumgartner, Frank R., Jeffrey M. Berry, Marie Hojnacki, David C. Kimball, and Beth L. Leech. *Lobbying and Policy Change: Who Wins, Who Loses, and Why*. Chicago: University of Chicago Press, 2009.

Baumgartner, Frank R., and Beth L. Leech. *Basic Interests: The Importance of Groups in Politics and in Political Science*. Princeton: Princeton University Press, 1998.

Bennett, W. Lance. "Toward a Theory of Press-State Relations in the United States." *Journal of Communication* 40, no. 2 (1990): 103–25.

Berelson, Bernard R., Paul F. Lazarsfeld, and William N. McPhee. *Voting: A Study of Opinion Formation in a Presidential Campaign*. Chicago: University of Chicago Press, 1954.

Berinsky, Adam J. *Silent Voices: Public Opinion and Political Participation in America*. Princeton: Princeton University Press, 2004.

Berk, Richard A. *Regression Analysis: A Constructive Critique*. Thousand Oaks, CA: Sage, 2004.

Berry, Christopher R., Barry C. Burden, and William G. Howell. "After Enactment: The Lives and Deaths of Federal Programs." *American Journal of Political Science* 54, no. 1 (2010): 1–17.

Berry, Jeffrey M. *The Interest Group Society*. Boston: Little, Brown, 1984.

———. *The New Liberalism: The Rising Power of Citizen Groups*. Washington, DC: Brookings Institution Press, 1999.

Besley, Timothy, and Anne Case. "Political Institutions and Policy Choices: Evidence from the United States." *Journal of Economic Literature* 41, no. 1 (2003): 7–73.

Binder, Sarah A. "The Dynamics of Legislative Gridlock, 1947–96." *American Political Science Review* 93, no. 3 (1999): 519–33.

———. *Stalemate: Causes and Consequences of Legislative Gridlock*. Washington, DC: Brookings Institution Press, 2003.

Bishop, George F., Alfred J. Tuchfarber, and Robert W. Oldendick. "Opinions on Fictitious Issues—the Pressure to Answer Survey Questions." *Public Opinion Quarterly* 50, no. 2 (1986): 240–50.

Bobo, Lawrence, and Frank D. Gilliam. "Race, Sociopolitical Participation, and Black Empowerment." *American Political Science Review* 84, no. 2 (1990): 377–93.

Brady, David, and Barbara Sinclair. "Building Majorities for Policy Changes in the House of Representatives." *Journal of Politics* 46, no. 4 (1984): 1033–60.

Brady, Henry E. "The Perils of Survey Research: Inter-Personally Incomparable Responses." *Political Methodology* 11, nos. 3–4 (1985): 269–91.

Breedlove, James. "Money, Politics, and Government Corruption." truthclinic .com, 2009.

Brody, Richard A., and Paul M. Sniderman. "Life Space to Polling Place—Relevance of Personal Concerns for Voting-Behavior." *British Journal of Political Science* 7 (July 1977): 337–60.

Buckley, William F., Jr. "Crucial Steps in Combating the Aids Epidemic; Identify All the Carriers." *New York Times*, March 18, 1986, A27.

Burden, Barry C. *Personal Roots of Representation*. Princeton: Princeton University Press, 2007.

Burman, Leonard, and Deborah Kobes. "Preferential Capital Gains Tax Rates." Tax Policy Center, 2004.

Burstein, Paul. "Why Estimates of the Impact of Public Opinion on Public Policy Are Too High: Empirical and Theoretical Implications." *Social Forces* 84, no. 4 (2006): 2273–89.

Butler, Katy. "George Lakoff Says Environmentalists Need to Watch Their Language." *Sierra Magazine* 89 (July/August 2004): 54–56.

Campbell, Andrea L. "The Public's Role in Winner-Take-All Politics." *Politics & Society* 38, no. 2 (2010): 227–32.

Canes-Wrone, Brandice. *Who Leads Whom? Presidents, Policy, and the Public*. Chicago: University of Chicago Press, 2006.

Canes-Wrone, Brandice, and Kenneth W. Shotts. "The Conditional Nature of Presidential Responsiveness to Public Opinion." *American Journal of Political Science* 48, no. 4 (2004): 690–706.

Carmines, Edward G., and James H. Kuklinski. "Incentives, Opportunities, and the Logic of Public Opinion in American Political Representation." In *Information and Democratic Processes*, edited by John A. Ferejohn and James H. Kuklinski, 240–68. Urbana: University of Illinois Press, 1990.

Carmines, Edward G., and Richard A. Zeller. *Reliability and Validity Assessment.* Newbury Park, CA: Sage, 1979.

Carnes, Nicholas. "Class and Representation: Legislators' Social Backgrounds and Economic Policy Choices." Ph.D. dissertation, Princeton University, 2010.

Carter, Gregg Lee. *Gun Control in the United States: A Reference Handbook*, Contemporary World Issues. Santa Barbara, CA: ABC-CLIO, 2006.

Chaikind, Hinda Ripps, Sibyl Tilson, Jennifer O'Sullivan, Carolyn Merck, and Madeleine Smith. "Medicare Provisions in the Medicare, Medicaid, and Schip Benefits Improvement and Protection Act of 2000 (Bipa, P.L. 106-554)." Washington, DC: Congressional Research Service, 2001.

Chamberlain, Andrew, Gerald Prante, and Patrick Fleenor. "Death and Taxes: The Economics of the Federal Estate Tax." Washington, DC: Tax Foundation, 2006.

Citrin, Jack, and Donald P. Green. "The Self-Interest Motive in American Public Opinion." *Research in Micropolitics* 3 (1990): 1–28.

Cohen, Henry. "Regulation of Broadcast Indecency: Background and Legal Analysis." Washington DC: Congressional Research Service, 2006.

Cohen, Marty, David Karol, Hans Noel, and John Zaller. *The Party Decides: Presidential Nominations before and after Reform.* Chicago Studies in American Politics. Chicago: University of Chicago Press, 2008.

Congressional Budget Office. *Effective Federal Tax Rates under Current Law, 2001 to 2014.* Washington, DC, 2004. http://www.cbo.gov/doc.cfm?index=5746.

———. "Historical Effective Federal Tax Rates: 1979 to 2003." Washington, DC, 2005.

———. *How Capital Gains Tax Rates Affect Revenues: The Historical Evidence.* Washington, DC, 1988. http://www.cbo.gov/doc.cfm?index=8449.

———. *Trends in Public Spending on Transportation and Water Infrastructure, 1956 to 2004.* Washington, DC, 2007. http://www.cbo.gov/ftpdocs/85xx/doc 8517/08-08-Infrastructure.pdf.

Converse, Philip E. "Assessing the Capacity of Mass Electorates." *Annual Review of Political Science* 3 (2000): 331–53.

———. "The Nature of Belief Systems in Mass Publics." In *Ideology and Discontent*, edited by David E. Apter, 206–61. New York: Free Press, 1964.

———. "Popular Representation and the Distribution of Information." In *Information and Democratic Processes*, edited by John A. Ferejohn and James H. Kuklinksi, 369–88. Urbana: University of Illinois Press, 1990.

Conway, Margaret M., Joanne Connor Green, and Marian Currinder. "Interest Group Money in Elections." In *Interest Group Politics*, edited by Allan J. Cigler and Burdett A. Loomis, 117–40. Washington, DC: CQ Press, 2002.

Cottrill, James. "The Effects of Independent Redistricting Commissions on Competition in Congressional Elections." Paper presented at annual meeting of the Midwest Political Science Association, Chicago, April 2006.

Cox, Gary W., and Mathew D. McCubbins. *Legislative Leviathan: Party Government in the House*. Berkeley: University of California Press, 1993.

———. *Setting the Agenda: Responsible Party Government in the U.S. House of Representatives*. Cambridge: Cambridge University Press, 2005.

Crespin, Michael H. "Serving Two Masters: Redistricting and Voting in the U.S. House of Representatives." *Political Research Quarterly* (2009): 1–9.

Dahl, Robert A. *Polyarchy: Participation and Opposition*. New Haven: Yale University Press, 1971.

———. *A Preface to Democratic Theory*. Chicago: University of Chicago Press, 1956.

———. *Who Governs? Democracy and Power in an American City*. Yale Studies in Political Science. New Haven: Yale University Press, 1961.

Delli Carpini, Michael X., and Scott Keeter. *What Americans Know about Politics and Why It Matters*. New Haven: Yale University Press, 1996.

DiIulio, John J., Jr. "Why Judging George W. Bush Is Never as Easy as It Seems." In *Judging Bush*, edited by Robert Maranto, Tom Lansford and Jeremy Johnson, 294–310. Stanford: Stanford University Press, 2009.

Domhoff, G. William. *Who Rules America? Power, Politics, and Social Change*. 6th ed. Boston: McGraw-Hill Higher Education, 2009.

Donnay, Patrick D., and Graham P. Ramsden. "Public Financing of Legislative Elections—Lessons from Minnesota." *Legislative Studies Quarterly* 20, no. 3 (1995): 351–64.

Donovan, Todd, and Shaun Bowler. *Reforming the Republic: Democratic Institutions for the New America*. Real Politics in America. Upper Saddle River, NJ: Pearson/Prentice Hall, 2004.

Downs, Anthony. *An Economic Theory of Democracy*. New York: Harper Collins, 1957.

Dreyfuss, Barbara T. "The Shocking Story of How AARP Backed the Medicare Bill." *American Prospect*, May 12, 2004.

Druckman, James N. "Political Preference Formation: Competition, Deliberation, and the (Ir)Relevance of Framing Effects." *American Political Science Review* 98, no. 4 (2004): 671–86.

Druckman, James N., and Lawrence R. Jacobs. "Presidential Responsiveness to Public Opinion." In *The Oxford Handbook of the American Presidency*, edited by George C. Edwards and William G. Howell, 160–81. New York: Oxford University Press, 2009.

Eddy, Mark. "Medical Marijuana: Review and Analysis of Federal and State Policies." Washington, DC: Congressional Research Service, 2005.

Elling, Richard C. "Ideological Change in the United States Senate: Time and Electoral Responsiveness." *Legislative Studies Quarterly* 7, no. 1 (1982): 75–92.

Enelow, James M., and Melvin J. Hinich. *The Spatial Theory of Voting: An Introduction*. Cambridge: Cambridge University Press, 1984.

Eom, Kihong, and Donald A. Gross. "Contribution Limits and Disparity in Contributions between Gubernatorial Candidates." *Political Research Quarterly* 59, no. 1 (2006): 99–110.

Erikson, Robert S. "Economic Conditions and the Congressional Vote: A Review of Macrolevel Evidence." *American Journal of Political Science* 34, no. 2 (1990): 373–99.

Erikson, Robert S., Michael B. MacKuen, and James A. Stimson. *The Macro Polity*. New York: Cambridge University Press, 2002.

Executive Office of the President. "National Drug Control Strategy, FY 2007 Budget Summary." White House, 2006.

Faler, Brian, and Amanda Coyne. "Alaska Senator Murkowski Loses Nomination Bid to Tea Party-Backed Miller." *Bloomberg News*, August 31, 2010.

Feldman, Stanley. "Economic Self-Interest and Political-Behavior." *American Journal of Political Science* 26, no. 3 (1982): 446–66.

———. "Measuring Issue Preferences: The Problem of Response Instability." In *Political Analysis*, edited by James A. Stimson, 25–60. Ann Arbor: University of Michigan Press, 1989.

Feldman, Stanley, Leonie Huddy, and George Marcus. "Going to War: When Citizens Matter." Paper presented at New York Area Political Psychology Meeting, Columbia University, October 27, 2007.

Fenno, Richard F. *Home Style: House Members in Their Districts*. New York: Longman, 2003.

Ferguson, Thomas. *Golden Rule: The Investment Theory of Party Competition and the Logic of Money-Driven Political Systems*. Chicago: University of Chicago Press, 1995.

Fiorina, Morris P. *Retrospective Voting in American National Elections*. New Haven: Yale University Press, 1981.

Fiorina, Morris P., and Samuel J. Abrams. *Disconnect: The Breakdown of Representation in American Politics*. Norman: University of Oklahoma Press, 2009.

Fishkin, James S., and Robert C. Luskin. "Bringing Deliberation to the Democratic Dialogue." In *A Poll with a Human Face*, edited by Max McCombs and Amy Reynolds, 3–38. Mahwah, NJ: Lawrence Erlbaum Associates, 1999.

———. "Experimenting with a Democratic Ideal: Deliberative Polling and Public Opinion." *Acta Politica* 40, no. 3 (2005): 284–98.

Fligstein, Neil. "Politics, the Reorganization of the Economy, and Income Inequality, 1980—2009." *Politics & Society* 38, no. 2 (2010): 233–42.

Fortier, John C., and Norman J. Ornstein. "President Bush: Legislative Strategist." In *The George W. Bush Presidency: An Early Assessment*, edited by Fred I. Greenstein, 138–72. Baltimore: Johns Hopkins University Press, 2003.

Francia, Peter L., John C. Green, Paul S. Herrnson, Lynda W. Powell, and Clyde Wilcox. *The Financiers of Congressional Elections: Investors, Ideologues, and Intimates*, Power, Conflict, and Democracy. New York: Columbia University Press, 2003.

Freeman, Richard Barry, and James L. Medoff. *What Do Unions Do?* New York: Basic Books, 1984.

Fried, Marlene Gerber. "Abortion in the United States: Barriers to Access." *Health and Human Rights* 4, no. 2 (2000): 174–94.

Gerber, Alan. "Estimating the Effect of Campaign Spending on Senate Election Outcomes Using Instrumental Variables." *American Political Science Review* 92, no. 2 (1998): 401–11.

Gerber, Elizabeth R., and Jeffrey B. Lewis. "Beyond the Median: Voter Preferences, District Heterogeneity, and Political Representation." *Journal of Political Economy* 112, no. 6 (2004): 1364–83.

Gershkoff, Amy R. "How Issue Interest Can Rescue the American Public." Ph.D. dissertation, Princeton University, 2006.

Gershkoff, Amy, and Shana Kushner. "Shaping Public Opinion: The 9/11-Iraq Connection in the Bush Administration's Rhetoric." *Perspectives on Politics* 3, no. 3 (2005): 525–37.

Gilens, Martin. "Political Ignorance and Collective Policy Preferences." *American Political Science Review* 95, no. 2 (2001): 379–96.

———. "Preference Gaps and Inequality in Representation." *PS: Political Science and Politics* 42, no. 2 (2009): 335–41.

———. *Why Americans Hate Welfare: Race, Media, and the Politics of Antipoverty Policy*. Chicago: University of Chicago Press, 1999.

Gilens, Martin, and Naomi Murakawa. "Elite Cues and Political Decision-Making." In *Research in Micropolitics*, edited by Michael X. Delli Carpini, Leonie Huddy and Roberty Y. Shapiro, 15–50. Oxford: Elsevier, 2002.

Gilens, Martin, Lynn Vavreck, and Martin Cohen. "The Mass Media and the Public's Assessments of Presidential Candidates, 1952–2000." *Journal of Politics* 69, no. 4 (2007): 1160–75.

Glynn, Carroll J., Susan Herbst, Garrett J. O'Keefe, Robert Y. Shapiro, and Mark Lindeman. *Public Opinion*. 2nd ed. Boulder: Westview Press, 2004.

Gottschalk, Marie. *The Shadow Welfare State: Labor, Business, and the Politics of Health-Care in the United States*. Ithaca: ILR Press, 2000.

Graetz, Michael J., and Ian Shapiro. *Death by a Thousand Cuts: The Fight over Taxing Inherited Wealth*. Princeton: Princeton University Press, 2005.

Green, Donald P., and Jack Citrin. "Measurement Error and the Structure of Attitudes: Are Positive and Negative Judgments Opposites?" *American Journal of Political Science* 38, no. 1 (1994): 256–81.

Green, Donald P., and Jonathan S. Krasno. "Rebuttal to Jacobson's 'New Evidence for Old Arguments.'" *American Journal of Political Science* 34, no. 2 (1990): 363–72.

———. "Salvation for the Spendthrift Incumbent: Reestimating the Effects of Campaign Spending in House Elections." *American Journal of Political Science* 32, no. 4 (1988): 884–907.

Green, Donald P., and Bradley Palmquist. "Of Artifacts and Partisan Instability." *American Journal of Political Science* 34, no. 3 (1990): 871–902.

Green, Donald P., Bradley Palmquist, and Eric Schickler. *Partisan Hearts and Minds: Political Parties and the Social Identities of Voters*. Yale Isps Series. New Haven: Yale University Press, 2002.

Green, Donald P., and Ian Shapiro. *Pathologies of Rational Choice Theory: A Critique of Applications in Political Science*. New Haven: Yale University Press, 1994.

Green, John, Paul Herrnson, Lynda Powell, and Clyde Wilcox. "Individual Congressional Campaign Contributors: Wealthy, Conservative and Reform Minded." http://www.opensecrets.org/pubs/donors/donors.htm, 1998.

Griffin, John D., and Brian Newman. *Minority Report: Evaluating Political Equality in America*. Chicago: University of Chicago Press, 2008.

Grofman, Bernard. "Downs and Two-Party Convergence." *Annual Review of Political Science* 7 (2004): 25–46.

Guttmacher Institute. "State Policies in Brief: Counseling and Waiting Periods for Abortion." New York, 2008.

Hacker, Jacob S. *Health at Risk: America's Ailing Health System—and How to Heal It*. New York: Columbia University Press, 2008.

Hacker, Jacob S., Suzanne Mettler, and Dianne Pinderhughes. "Inequality and Public Policy." In *Inequality and American Democracy: What We Know and What We Need to Learn*, edited by Lawrence R. Jacobs and Theda Skocpol, 156–213. New York: Russell Sage Foundation, 2005.

Hacker, Jacob S., and Paul Pierson. *Off Center: The Republican Revolution and the Erosion of American Democracy*. New Haven: Yale University Press, 2006.

———. *Winner-Take-All Politics: How Washington Made the Rich Richer and Turned Its Back on the Middle Class*. New York: Simon & Schuster, 2010.

———. "Winner-Take-All Politics: Organizations, Policy, and the New American Political Economy." Ms., 2007.

———. "Winner-Take-All Politics: Public Policy, Political Organization, and the Precipitous Rise of Top Incomes in the United States." *Politics & Society* 38, no. 2 (2010): 152–204.

———. "Winner-Take-All Politics and Political Science: A Response." *Politics & Society* 38, no. 2 (2010): 266–82.

Hall, Richard L., and Frank W. Wayman. "Buying Time: Moneyed Interests and the Mobilization of Bias in Congressional Committees." *American Political Science Review* 84, no. 3 (1990): 797–820.

Herbst, Susan. *Reading Public Opinion: How Political Actors View the Democratic Process*. Chicago: University of Chicago Press, 1998.

Hibbs, Douglas A. *The American Political Economy: Macroeconomics and Electoral Politics*. Cambridge: Harvard University Press, 1987.

Hirsch, Barry T., and David A. Macpherson. "Union Membership and Coverage Database from the Current Population Survey: Note." *Industrial and Labor Relations Review* 56, no. 2 (2003): 349–54.

Hochschild, Jennifer, Benjamin I. Page, and James A. Stimson. "Perspectives on Unequal Democracy: The Political Economy of the New Guilded Age." *Perspectives on Politics* 7, no. 1 (2009): 145–53.

Hogan, Julie A. "The Life of the Abortion Pill in the United States." *Harvard Law School Legal Electronic Document Archive*. Cambridge: Harvard Law School Library, 2000. http://leda.law.harvard.edu/leda/data/247/Hogan,_Julie.pdf.

Howell, William G. Personal communication, 2010.

Hussey, Wesley, and John Zaller. "Who Do Parties Represent?" In *Who Gets Represented?* edited by Peter K. Enns and Christopher Wlezien, 311–44. New York: Russell Sage Foundation, 2011.

Hutchings, Vincent L., Harwood K. McClerking, and Guy-Uriel Charles. "Congressional Representation of Black Interests: Recognizing the Importance of Stability." *Journal of Politics* 66, no. 2 (2004): 450–68.

Iyengar, Shanto, Kyu S. Hahn, Jon A. Krosnick, and John Walker. "Selective Exposure to Campaign Communication: The Role of Anticipated Agreement and Issue Public Membership." *Journal of Politics* 70, no. 1 (2008): 186–200.

Jackson, Pamela J. "The Federal Excise Tax on Gasoline and the Highway Trust Fund: A Short History." Washington, DC: Congressional Research Service, 2006.

Jacobs, Lawrence R. "Democracy and Capitalism: Structure, Agency, and Organized Combat." *Politics & Society* 38, no. 2 (2010): 243–54.

———. "The Medicare Approach: Political Choice and American Institutions." *Journal of Health Politics, Policy and Law* 32, no. 2 (2007): 159–86.

Jacobs, Lawrence R., and Benjamin I. Page. "Who Influences US Foreign Policy?" *American Political Science Review* 99, no. 1 (2005): 107–23.

Jacobs, Lawrence R., and Robert Y. Shapiro. "Bush's Democratic Ambivalence: Responsiveness and Policy Promotion in Republican Government." In *The George W. Bush Legacy*, edited by Colin Campbell, Bert A. Rockman, and Andrew Rudalevige, 45–61. Washington, DC: CQ Press, 2008.

———. *Politicians Don't Pander: Political Manipulation and the Loss of Democratic Responsiveness*. Chicago: University of Chicago Press, 2000.

———. "The Rise of Presidential Polling—the Nixon White-House in Historical-Perspective." *Public Opinion Quarterly* 59, no. 2 (1995): 163–95.

Jacobson, Gary C. "Campaign Spending Effects in US Senate Elections: Evidence from the National Annenberg Election Survey." *Electoral Studies* 25, no. 2 (2006): 195–226.

———. *A Divider, Not a Uniter: George W. Bush and the American People*. 2nd ed. New York: Pearson, 2010.

———. "The Effects of Campaign Spending in House Elections: New Evidence for Old Arguments." *American Journal of Political Science* 34, no. 2 (1990): 334–62.

Jamieson, Kathleen Hall. "When Harry Met Louise." *Washington Post*, August 15, 1994.

Jelen, Ted G., and Clyde Wilcox. "Causes and Consequences of Public Attitudes toward Abortion: A Review and Research Agenda." *Political Research Quarterly* 56, no. 4 (2003): 489–500.

Johnson, David S. "Webinar on 2008 Income, Poverty, and Health Insurances Estimates from the Current Population Survey." United States Census Bureau, 2009.

Johnson, Judith A., and Pamela W. Smith. "Aids: An Overview of Issues." Washington, DC: Congressional Research Service, 1988.

Jones, Bradford S., and Barbara Norrander. "The Reliability of Aggregated Public Opinion Measures." *American Journal of Political Science* 40, no. 1 (1996): 295–309.

Jones, Rachel K., and Heather Boonstra. "Confidential Reproductive Health Services for Minors: The Potential Impact of Mandated Parental Involvement for Contraception." *Perspectives on Sexual and Reproductive Health* 36, no. 5 (2004): 182–91.

Kenworthy, Lane. "Business Political Capacity and the Top-Heavy Rise in Income Inequality: How Large an Impact?" *Politics & Society* 38, no. 2 (2010): 255–65.

Kernell, Samuel. *Going Public: New Strategies of Presidential Leadership.* 3rd ed. Washington, DC: CQ Press, 1997.

Key, V. O. *Politics, Parties and Pressure Groups.* New York: Thomas Y. Crowell, 1942.

———. *Public Opinion and American Democracy.* New York: Knopf, 1961.

Kingdon, John W. *Agendas, Alternatives, and Public Policies.* 2nd ed. New York: Longman, 1995.

———. *Congressmen's Voting Decisions.* 3rd ed. Ann Arbor: University of Michigan Press, 1989.

Kollman, Ken. *Outside Lobbying: Public Opinion and Interest Group Strategies.* Princeton: Princeton University Press, 1998.

Kollmann, Geoffrey. "Social Security: Raising the Retirement Age Background and Issues." Washington, DC: Congressional Research Service, 2000.

Kramer, Gerald H. "Short-Term Fluctuations in U.S. Voting Behavior." *American Political Science Review* 65, no. 1 (1971): 131–43.

Krehbiel, Keith. *Pivotal Politics: A Theory of U.S. Lawmaking.* Chicago: University of Chicago Press, 1998.

Krippendorff, Klaus. *Content Analysis: An Introduction to Its Methodology.* Beverly Hills: Sage, 1980.

Krosnick, Jon A. "Government Policy and Citizen Passion: A Study of Issue Publics in Contemporary America." *Political Behavior* 12, no. 1 (1990): 59–92.

———. "The Stability of Political Preferences: Comparisons of Symbolic and Nonsymbolic Attitudes." *American Journal of Political Science* 35 (1991): 547–76.

Kuklinski, James H. "Representativeness and Elections: Policy Analysis." *American Political Science Review* 72, no. 1 (1978): 165–77.

Kuklinski, James H., Paul J. Quirk, Jennifer Jerit, David Schwieder, and Robert F. Rich. "Misinformation and the Currency of Democratic Citizenship." *Journal of Politics* 62, no. 3 (2000): 790–816.

Kull, Steven, and I. M. Destler. *Misreading the Public: The Myth of a New Isolationism.* Washington, DC: Brookings Institution Press, 1999.

Kull, Steven, Clay Ramsay, and Evan Lewis. "Misperceptions, the Media, and the Iraq War." *Political Science Quarterly* 118, no. 4 (2003): 569–98.

Langworth, Richard M. *Churchill by Himself: The Definitive Collection of Quotations.* New York: PublicAffairs, 2008.

Lau, Richard R., and David P. Redlawsk. *How Voters Decide: Information Processing during Election Campaigns.* Cambridge Studies in Public Opinion and Political Psychology. Cambridge: Cambridge University Press, 2006.

———. "Voting Correctly." *American Political Science Review* 91, no. 3 (1997): 585–98.

Layman, Geoffrey C. "'Culture Wars' in the American Party System: Religious and Cultural Change among Partisan Activists since 1972." *American Politics Quarterly* 27, no. 1 (1999): 89–121.

Lee, Taeku. "The Sovereign Status of Survey Data." In *Navigating Public Opinion*, edited by Jeff Manza, Fay Lomax Cook, and Benjamin I. Page, 290–312. Oxford: Oxford University Press, 2002.

Levitt, Steven D. "How Do Senators Vote? Disentangling the Role of Voter Preferences, Party Affiliation, and Senator Ideology." *American Economic Review* 86, no. 3 (1996): 425–41.

Lewis-Beck, Michael S., and Mary Stegmaier. "Economic Determinants of Electoral Outcomes." *Annual Review of Political Science* 3 (2000): 183–219.

Lichtblau, Eric, and Michael Luo. "Big Gifts to G.O.P. Groups Push Donor to New Level." *New York Times*, October 22, 2010, A18.

Lindblom, Charles Edward. *Politics and Markets: The World's Political Economic Systems*. New York: Basic Books, 1977.

Lipset, Seymour Martin, and Stein Rokkan. *Party Systems and Voter Alignments: Cross-National Perspectives*. International Yearbook of Political Behavior Research. New York: Free Press, 1967.

Lowery, David, and Virginia Gray. "Bias in the Heavenly Chorus—Interests in Society and before Government." *Journal of Theoretical Politics* 16, no. 1 (2004): 5–29.

Luckey, John R. "A History of Federal Estate, Gift, and Generation-Skipping Taxes." Washington, DC: Congressional Research Service, 2003.

Lupia, Arthur. "Shortcuts versus Encyclopedias: Information and Voting-Behavior in California Insurance Reform Elections." *American Political Science Review* 88, no. 1 (1994): 63–76.

———. "Who Can Persuade? A Formal Theory, a Survey and Implications for Democracy." 1995.

Lupia, Arthur, Adam Seth Levine, Jesse O. Menning, and Gisela Sin. "Were Bush Tax Cut Supporters 'Simply Ignorant'? A Second Look at Conservatives and Liberals in 'Homer Gets a Tax Cut.'" *Perspectives on Politics* 5, no. 4 (2007): 773–84.

Lupia, Arthur, and Mathew D. McCubbins. *The Democratic Dilemma: Can Citizens Learn What They Need to Know?* Cambridge: Cambridge University Press, 1998.

Lupu, Noam, and Jonas Pontusson. "The Structure of Inequality and the Politics of Redistribution." *American Political Science Review* 105, no. 2 (2011): 316–36.

Luskin, Robert C., and James S. Fishkin. "Deliberative Polling, Public Opinion, and Democracy: The Case of the National Issues Convention." Paper presented at annual meeting of the American Political Science Association, Boston, 1998.

Makinson, Larry. *Speaking Freely: Washington Insiders Talk about Money in Politics*. 2nd ed. Washington, DC: Center for Responsive Politics, 2003.

Mansbridge, Jane J. "Should Blacks Represent Blacks and Women Represent Women? A Contingent 'Yes.'" *Journal of Politics* 61, no. 3 (1999): 628–57.

Manza, Jeff, and Fay Lomax Cook. "A Democratic Polity? Three Views of Policy Responsiveness to Public Opinion in the United States." *American Politics Research* 30, no. 6 (2002): 630–67.

Masters, Marick F., and John T. Delaney. "Organized Labor's Political Scorecard." *Journal of Labor Research* 26, no. 3 (2005): 365–92.

Mayer, Jane. "Covert Operations: The Billionaire Brothers Who Are Waging a War against Obama." *New Yorker*, August 30, 2010.

Mayhew, David R. *Congress: The Electoral Connection*. 2nd ed. New Haven: Yale University Press, 2004.

———. *Divided We Govern: Party Control, Lawmaking, and Investigations, 1946–1990*. New Haven: Yale University Press, 1991.

———. *Placing Parties in American Politics: Organization, Electoral Settings, and Government Activity in the Twentieth Century*. Princeton: Princeton University Press, 1986.

McCall, Leslie, and Lane Kenworthy. "Americans' Social Policy Preferences in the Era of Rising Inequality." *Perspectives on Politics* 7, no. 3 (2009): 459–84.

McCarty, Nolan M. "The Policy Effects of Political Polarization." In *The Transformation of American Politics: Activist Government and the Rise of Conservatism*, edited by Paul Pierson and Theda Skocpol, 223–55. Princeton: Princeton University Press, 2007.

McCarty, Nolan M., Keith T. Poole, and Howard Rosenthal. *Polarized America: The Dance of Ideology and Unequal Riches*, Walras-Pareto Lectures. Cambridge: MIT Press, 2006.

McDonald, Michael P., and John Samples. *The Marketplace of Democracy: Electoral Competition and American Politics*. Washington, DC: Brookings Institution Press, 2006.

McKelvey, Richard D., and Peter C. Ordeshook. "Information, Electoral Equilibria, and the Democratic Ideal." *Journal of Politics* 48, no. 4 (1986): 909–37.

Meyerson, Denise. *False Consciousness*. Oxford Philosophical Monographs. New York: Oxford University Press, 1991.

Milbank, Dana. "Serious 'Strategery': as Rove Launches Elaborate Political Effort, Some See a Nascent Clintonian 'War Room.'" *Washington Post*, April 22, 2001, A1.

Miller, Nicholas R. "Information, Electorates, and Democracy: Some Extensions and Interpretations of the Condorcet Jury Theorem." In *Information Pooling and Group Decision Making*, edited by Bernard Grofman and Guillermo Owen, 172–92. Greenwich, CT: JAI, 1986.

Miller, Warren E., and Donald E. Stokes. "Constituency Influence in Congress." *American Political Science Review* 57, no. 1 (1963): 45–56.

Monroe, Alan D. "Consistency between Public Preferences and National Policy Decisions." *American Politics Quarterly* 7, no. 1 (1979): 3–19.

———. "Public Opinion and Public Policy 1960–1999." Paper presented at annual meeting of the American Political Science Association, San Francisco, 2001.

———. "Public Opinion and Public Policy, 1980–1993." *Public Opinion Quarterly* 62, no. 1 (1998): 6–28.

Monroe, Alan D., and Paul J. Gardner. "Public Policy Linkages." In *Research in Micropolitics*, edited by Samuel Long, 207–32. Greenwich, CT: JAI Press, 1987.

Montopoli, Brian. "237 Millionaires in Congress." CBS News: Political Hotsheet, 2009. http://www.cbsnews.com/8301-503544_162-5553408-503544.html.

Morris, Charles R. *The AARP: America's Most Powerful Lobby and the Clash of Generations*. New York: Times Books, 1996.

Mutz, Diana C. "Contextualizing Personal Experience: The Role of Mass-Media." Ms., 1994.

Mycoff, Jason D., and Joseph August Pika. *Confrontation and Compromise: Presidential and Congressional Leadership, 2001–2006*. Lanham, MD: Rowman & Littlefield, 2008.

National Bureau of Economic Research. "Summary Measures of the US Income Tax System, 1960–2005." Cambridge, MA, 2006.

Newman, Katherine S., and Elisabeth S. Jacobs. *Who Cares? Public Ambivalence and Government Activism from the New Deal to the Second Gilded Age*. Princeton: Princeton University Press, 2010.

Nie, Norman H., Jane Junn, and Kenneth Stehlik-Barry. *Education and Democratic Citizenship in America*. Chicago: University of Chicago Press, 1996.

Nozick, Robert. "Interpersonal Utility Theory." *Social Choice and Welfare* 2, no. 3 (1985): 161–79.

O'Brien, Robert M. "Correcting Measures of Relationship between Aggregate-Level Variables." *Sociological Methodology* 21 (1991): 125–65.

———. "Correcting Measures of Relationship between Aggregate-Level Variables for Both Unreliability and Correlated Errors: An Empirical Example." *Social Science Research* 27, no. 2 (1998): 218–34.

O'Connor, Karen. *No Neutral Ground? Abortion Politics in an Age of Absolutes*, Dilemmas in American Politics. Boulder: Westview Press, 1996.

"Ohio Voters Cut through Pricey Baloney." *Dayton Daily News*, November 11, 2008, A12.

Olson, Mancur. *The Logic of Collective Action: Public Goods and the Theory of Groups*. Harvard Economic Studies, vol. 124. Cambridge: Harvard University Press, 1965.

Page, Benjamin I. "The Semi-Sovereign Public." In *Navigating Public Opinion*, edited by Jeff Manza, Fay Lomax Cook and Benjamin I. Page, 325–44. Oxford: Oxford University Press, 2002.

Page, Benjamin I., and Jason Barabas. "Foreign Policy Gaps between Citizens and Leaders." *International Studies Quarterly* 44, no. 3 (2000): 339–64.

Page, Benjamin I., and Marshall M. Bouton. *The Foreign Policy Disconnect: What Americans Want from Our Leaders but Don't Get*. American Politics and Political Economy. Chicago: University of Chicago Press, 2006.

Page, Benjamin I., and Cari Lynn Hennessy. "What Affluent Americans Want from Politics." Paper presented at annual meeting of the American Political Science Association, Washington, DC, September 2010.

Page, Benjamin I., and Lawrence R. Jacobs. *Class War? What Americans Really Think about Economic Inequality*. Chicago: University of Chicago Press, 2009.

Page, Benjamin I., and Robert Y. Shapiro. "Effects of Public Opinion on Policy." *American Political Science Review* 77, no. 1 (1983): 175–90.

———. *The Rational Public: Fifty Years of Trends in Americans' Policy Preferences*. Chicago: University of Chicago Press, 1992.

Panagopoulos, Costas, and Donald P. Green. "Field Experiments Testing the Impact of Radio Advertisements on Electoral Competition." *American Journal of Political Science* 52, no. 1 (2008): 156–68.

Patashnik, Eric M. *Reforms at Risk: What Happens after Major Policy Changes Are Enacted*. Princeton: Princeton University Press, 2008.

Piketty, Thomas, and Emmanuel Saez. "Income Inequality in the United States." http://emlab.berkeley.edu/users/saez/.

———. "Income Inequality in the United States, 1913–1998." *Quarterly Journal of Economics* 118, no. 1 (2003): 1–39.

Pines, Christopher L. *Ideology and False Consciousness: Marx and His Historical Progenitors*. Albany: State University of New York Press, 1993.

Planned Parenthood. "History & Successes." http://www.plannedparenthood.org/about-us/who-we-are/history-and-successes.htm#bushii.

Polsby, Nelson W., and Aaron Wildavsky. *Presidential Elections: Strategies and Structures of American Politics*. 11th ed. New York: Rowman and Littlefield, 2004.

Popkin, Samuel L. *The Reasoning Voter: Communication and Persuasion in Presidential Campaigns*. Chicago: University of Chicago Press, 1991.

Primo, David M., Jeffrey Milyo, and Timothy Groseclose. "State Finance Reform, Competitiveness, and Party Advantage in Gubernatorial Elections." In *The Marketplace of Democracy: Electoral Competition and American Politics*, edited by Michael P. McDonald and John Samples, 268–85. Washington, DC: Brookings Institution Press, 2006.

Przeworski, Adam. "The Minimalist Conception of Democracy: A Defense." In *Democracy's Value*, edited by Ian Shapiro and Casiano Hacker-Cordón, 23–55. New York: Cambridge University Press, 1999.

Quadagno, Jill S. *One Nation, Uninsured: Why the U.S. Has No National Health Insurance*. New York: Oxford University Press, 2005.

Quattrone, George A., and Amos Tversky. "Contrasting Rational and Psychological Analyses of Political Choice." *American Political Science Review* 82, no. 3 (1988): 719–36.

Quirk, Paul J. "Politicians Do Pander: Mass Opinion, Polarization, and Law Making." *Forum—a Journal of Applied Research in Contemporary Politics* 7, no. 4 (2009).

Quirk, Paul J., and Joseph Hinchliffe. "The Rising Hegemony of Mass Opinion." *Journal of Policy History* 10, no. 1 (1998).

Riffe, Daniel, Stephen Lacy, and Frederick G. Fico. *Analyzing Media Messages: Using Quantitative Content Analysis in Research*. Mahwah, NJ: Lawrence Erlbaum Associates, 1998.

Rigby, Elizabeth, and Gerald C. Wright. "Political Parties and Representation of the Poor in the American States." Ms., Department of Political Science, George Washington University, 2010.

———. "Whose Statehouse Democracy? Policy Responsiveness to Poor Versus Rich Constituents in Poor Versus Rich States." In *Who Gets Represented?* edited by Peter K. Enns and Christopher Wlezien, 189–222. New York: Russell Sage Foundation, 2011.

Riker, William H. *Liberalism against Populism: A Confrontation between the Theory of Democracy and the Theory of Social Choice*. San Francisco: W. H. Freeman, 1982.

Saez, Emmanuel. "Striking It Richer: The Evolution of Top Incomes in the United States," Ms., Department of Economics, University of California, Berkeley, 2009.

Schattschneider, E. E. *The Semisovereign People*. New York: Holt Rinehart and Winston, 1960.

Schlozman, Kay Lehman. "Who Sings in the Heavenly Chorus? The Shape of the Organized Interest System." In *The Oxford Handbook of American Political Parties and Interest Groups*, edited by Louis Sandy Maisel and Jeffrey M. Berry, 425–50. New York: Oxford University Press, 2010.

Schlozman, Kay Lehman, and John T. Tierney. *Organized Interests and American Democracy*. New York: Harper and Row, 1986.

Schlozman, Kay Lehman, Sidney Verba, Henry E. Brady, Philip Jones, and Traci Burch. "Who Sings in the Heavenly Chorus? The Shape of the Organized Interest System." Paper presented at annual meeting of the American Political Science Association, Boston, August 2008.

Schuman, Howard, and Stanley Presser. "Public-Opinion and Public Ignorance: The Fine Line between Attitudes and Non-Attitudes." *American Journal of Sociology* 85, no. 5 (1980): 1214–25.

———. *Questions and Answers in Attitude Surveys*. San Diego: Academic Press, 1981.

Schumpeter, Joseph Alois. *Capitalism, Socialism, and Democracy*. New York: Harper & Brothers, 1942.

Sears, David O., and Carolyn L. Funk. "The Role of Self-Interest in Social and Political Attitudes." *Advances in Experimental Social Psychology* 24 (1991): 1–91.

Sen, Amartya. *Collective Choice and Social Welfare*. Mathematical Economics Texts. San Francisco: Holden-Day, 1970.

Shimabukuro, Jon O. "Background and Legal Issues Related to Stem Cell Research." Washington, DC: Congressional Research Service, Library of Congress, 2007.

Simon, Herbert A. *Models of Discovery*. Boston: D. Reidel, 1977.

Skocpol, Theda. *Boomerang: Health Care Reform and the Turn against Government*. New York: Norton, 1997.

———. *Diminished Democracy: From Membership to Management in American Civic Life*. Norman: University of Oklahoma Press, 2003.

———. "Targeting within Universalism." In *The Urban Underclass*, edited by Christopher Jencks and Paul E. Peterson, 411–36. Washington, DC: Brookings Institution, 1991.

Slivinski, Stephen A. "The Corporate Tax Burden." In *Special Report* no. 126 (November). Washington, DC: Tax Foundation, 2003.

Smith, Marcia. "V-Chip and TV Ratings: Helping Parents Supervise Their Children's Television Viewing." Washington, DC: Congressional Research Service, 2002.

Smith, Mark A. *American Business and Political Power: Public Opinion, Elections, and Democracy*. Chicago: University of Chicago Press, 2000.

Smith, Tom W. "That Which We Call Welfare by Any Other Name Would Smell Sweeter: An Analysis of the Impact of Question Wording on Response Patterns." *Public Opinion Quarterly* 51, no. 1 (1987): 75–83.

Sniderman, Paul M., Richard A. Brody, and Philip E. Tetlock. *Reasoning and Choice: Explorations in Political Psychology*. Cambridge: Cambridge University Press, 1991.

Sniderman, Paul M., and Sean M. Theriault. "The Structure of Political Argument and the Logic of Issue Framing." In *Studies in Public Opinion: Attitudes, Non-attitudes, Measurement Error, and Change*, edited by Willem E. Saris and Paul M. Sniderman, 133–65. Princeton: Princeton University Press, 2004.

Snyder, James M. "Long-Term Investing in Politicians—or, Give Early, Give Often." *Journal of Law & Economics* 35, no. 1 (1992): 15–43.

Solinger, Rickie. *Abortion Wars: A Half Century of Struggle, 1950–2000*. Berkeley: University of California Press, 1998.

Soroka, Stuart N., and Christopher Wlezien. "On the Limits to Inequality in Representation." *PS: Political Science and Politics* 41, no. 2 (2008): 319–27.

Stimson, James A. *Public Opinion in America: Moods, Cycles, and Swings*. Boulder: Westview Press, 1991.

Stimson, James A., Michael B. MacKuen, and Robert S. Erikson. "Dynamic Representation." *American Political Science Review* 89, no. 3 (1995): 543–65.

Stokes, Donald E. "Spatial Models of Party Competition." *American Political Science Review* 57, no. 2 (1963): 368–77.

Stratmann, Thomas. "Some Talk: Money in Politics. A (Partial) Review of the Literature." *Public Choice* 124, no. 1–2 (2005): 135–56.

Stratmann, Thomas, and Francisco J. Aparicio-Castillo. "Competition Policy for Elections: Do Campaign Contribution Limits Matter?" *Public Choice* 127, no. 1–2 (2006): 177–206.

Strolovitch, Dara Z. *Affirmative Advocacy: Race, Class, and Gender in Interest Group Politics*. Chicago: University of Chicago Press, 2007.

Sturgis, Patrick, and Patten Smith. "Fictitious Issues Revisited: Political Interest, Knowledge and the Generation of Nonattitudes." *Political Studies* 58, no. 1 (2010): 66–84.

Sundquist, James L. *Back to Gridlock? Governance in the Clinton Years*. Washington, DC: Brookings Institution, Committee on the Constitutional System, 1995.

Thomas, Martin. "Election Proximity and Senatorial Roll Call Voting." *American Journal of Political Science* 29, no. 1 (1985): 96–111.

Treier, Shawn. "Explaining Policy Change: Conversion or Replacement?" Paper presented at annual meeting of the American Political Science Association, Toronto, September 2009.

Truman, David B. *The Governmental Process: Political Interests and Public Opinion*. New York: Knopf, 1951.

Tufte, Edward R. *Political Control of the Economy*. Princeton: Princeton University Press, 1978.

U.S. Bureau of the Census. "U.S. Foreign Economic and Military Aid Programs: 1980 to 2005," table 1270. In *Statistical Abstract*. Washington, DC, 2008.

U.S. Department of Defense. "Missile Defense Agency, FY85–FY07 Historical Funding Chart." Washington, DC, 2006.

U.S. Department of Justice. "Drug Demand Reduction Activities, Report No. 03-12." Washington, DC: Office of the Inspector General, 2003.

U.S. Department of Labor. "Drug-Free Workforce Conference: Workplace-Related Policies, Programs and Laws." Washington, DC, 2003.

U.S. Department of the Treasury. "U.S. Individual Income Tax: Personal Exemptions and Lowest and Highest Bracket Tax Rates, and Tax Base for Regular Tax, Tax Years 1913–2006." Washington, DC, 2006.

U.S. International Trade Commission. *Value of U.S. Imports for Consumption, Duties Collected, and Ratio of Duties to Values 1891–2005*. Washington, DC: Statistical Services Division, Office of Operations, 2006.

U.S. Social Security Administration. "Annual Statistical Supplement: History of SSI, Medicare, and Medicaid Provisions," table 2.C1. Washington, DC, 2006.

Vavreck, Lynn. *The Message Matters: The Economy and Presidential Campaigns.* Princeton: Princeton University Press, 2009.

Verba, Sidney, Kay Lehman Schlozman, and Henry E. Brady. *Voice and Equality: Civic Voluntarism in American Politics.* Cambridge: Harvard University Press, 1995.

Villar, Ana, and Jon A. Krosnick. "Global Warming vs. Climate Change, Taxes vs. Prices: Does Word Choice Matter?" *Climate Change* 105, no. 1 (2010): 1–12.

Ware, Alan. *The Breakdown of Democratic Party Organization, 1940–1980.* Oxford: Oxford University Press, 1985.

Washington, Ebonya L. "Female Socialization: How Daughters Affect Their Legislator Fathers' Voting on Women's Issues." *American Economic Review* 98, no. 1 (2008): 311–32.

Watson, W. Marvin, and Sherwin Markman. *Chief of Staff: Lyndon Johnson and His Presidency.* New York: Thomas Dunne Books, 2004.

White House, The. "The Quiet Revolution: The President's Faith-Based and Community Initiative: A Seven-Year Progress Report." Washington, DC, 2008.

Wildavsky, Aaron. "The Two Presidencies." *Trans-Action* 4 (1966): 7–14.

Wiley, David E., and James A. Wiley. "The Estimation of Measurement Error in Panel Data." *American Sociological Review* 35 (1970): 112–16.

Wilson, James Q. *The Amateur Democrat: Club Politics in Three Cities.* Chicago: University of Chicago Press, 1966.

Winters, Jeffrey A. *Oligarchy.* Cambridge: Cambridge University Press, 2011.

Winters, Jeffrey A., and Benjamin I. Page. "Oligarchy in the United States?" *Perspectives on Politics* 7, no. 4 (2009): 731–51.

Witko, Christopher, and Sally Friedman. "Business Backgrounds and Congressional Behavior." *Congress & the Presidency* 35, no. 1 (2008): 71–86.

Wlezien, Christopher. "Patterns of Representation: Dynamics of Public Preferences and Policy." *Journal of Politics* 66, no. 1 (2004): 1–24.

———. "The Public as Thermostat—Dynamics of Preferences for Spending." *American Journal of Political Science* 39, no. 4 (1995): 981–1000.

Wolfers, Justin. "Are Voters Rational? Evidence from Gubernatorial Elections." Stanford: GSB, 2002.

Wood, B. Dan, and Angela H. Andersson. "The Dynamics of Senatorial Representation, 1952–1991." *Journal of Politics* 60, no. 3 (1998): 705–36.

Wright, Gerald C., and Michael B. Berkman. "Candidates and Policy in United States Senate Elections." *American Political Science Review* 80, no. 2 (1986): 567–88.

Wright, John R. *Interest Groups and Congress.* Needham Heights, MA: Allyn and Bacon, 1996.

Zaller, John R. "Coming to Grips with V. O. Key's Concept of Latent Opinion." In *Electoral Democracy*, edited by Michael B. MacKuen and George Rabinowitz, 311–36. Ann Arbor: University of Michigan Press, 2003.

———. *The Nature and Origins of Mass Opinion.* Cambridge: Cambridge University Press, 1992.

Zaller, John, and Stanley Feldman. "A Simple Theory of the Survey Response: Answering Questions versus Revealing Preferences." *American Journal of Political Science* 36, no. 3 (1992): 579–616.

Index

Note: Page numbers in *italics* indicate illustrations; those with a *t* indicate tables.

AARP. *See* American Association of Retired People

abortion, 16, 47, 52; and birth control issues, 110*t*, 111, 113; and congressional partisan control, 186, 297n34; interest group alignments on, 129–30, 132; "partial-birth," 110*t*; RU-486 pill for, 110*t*, 111, 113; support across income groups for, 109, 110*t*, 112–13

Ackerman, Bruce, 249

Advocacy and Public Policymaking project, 127, 292nn7–8

Afghanistan War, 8; and Bush's tax cuts, 232; public support for, 39, 229

AFL-CIO, 156*t*, 158, 237, 263*t*. *See also* unions

aggregation, preference, 21–24, 30–32, 66

agricultural policies, 38, 153

Aid for Families with Dependent Children, 117. *See also* social welfare policies

AIDS testing, 109, 110*t*, 111

Althaus, Scott, 28, 31–32, 284n12

Alwin, Duane, 65

American Association of Retired People (AARP), 7, 155, 244, 263*t*; on Medicare reform, 121, 123, 131, 158; on poverty-related issues, 156*t*, 160–61; on Social Security reform, 153, 158

American Association of University Women, 236

American Bankers Association, 157*t*, 263*t*

American Civil Liberties Union, 154, 155

American Council of Life Insurance, 157*t*, 263*t*

American Crossroads (organization), 247

American Farm Bureau Federation, 156*t*, 263*t*

American Federation of State, County, and Municipal Employees, 156*t*, 263*t*

American Federation of Teachers, 121

American Hospital Association, 154, 156*t*, 263t

American Israel Public Affairs Committee (AIPAC), 152, 156*t*, 263*t*

American Legion, 263*t*

American National Election Study, 91, 186–88, 287n16; and Bush's tax cut, 300n55; and political party characteristics, 297n39

Ansolabehere, Stephen, 245, 298n6

Aparicio-Castillo, Francisco, 249

Arnold, Douglas, 246

Association of Trial Lawyers, 157*t*, 263*t*

automobile companies, 60; and air pollution, 146; lobbying by, 156*t*, 263*t*

AWACS (airborne warning and control systems), 63, 64*t*

Ayres, Ian, 249

Baldwin, Robert, 245

Bartels, Larry, 31, 43, 167, 243; on American National Election Study, 287n16; on campaign spending, 245; on posttax inequality, 252; on Senators' voting, 239, 301n10

Baumgartner, Frank R., 127, 129–31, 161

Berelson, Bernard, 14, 18–19, 30

Berinsky, Adam, 36–37

Berry, Christopher, 173

Berry, Jeffrey M., 161

Besley, Timothy, 249

Binder, Sarah, 44–45, 209

Bipartisan Campaign Reform Act (2002), 247

birth control issues, 110*t*, 111, 113. *See also* abortion

Bosnia, 105, 106*t*, 130, 286n4

Brady Bill (1993), 151, 295n17. *See also* gun control

Brandeis, Louis, 1

Buchanan, Patrick, 19–20

Buchanan, Vernon, 237

Buffet, Warren, 230

Burden, Barry, 173, 236

Burstein, Paul, 54–55

Bush, George H. W., 111; congressional partisan control under, 179*t*, 296n27; policy responsiveness under, 199–204,

Bush, George H. W. (*continued*)
  200, 200*t*, 204*t*, 218–21, 219*t*, 220;
  popularity of, 225; and religious issues,
  185–86; tax increase under, 296n32
Bush, George W., 9, 54, 107; campaign
  financing of, 245, 248; congressional
  partisan control under, 178–80, 179*t*;
  defense strategies of, 107; estate tax
  elimination by, 26; faith-based initiatives
  of, 8, 64*t*, 109, 110*t*, 152–53, 186,
  194; health care policies of, 121; and
  Homeland Security Department, 24–25;
  and Iraq War, 39, 166, 229; and medical
  marijuana, 109, 110*t*; as polarizing
  figure, 193–94; policy responsiveness
  under, 199–205, 200–203, 200–204*t*,
  218–21, 219*t*, 220, 224–29; popularity
  of, 224, 225; on stem cell research, 112,
  226; tax policies of, 26, 150, 183, 194,
  229–32, 300n60; as Texas governor,
  227–28

Campaign Finance Institute, 298n7
campaign financing, 196–97, 243–47; by
  anonymous contributors, 303n42; by
  political action committees, 245–49,
  298nn7–8; public funding for, 248–49,
  303n40, 303n43; reform of, 10, 247–50,
  302n19
Canes-Wrone, Brandice, 95, 288n27
Carnes, Nicholas, 237–38
Carter, Jimmy, 167
Case, Anne, 249
censorship, and TV ratings, 109, 110*t*
Chambers of Commerce, 53, 146, 156*t*,
  237, 263*t*
Charles, Guy-Uriel, 46
Cheney, Dick, 179*t*, 226–27
child care, 33, 78, 189, 251; and welfare
  reform, 118*t*, 119
Chile, 283n6
China, 55, 245
chi-square test, 298n18
Christian Coalition, 129, 132, 153, 155–57,
  156*t*, 263*t*. *See also* religious issues
Churchill, Winston, 40
"clean elections" programs, 303n43
Clinton, Bill, 109, 110*t*, 111; congressional
  partisan control under, 178–80, 179*t*;
  family-leave policy of, 113, 114*t*, 150;
  free-trade policies of, 167, 185; health

care reform of, 25, 58, 117, 118*t*, 119,
  169; policy responsiveness under,
  199–205, 200–203, 200–204*t*, 218–21,
  219*t*, 220; popularity of, 169, 225; and
  religious issues, 185–86; tax rates under,
  25, 115, 183, 296n32; welfare reforms
  of, 117, 118*t*
Cohen, Martin, 206
computer industry, 156*t*, 263*t*
Condorcet, Marquis de, 21–22
Congressional Campaign Finance Study,
  302n19
Converse, Philip, 17, 20–21, 31, 279n22
correlated measurement error, 287n14
Credit Union National Association, 157*t*,
  263*t*
Crespin, Michael, 46
Crime Control Act (1990), 151
cue taking for policy preferences, 18–21,
  30–32, 40–41, 52–53

Dahl, Robert, 1, 37
"death tax." *See* taxes, inheritance
defense contractors, 91, 156*t*, 263*t*. *See
  also* military
de Figueiredo, John, 245
Delli Carpini, Michael, 17–18
democracy, 4–5, 40–41, 47–48; characteristics of, 1, 37; citizens' role in, 14–17;
  decision making in, 12–13, 27; defini-
  tions of, 13–15; enhancing of, 250–52;
  policy responsiveness in, 70–72, 71; and
  theocracy, 66
Democrats. *See* partisan control of
  Congress
DiIulio, John, 227
Don't Ask, Don't Tell policy, 57, 169, 186
Downs, Anthony, 19, 162
Druckman, James, 35
drug abuse, 33, 52, 64*t*, 109, 110*t*
dyadic analysis, 42, 44–46

Economic Growth and Tax Relief
  Reconciliation Act (2001), 115
economic policies, 15–16; and congressional partisan control, 183, 184*t*; democratic responsiveness in, 97–104, 98*t*,
  99*t*; interest group alignments on, 131,
  144–45, 144*t*, 148*t*, 149–50; support
  across income groups for, 101–4, 102*t*,
  106*t*, 107–8, 113–17, 114*t*

Economic Recovery Act (1981), 115
education, 48, 61–62; federal aid to, 9,
118t, 120, 189, 228, 251; income
percentiles by, 93–95, 94; and No Child
Left Behind, 50, 194, 226, 291n42; and
school prayer, 109, 110t; and school
vouchers, 6–7, 50, 118t, 120–22, 153,
236, 249
Egypt, 283n6
elections: of 1992, 169; of 2000, 9, 224,
227, 245, 299n41; of 2006, 166; of
2008, 248; national study of, 91,
186–88, 287n16, 297n39, 300n55;
policy responsiveness after, 162–68,
170–74, 171t, 172, 190–92, 191t. See
also campaign financing
elite persuasion, 24–29; framing effects of,
35; public receptiveness to, 93–96, 94
El Salvador, 24, 64t, 105, 106t
Enron scandal, 113, 114t, 150
environmentalism, 16, 91, 136; and global
warming, 34–35; interest group alignments on, 144t, 146
Eom, Kihong, 249
equivalency frames, 34
Erikson, Robert, 165–66

faith-based initiatives, 8, 64t, 109, 110t,
152–53, 186, 194. See also religious
issues
false consciousness, 190; and elite
manipulation, 25–26; about inheritance
tax, 115
family-leave policy, 150, 295n17; support
across income groups for, 113, 114t
Federal Election Commission, 196–97,
242, 247, 298n8; "laundering"
contributions through, 303n42
filibusters, 167–68
financial institutions, 2; lobbying by, 128,
243, 244
Fiorina, Morris P., 15–16
flat tax, 114t, 116, 290n34. See also taxes
force multipliers, 140–43, 141t, 142
foreign policy, 16, 98t; and congressional
partisan control, 184–85, 184t; democratic responsiveness in, 97–104, 98t,
99t; and development aid, 106t, 108;
elite manipulation of, 24–25; interest
group alignments on, 130, 144t; and
status quo bias, 98; support across

income groups for, 101–4, 102t, 105–8,
106t
Fortune magazine. See "Power 25" list
framing effects, 32–36, 63–65, 64t
free-trade policies, 157; and GATT, 106t,
107–8; and NAFTA, 8, 54, 106t, 107–8,
161, 167, 185

Gallup polls, 57
Gates, Bill, 26
gay rights, 47, 136; in military, 57, 169,
186; support across income groups for,
109, 110t, 111
General Agreement on Tariffs and Trade
(GATT), 106t, 107–8
General Social Survey, 33, 243, 288n24
gerrymandering, partisan, 250
globalization, 48, 251
global warming, 34–35, 146. See also
environmentalism
Goldwater, Barry, 222
Gorbachev, Mikhail, 289n3
Great Society programs, 9, 222. See also
social welfare policies
Green, Donald, 187, 250
gridlock, 9, 170, 194, 208–14, 210–13,
234; definition of, 210. See also partisan
control of Congress
Griffin, John, 43
Gross, Donald, 249
Gulf of Tonkin incident (1964), 24
gun control, 16, 91; Brady Bill for, 151,
295n17; interest group alignments on,
144t, 146–51, 148t, 154, 156t, 244,
263t

habeas corpus, suspension of, 106t, 107
Hacker, Jacob, 44, 231, 252, 291n44
Haiti, 57, 105, 106t, 286n4
Harris polls, 57
health care, 7, 57, 91, 189; Clintons'
reform of, 25, 58, 117, 118t, 119, 169;
Obama's reform of, 291n36; of poor,
154; religious issues with, 108; and stem
cell research, 109–12, 110t, 226
Health Insurance Association, 131–32,
156t, 263t
health maintenance organizations (HMOs),
118t, 119–20
Hennessy, Cari, 242–43
HIV testing, 109, 110t, 111

Homeland Security Department, 24–25
House of Representatives. *See* partisan control of Congress
Howell, William, 173
Humphrey, Hubert, 166
Hussein, Saddam, 24, 26
Hutchings, Vincent, 46

immigration policies, 8, 9, 54, 222
income percentiles: and cross-class coalitions, 83–85, 84*t*; and economic policies, 113–17, 114*t*; and educational level, 93–95, 94; and foreign policy issues, 105–8, 106*t*; imputing preferences by, 61–62, 62*t*; and interest group alignments, 137*t*; by policy domain, 97–104, 98*t*, 99*t*, 101–4; policy responsiveness by, 77–87; and political engagement, 239–43, 240; preferences across, 79*t*, 87–96, 92, 94; and religious issues, 108–13, 110*t*; and social welfare issues, 117–22, 118*t*
incumbency, advantage of, 15–16, 194, 250
Independent Insurance Agents of America, 157*t*, 263*t*
Institute for Social Science Research, 57
interest groups, 123–61, 244; campaign financing by, 245–49; as force multipliers, 140–43, 141*t*, 142; as omitted variable, 135–37; and policy outcomes, 133, 133–35, 152–54, 245–46; and policy preferences, 125, 135–37, 137*t*, 154–60, 156–57*t*; and policy responsiveness, 137–39, 139*t*, 149–51; proliferation of, 194–95
Interest Group Alignment Index, 126–38, 131*t*, 133, 154–60, 156–57*t*; across issue domains, 143–51, 144*t*, 148*t*; as policy change predictor, 140–42, 141*t*, 142
International Brotherhood of Teamsters, 156*t*, 263*t*
Inter-University Consortium for Political and Social Research, 57
iPOLI database, 57, 58, 284n12
Iran, 105, 106*t*
Iraq War, 8, 24, 26, 54, 105, 106*t*; and Bush's tax cuts, 232; public support for, 39, 166, 229
Israel, 152
Issa, Darrell, 237

issue publics, 20–21. *See also* policy domains

Jackson, Jesse, 19–20
Jacobs, Lawrence R., 25, 300n51; on policy preferences, 229; on policy responsiveness, 196; on political context, 194
Japanese imports, 153
Jeffords, Jim, 179t, 226–27, 295n15
job training, 64*t*, 118*t*, 189, 251
Johnson, Lyndon, 9; congressional partisan control under, 178–80, 179*t*; and Gulf of Tonkin incident, 24; policy responsiveness under, 193, 199–205, *200–203*, 200–204*t*, 218–24, 219*t*, 220; popularity of, 169; and religious issues, 185; tax increase under, 183
jury theorem, 21–22

Kaiser Family Foundation, 57
Keeter, Scott, 17–18
Kennedy, Edward "Ted," 226
Kennedy, John F., 24, 222
Kerry, John, 237, 241, 247, 248
Key, V. O., 40
King, Martin Luther, 54
Kingdon, John, 51–52, 55
Kohl, Herb, 237
Krehbiel, Keith, 165
Krosnick, Jon, 21, 65
Kyoto Accord, 146

Law Enforcement Officers Protection Act (1986), 151. *See also* gun control
Lazarsfeld, Paul, 14, 18–19, 30
Lewis, Peter, 241
Libya, 105, 106*t*
lobbying. *See* interest groups
Lupia, Arthur, 19
Lupu, Noam, 83–85, 84*t*

MacKuen, Michael, 165–66
macro-polity perspective, 165–66
Madison, James, 286n2
Magee, Christopher, 245
marijuana laws, 109, 110*t*
Mayhew, David, 209
McCain, John, 247, 248, 303n40
McClerking, Harwood, 46
McPhee, William, 14, 18–19, 30
median voter theorem, 83

Medicaid, 110t, 111, 153, 158
Medicare, 6–7, 9; interest group alignments on, 131–32, 157t, 263t; and partisan politics, 187; reform of, 117–23, 118t, 194, 226, 227
Mexican loan guarantees, 106t
Milbank, Dana, 227
military, 16, 98t; and defense contractors, 91, 156t, 263t; and foreign arms sales, 283n6; lesbians and gays in, 57, 169, 186; support across income groups for, 101–4, 102t, 105–8, 106t
minimum wage, 57, 59, 60, 251; partisan politics of, 167, 189; support across income groups for, 114t, 116–17
"missile gap," 24
Monroe, Alan D., xiii, 43, 60, 196, 286n5
Moral Majority, 186
Motion Picture Association of America, 157t, 263t
Moveon.org, 301n12
multivariate analysis, 85–86, 87t, 125–26; definition of, 78; of policy responsiveness, 190, 191t, 270t
Murkowski, Lisa, 273
MX missiles, 106t, 107. See also nuclear weapons

NAFTA. See North American Free Trade Agreement
National Association of Manufacturers, 146, 156t, 263t
National Education Association, 123, 158–59, 263t; on poverty-related issues, 156t; on school vouchers, 121
National Governors' Association, 153, 156t, 158–59, 263t
National Issues Convention, 30–31
National Labor Relations Board, 189
National Organization for Women, 236
National Rifle Association, 146, 147, 150, 154, 156t, 244, 263t. See also gun control
National Right to Life Committee, 129, 132, 155–57, 156t, 263t
Net Interest Group Alignment Index, 133, 133–38, 144t, 147–51, 148t
Newman, Brian, 43
Nicaragua, 24, 64t, 105, 106t, 130
9/11. See September 11 attacks
Nixon, Richard, 166, 245

No Child Left Behind Act (2001), 50, 194, 226, 291n42. See also education
North American Free Trade Agreement (NAFTA), 8, 54, 185; partisan politics of, 167; support across income groups for, 106t, 107–8; union opposition to, 161
Nozick, Robert, 282n71
nuclear weapons, 24, 105–7, 106t, 289n3

Obama, Barack, 248, 291n36, 303n40
O'Brien, Robert M., 287n14
Odum Institute, 57
Office of Strategic Initiatives, 227
oil industry, 128, 146, 157t, 263t; and energy tax, 114t, 116, 153
Opensecrets.org, 301n12

PACs. See political action committees
Page, Benjamin, 42; on moneyed interests, 241–43; The Rational Public, 23–24, 27, 40; on survey questions, 54–55
Pakistan, 283n6
Palmquist, Bradley, 187
Panagopoulos, Costos, 250
partisan change hypothesis, 165–68, 174–78, 176t, 177, 211, 295n12
partisan control of Congress, 9, 165, 178–92, 179t, 181t, 182, 184t, 191t, 270t; gridlock from, 9, 170, 194, 208–14, 210–13, 234
partisan gerrymandering, 250
Perry, Robert, 241
Pew Research Center for the People and the Press, 57
pharmaceutical industry, 123, 157t, 263t
Pierson, Paul, 44, 231, 252, 291n44
pivotal politics theory, 165
Plato, 12, 17, 22
policy domains, 20–21, 57–60; and congressional partisan control, 183–90, 184t; interest group alignments across, 143–51, 144t, 148t; responsiveness by, 97–104, 98t, 99t, 101–4
policy maximizers, 9, 162–63, 173–74, 191, 193, 215–16, 223–24, 232
policy preferences, 3–4, 17–18; aggregation of, 21–24, 30–32, 66; cue taking for, 18–21, 30–32, 40–41, 52–53; datasets of, 50–54, 57–60; feigned, 35–37; homogeneity of, 91–92, 92; intensity of,

policy preferences (*continued*)
37–39, 88–91, *89*; and interest groups,
125–27, 135–39, 137*t*, 139*t*, 154–60,
156–57*t*; by issue, 97–104, 98*t*, 99*t*,
101–4; manifest versus latent, 39–40,
62*t*; quality of, 21–22; reliability measures of, 62–66, 64*t*, 88; and survey
agenda, 54–56
policy responsiveness, 4–6, 37–39;
assessing of, 41–42, 66–69, 68*t*; coding
of, 60; and congressional partisan
control, 180–92, 181*t*, *182*, 184*t*, 191*t*;
by domain, 97–104, 98*t*, 99*t*, *101–4*;
and electoral cycle, 170–74, 171*t*, *172*,
190–92, 191*t*; empirical evidence of,
73–77; enhancing of, 250–52; and
gridlock, 194, 208–14, *210–13*; by
income groups, 76–87, 76*t*, 77, 79*t*,
80, 82, 87*t*; and interest groups, *133*,
133–39, 139*t*, 149–51, 152–54; models
of, 70–72, *71*; observed versus predicted,
75, 76*t*, 77; over time, 60, 198–205,
199–203, 200–204*t*, 218–21, 219*t*, *220*;
and presidential regime length, 174–78,
176*t*, *177*, 190–92, 191*t*; status quo bias
in, 72–74, *73*, 98*t*, 99, 286n5
political action committees (PACs): campaign financing by, 245–49, 298nn7–8;
donations to, 45–46, 241, 242, 244,
302n20; and policy outcomes, 245–46.
See also interest groups
political parties, 25, 162–68, 249; congressional control by, 178–90, 179*t*, 181*t*,
182, 184*t*; as policy maximizers, 9,
162–63, 173–74, 191, 193, 215–16,
223–24, 232
Pontusson, Jonas, 83–85, 84*t*
poverty issues, 8–9, 33, 222; interest group
alignments on, 154–60, 156–57*t*. *See
also* social welfare policies
"Power 25" list (expanded), 127–28,
130–32, 146, 153–54, 161, 263*t*
presidency, 100; and partisan regime
length, 174–78, 176*t*, *177*, 190–92, 191*t*;
popularity of, 165, 289n27. *See also*
campaign financing
Presser, Stanley, 32–33
privacy issues, 64*t*, 106*t*, 185
public opinion, 4–5; and interest groups,
140–43, 141*t*, *142*; manifest versus
latent, 39–40, 62*t*; and policy preferences, 17–18

Public Opinion Poll Question database,
57, 58
public works projects, 6–7, 118*t*, 120–22,
291n47

Quattrone, George, 33–34
questions, wording of, 29, 32–36, 63–65,
64*t*
Quirk, Paul, 195, 214

racial issues, 20, 24, 27, 37, 43, 46
Reagan, Ronald, 54; arms reduction treaty
under, 289n3; Central American policies
of, 24, 64*t*; congressional partisan
control under, 179*t*; defense spending
under, 8, 105–7; Medicaid proposals
under, 153; policy responsiveness under,
199–205, *200–203*, 200–204*t*, 218–21,
219*t*, *220*; popularity of, *225*; and
religious issues, 185–86; tax rates
under, 115, 183
reliability measures, 62–66
religious issues, *101–4*, 102*t*, 108–13,
110*t*; and Christian Coalition, 129, 132,
153, 155–57, 156*t*, 263*t*; and congressional partisan control, 184*t*, 185–86;
democratic responsiveness in, 97–105,
98*t*, 99*t*; interest group alignments on,
144*t*, 145–46, 148*t*. *See also* faith-based
initiatives
Republicans. *See* partisan control of
Congress
Rigby, Elizabeth, 303n47
Romney, Mitt, 243
Roper Center, 55, 57
Rousseau, Jean-Jacques, 13–14
Rove, Karl, 227, 241, 247
RU-486 (drug), 110*t*, 111, 113. *See also*
abortion
Russia, 106*t*, 107–8, 131, 145, 185. *See
also* Union of Soviet Socialist Republics

Sanders, Bernie, 226–27
Sarbanes-Oxley Act (2002), 113, 114*t*
Saudi Arabia, 63, 64*t*
Scaife, Richard, 135
Schickler, Eric, 187
schools: prayer in, 109, 110*t*; vouchers for,
6–7, 50, 118*t*, 120–22, 153, 236, 249.
See also education
Schuman, Howard, 32–33
Schumpeter, Joseph, 14–15

Senate. *See* partisan control of Congress

September 11 attacks, 24, 26, 224; privacy issues after, 64*t*, 106*t*, 185; war on terror after, 24–25, 105–8, 106*t*

Serbia, 105, 106*t*

Shapiro, Robert, 23–24, 27, 40, 42, 300n51; on policy responsiveness, 196; on political context, 194

Shotts, Kenneth, 95, 288n27

Sierra Club, 154, 155

Simon, Herbert, 51

Smith, Mark A., 142

Smith, Tom W., 32

smoking. *See* tobacco companies

Snyder, James M., 245, 246, 298n6

Social Security, 6–7; interest group alignments on, 153, 158; and partisan politics, 187; reform of, 58–59, 117–22, 118*t*, 131–32

social welfare policies, 33, 36–37, 91, 251; and child care, 118*t*, 119; and congressional partisan control, 183–84, 184*t*; democratic responsiveness in, 97–104, 98*t*, 99*t*; interest group alignments in, 144*t*, 145, 148*t*; representational inequality in, 121–22; status quo bias in, 99, 121; support across income groups for, *101–4*, 102*t*, 117–21, 118*t*; time limits on, 117, 130, 189

Soros, George, 26, 135, 230, 241

status quo bias, 72–74, 73, 73, 98*t*, 99, 286n5; and foreign policy issues, 98; and policy drift, 291n44; and social welfare issues, 99, 121

stem cell research, 109–12, 110*t*, 226

Stewart, Charles, III, 298n6

Stimson, James, 165–66

Strategic Arms Reduction Treaty (START), 289n3. *See also* nuclear weapons

Stratmann, Thomas, 245, 249, 302

Strolovitch, Dara, 154–55

substance abuse, 33, 52, 58, 64*t*, 109, 110*t*

taxes, 16, 23, 48; alternative minimum, 150; during Bush's presidency, 26, 150, 183, 194, 229–32, 300n60; capital gains, 3, 114*t*, 115–16, 189, 241; child deduction on, 130; during Clinton's presidency, 25, 115, 183, 296n32; energy, 114*t*, 116, 153; flat, 114*t*, 116,

290n34; income, 114*t*, 116; inheritance, 26, 34, 114*t*, 115–16, 125, 183, 189, 230, 290n32; interest group alignments on, 144–45, 144*t*, 148*t*, 149–50; during Johnson's presidency, 183, 222; and partisan control, 183, 296n32; and religious issues, 108; unions on, 156*t*, 157; value-added, 113, 114*t*, 150

Taxpayer Protection Act (1997), 115

Teamsters union, 156*t*, 263*t*

telecommunications industry, 55; lobbying by, 128, 156*t*, 263*t*

television, 34, 52, 58; rating systems for, 109, 110*t*

Temporary Assistance for Needy Families, 117. *See also* social welfare policies

terrorism, 24–25, 105–8, 106*t*. *See also* September 11 attacks

tobacco companies, 34, 109, 110*t*, 236, 263*t*

trade unions. *See* unions

Tversky, Amos, 33–34

Tyco Corporation, 113

unemployment, 16, 23, 33, 34, 114*t*

Union of Soviet Socialist Republics (USSR), 24; arms reduction treaties with, 106*t*, 107, 289n3; Central American policies of, 64*t*. *See also* Russia

unions, 48; campaign financing by, 249; and Democratic Party, 8, 169; lobbying by, 61, 156*t*, 157–58, 237, 263*t*; teachers', 7, 121, 123

utility theory, 282n71

Vavreck, Lynn, 206

V-chip, for television sets, 109, 110*t*

Vietnam War, 24, 36–37, 183, 222

vote maximizers, 162–63, 173–74

voting rights, 10, 14

vouchers, school, 6–7, 50, 118*t*, 120–22, 153, 236, 249. *See also* education

Washington, Ebonya, 236

welfare. *See* social welfare policies

Winters, Jeffrey, 241

Wright, Gerald C., 303n47

Yugoslavia, breakup of, 105, 106*t*, 130

Zaller, John, 232